TSUYOSHI WATANABE

DRAGONS RIOTING

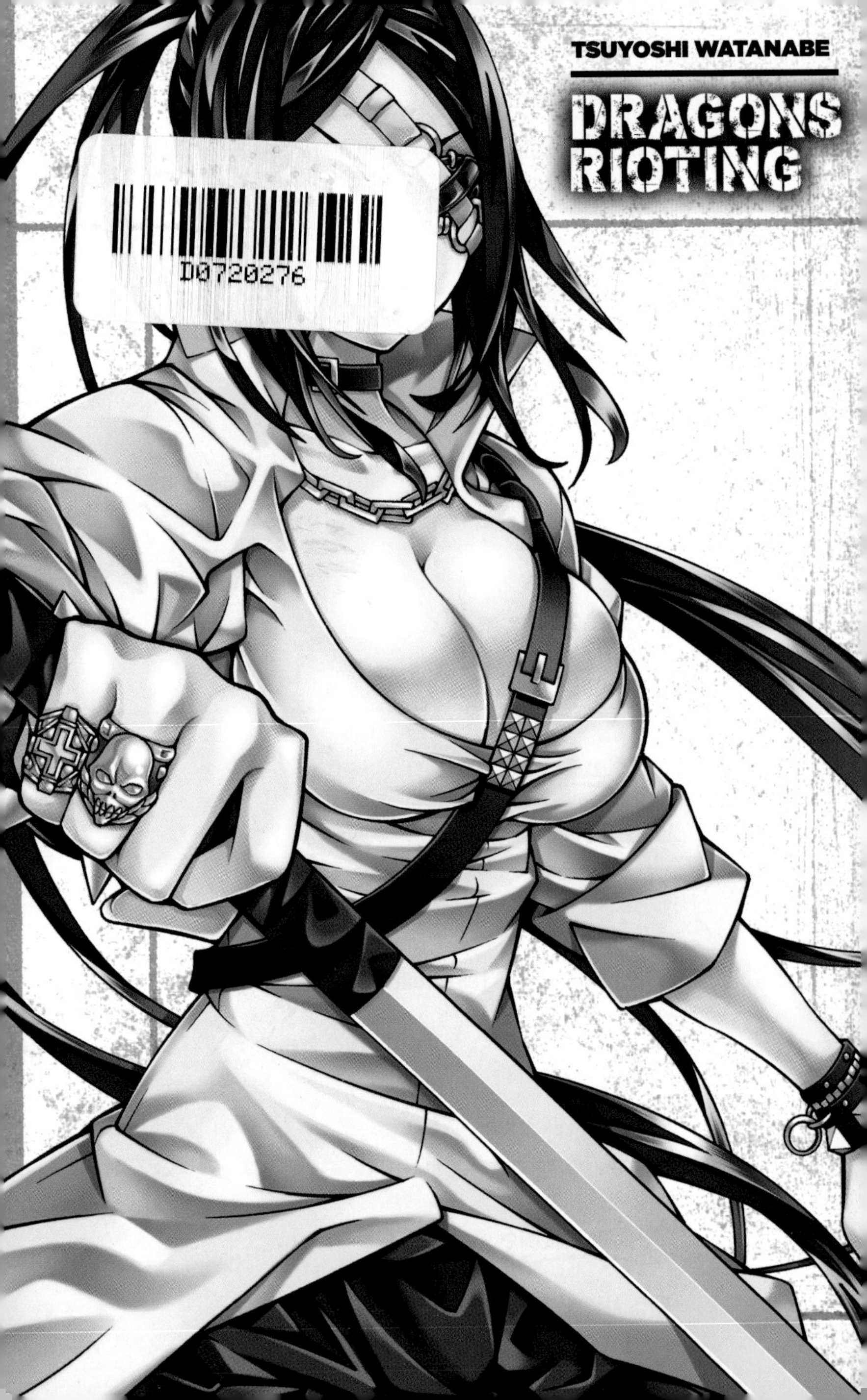

男獄煉

SEP-
TEM-
BER
1ST

OPEN-
ING
CERE-
MONY

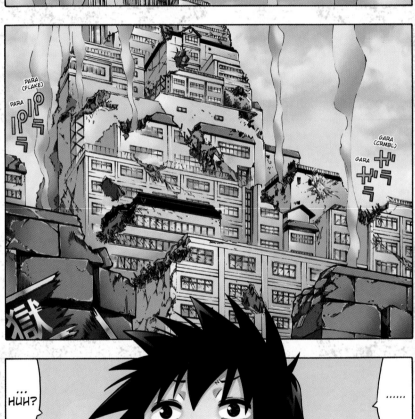

PARA
(FLAKE)

PARA

パ
ラ
パ
ラ

GARA
(CRMBL)

GARA

ガ
ラ
ガ
ラ

...

HUH?

......

DRAGON 25
BATTLE
ROYAL

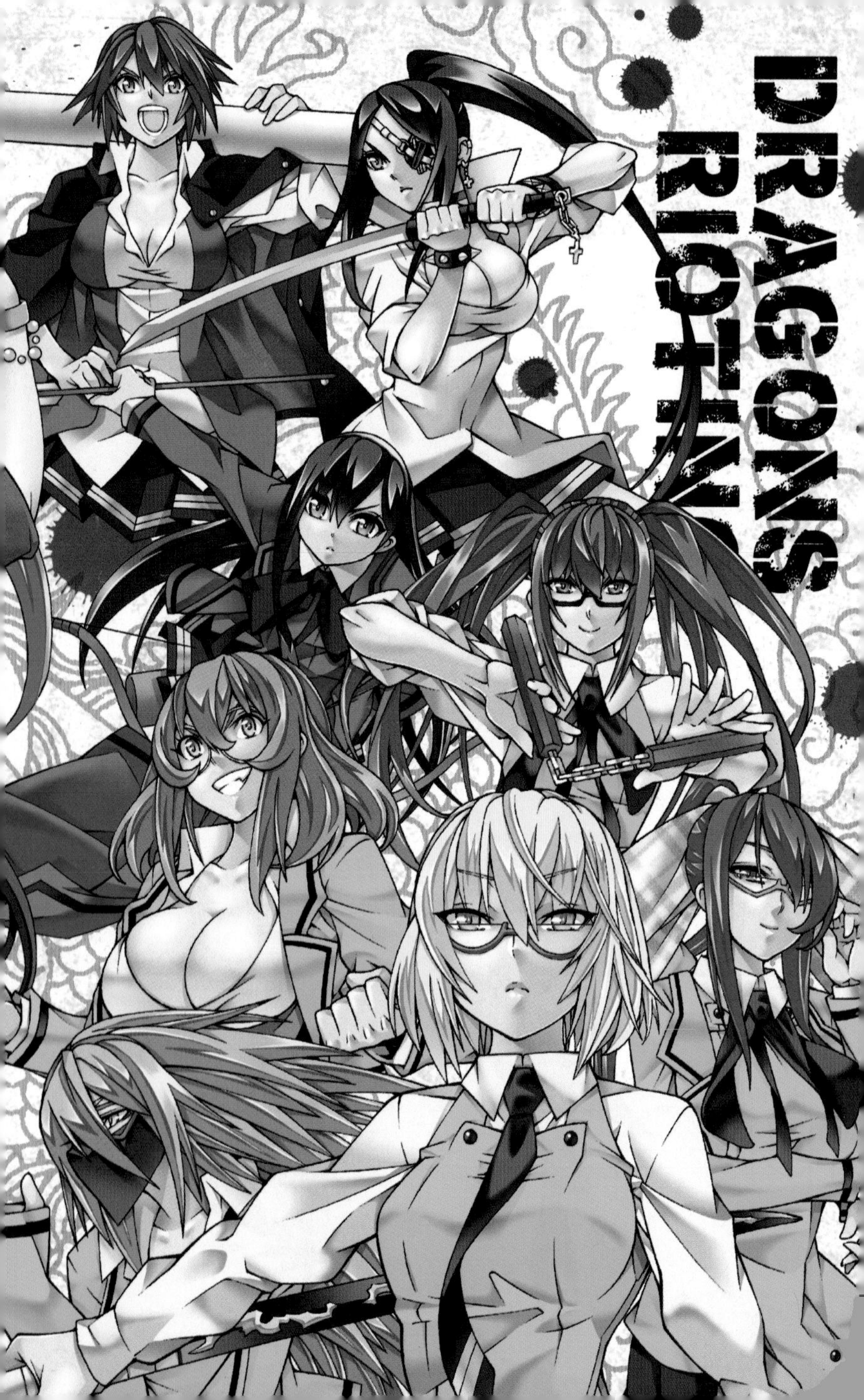
DRAGONS RIOTING

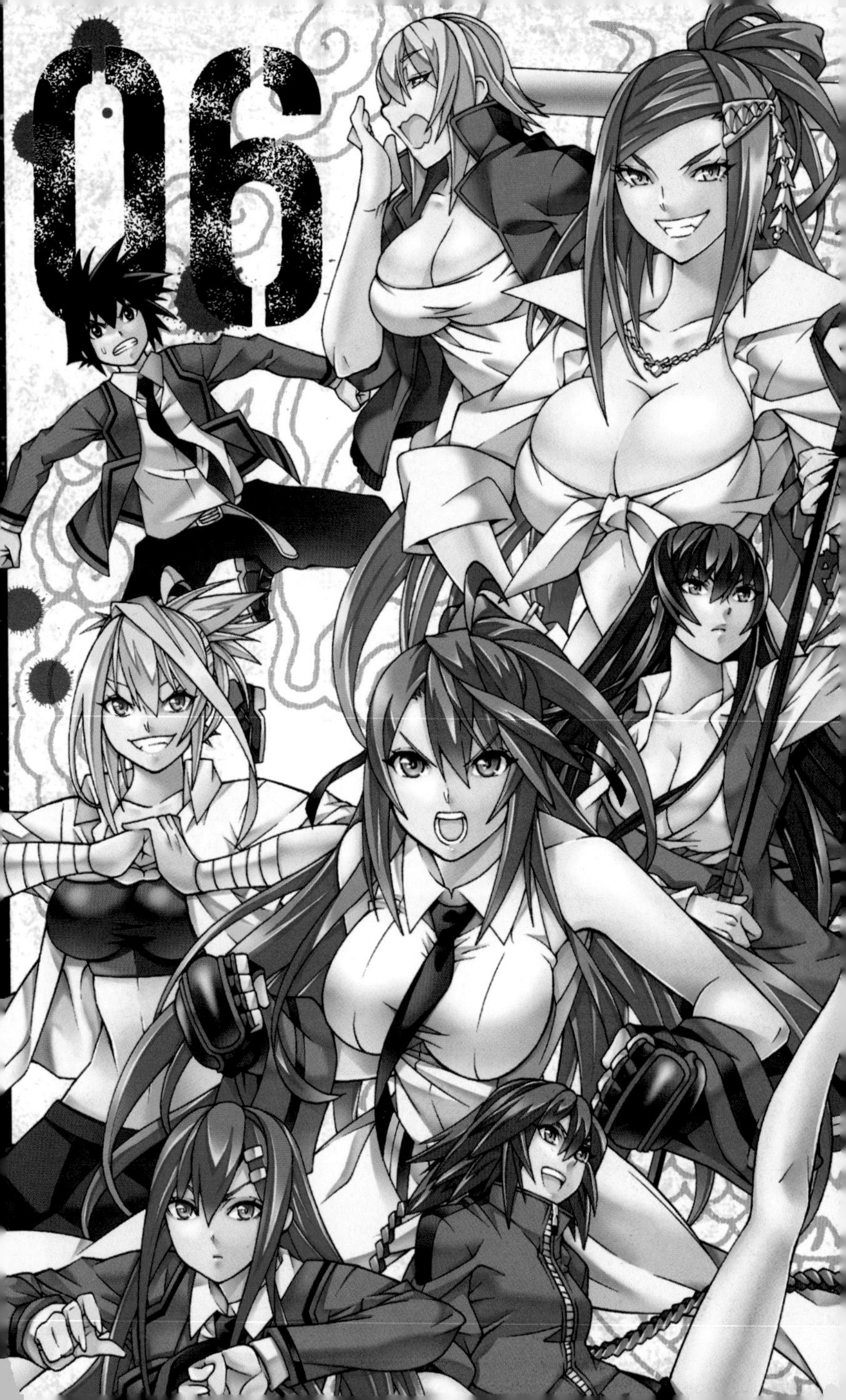
06

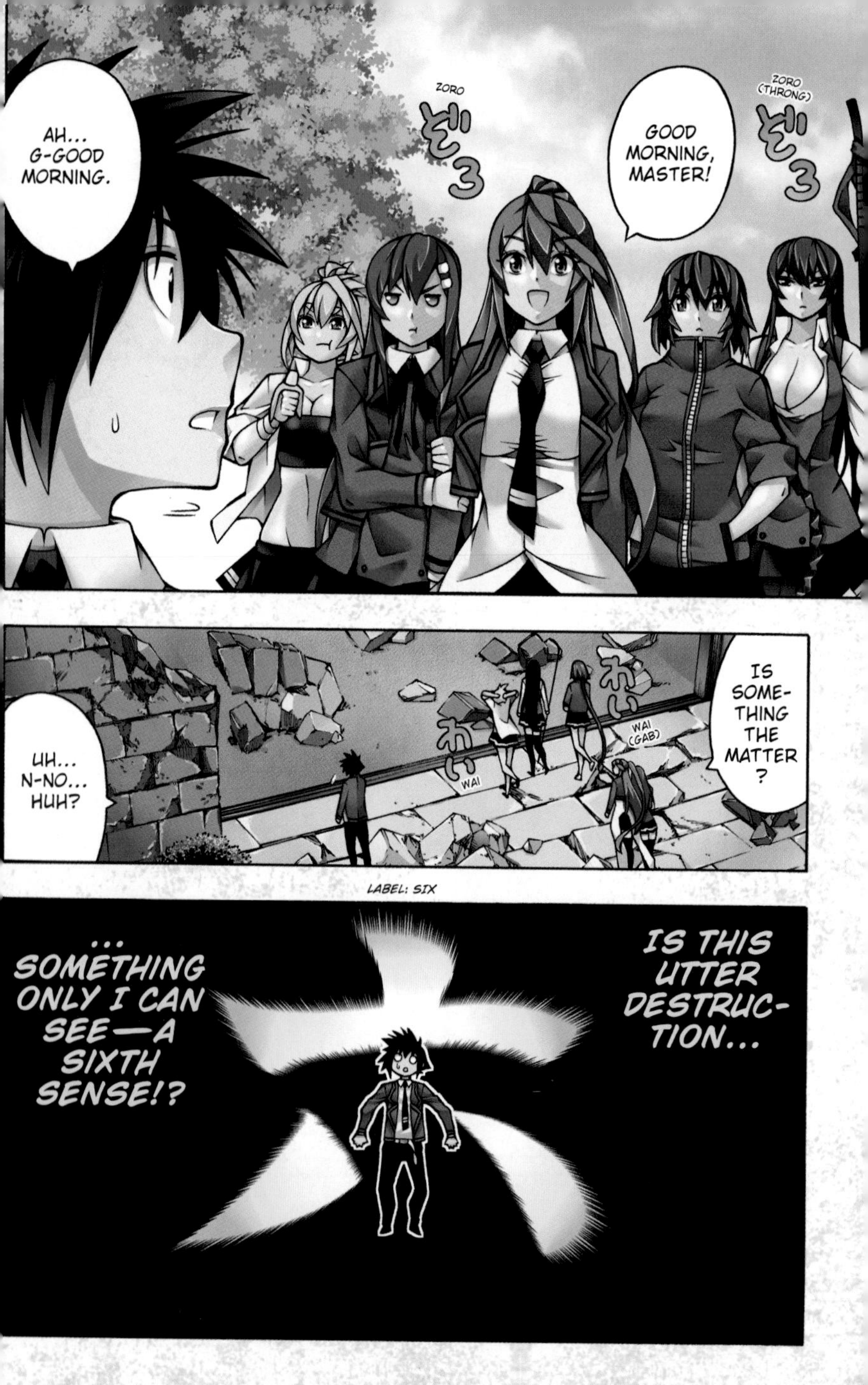
ぞろ
ZORO (THRONG)
GOOD MORNING, MASTER!
ぞろ
ZORO
AH... G-GOOD MORNING.
IS SOMETHING THE MATTER?
わい
WAI (GAB)
わい
WAI
UH... N-NO... HUH?
LABEL: SIX
IS THIS UTTER DESTRUCTION...
...SOMETHING ONLY I CAN SEE—A SIXTH SENSE!?

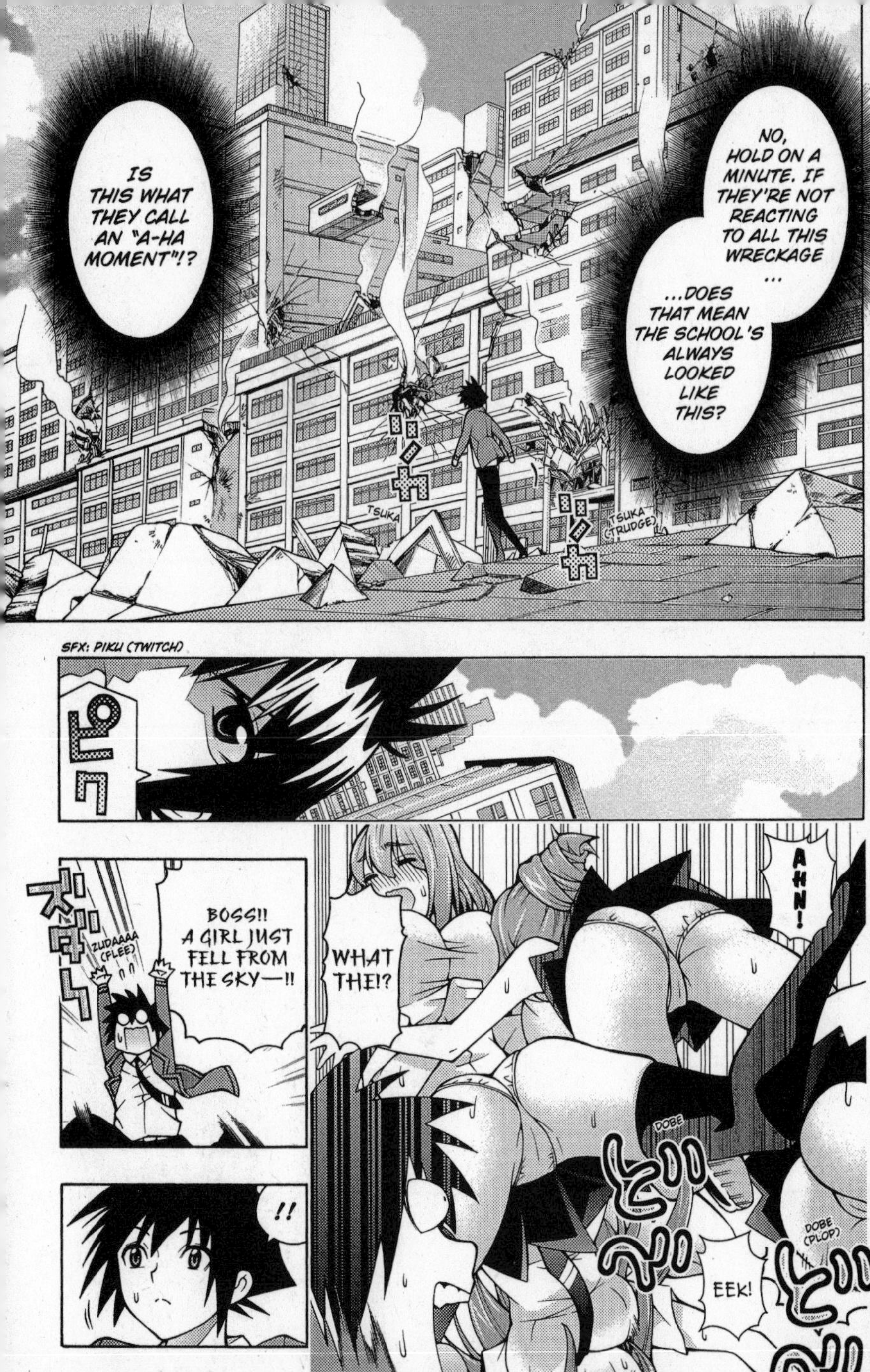
NO, HOLD ON A MINUTE. IF THEY'RE NOT REACTING TO ALL THIS WRECKAGE ...
...DOES THAT MEAN THE SCHOOL'S ALWAYS LOOKED LIKE THIS?
IS THIS WHAT THEY CALL AN "A-HA MOMENT"!?
TSUKA (TRUDGE)
TSUKA
SFX: PIKU (TWITCH)
AHN!
WHAT THE!?
DOBE
DOBE (PLOP)
EEK!
BOSS!! A GIRL JUST FELL FROM THE SKY—!!
ZUDAAAA (FLEE)
!!

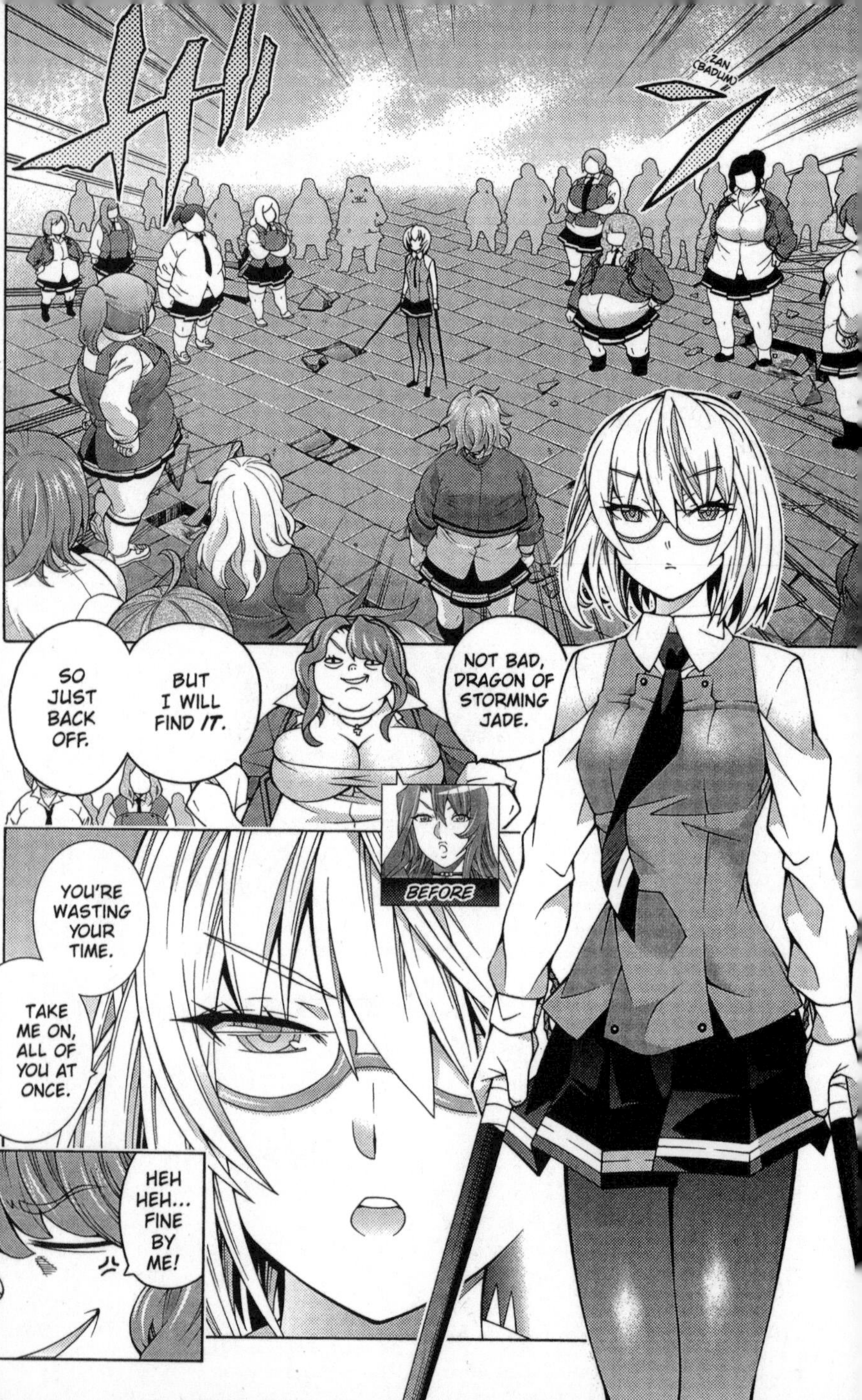
ZAN (BADUM)
NOT BAD, DRAGON OF STORMING JADE.
BUT I WILL FIND *IT*.
SO JUST BACK OFF.
BEFORE
YOU'RE WASTING YOUR TIME.
TAKE ME ON, ALL OF YOU AT ONCE.
HEH HEH... FINE BY ME!

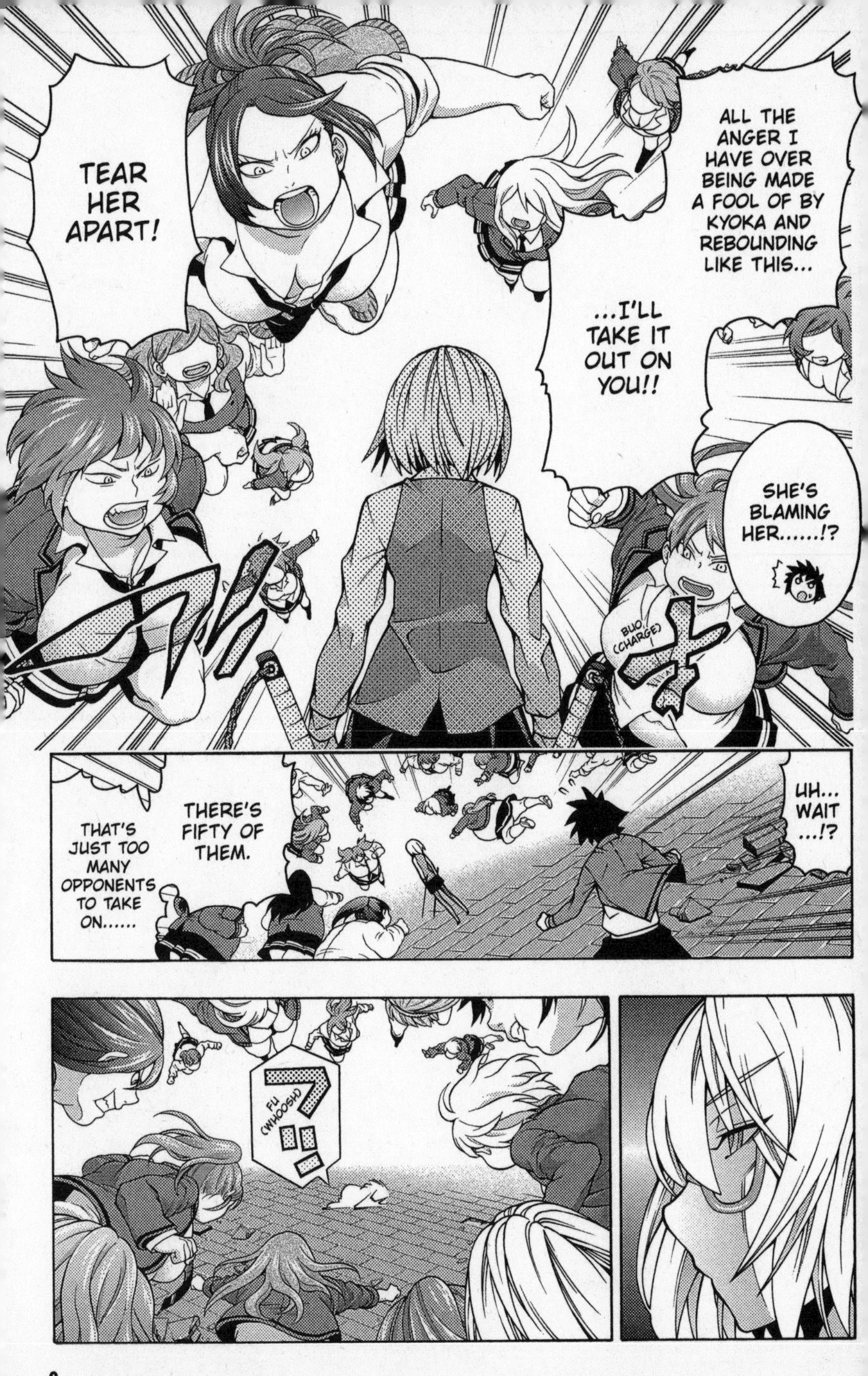
ALL THE ANGER I HAVE OVER BEING MADE A FOOL OF BY KYOKA AND REBOUNDING LIKE THIS...
...I'LL TAKE IT OUT ON YOU!!
TEAR HER APART!
SHE'S BLAMING HER......!?
BUO (CHARGE)
UH... WAIT ...!?
THERE'S FIFTY OF THEM.
THAT'S JUST TOO MANY OPPONENTS TO TAKE ON......
FU (WHOOSH)

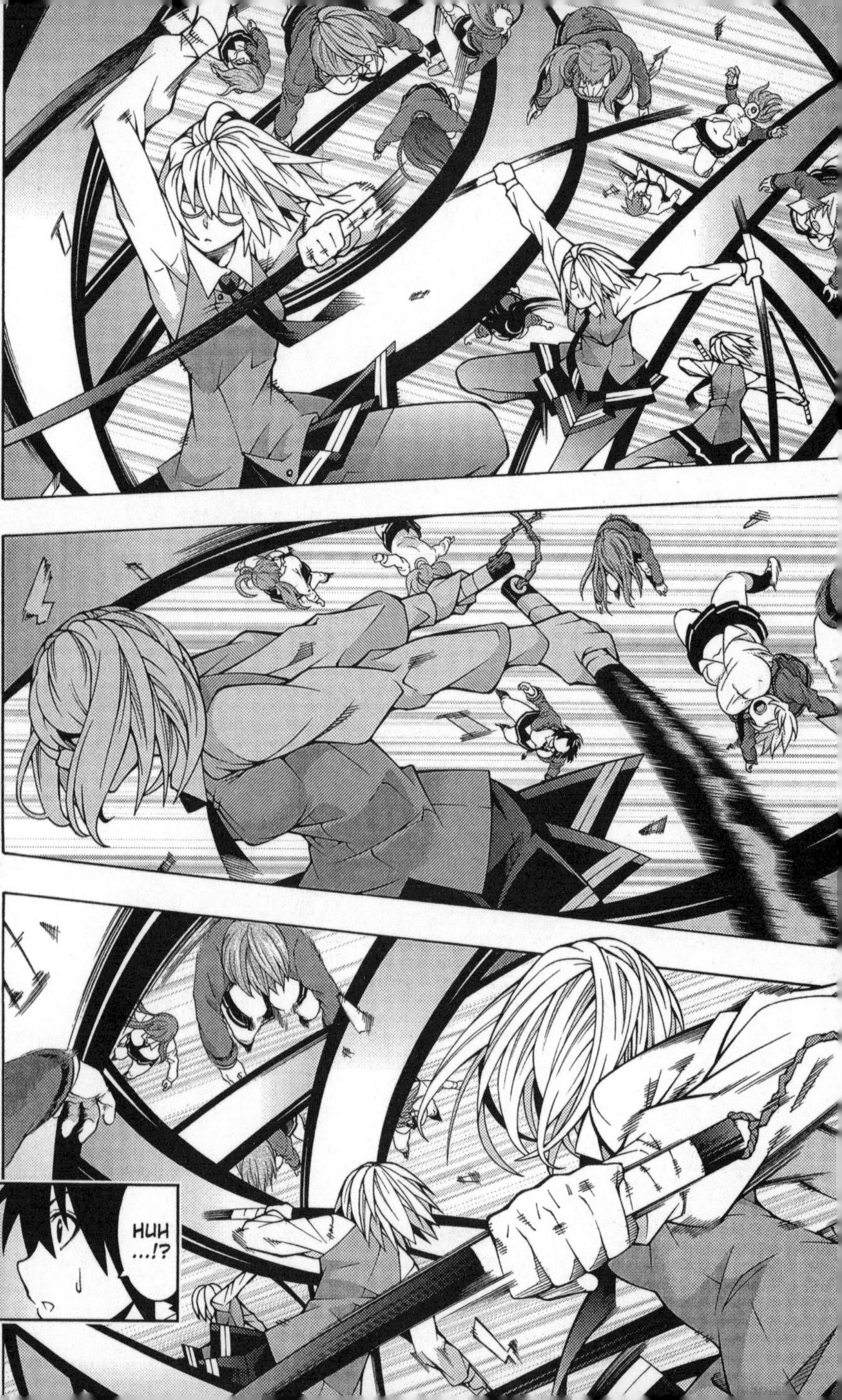
HUH ...!?

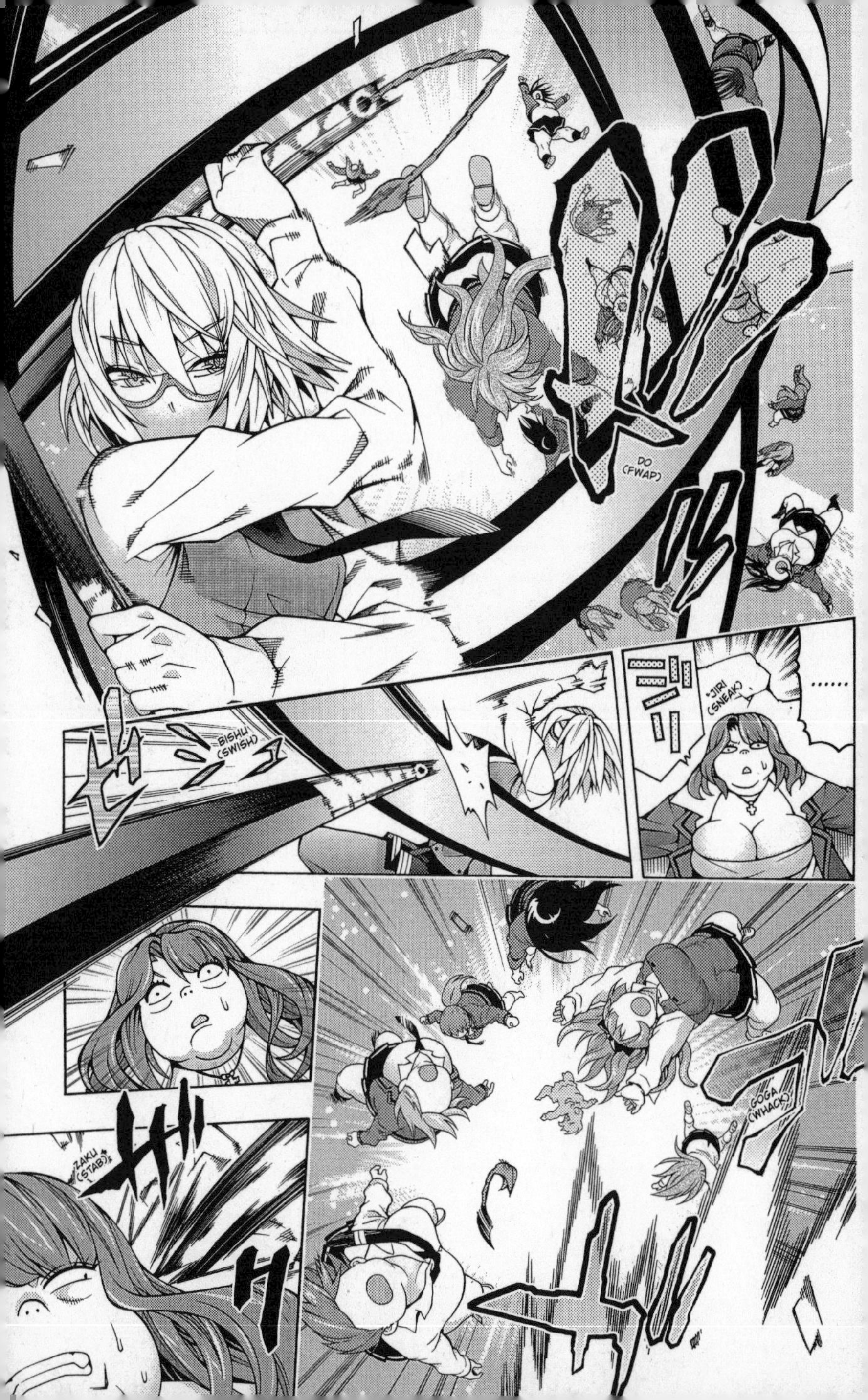
DO
(FWAP)
......
JIRI
(SNEAK)
BISHU
(SWISH)
GOGA
(WHACK)
ZAKU
(STAB)

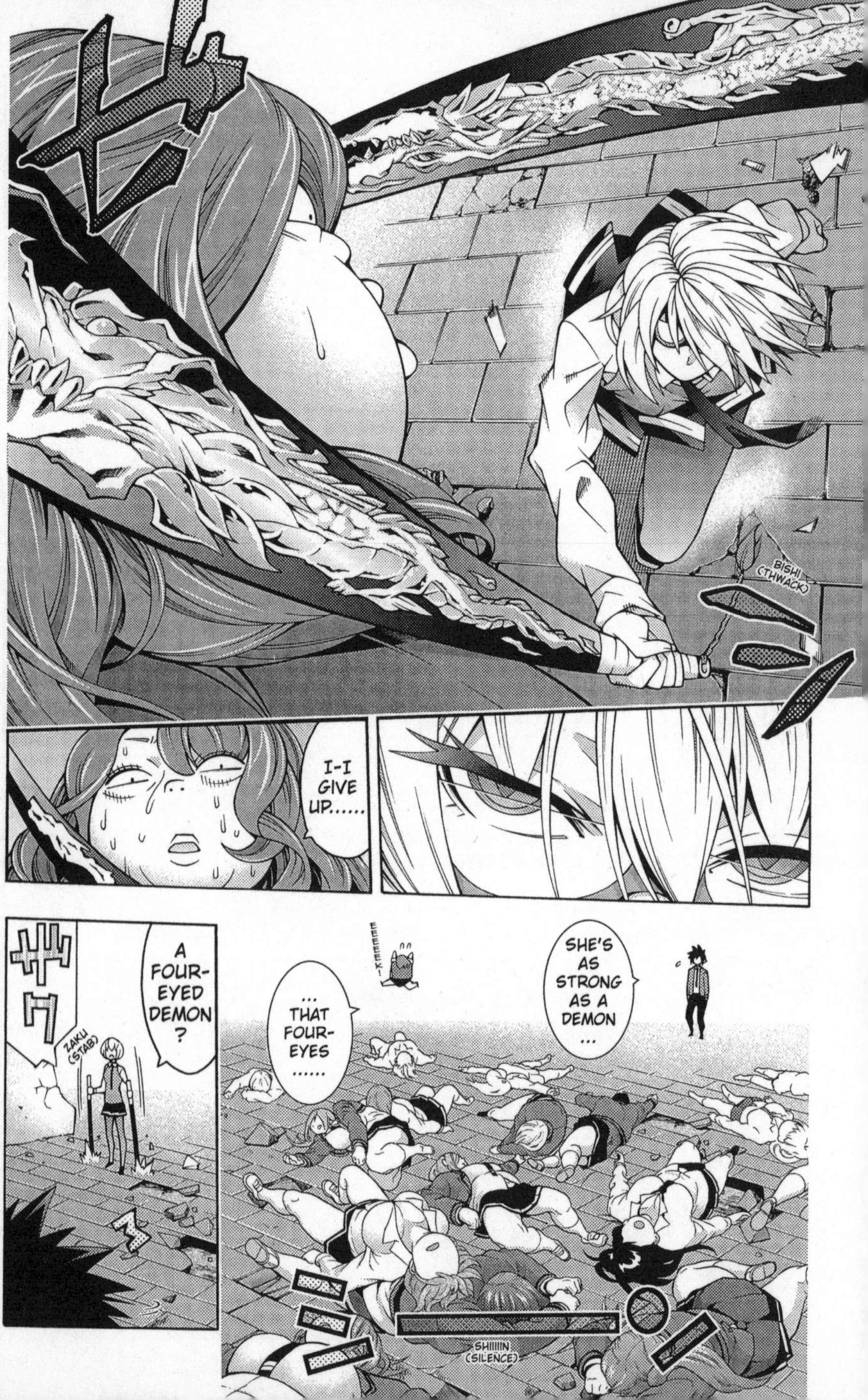
BISHI
(THWACK)
I-I GIVE UP......
SHE'S AS STRONG AS A DEMON ...
EEEEEK!
... THAT FOUR-EYES ......
SHIIIIIN
(SILENCE)
A FOUR-EYED DEMON ?
ZAKU
(STAB)

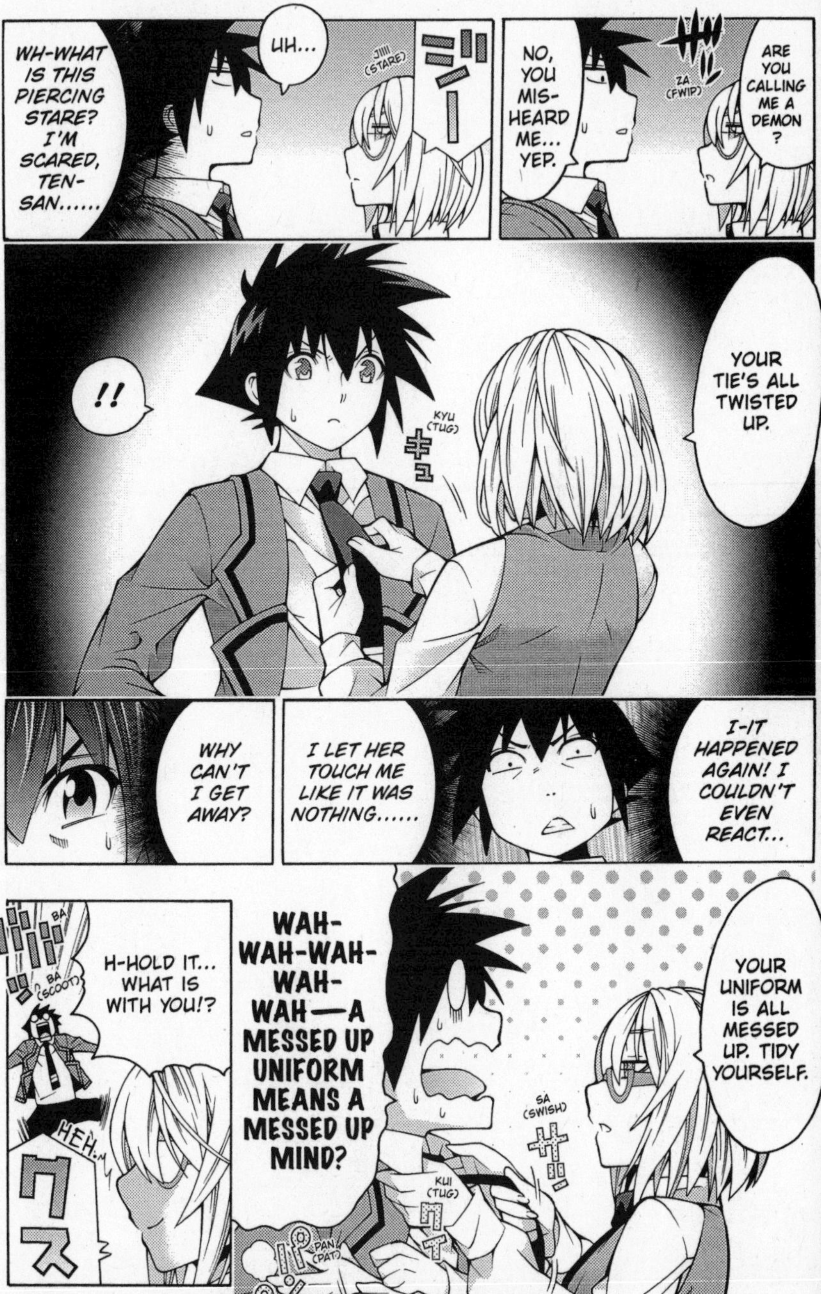
ARE YOU CALLING ME A DEMON?
ZA (FWIP)
NO, YOU MIS-HEARD ME... YEP.
JIIII (STARE)
UH...
WH-WHAT IS THIS PIERCING STARE? I'M SCARED, TEN-SAN......
YOUR TIE'S ALL TWISTED UP.
KYU (TUG)
!!
I-IT HAPPENED AGAIN! I COULDN'T EVEN REACT...
I LET HER TOUCH ME LIKE IT WAS NOTHING......
WHY CAN'T I GET AWAY?
YOUR UNIFORM IS ALL MESSED UP. TIDY YOURSELF.
SA (SWISH)
WAH-WAH-WAH-WAH-WAH—A MESSED UP UNIFORM MEANS A MESSED UP MIND?
KUI (TUG)
PAN (PAT)
PAN
BA
BA (SCOOT)
H-HOLD IT... WHAT IS WITH YOU!?
HEH...

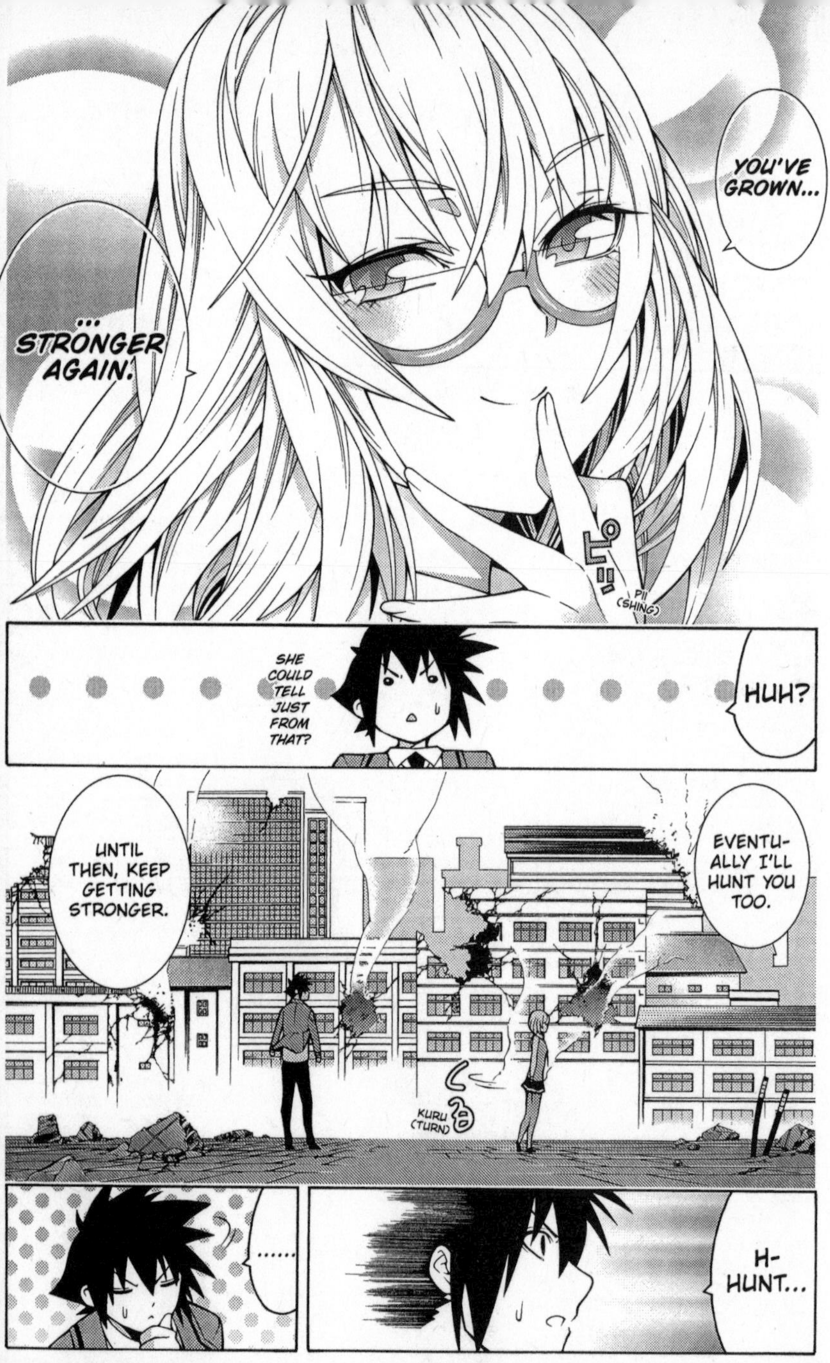
YOU'VE GROWN...
...STRONGER AGAIN.
PII (SHING)
HUH?
SHE COULD TELL JUST FROM THAT?
EVENTU-ALLY I'LL HUNT YOU TOO.
UNTIL THEN, KEEP GETTING STRONGER.
KURU (TURN)
H-HUNT...
......

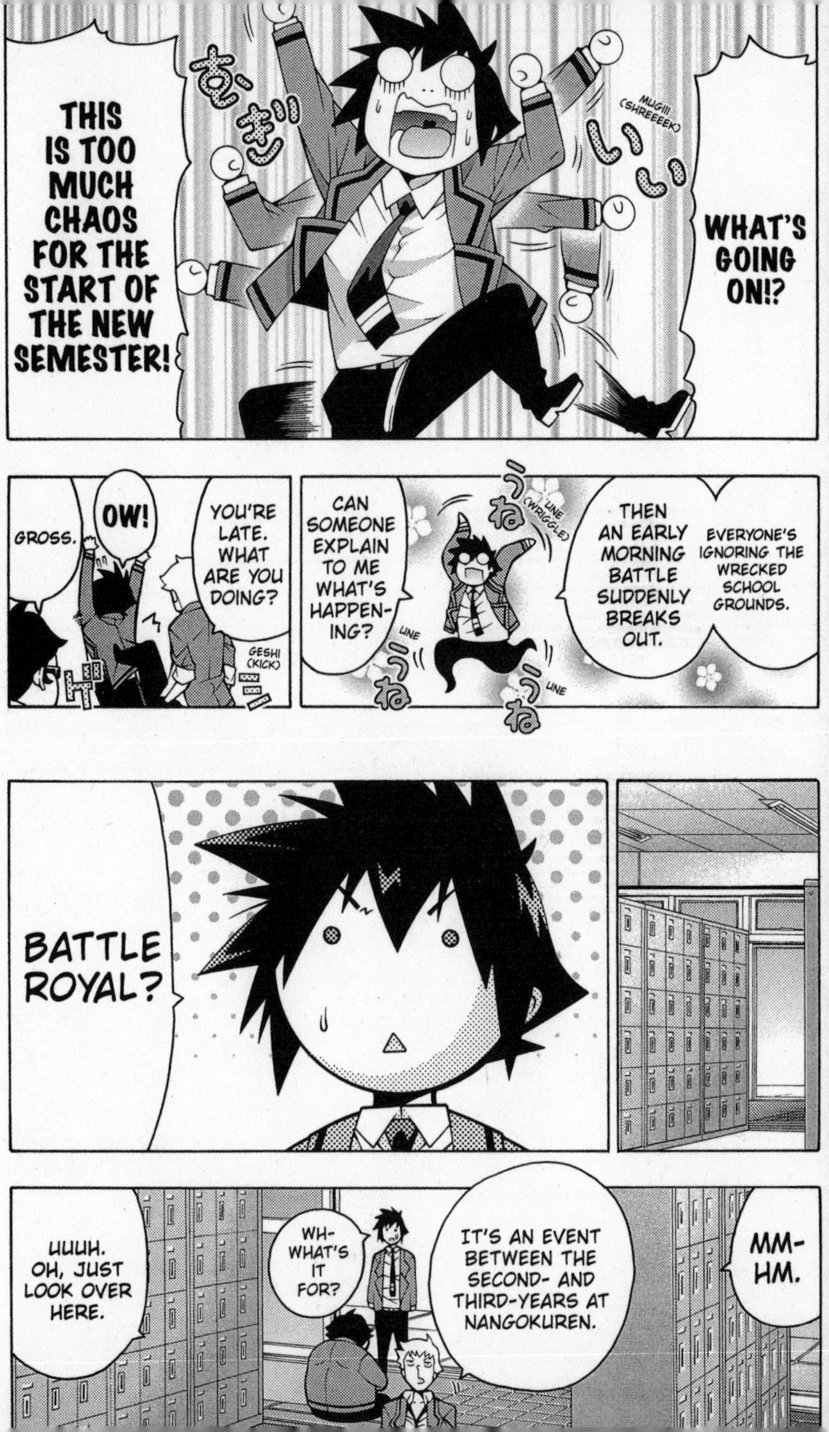
WHAT'S GOING ON!?
MUGIII (SHREEEEK)
THIS IS TOO MUCH CHAOS FOR THE START OF THE NEW SEMESTER!
EVERYONE'S IGNORING THE WRECKED SCHOOL GROUNDS.
THEN AN EARLY MORNING BATTLE SUDDENLY BREAKS OUT.
UNE (WRIGGLE)
CAN SOMEONE EXPLAIN TO ME WHAT'S HAPPEN-ING?
UNE
UNE
YOU'RE LATE. WHAT ARE YOU DOING?
OW!
GESHI (KICK)
GROSS.
BATTLE ROYAL?
MM-HM.
IT'S AN EVENT BETWEEN THE SECOND- AND THIRD-YEARS AT NANGOKUREN.
WH-WHAT'S IT FOR?
UUUH. OH, JUST LOOK OVER HERE.

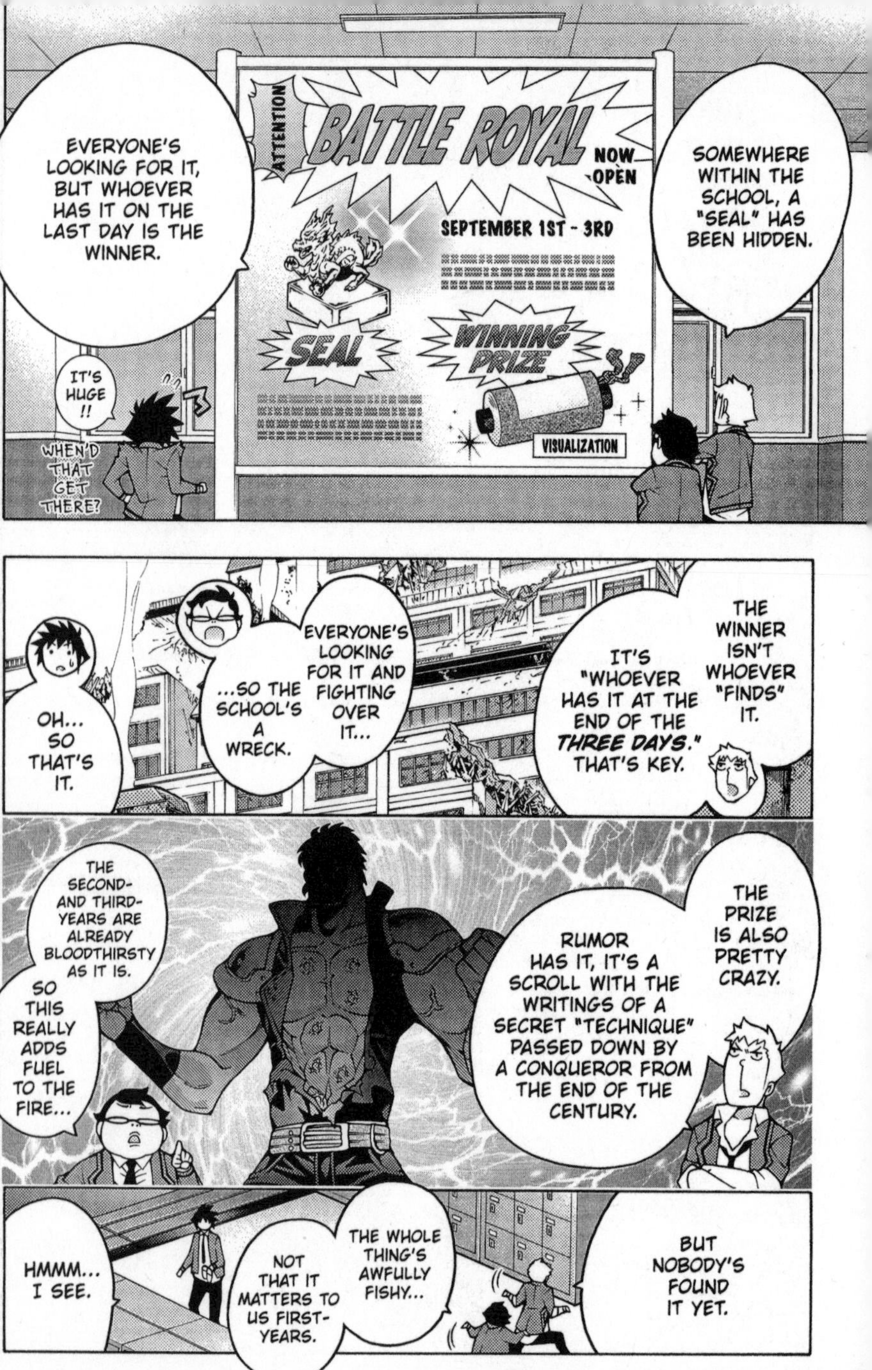
SOMEWHERE WITHIN THE SCHOOL, A "SEAL" HAS BEEN HIDDEN.
ATTENTION
BATTLE ROYAL
NOW OPEN
SEPTEMBER 1ST - 3RD
SEAL
WINNING PRIZE
VISUALIZATION
EVERYONE'S LOOKING FOR IT, BUT WHOEVER HAS IT ON THE LAST DAY IS THE WINNER.
IT'S HUGE!!
WHEN'D THAT GET THERE?
THE WINNER ISN'T WHOEVER "FINDS" IT.
IT'S "WHOEVER HAS IT AT THE END OF THE *THREE DAYS*." THAT'S KEY.
EVERYONE'S LOOKING FOR IT AND FIGHTING OVER IT...
...SO THE SCHOOL'S A WRECK.
OH... SO THAT'S IT.
THE PRIZE IS ALSO PRETTY CRAZY.
RUMOR HAS IT, IT'S A SCROLL WITH THE WRITINGS OF A SECRET "TECHNIQUE" PASSED DOWN BY A CONQUEROR FROM THE END OF THE CENTURY.
THE SECOND- AND THIRD-YEARS ARE ALREADY BLOODTHIRSTY AS IT IS.
SO THIS REALLY ADDS FUEL TO THE FIRE...
BUT NOBODY'S FOUND IT YET.
THE WHOLE THING'S AWFULLY FISHY...
NOT THAT IT MATTERS TO US FIRST-YEARS.
HMMM... I SEE.

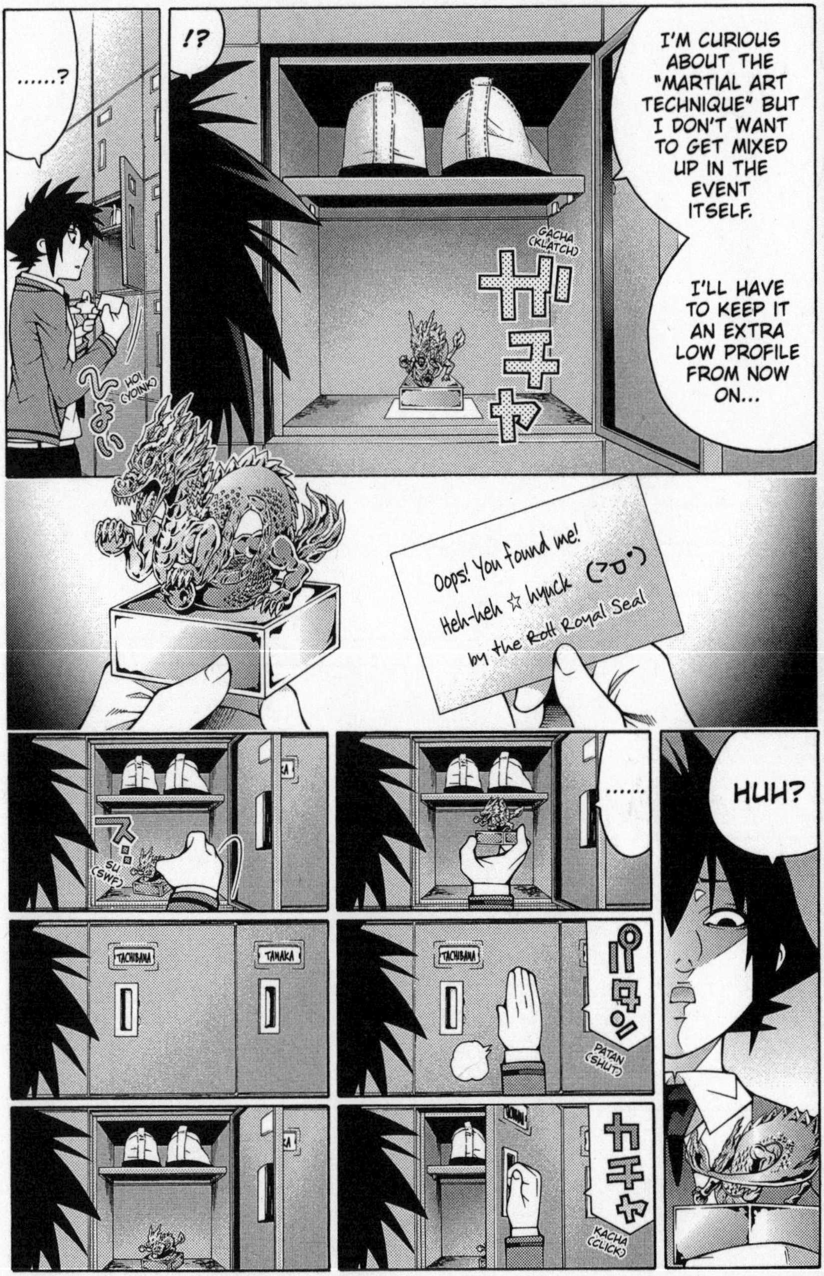
I'M CURIOUS ABOUT THE "MARTIAL ART TECHNIQUE" BUT I DON'T WANT TO GET MIXED UP IN THE EVENT ITSELF.
I'LL HAVE TO KEEP IT AN EXTRA LOW PROFILE FROM NOW ON...
GACHA (KLATCH)
!?
......?
HOI (YOINK)
Oops! You found me!
Heh-heh ☆ hyuck
by the Roll Royal Seal
HUH?
......
SU (SWF)
TACHIBANA
PATAN (SHUT)
TACHIBANA
TAMAKA
KACHA (CLICK)

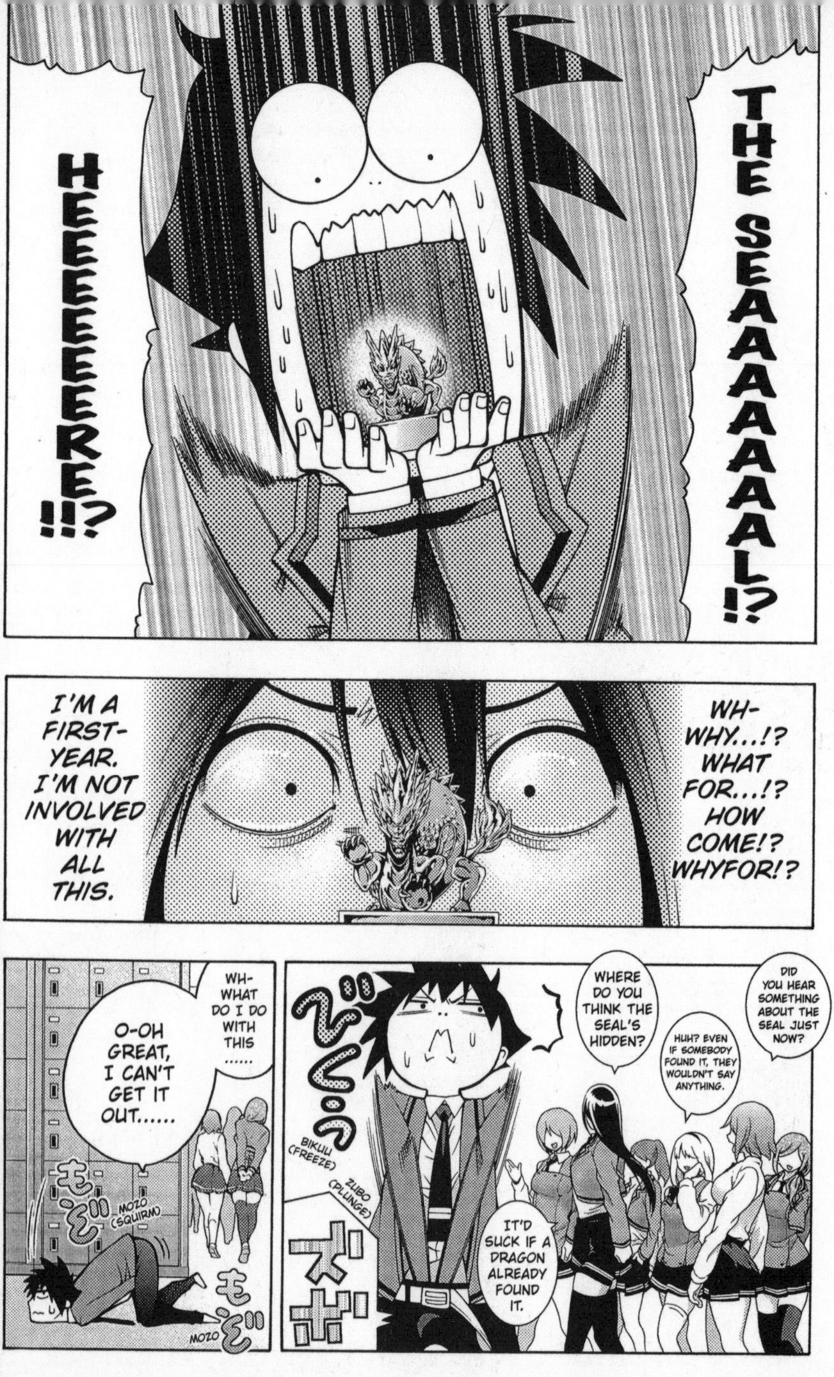
THE SEAAAAAAAL!?
HEEEEEEERE!!?
WH-WHY...!? WHAT FOR...!? HOW COME!? WHYFOR!?
I'M A FIRST-YEAR. I'M NOT INVOLVED WITH ALL THIS.
DID YOU HEAR SOMETHING ABOUT THE SEAL JUST NOW?
HUH? EVEN IF SOMEBODY FOUND IT, THEY WOULDN'T SAY ANYTHING.
WHERE DO YOU THINK THE SEAL'S HIDDEN?
BIKUU (FREEZE)
IT'D SUCK IF A DRAGON ALREADY FOUND IT.
ZUBO (PLUNGE)
WH-WHAT DO I DO WITH THIS ......
O-OH GREAT, I CAN'T GET IT OUT......
MOZO (SQUIRM)
MOZO

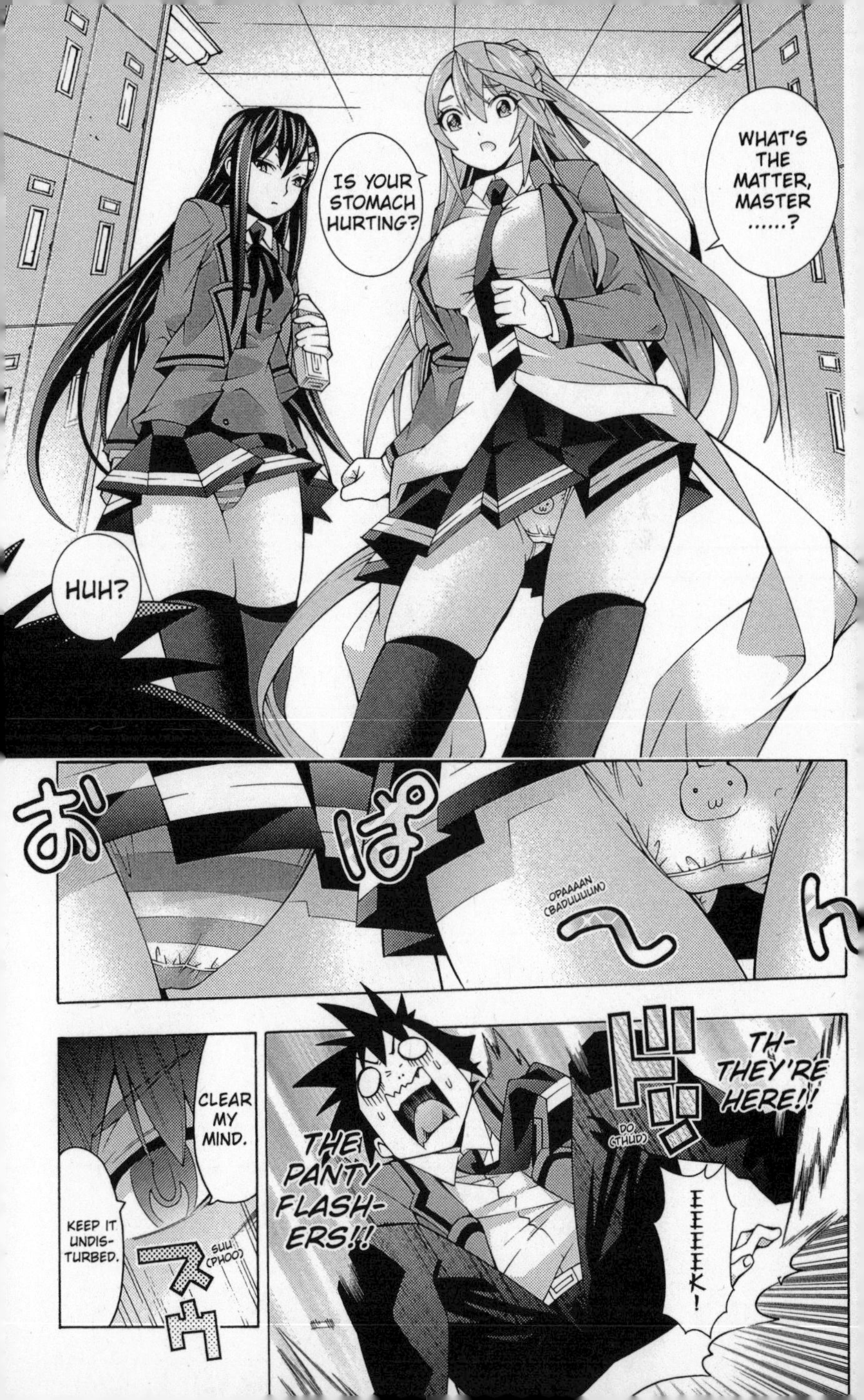
WHAT'S THE MATTER, MASTER ......?
IS YOUR STOMACH HURTING?
HUH?
おぱ〜ん
OPAAAAN (BADUUUUM)
TH- THEY'RE HERE!!
ド
DO (THUD)
EEEEEK!
THE PANTY FLASH- ERS!!
CLEAR MY MIND.
KEEP IT UNDIS- TURBED.
すう
SUU (PHOO)

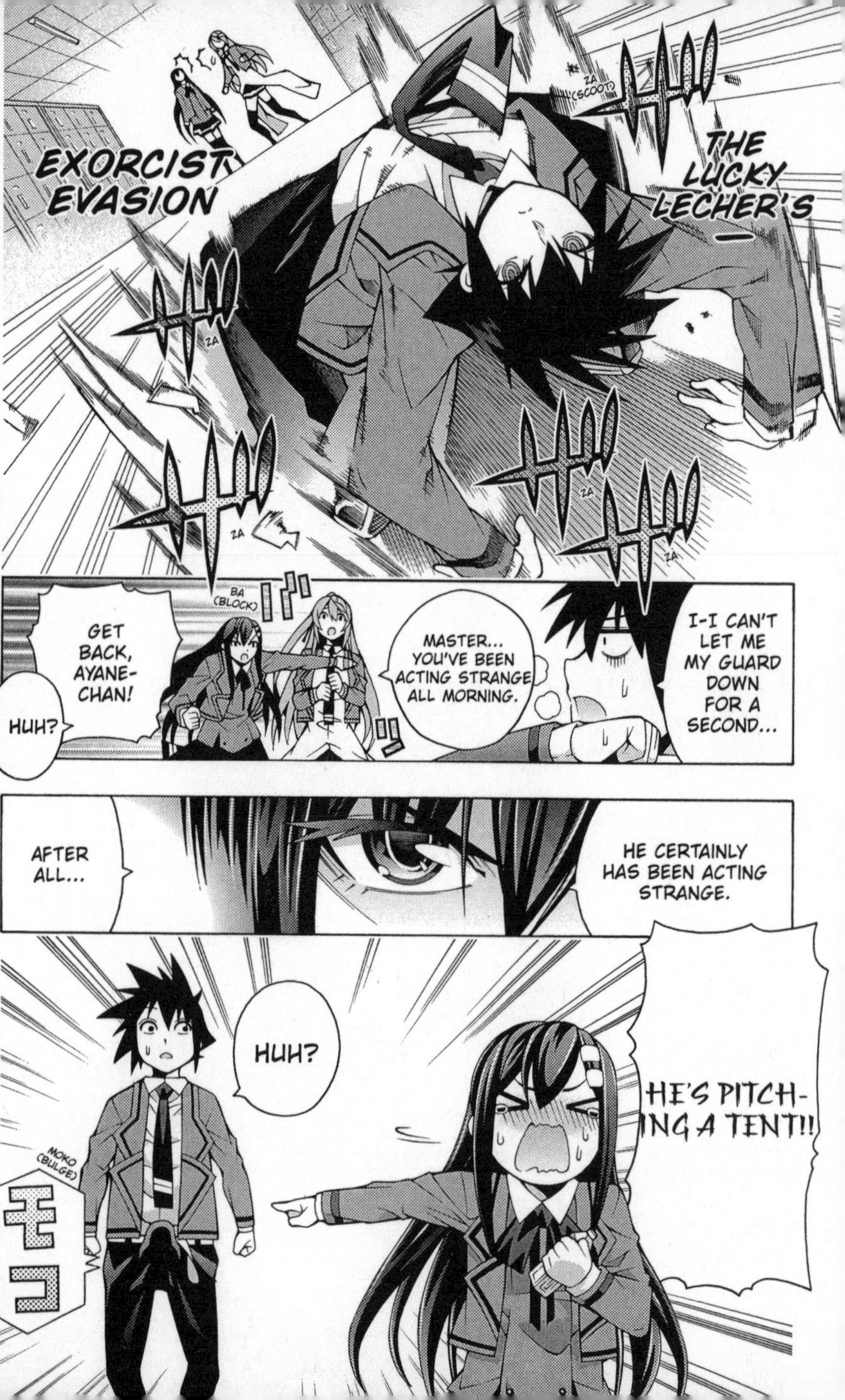
ZA (SCOOT)
THE LUCKY LECHER'S—
EXORCIST EVASION
ZA
ZA
ZA
ZA
I-I CAN'T LET ME MY GUARD DOWN FOR A SECOND...
BA (BLOCK)
MASTER... YOU'VE BEEN ACTING STRANGE ALL MORNING.
GET BACK, AYANE-CHAN!
HUH?
HE CERTAINLY HAS BEEN ACTING STRANGE.
AFTER ALL...
HE'S PITCHING A TENT!!
HUH?
MOKO (BULGE)

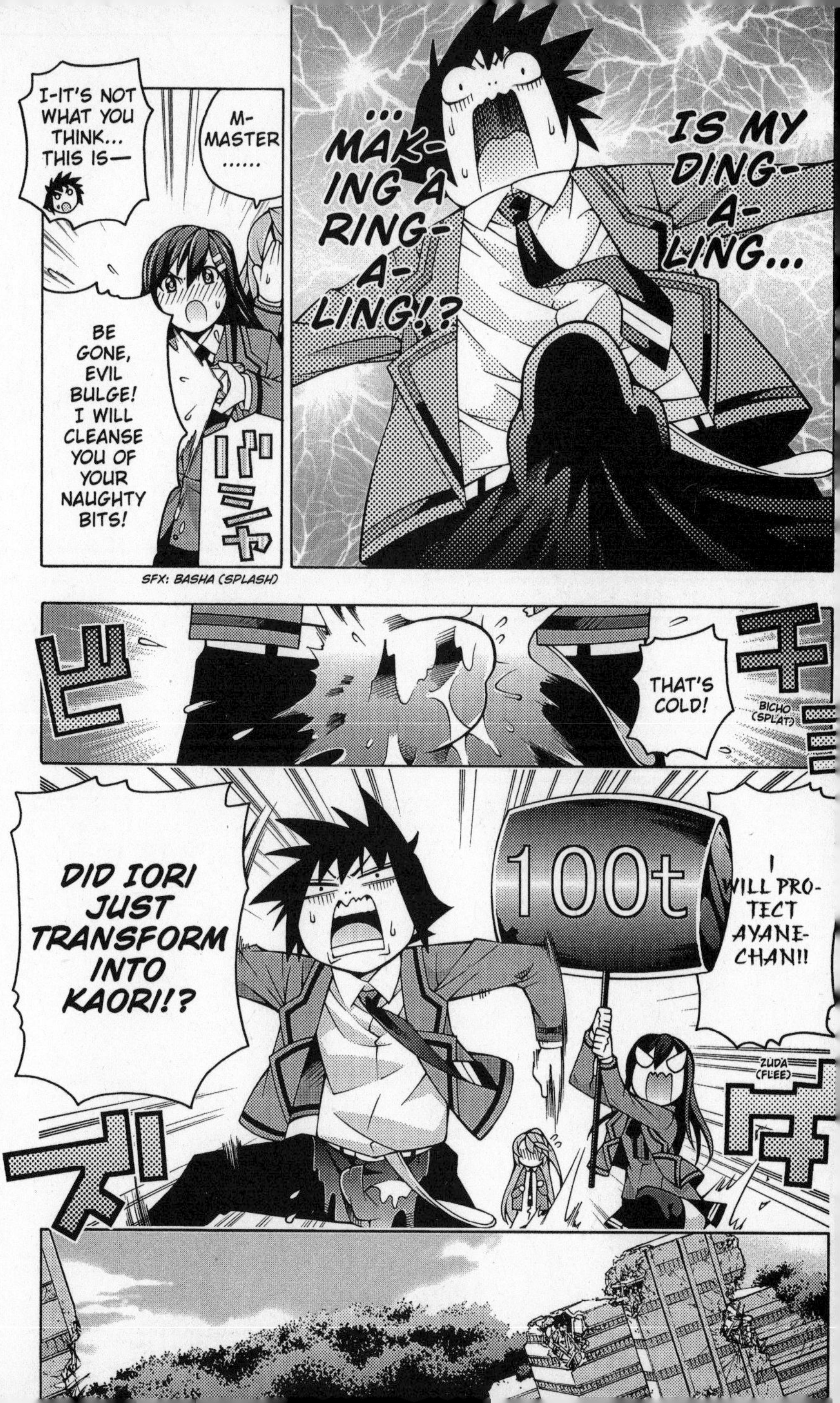
IS MY DING-A-LING...
...MAKING A RING-A-LING!?
M-MASTER ......
I-IT'S NOT WHAT YOU THINK... THIS IS—
BE GONE, EVIL BULGE! I WILL CLEANSE YOU OF YOUR NAUGHTY BITS!
SFX: BASHA (SPLASH)
BICHO (SPLAT)
THAT'S COLD!
I WILL PROTECT AYANE-CHAN!!
100t
ZUDA (FLEE)
DID IORI JUST TRANSFORM INTO KAORI!?

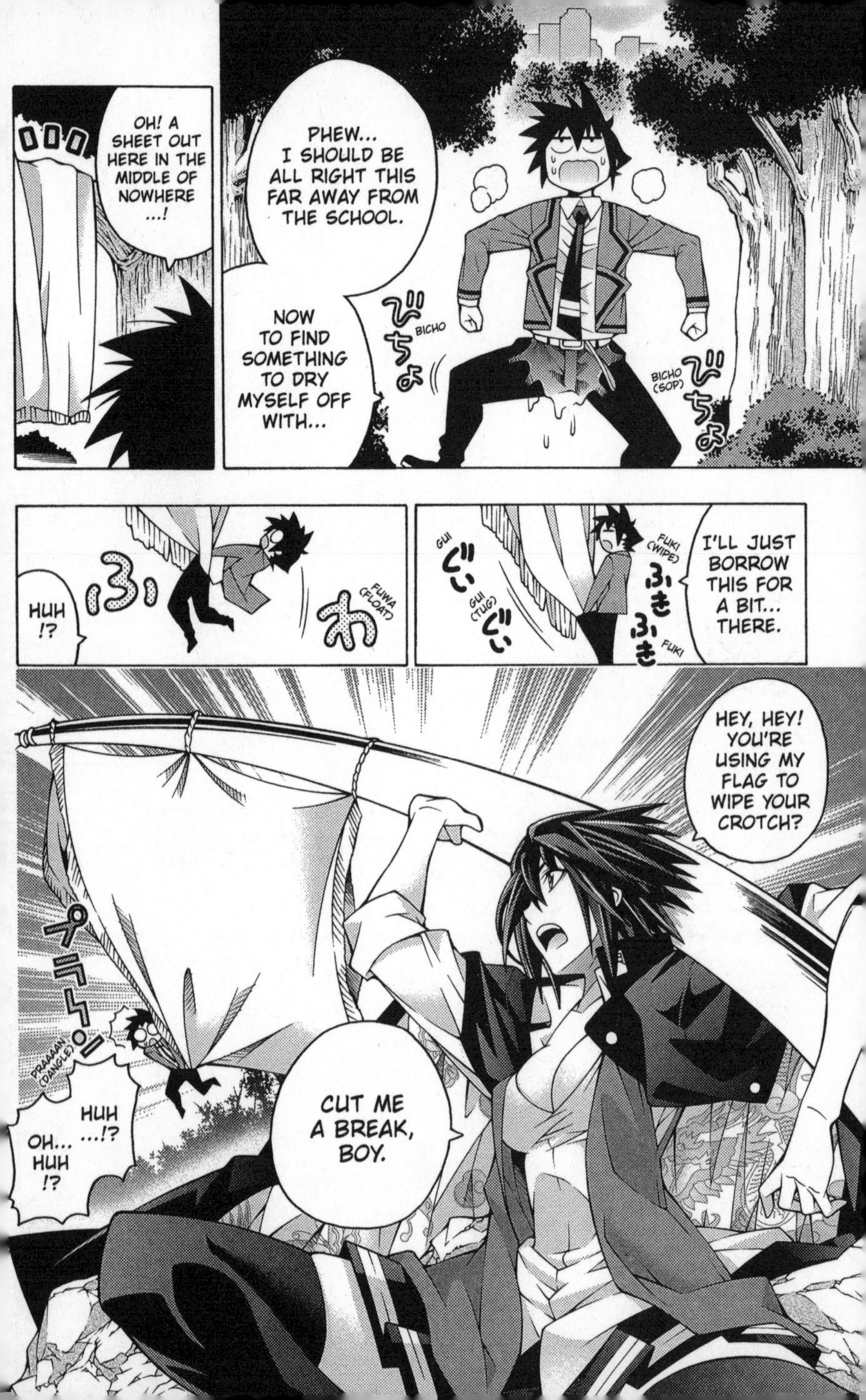
PHEW... I SHOULD BE ALL RIGHT THIS FAR AWAY FROM THE SCHOOL.
NOW TO FIND SOMETHING TO DRY MYSELF OFF WITH...
びちょ
BICHO (SOP)
びちょ
BICHO
OH! A SHEET OUT HERE IN THE MIDDLE OF NOWHERE ...!
I'LL JUST BORROW THIS FOR A BIT... THERE.
ふき
FUKI (WIPE)
ふき
FUKI
ぐい
GUI
ぐい
GUI (TUG)
ふわ
FUWA (FLOAT)
HUH !?
HEY, HEY! YOU'RE USING MY FLAG TO WIPE YOUR CROTCH?
CUT ME A BREAK, BOY.
プラ〜ン
PRAAAAN (DANGLE)
HUH ...!?
OH... HUH !?

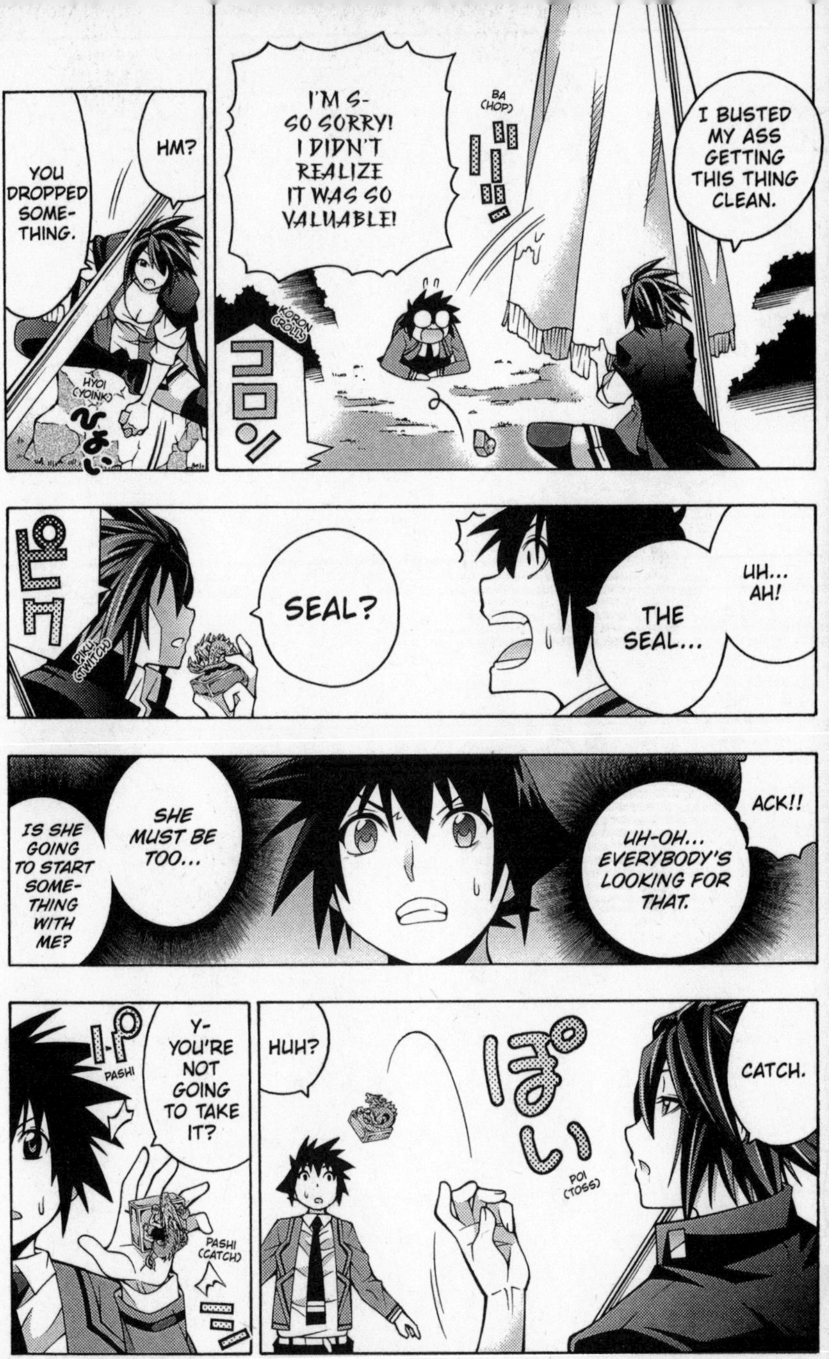
I BUSTED MY ASS GETTING THIS THING CLEAN.
BA (HOP)
I'M S- SO SORRY! I DIDN'T REALIZE IT WAS SO VALUABLE!
KORON (ROLL)
HM?
YOU DROPPED SOME-THING.
HYOI (YOINK)
UH... AH!
THE SEAL...
SEAL?
PIKU (TWITCH)
ACK!!
UH-OH... EVERYBODY'S LOOKING FOR THAT.
SHE MUST BE TOO...
IS SHE GOING TO START SOME-THING WITH ME?
CATCH.
POI (TOSS)
HUH?
PASHI
Y- YOU'RE NOT GOING TO TAKE IT?
PASHI (CATCH)

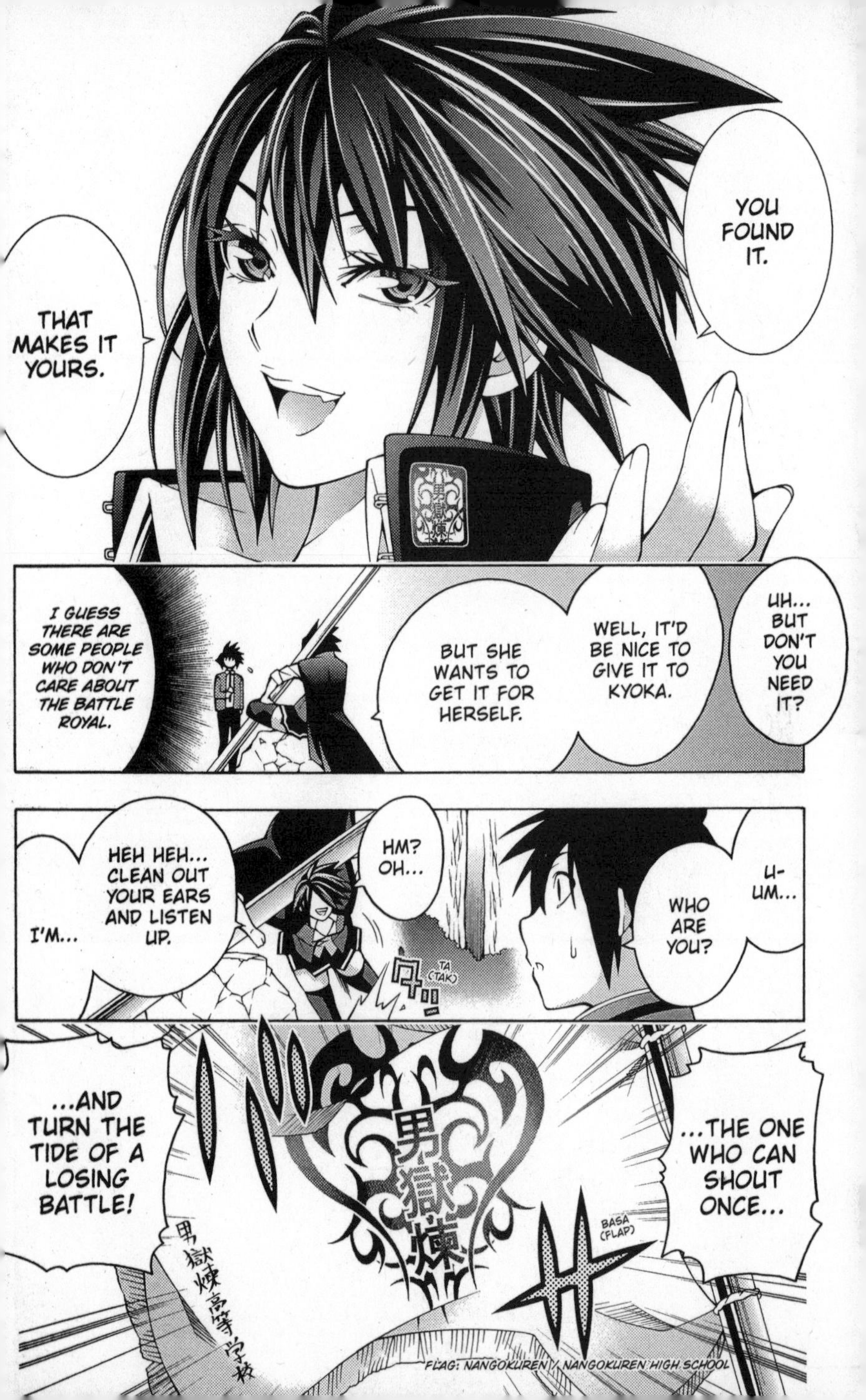
YOU FOUND IT.
THAT MAKES IT YOURS.
UH... BUT DON'T YOU NEED IT?
WELL, IT'D BE NICE TO GIVE IT TO KYOKA.
BUT SHE WANTS TO GET IT FOR HERSELF.
I GUESS THERE ARE SOME PEOPLE WHO DON'T CARE ABOUT THE BATTLE ROYAL.
U-UM...
WHO ARE YOU?
HM? OH...
TA (TAK)
HEH HEH... CLEAN OUT YOUR EARS AND LISTEN UP.
I'M...
...THE ONE WHO CAN SHOUT ONCE...
BASA (FLAP)
男獄煉
...AND TURN THE TIDE OF A LOSING BATTLE!
男獄煉高等学校
FLAG: NANGOKUREN / NANGOKUREN HIGH SCHOOL

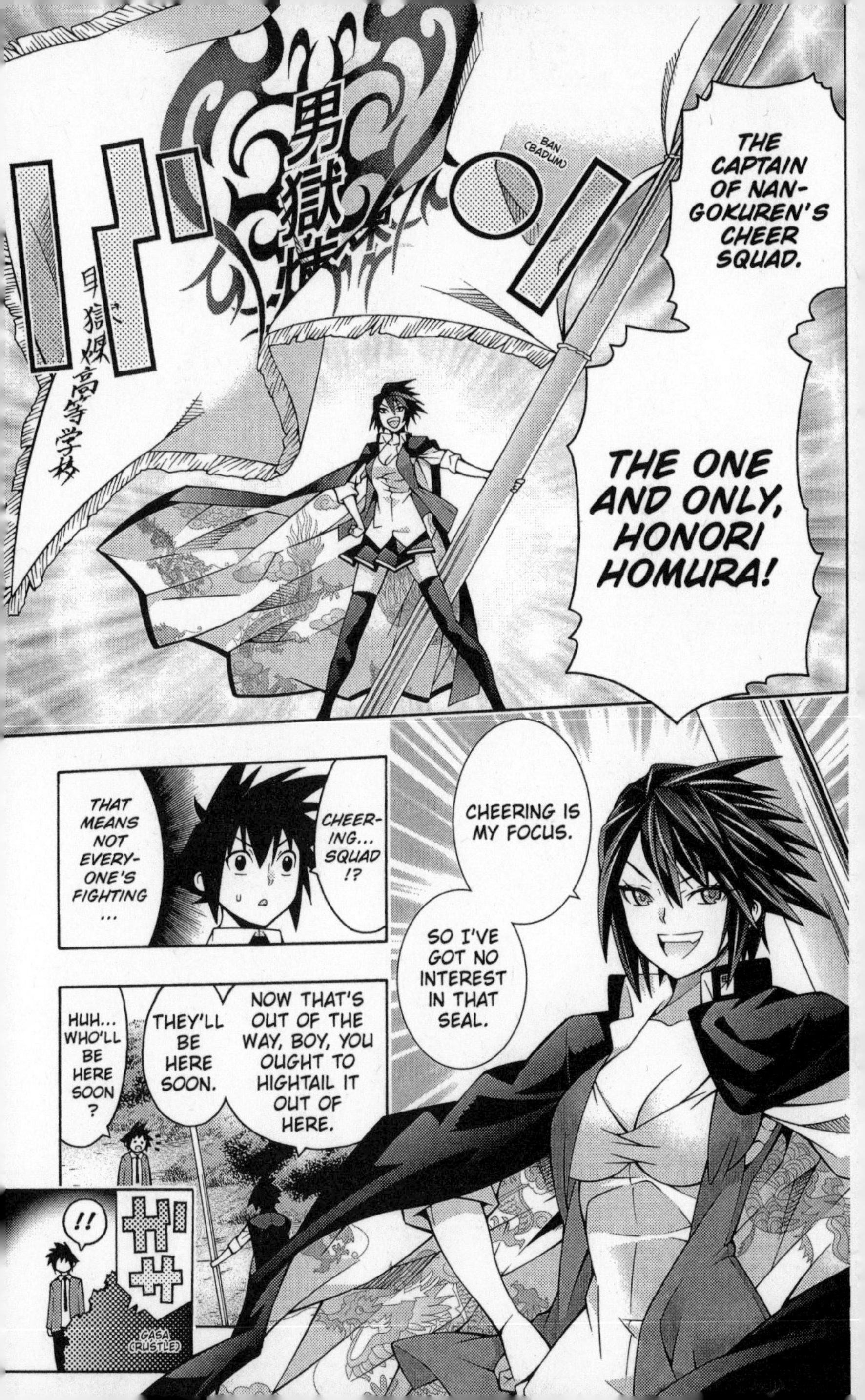
男獄
BAN (BADUM)
THE CAPTAIN OF NAN-GOKUREN'S CHEER SQUAD.
THE ONE AND ONLY, HONORI HOMURA!
CHEERING IS MY FOCUS.
SO I'VE GOT NO INTEREST IN THAT SEAL.
CHEER-ING... SQUAD!?
THAT MEANS NOT EVERY-ONE'S FIGHTING...
NOW THAT'S OUT OF THE WAY, BOY, YOU OUGHT TO HIGHTAIL IT OUT OF HERE.
THEY'LL BE HERE SOON.
HUH... WHO'LL BE HERE SOON?
!!
GASA (RUSTLE)

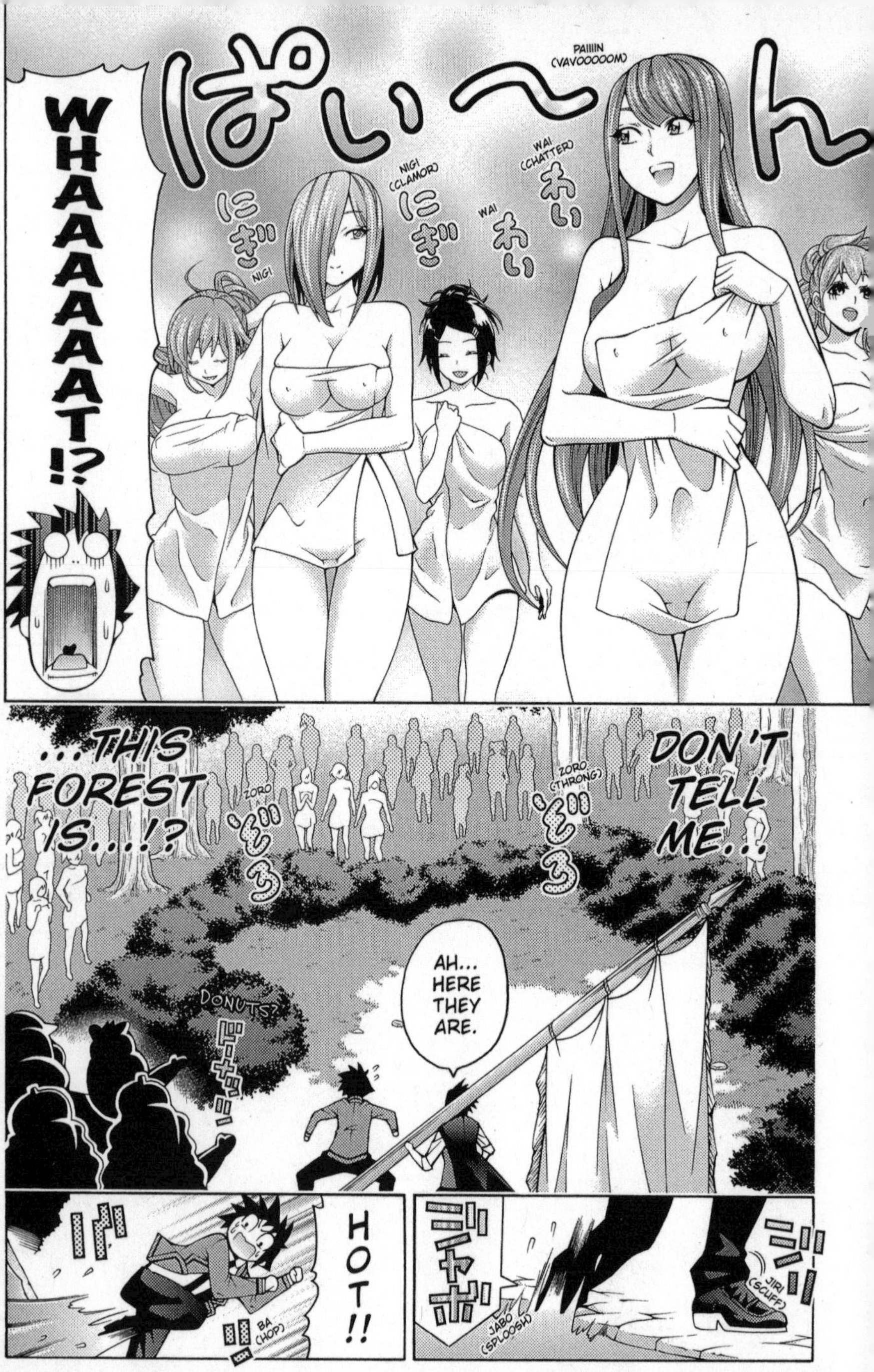
ぱい〜ん
PAIIIN (VAVOOOOOM)
わい わい
WAI (CHATTER)
WAI
にぎ にぎ
NIGI (CLAMOR)
NIGI
WHAAAAAAAT!?
DON'T TELL ME...
ぞろ ぞろ
ZORO (THRONG)
ZORO
...THIS FOREST IS...!?
AH... HERE THEY ARE.
DONUTS?
ジリ
JIRI (SCUFF)
ジャボ
JABO (SPLOOSH)
HOT!!
バッ
BA (HOP)

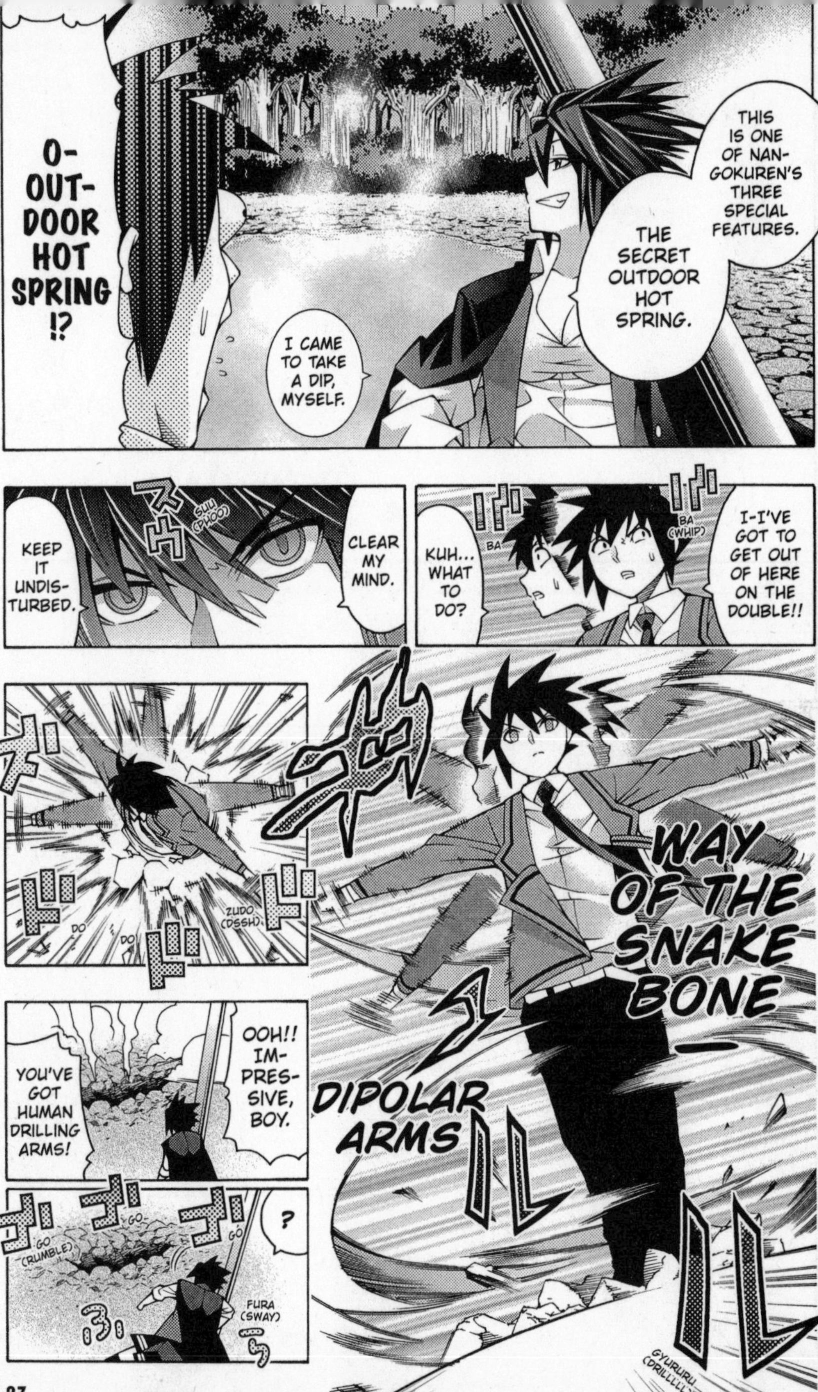

THIS IS ONE OF NAN-GOKUREN'S THREE SPECIAL FEATURES.
THE SECRET OUTDOOR HOT SPRING.
I CAME TO TAKE A DIP, MYSELF.
O-OUTDOOR HOT SPRING!?
I-I'VE GOT TO GET OUT OF HERE ON THE DOUBLE!!
BA (WHIP)
BA
KUH... WHAT TO DO?
CLEAR MY MIND.
SUU (PHOO)
KEEP IT UNDISTURBED.
WAY OF THE SNAKE BONE
DIPOLAR ARMS
GYURURU (DRILLLLL)
ZUDO (DSSH)
DO
DO
OOH!! IM-PRES-SIVE, BOY.
YOU'VE GOT HUMAN DRILLING ARMS!
?
GO
GO
GO (RUMBLE)
FURA (SWAY)

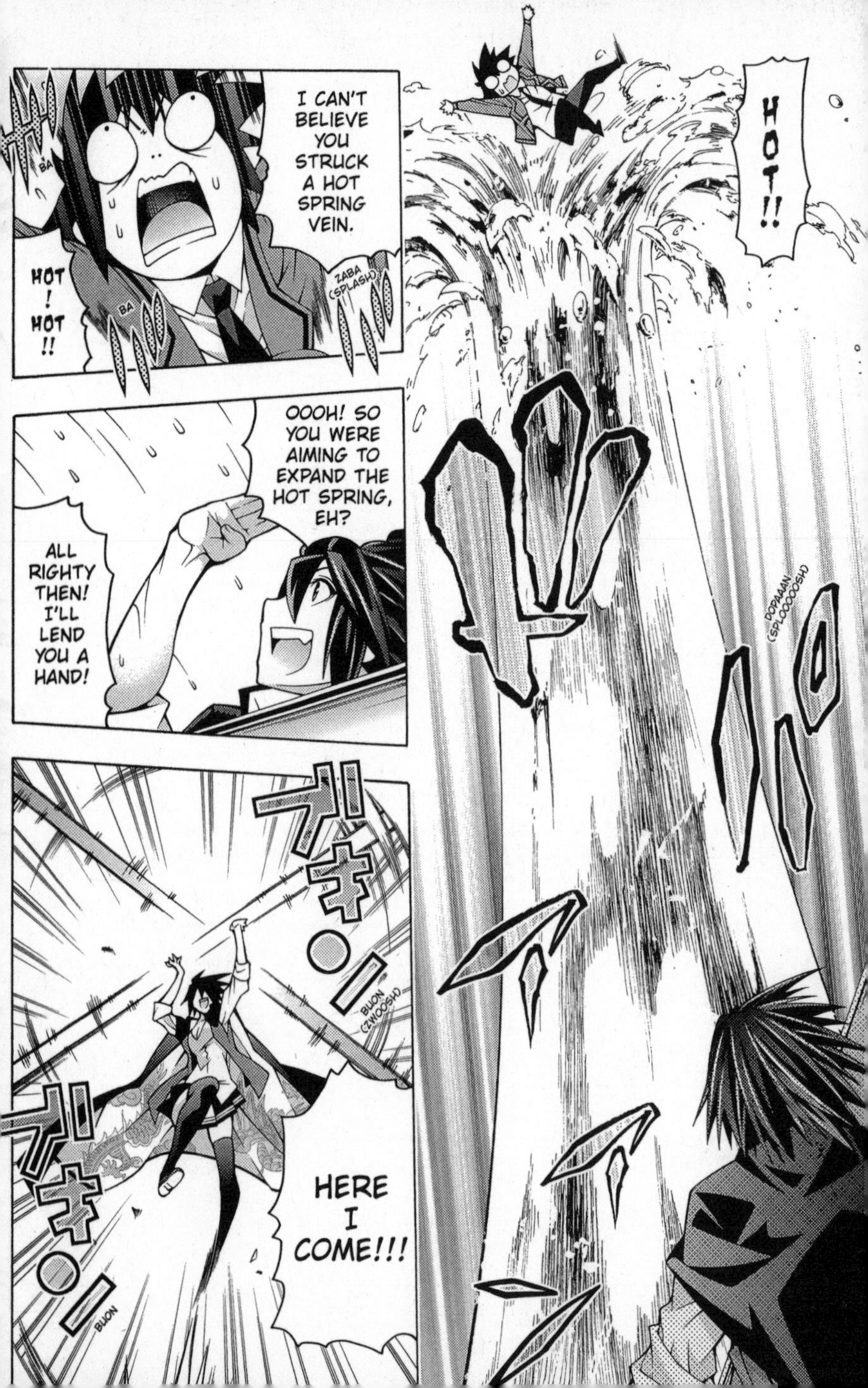
HOT!!
DOPAAAN (SPLOOOOOSH)
I CAN'T BELIEVE YOU STRUCK A HOT SPRING VEIN.
ZABA (SPLASH)
BA
BA
HOT! HOT!!
OOOH! SO YOU WERE AIMING TO EXPAND THE HOT SPRING, EH?
ALL RIGHTY THEN! I'LL LEND YOU A HAND!
BUON (ZWOOSH)
HERE I COME!!!
BUON

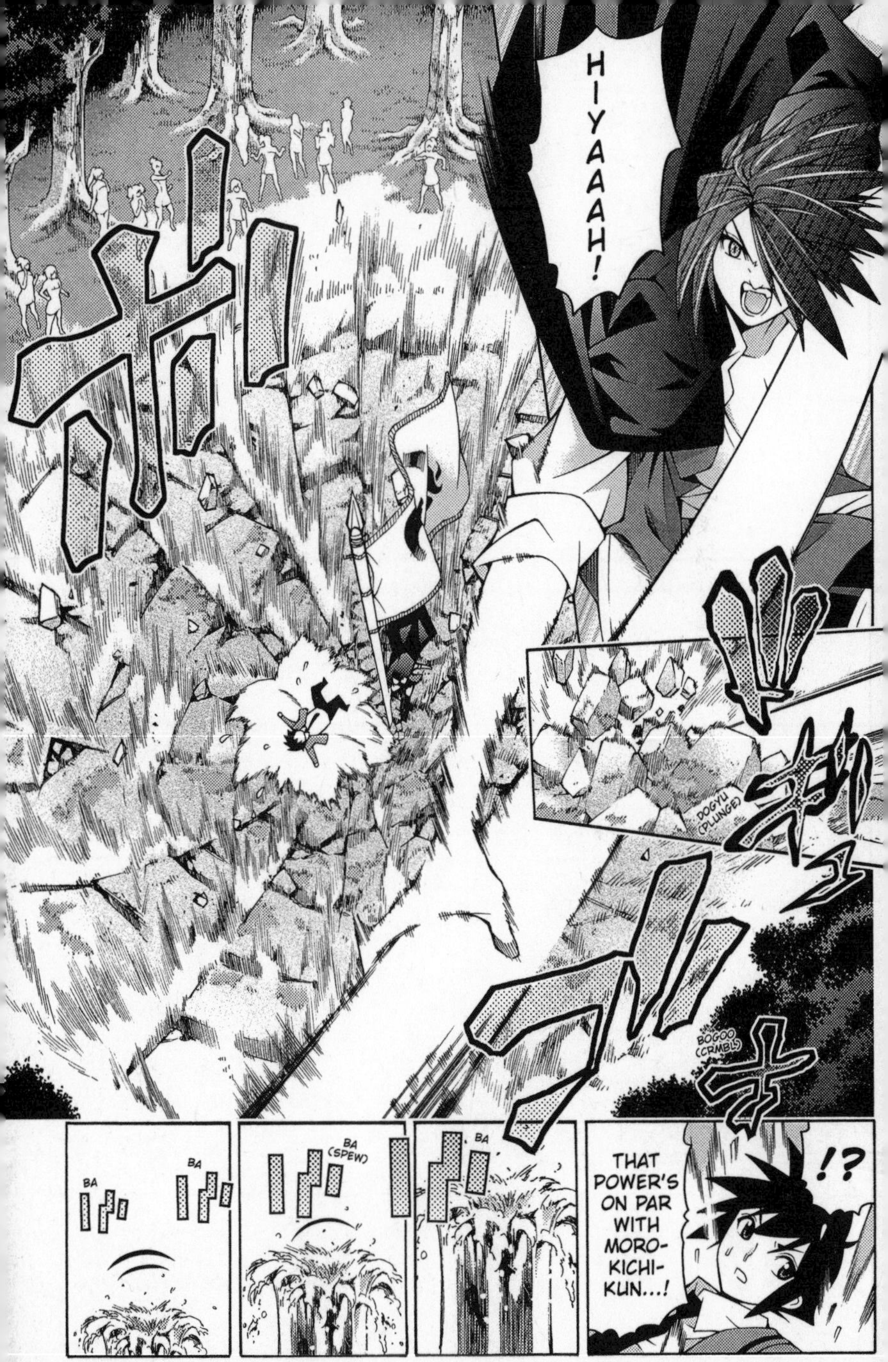
HIYAAAAH!
DOGYU (PLUNGE)
BOGOO (CRMBL)
!?
THAT POWER'S ON PAR WITH MORO-KICHI-KUN...!
BA
BA (SPEW)
BA
BA

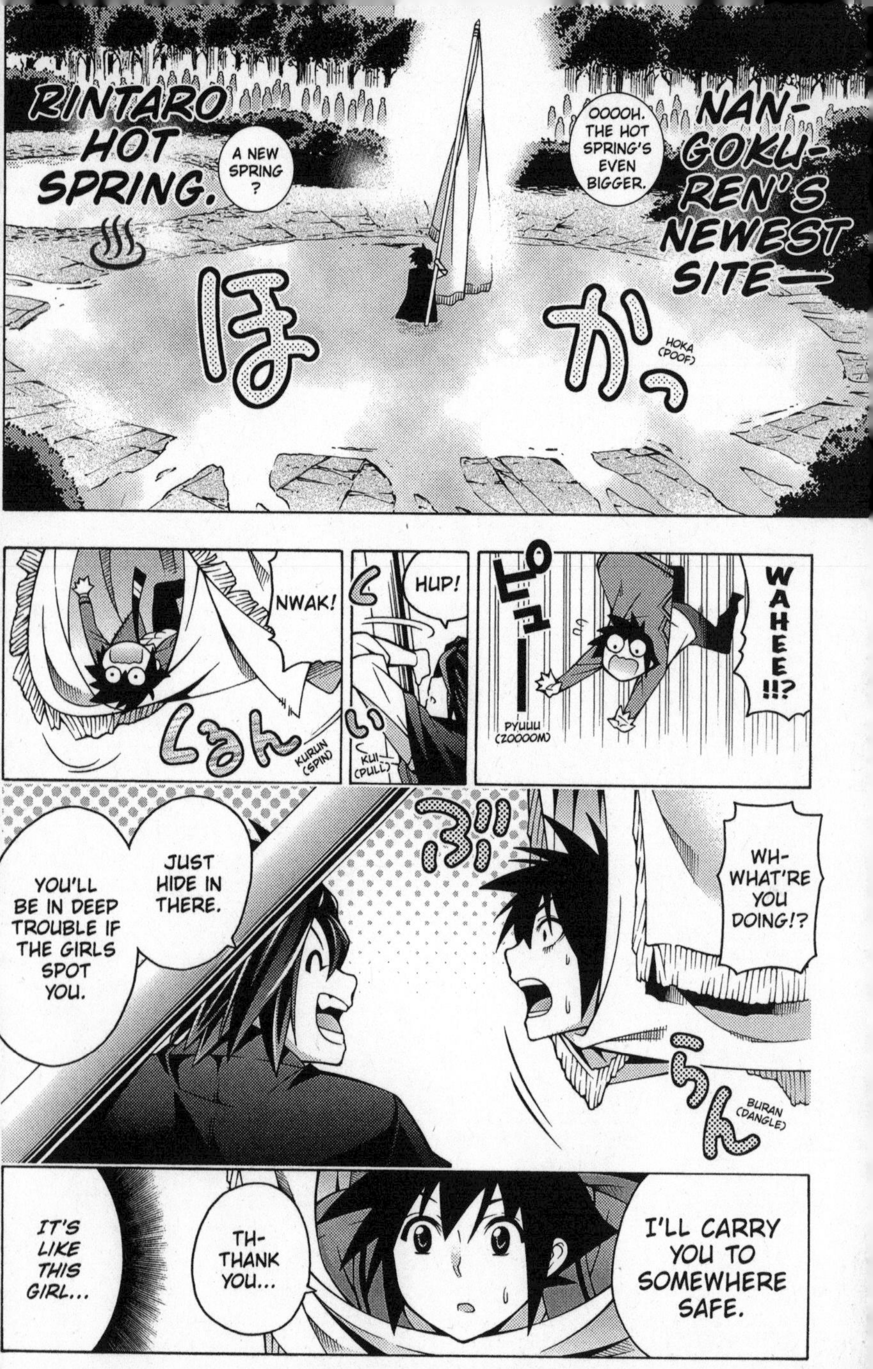
NAN-GOKU-REN'S NEWEST SITE—
OOOOH. THE HOT SPRING'S EVEN BIGGER.
A NEW SPRING ?
RINTARO HOT SPRING.
HOKA (POOF)
WAHEE!!?
PYUUU (ZOOOOM)
HUP!
KUI (PULL)
NWAK!
KURUN (SPIN)
WH-WHAT'RE YOU DOING!?
BURAN (DANGLE)
JUST HIDE IN THERE.
YOU'LL BE IN DEEP TROUBLE IF THE GIRLS SPOT YOU.
I'LL CARRY YOU TO SOMEWHERE SAFE.
TH-THANK YOU...
IT'S LIKE THIS GIRL...

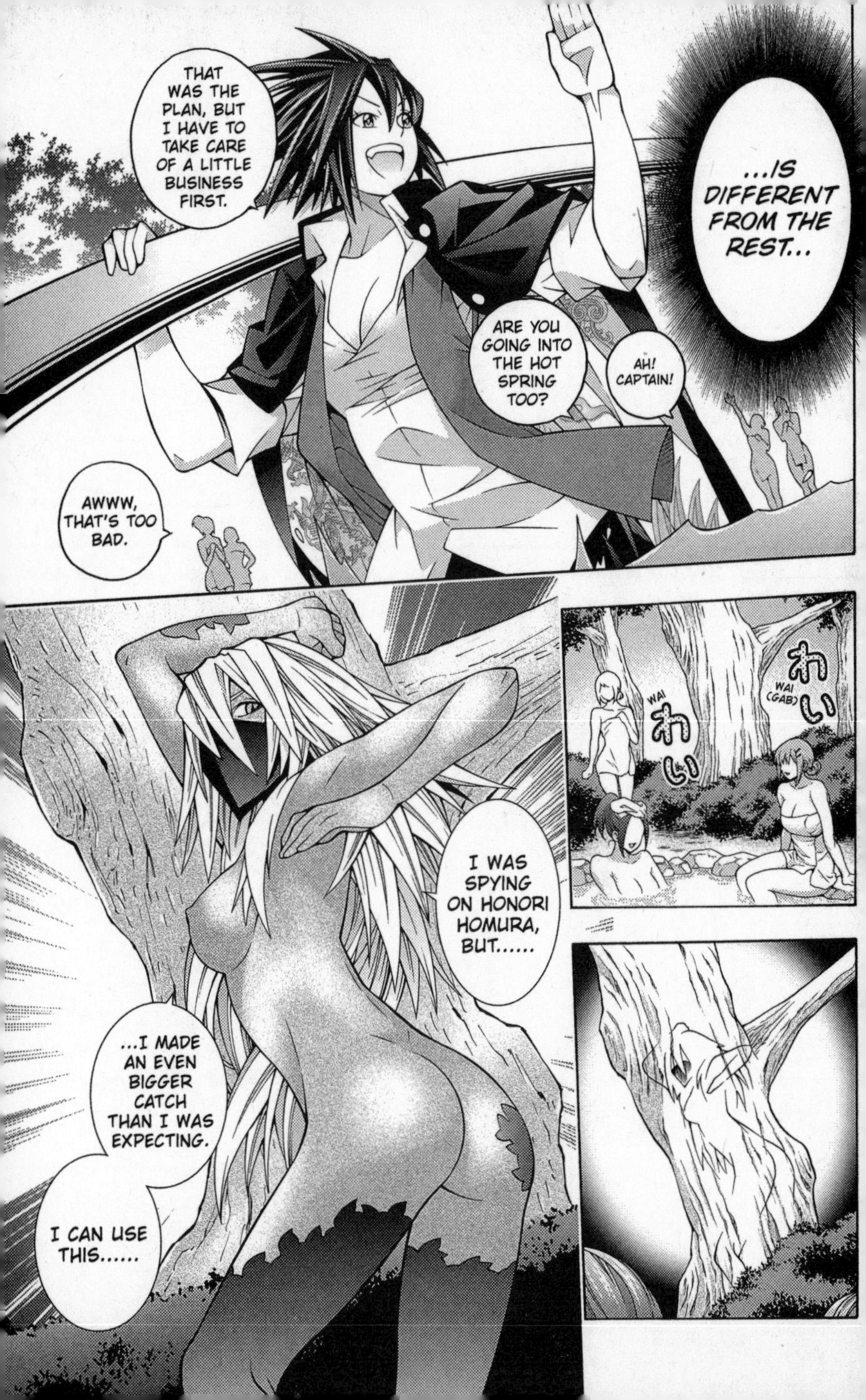
...IS DIFFERENT FROM THE REST...
AH! CAPTAIN!
ARE YOU GOING INTO THE HOT SPRING TOO?
THAT WAS THE PLAN, BUT I HAVE TO TAKE CARE OF A LITTLE BUSINESS FIRST.
AWWW, THAT'S TOO BAD.
わい
WAI (GAB)
わい
WAI
I WAS SPYING ON HONORI HOMURA, BUT......
...I MADE AN EVEN BIGGER CATCH THAN I WAS EXPECTING.
I CAN USE THIS......

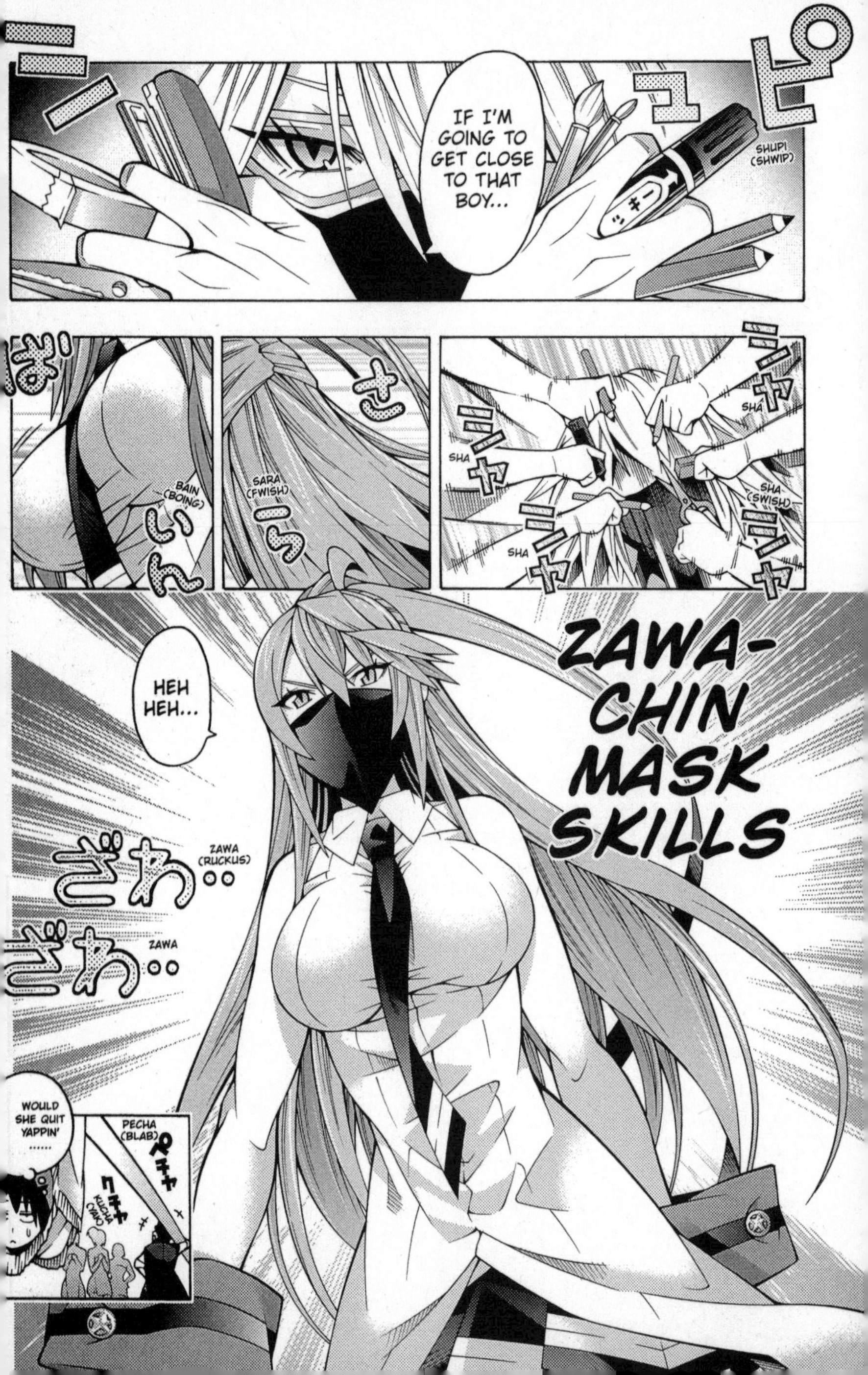

SHUPI (SHWIP)
IF I'M GOING TO GET CLOSE TO THAT BOY...
SHA
SHA
SHA (SWISH)
SHA
SARA (FWISH)
BAIN (BOING)
ZAWA-CHIN MASK SKILLS
HEH HEH...
ZAWA (RUCKUS)
ZAWA
PECHA (BLAB)
KUCHA (YAP)
WOULD SHE QUIT YAPPIN' ......

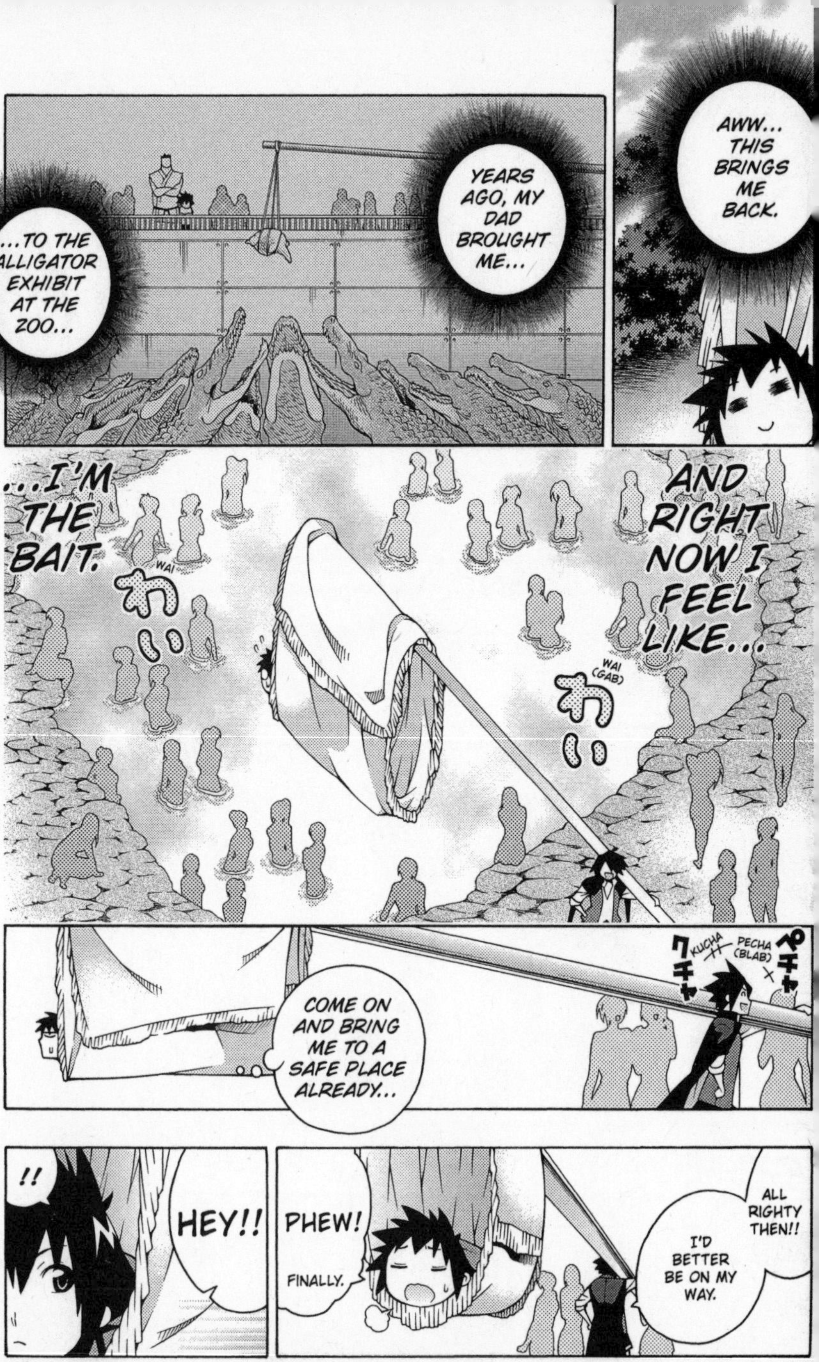
AWW... THIS BRINGS ME BACK.
YEARS AGO, MY DAD BROUGHT ME...
...TO THE ALLIGATOR EXHIBIT AT THE ZOO...
AND RIGHT NOW I FEEL LIKE...
わい
WAI (GAB)
わい
WAI
...I'M THE BAIT.
ペチャ
PECHA (BLAB)
クチャ
KUCHA
COME ON AND BRING ME TO A SAFE PLACE ALREADY...
ALL RIGHTY THEN!!
I'D BETTER BE ON MY WAY.
PHEW!
FINALLY.
HEY!!
!!

DRAGON 26 A WIFE FIERCELY GUARDS HER CHASTITY

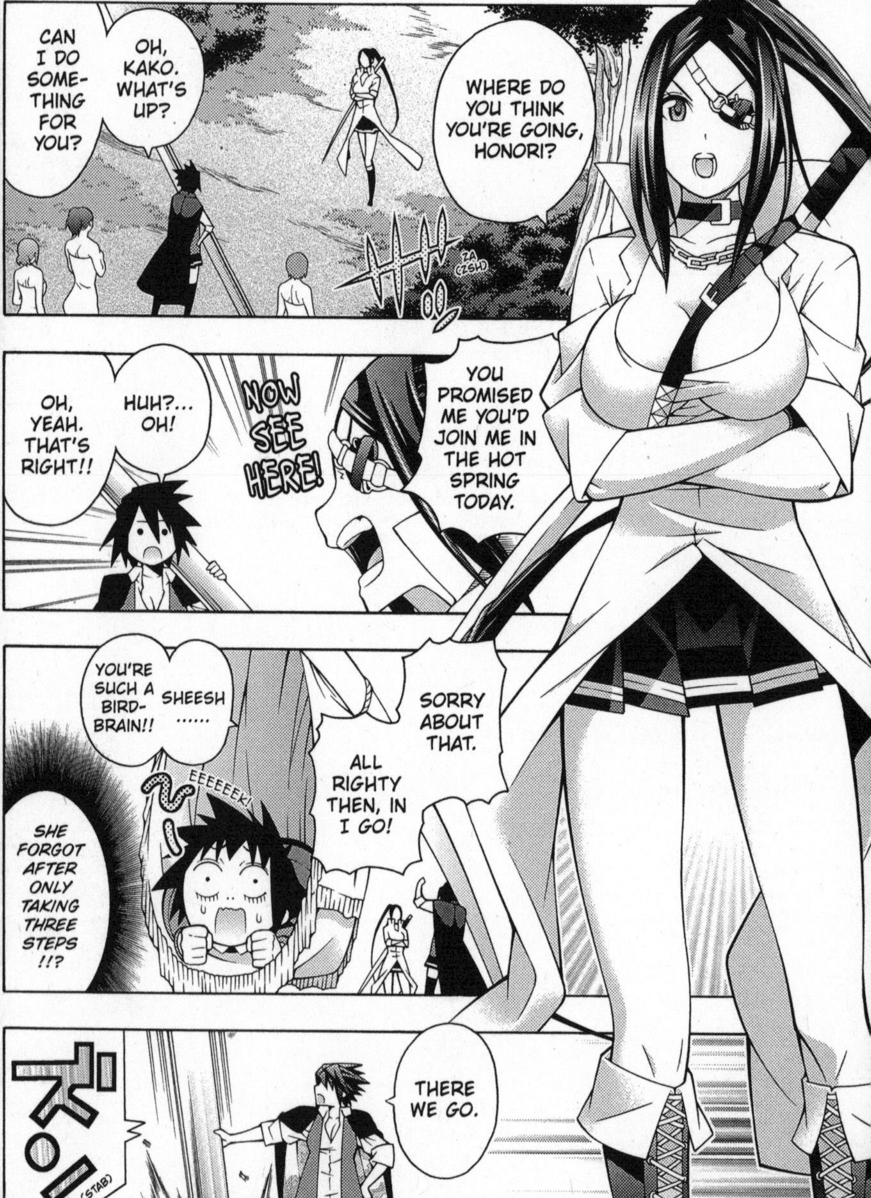
WHERE DO YOU THINK YOU'RE GOING, HONORI?
ZA (ZSH)
OH, KAKO. WHAT'S UP?
CAN I DO SOMETHING FOR YOU?
YOU PROMISED ME YOU'D JOIN ME IN THE HOT SPRING TODAY.
NOW SEE HERE!
HUH?... OH!
OH, YEAH. THAT'S RIGHT!!
SORRY ABOUT THAT.
ALL RIGHTY THEN, IN I GO!
SHEESH ......
YOU'RE SUCH A BIRD-BRAIN!!
EEEEEEK!
SHE FORGOT AFTER ONLY TAKING THREE STEPS!!?
THERE WE GO.
ZUN (STAB)

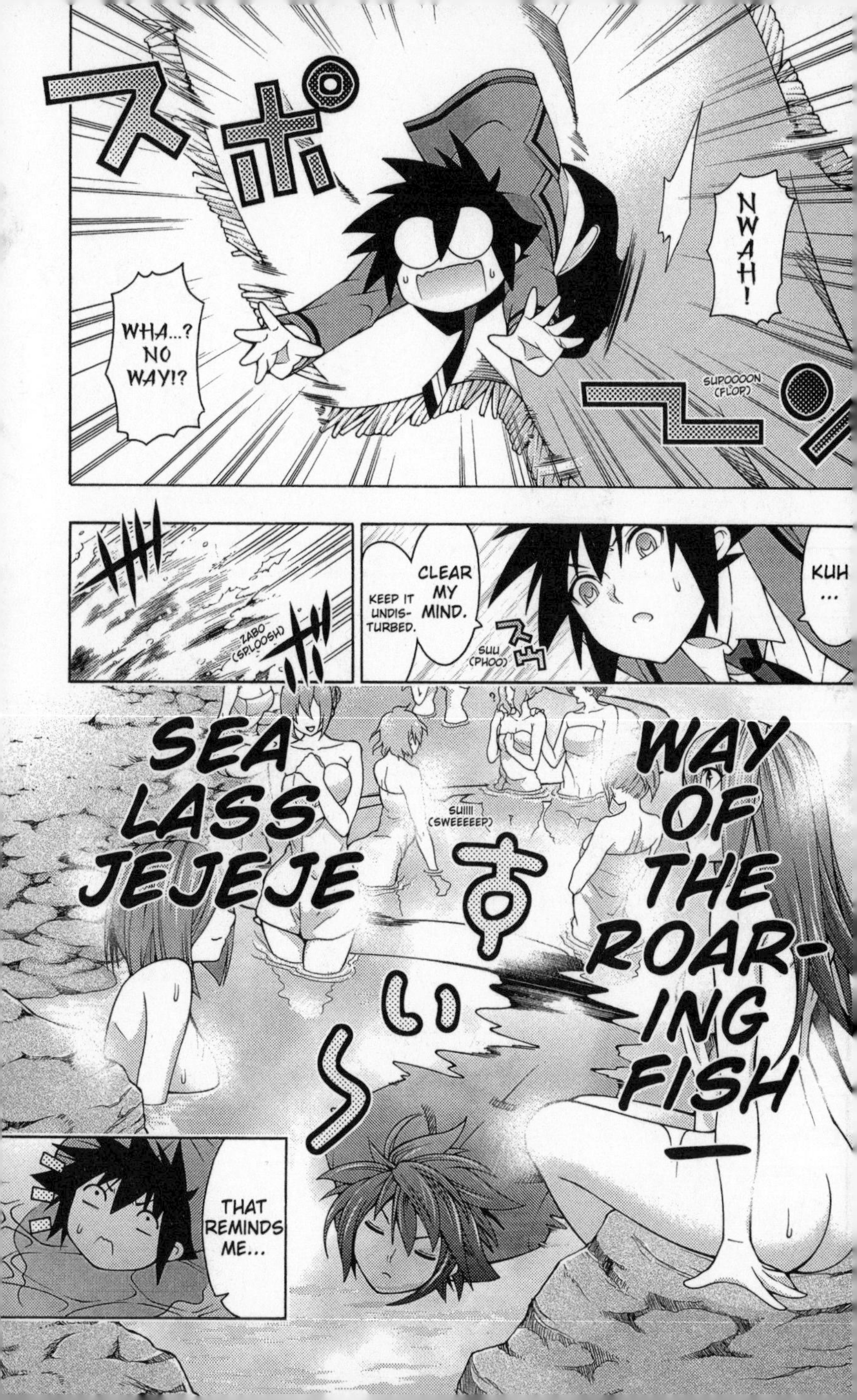

NWAH!
SUPOOOON (FLOP)
WHA...? NO WAY!?
KUH...
CLEAR MY MIND.
KEEP IT UNDIS-TURBED.
SUU (PHOO)
ZABO (SPLOOSH)
WAY OF THE ROAR-ING FISH
SUIIII (SWEEEEEP)
SEA LASS JEJEJE
THAT REMINDS ME...

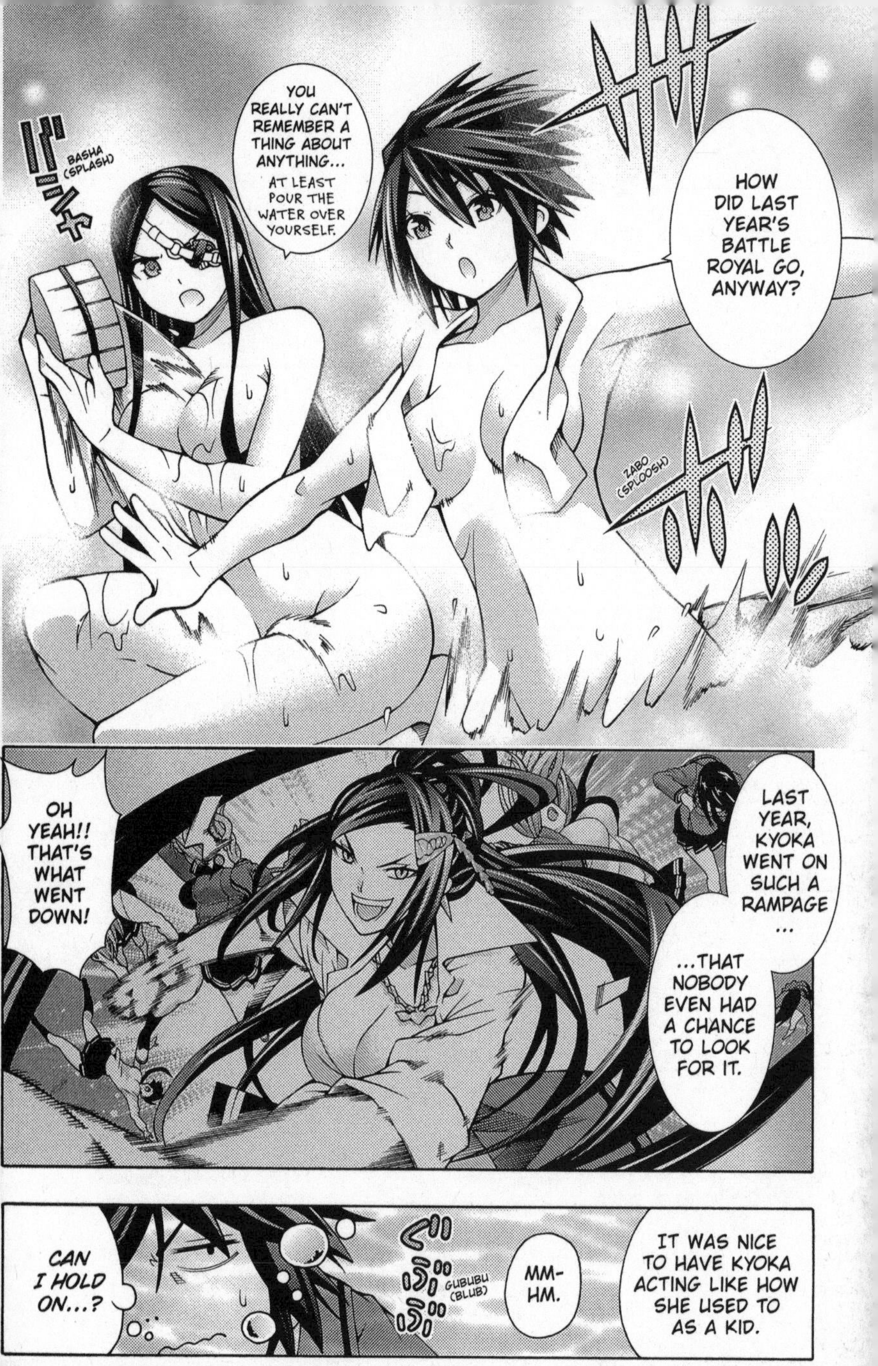

HOW DID LAST YEAR'S BATTLE ROYAL GO, ANYWAY?
ZABO (SPLOOSH)
YOU REALLY CAN'T REMEMBER A THING ABOUT ANYTHING...
AT LEAST POUR THE WATER OVER YOURSELF.
BASHA (SPLASH)
LAST YEAR, KYOKA WENT ON SUCH A RAMPAGE...
...THAT NOBODY EVEN HAD A CHANCE TO LOOK FOR IT.
OH YEAH!! THAT'S WHAT WENT DOWN!
IT WAS NICE TO HAVE KYOKA ACTING LIKE HOW SHE USED TO AS A KID.
MM-HM.
GUBUBU (BLUB)
CAN I HOLD ON...?

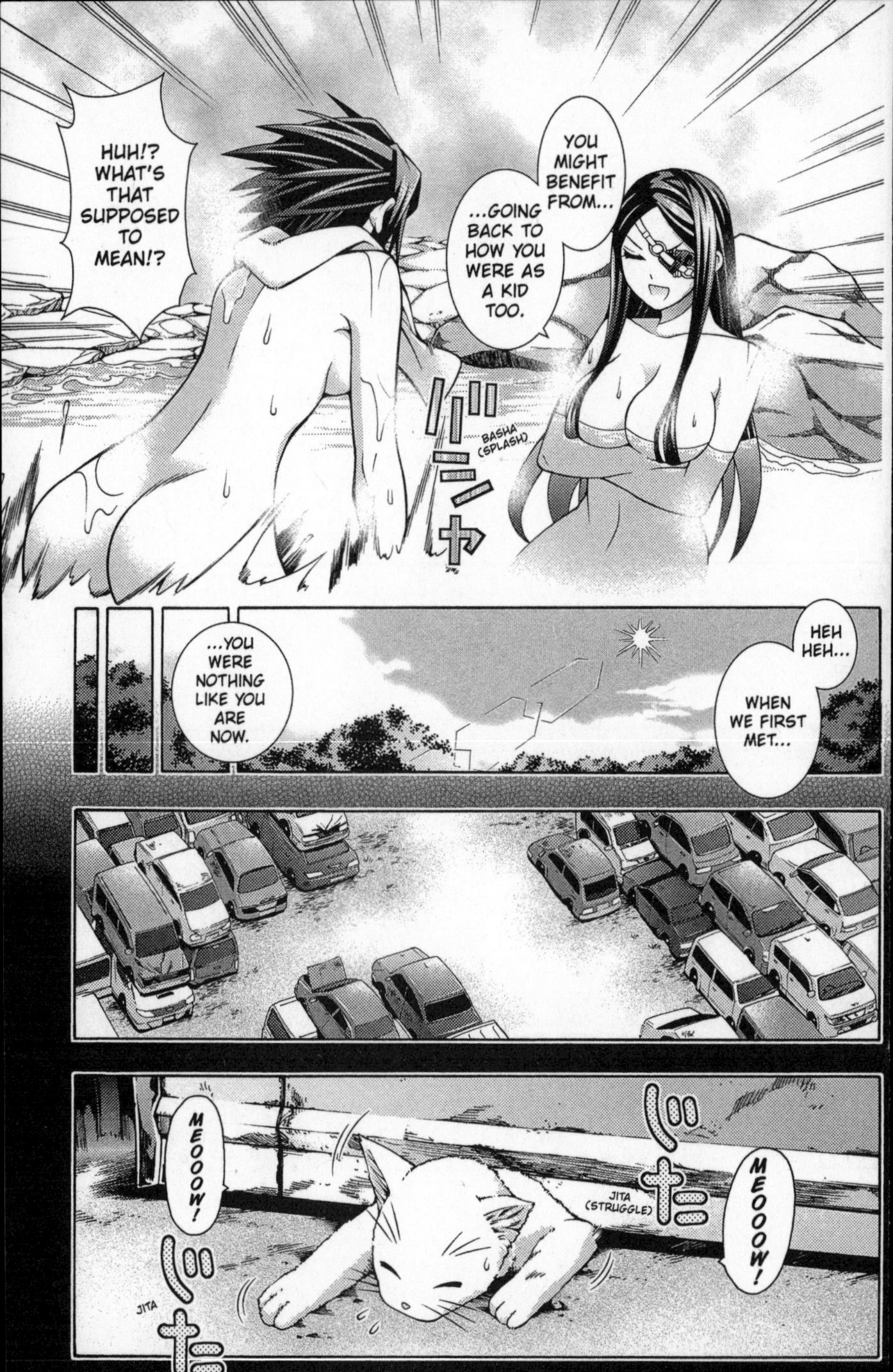
YOU MIGHT BENEFIT FROM...
...GOING BACK TO HOW YOU WERE AS A KID TOO.
BASHA (SPLASH)
HUH!? WHAT'S THAT SUPPOSED TO MEAN!?
HEH HEH...
WHEN WE FIRST MET...
...YOU WERE NOTHING LIKE YOU ARE NOW.
MEOOOW!
JITA (STRUGGLE)
MEOOOW!
JITA

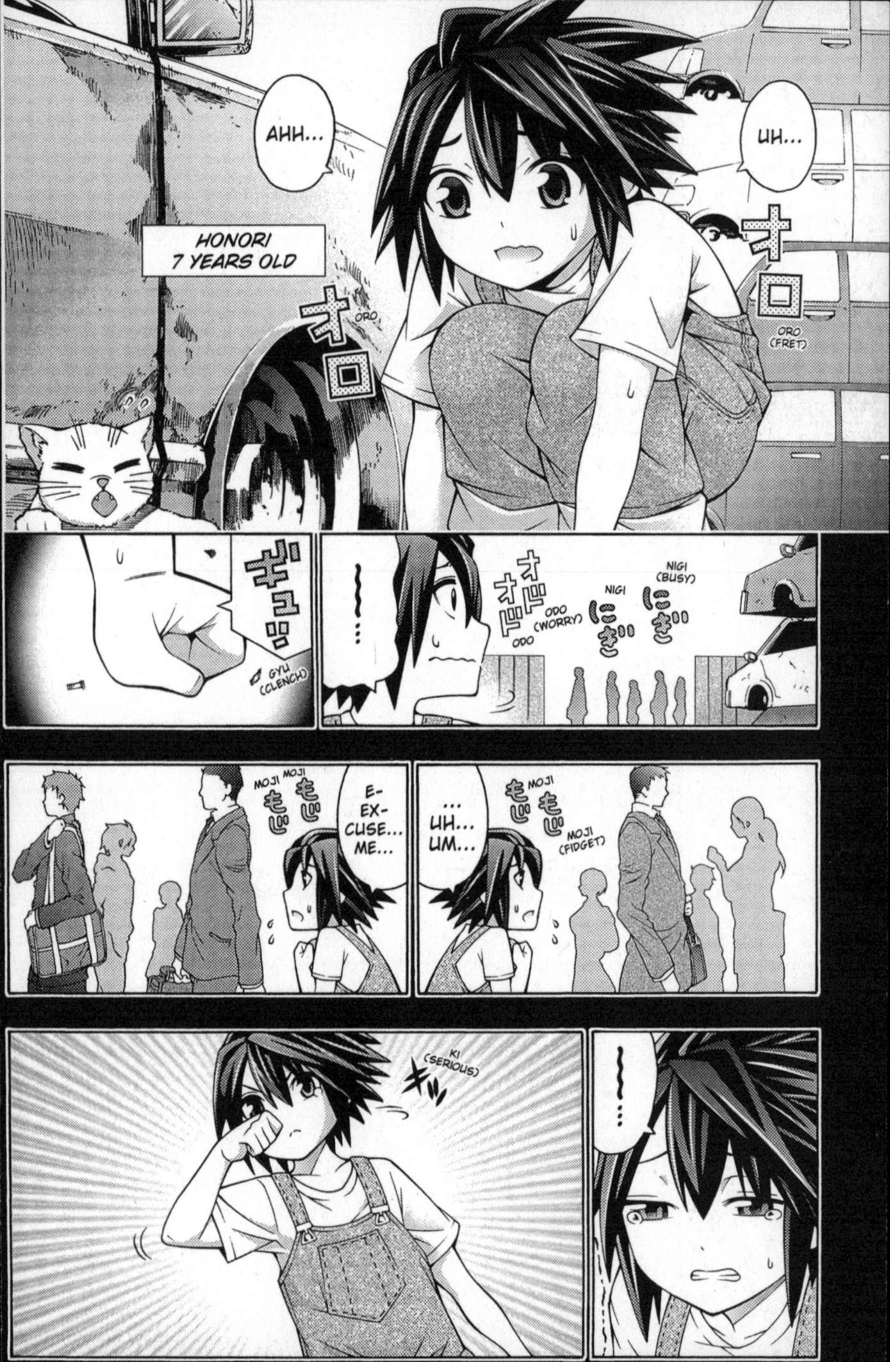
UH...
AHH...
HONORI
7 YEARS OLD
オロ
ORO (FRET)
オロ
ORO
にぎ
NIGI (BUSY)
にぎ
NIGI
オド
ODO (WORRY)
オド
ODO
...
ギュ
GYU (CLENCH)
もじ
MOJI
もじ
MOJI (FIDGET)
... UH... UM...
もじもじ
MOJI MOJI
E- EX- CUSE... ME...
...
キ
KI (SERIOUS)

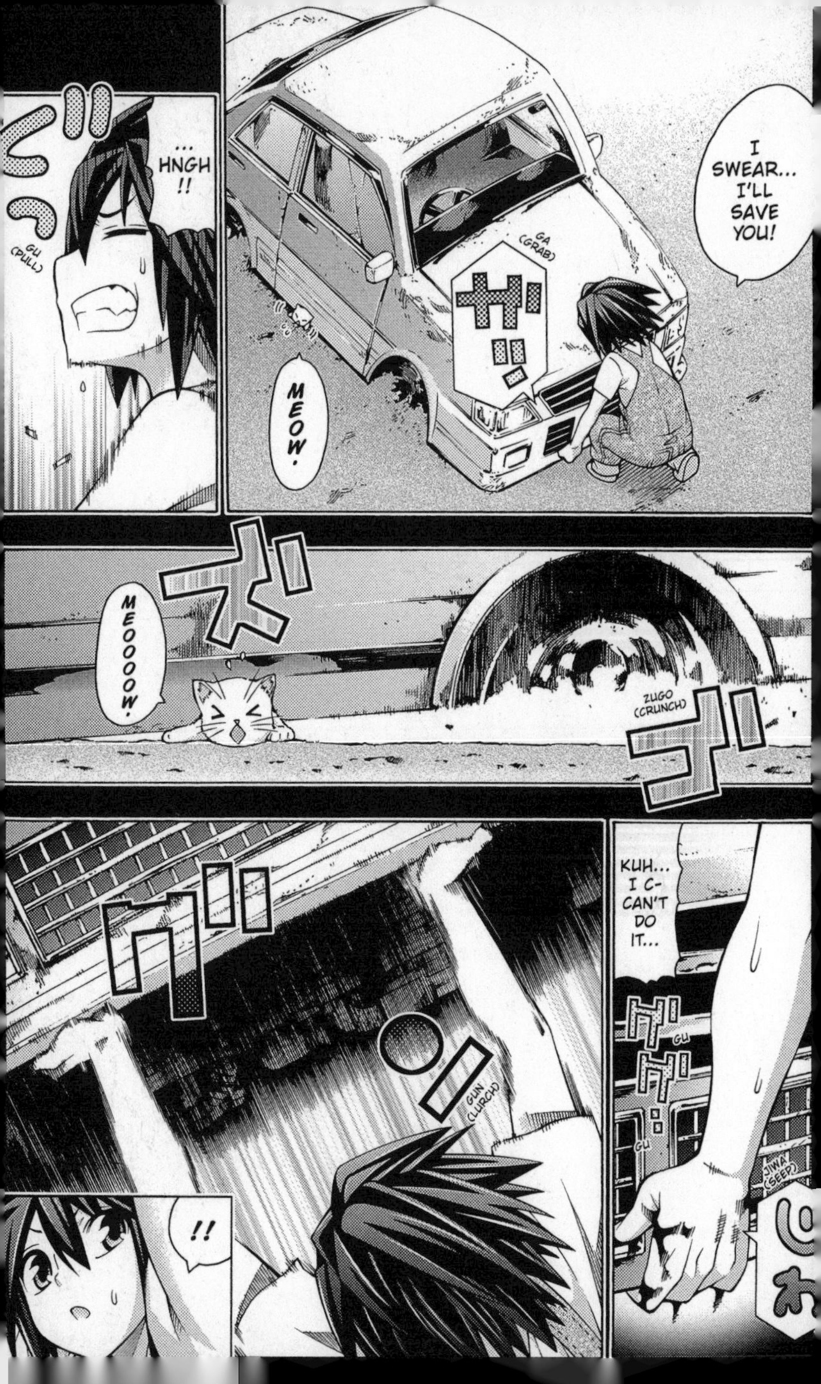
I SWEAR... I'LL SAVE YOU!
GA (GRAB)
MEOW.
...HNGH !!
GU (PULL)
MEOOOOOW.
ZUGO (CRUNCH)
KUH... I C-CAN'T DO IT...
GU
GU
JIWA (SEEP)
GUN (LURCH)
!!

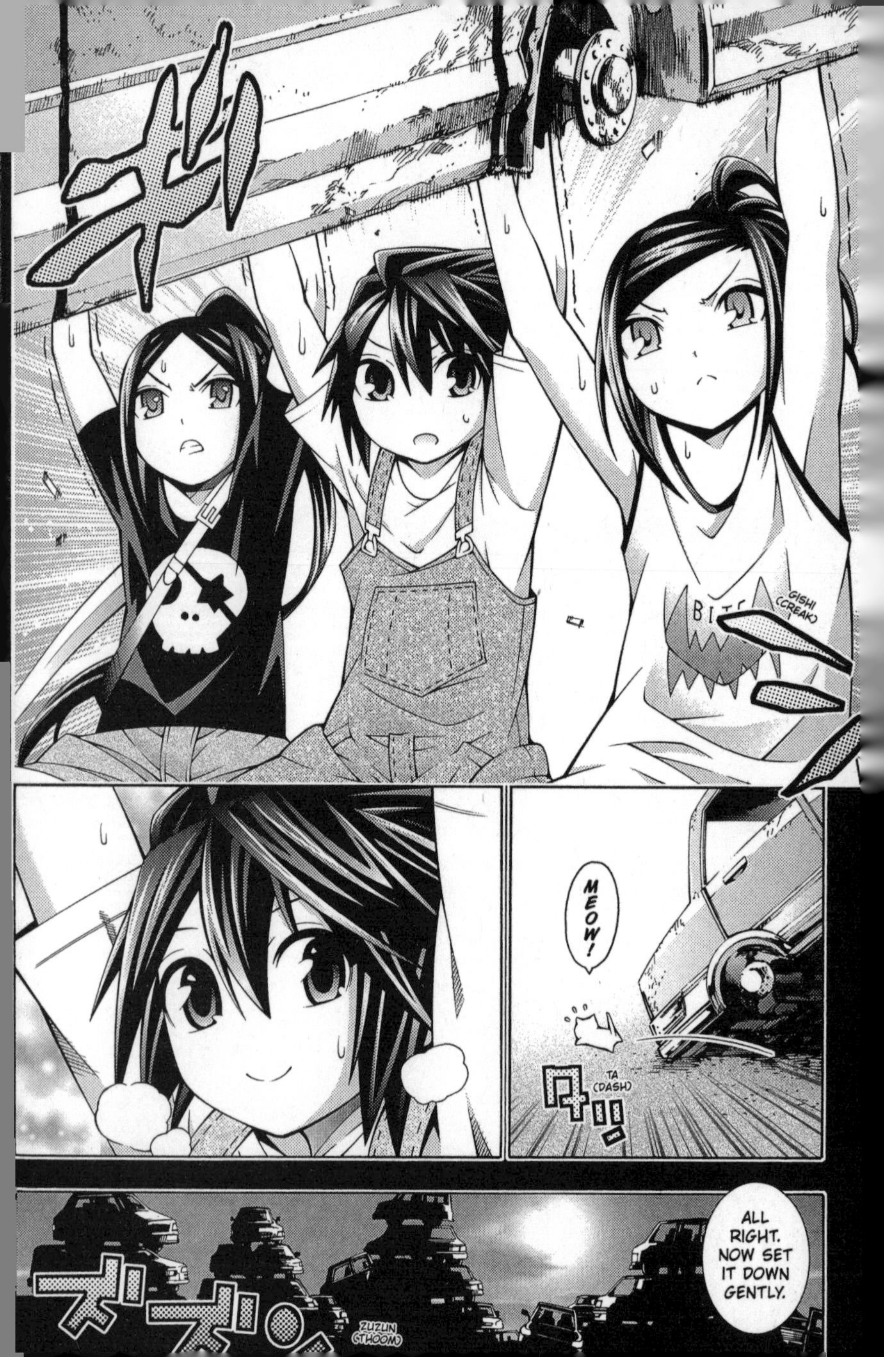
GISHI (CREAK)
MEOW!
TA (DASH)
ALL RIGHT. NOW SET IT DOWN GENTLY.
ZUZUN (THOOM)

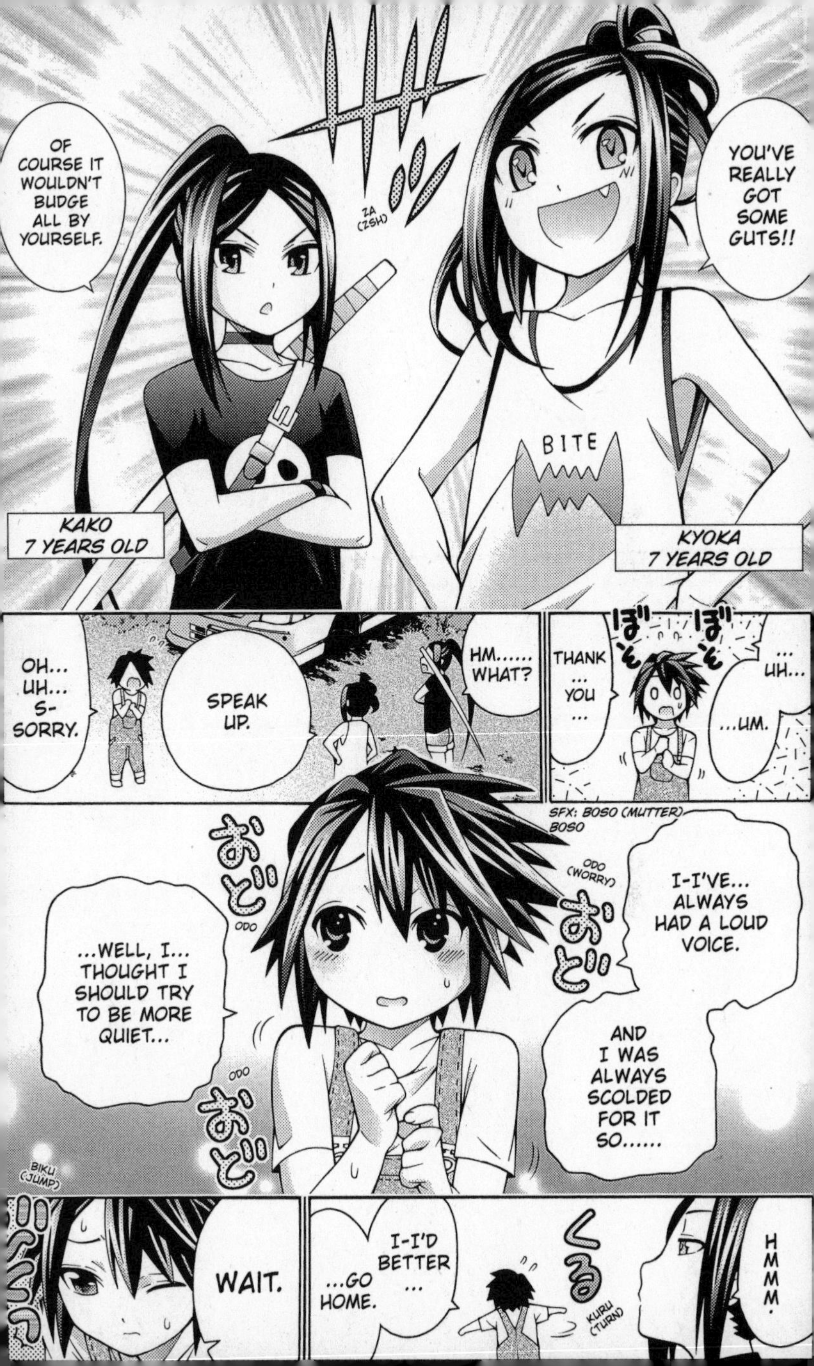
YOU'VE REALLY GOT SOME GUTS!!
ZA (ZSH)
OF COURSE IT WOULDN'T BUDGE ALL BY YOURSELF.
KYOKA 7 YEARS OLD
KAKO 7 YEARS OLD
ぼそ ぼそ
... UH...
...UM.
THANK ... YOU ...
HM...... WHAT?
SPEAK UP.
OH... UH... S-SORRY.
SFX: BOSO (MUTTER) BOSO
I-I'VE... ALWAYS HAD A LOUD VOICE.
おど
ODO (WORRY)
AND I WAS ALWAYS SCOLDED FOR IT SO......
おど
ODO
...WELL, I... THOUGHT I SHOULD TRY TO BE MORE QUIET...
おど
ODO
BIKU (JUMP)
HMMM.
くる
KURU (TURN)
I-I'D BETTER ...
...GO HOME.
WAIT.

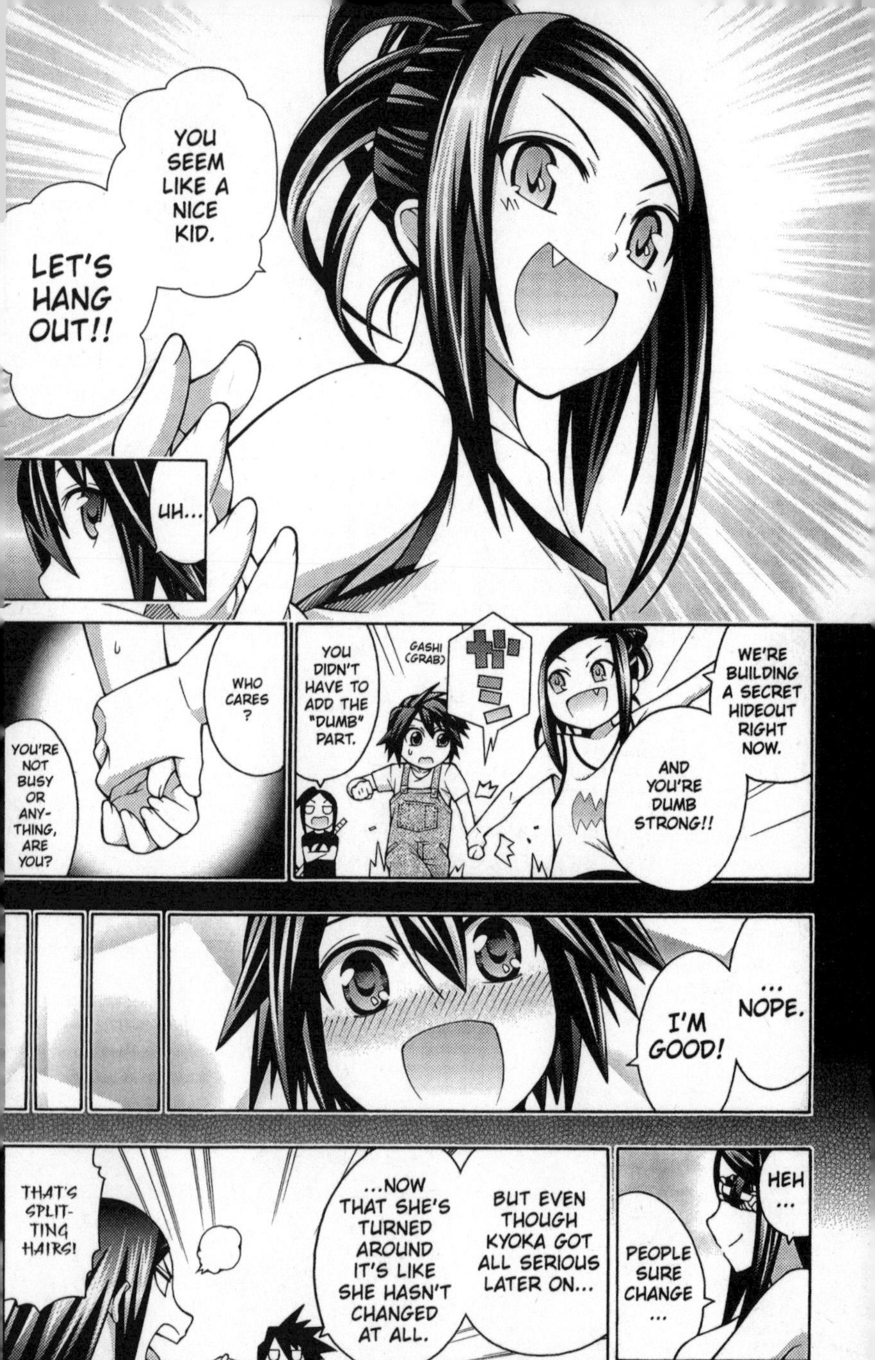
YOU SEEM LIKE A NICE KID.
LET'S HANG OUT!!
UH...
WE'RE BUILDING A SECRET HIDEOUT RIGHT NOW.
AND YOU'RE DUMB STRONG!!
GASHI (GRAB)
YOU DIDN'T HAVE TO ADD THE "DUMB" PART.
WHO CARES?
YOU'RE NOT BUSY OR ANY-THING, ARE YOU?
...NOPE.
I'M GOOD!
HEH...
PEOPLE SURE CHANGE...
BUT EVEN THOUGH KYOKA GOT ALL SERIOUS LATER ON...
...NOW THAT SHE'S TURNED AROUND IT'S LIKE SHE HASN'T CHANGED AT ALL.
THAT'S SPLIT-TING HAIRS!

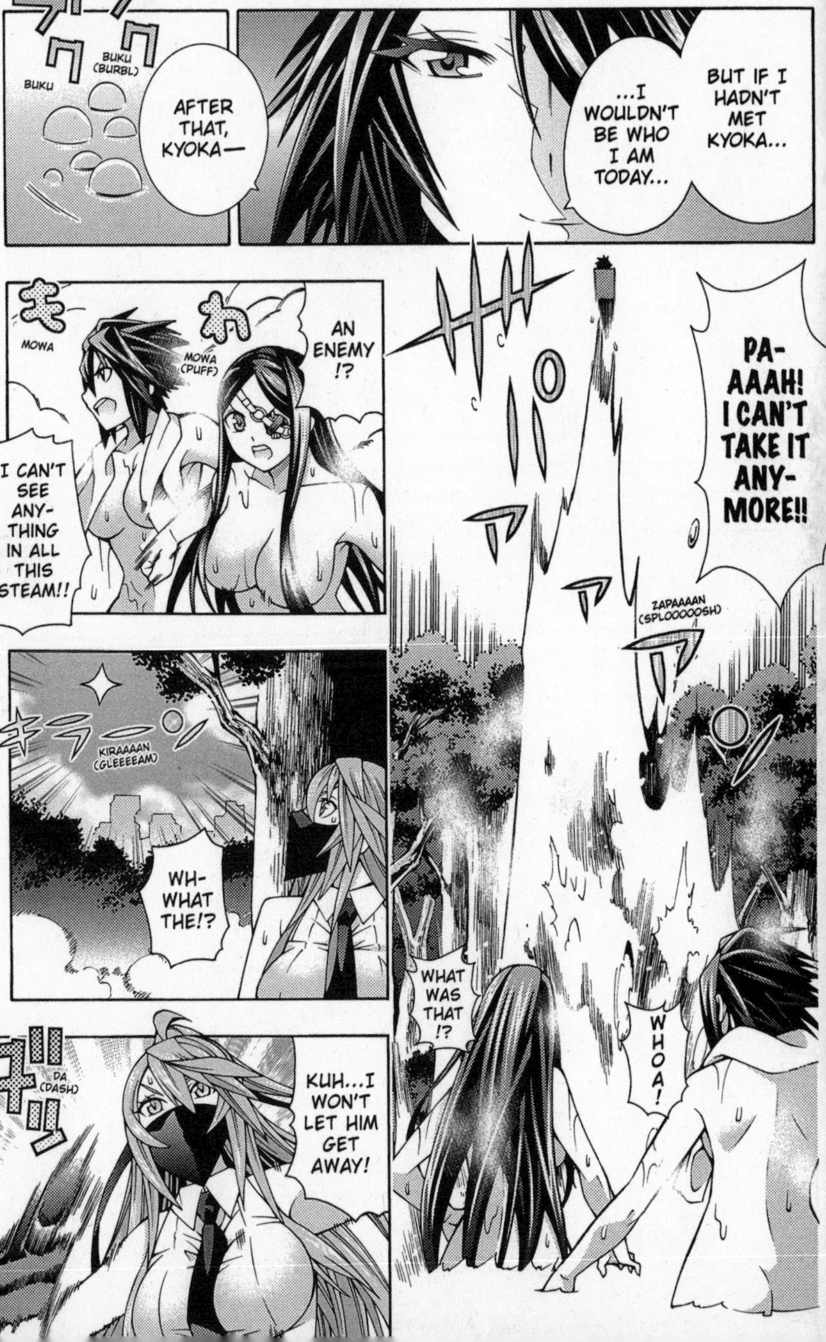
BUT IF I HADN'T MET KYOKA...
...I WOULDN'T BE WHO I AM TODAY...
BUKU
BUKU (BURBL)
AFTER THAT, KYOKA—
PA-AAAH! I CAN'T TAKE IT ANY-MORE!!
ZAPAAAAN (SPLOOOOOSH)
WHOA!
WHAT WAS THAT!?
AN ENEMY!?
MOWA (PUFF)
MOWA
I CAN'T SEE ANY-THING IN ALL THIS STEAM!!
KIRAAAAN (GLEEEEAM)
WH-WHAT THE!?
DA (DASH)
KUH...I WON'T LET HIM GET AWAY!

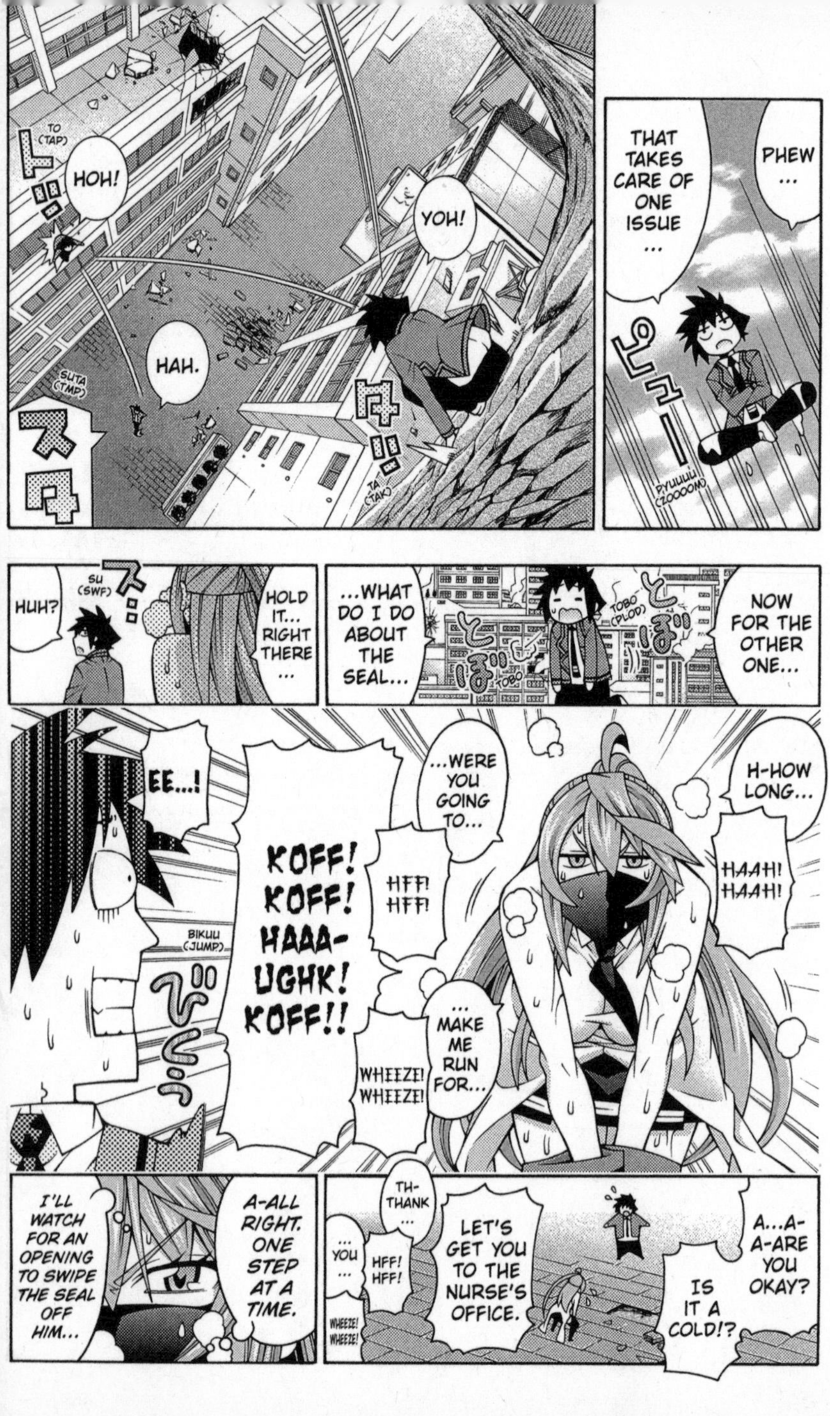
PHEW...
THAT TAKES CARE OF ONE ISSUE...
PYUUUU (ZOOOOM)
YOH!
TO (TAP)
HOH!
TA (TAK)
HAH.
SUTA (TMP)
NOW FOR THE OTHER ONE...
TOBO (PLOD)
TOBO
...WHAT DO I DO ABOUT THE SEAL...
HOLD IT... RIGHT THERE...
SU (SWF)
HUH?
H-HOW LONG...
HAAH! HAAH!
...WERE YOU GOING TO...
HFF! HFF!
...MAKE ME RUN FOR...
WHEEZE! WHEEZE!
KOFF! KOFF! HAAA-UGHK! KOFF!!
EE...!
BIKUU (JUMP)
A...A-A-ARE YOU OKAY?
IS IT A COLD!?
LET'S GET YOU TO THE NURSE'S OFFICE.
TH-THANK...
HFF! HFF!
...YOU...
WHEEZE! WHEEZE!
A-ALL RIGHT. ONE STEP AT A TIME.
I'LL WATCH FOR AN OPENING TO SWIPE THE SEAL OFF HIM...

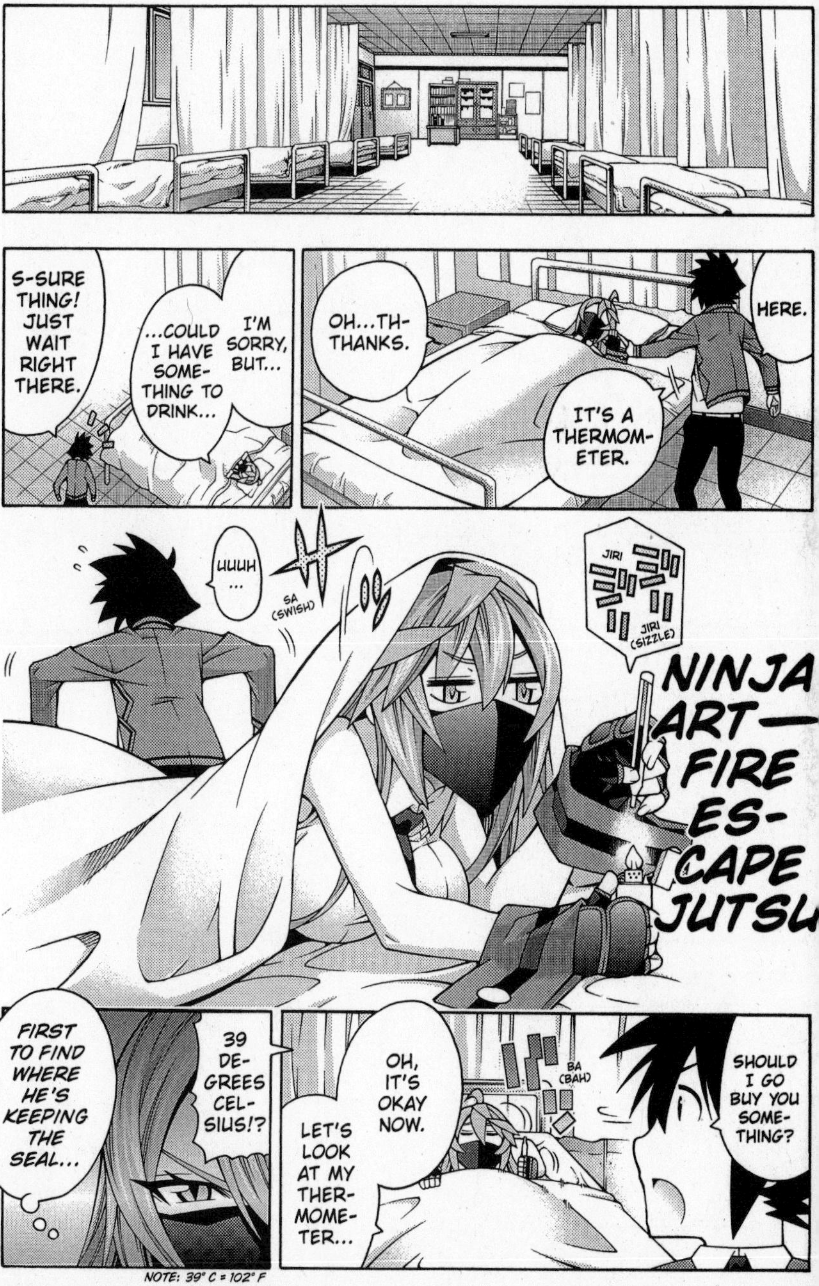
HERE.
OH...TH-THANKS.
IT'S A THERMOMETER.
I'M SORRY, BUT...
...COULD I HAVE SOMETHING TO DRINK...
S-SURE THING! JUST WAIT RIGHT THERE.
JIRI JIRI (SIZZLE)
NINJA ART—FIRE ESCAPE JUTSU
SA (SWISH)
UUUH...
SHOULD I GO BUY YOU SOMETHING?
BA (BAH)
OH, IT'S OKAY NOW.
LET'S LOOK AT MY THERMOMETER...
39 DEGREES CELSIUS!?
FIRST TO FIND WHERE HE'S KEEPING THE SEAL...

NOTE: 39° C = 102° F

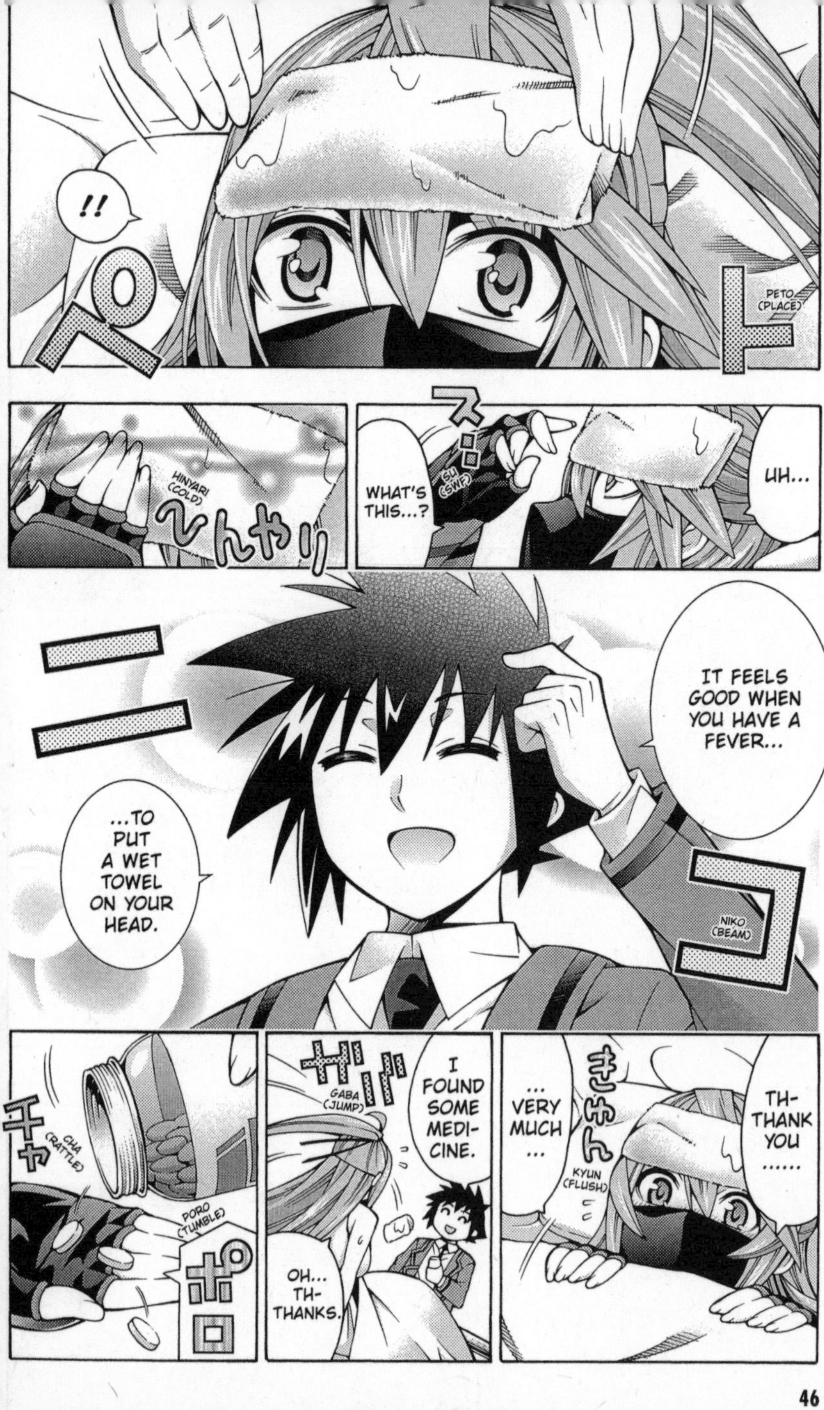
PETO (PLACE)
!!
UH...
WHAT'S THIS...?
SU (SWP)
HINYARI (COLD)
IT FEELS GOOD WHEN YOU HAVE A FEVER...
NIKO (BEAM)
...TO PUT A WET TOWEL ON YOUR HEAD.
TH-THANK YOU ......
KYUN (FLUSH)
... VERY MUCH ...
I FOUND SOME MEDI-CINE.
GABA (JUMP)
OH... TH-THANKS.
CHA (RATTLE)
PORO (TUMBLE)

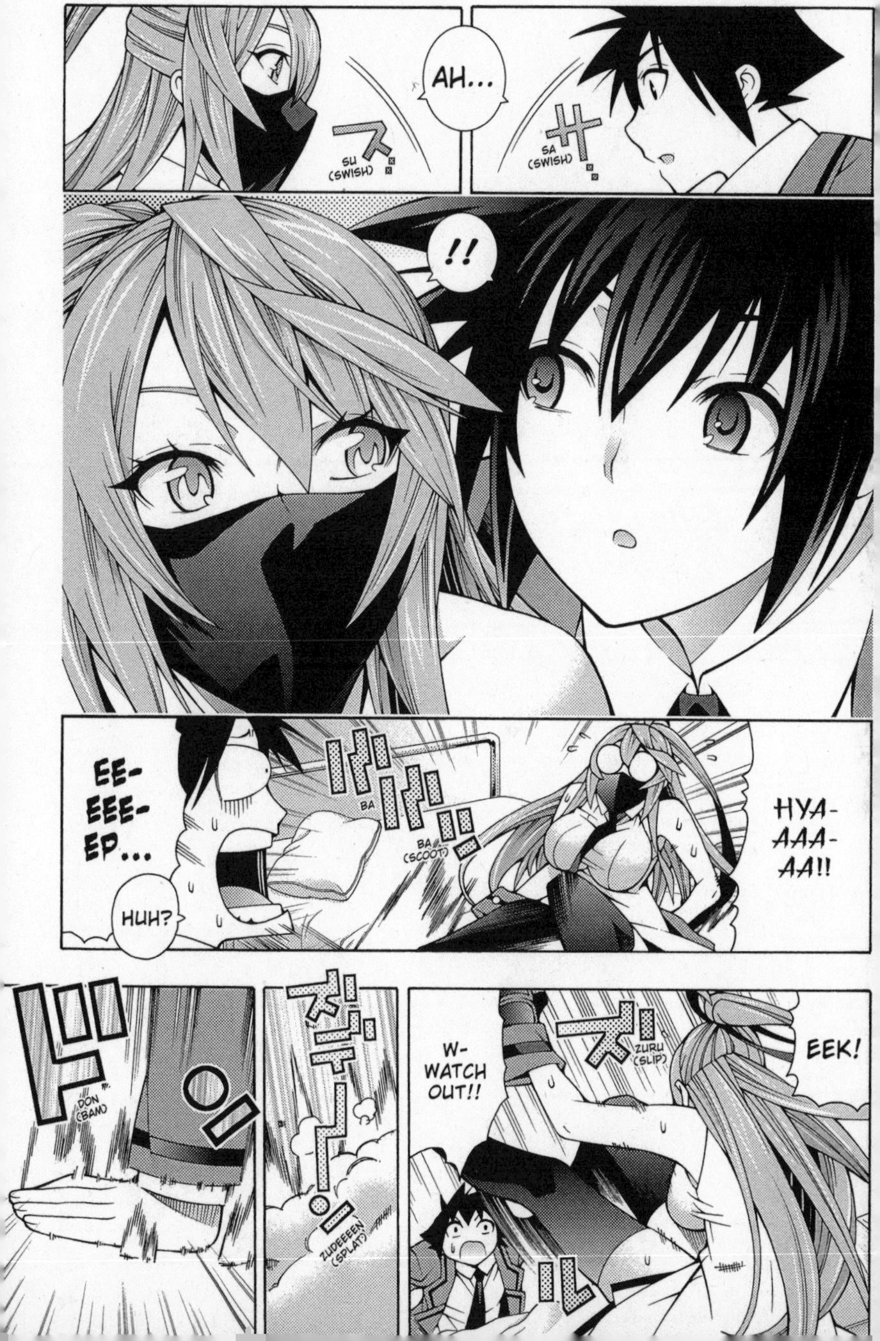
SA (SWISH)
AH...
SU (SWISH)
!!
HYA-AAA-AA!!
BA
BA (SCOOT)
EE-EEE-EP...
HUH?
EEK!
ZURU (SLIP)
W-WATCH OUT!!
ZUDEEEEN (SPLAT)
DON (BAM)

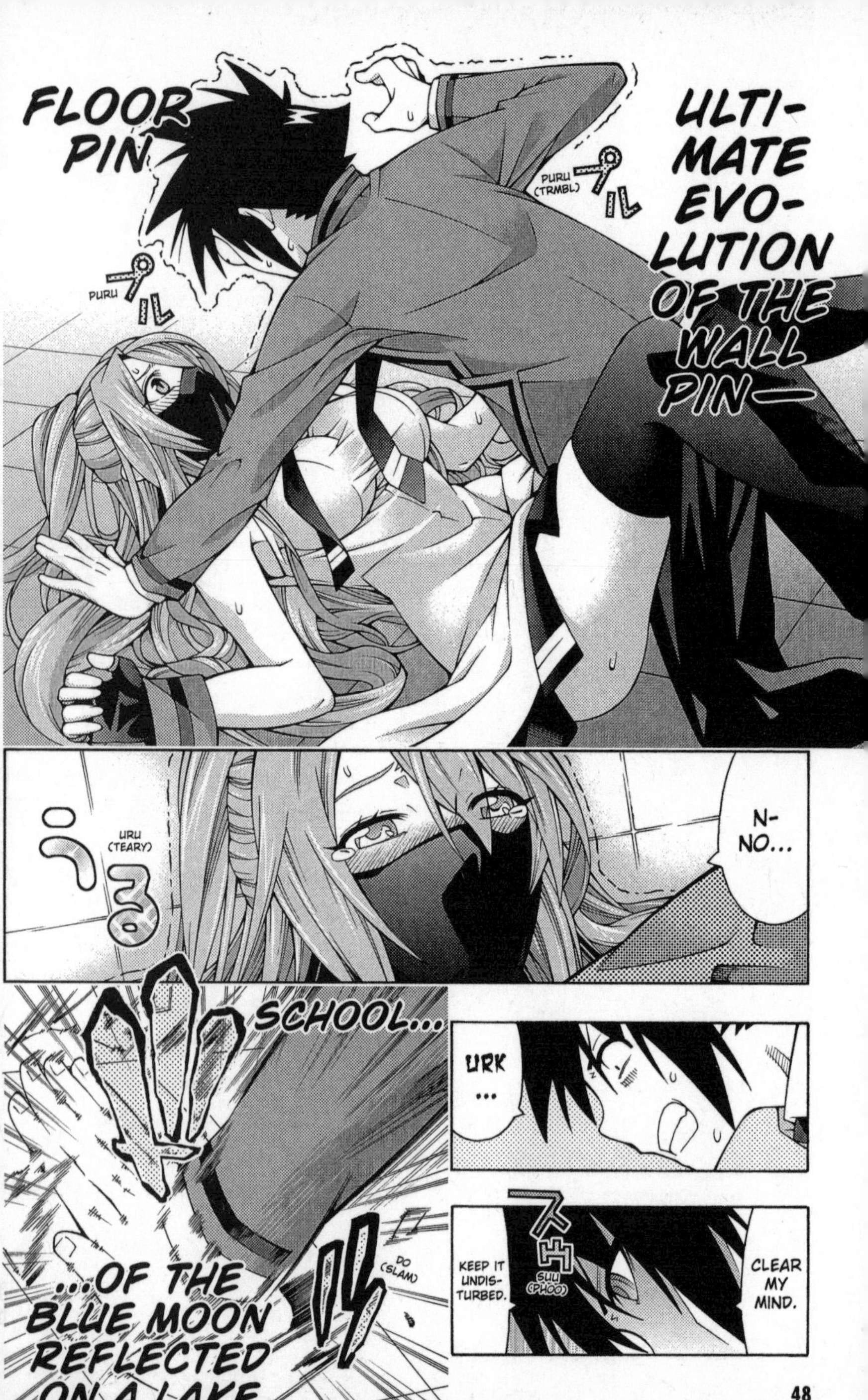
ULTIMATE EVOLUTION OF THE WALL PIN—
PURU (TRMBL)
FLOOR PIN
PURU
N-NO...
URU (TEARY)
URK ...
CLEAR MY MIND.
SUU (PHOO)
KEEP IT UNDISTURBED.
SCHOOL...
DO (SLAM)
...OF THE BLUE MOON REFLECTED ON A LAKE

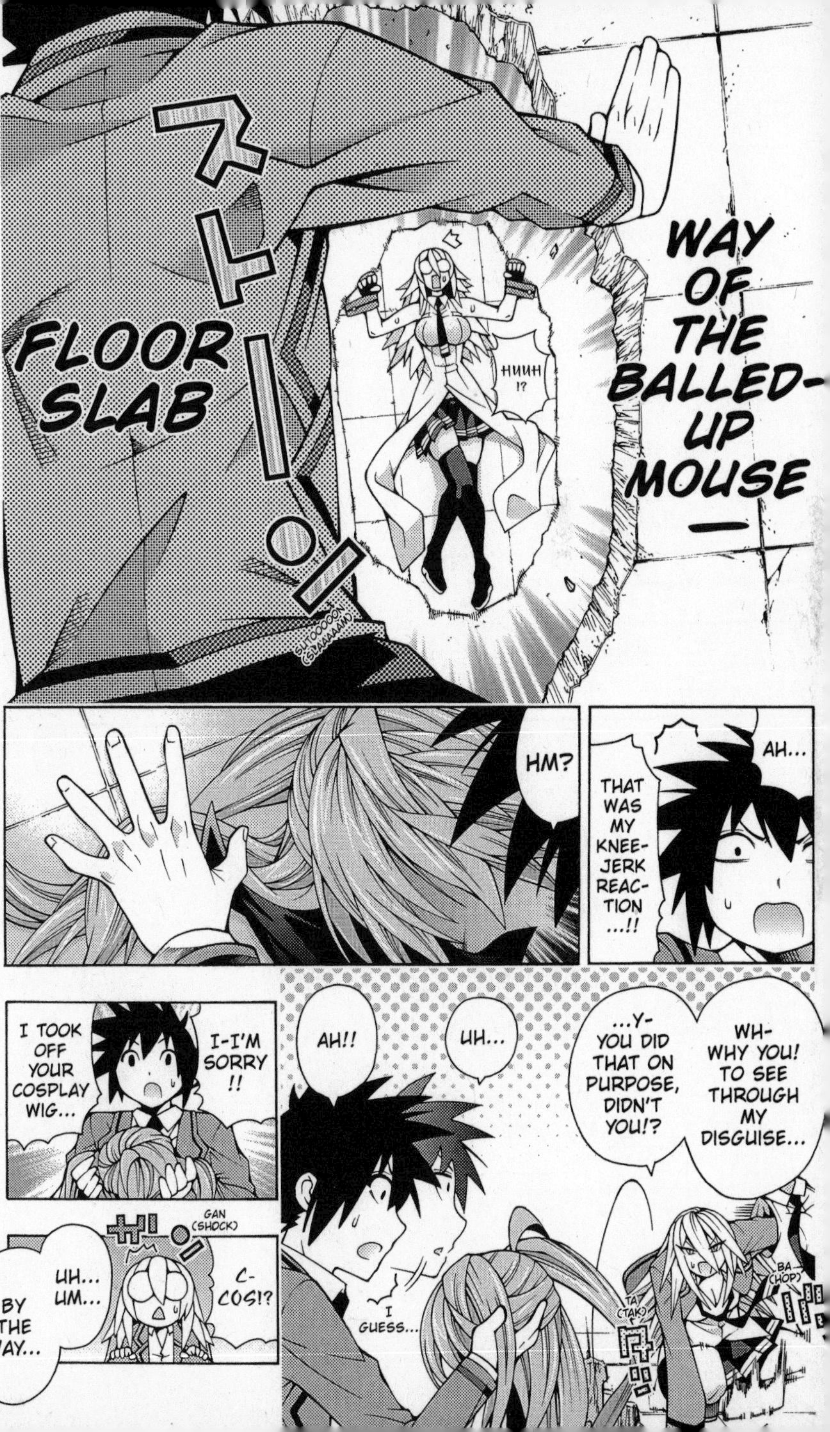
WAY OF THE BALLED-UP MOUSE —
HUUH !?
FLOOR SLAB
SUTOOOOON (SLAAAAAM)
AH...
THAT WAS MY KNEE-JERK REACTION ...!!
HM?
WH- WHY YOU! TO SEE THROUGH MY DISGUISE...
...Y- YOU DID THAT ON PURPOSE, DIDN'T YOU!?
UH...
AH!!
BA (CHOP)
TA (TAK)
I GUESS...
I-I'M SORRY !!
I TOOK OFF YOUR COSPLAY WIG...
GAN (SHOCK)
C- COS!?
UH... UM...
BY THE WAY...

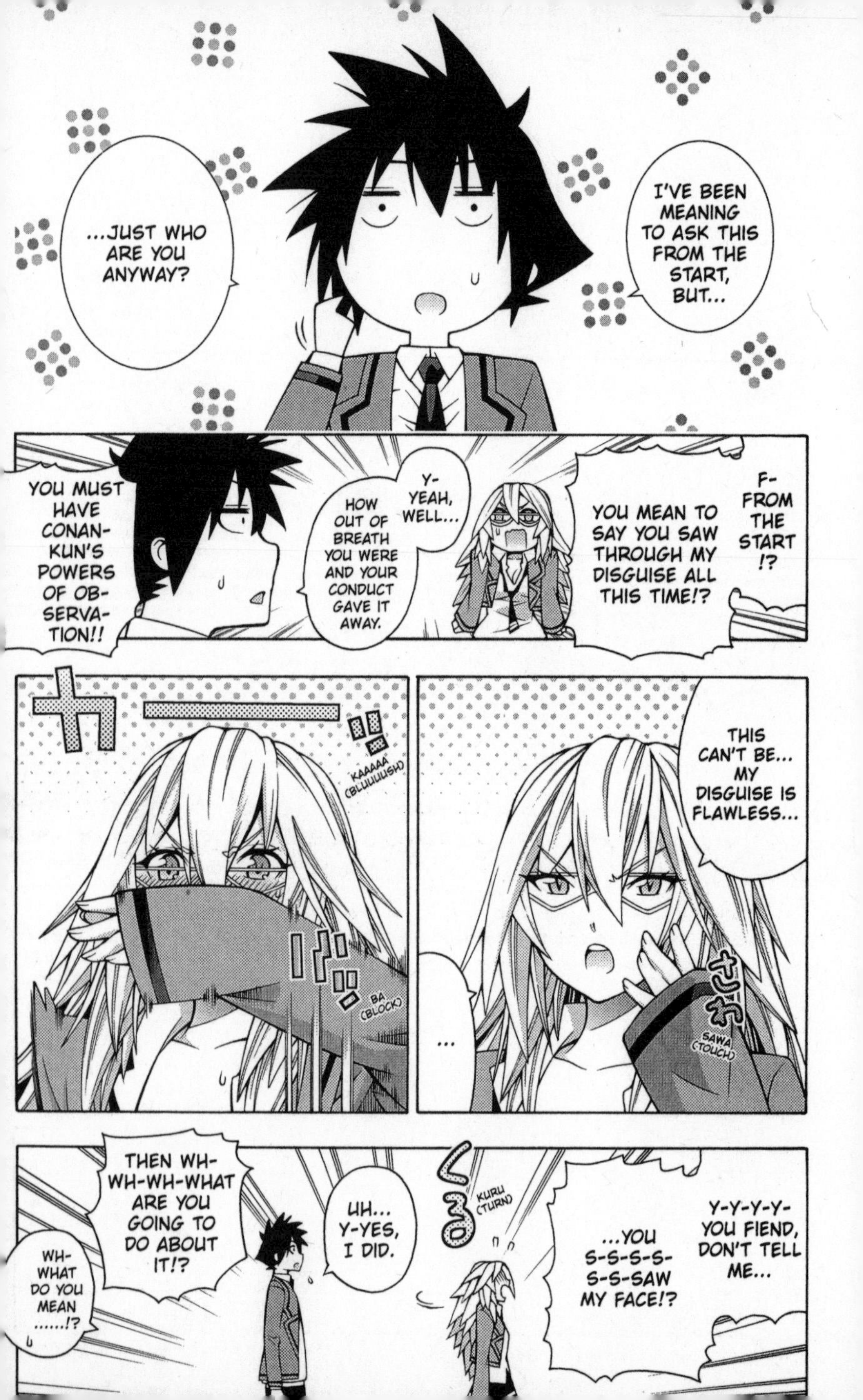
I'VE BEEN MEANING TO ASK THIS FROM THE START, BUT...
...JUST WHO ARE YOU ANYWAY?
F-FROM THE START!?
YOU MEAN TO SAY YOU SAW THROUGH MY DISGUISE ALL THIS TIME!?
Y-YEAH, WELL...
HOW OUT OF BREATH YOU WERE AND YOUR CONDUCT GAVE IT AWAY.
YOU MUST HAVE CONAN-KUN'S POWERS OF OB-SERVA-TION!!
THIS CAN'T BE... MY DISGUISE IS FLAWLESS...
SAWA (TOUCH)
...
KAAAAA (BLUUUUSH)
BA (BLOCK)
Y-Y-Y-Y-YOU FIEND, DON'T TELL ME...
...YOU S-S-S-S-S-S-SAW MY FACE!?
KURU (TURN)
UH... Y-YES, I DID.
THEN WH-WH-WH-WHAT ARE YOU GOING TO DO ABOUT IT!?
WH-WHAT DO YOU MEAN ......!?

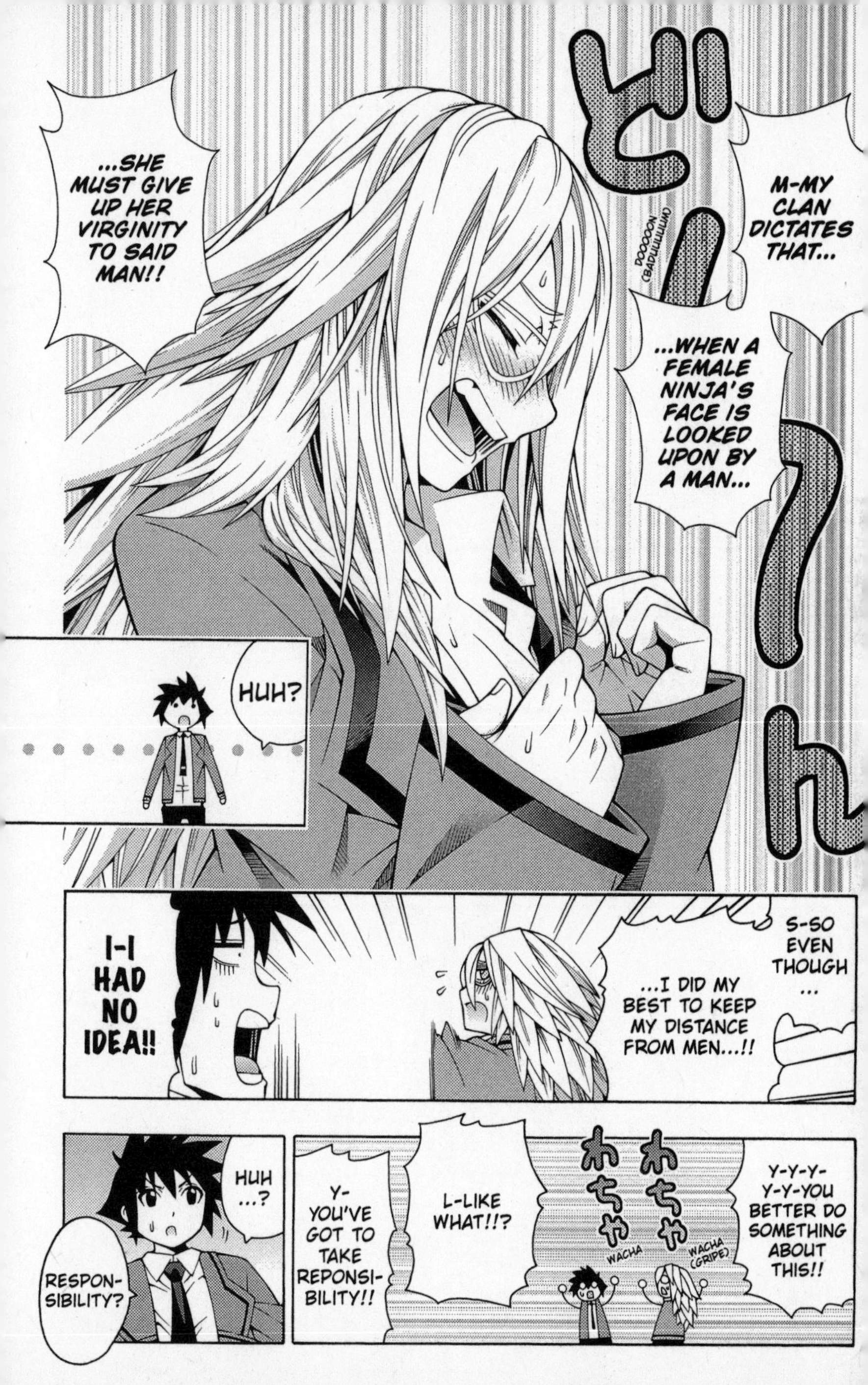

M-MY CLAN DICTATES THAT...
DOOOOOON (BADUUUUUUM)
...WHEN A FEMALE NINJA'S FACE IS LOOKED UPON BY A MAN...
...SHE MUST GIVE UP HER VIRGINITY TO SAID MAN!!
HUH?
......
S-SO EVEN THOUGH ...
...I DID MY BEST TO KEEP MY DISTANCE FROM MEN...!!
I-I HAD NO IDEA!!
Y-Y-Y-Y-Y-YOU BETTER DO SOMETHING ABOUT THIS!!
WACHA (GRIPE)
WACHA
L-LIKE WHAT!!?
Y-YOU'VE GOT TO TAKE REPONSIBILITY!!
HUH ...?
RESPON-SIBILITY?

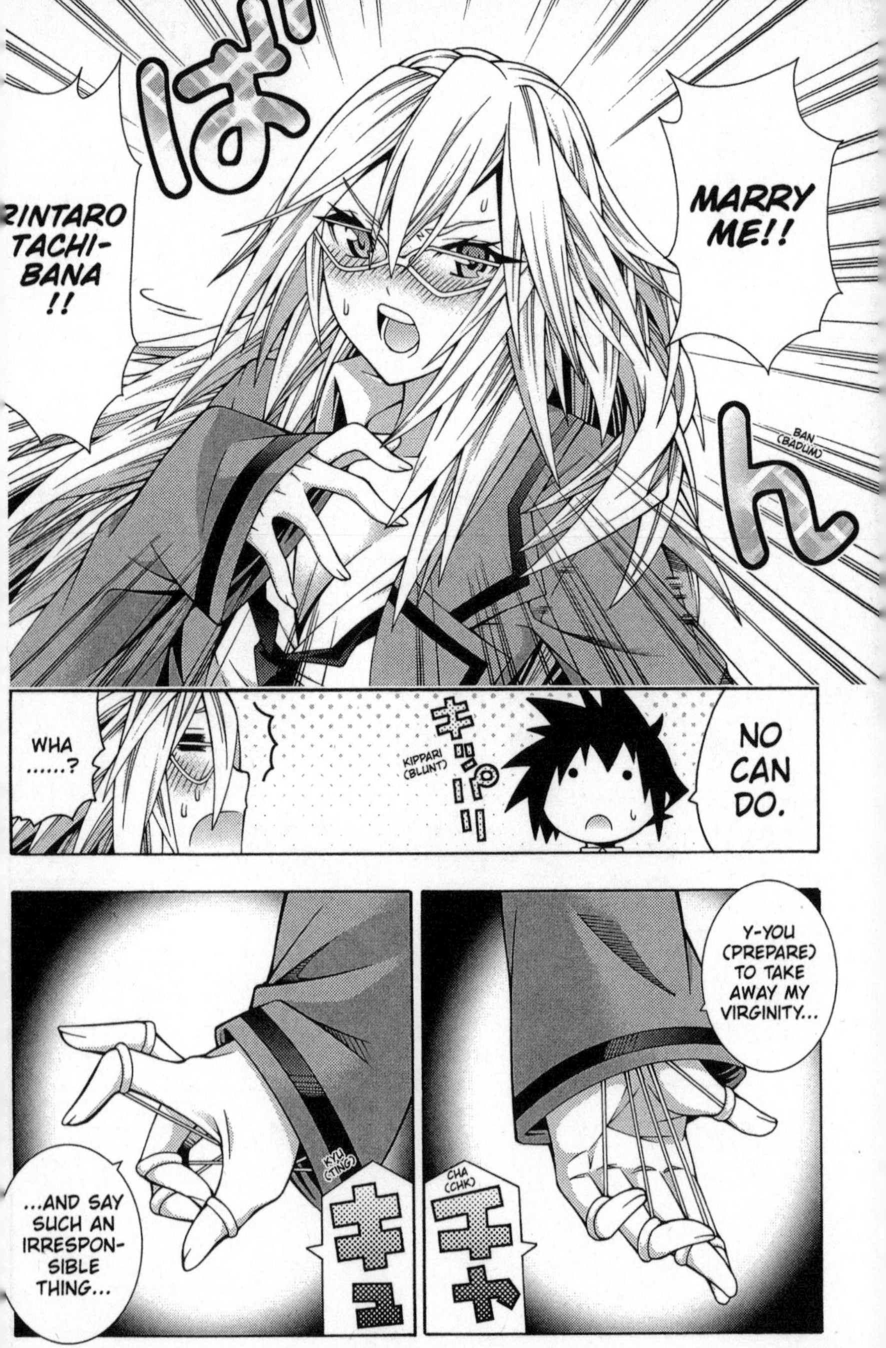

INTARO TACHI-BANA !!
MARRY ME!!
BAN (BADUM)
NO CAN DO.
KIPPARI (BLUNT)
WHA ......?
Y-YOU (PREPARE) TO TAKE AWAY MY VIRGINITY...
CHA (CHK)
KYU (TING)
...AND SAY SUCH AN IRRESPON-SIBLE THING...

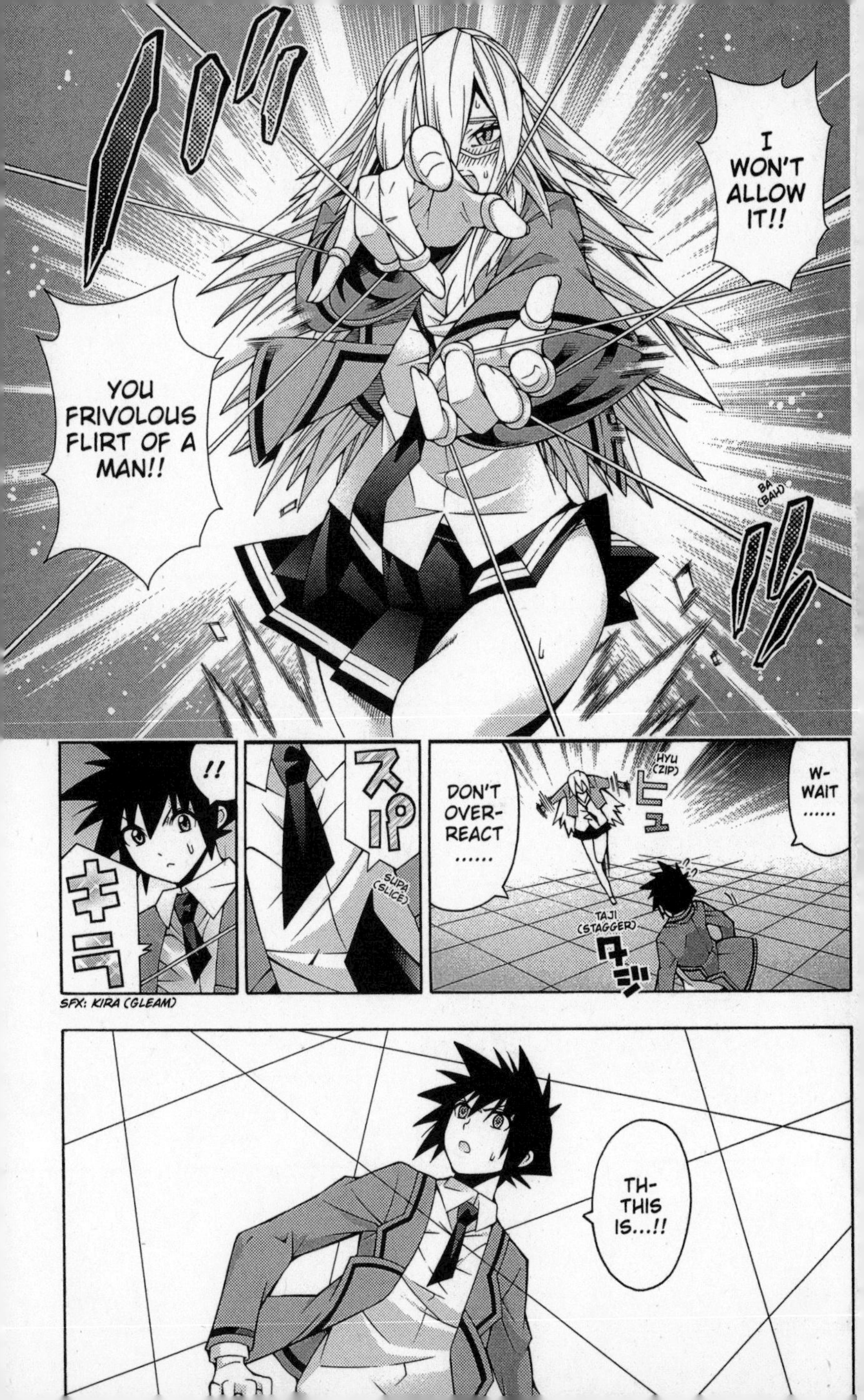
I WON'T ALLOW IT!!
YOU FRIVOLOUS FLIRT OF A MAN!!
BA (BAH)
W-WAIT ......
HYU (ZIP)
DON'T OVER-REACT ......
TAJI (STAGGER)
SUPA (SLICE)
!!
SFX: KIRA (GLEAM)
TH-THIS IS...!!

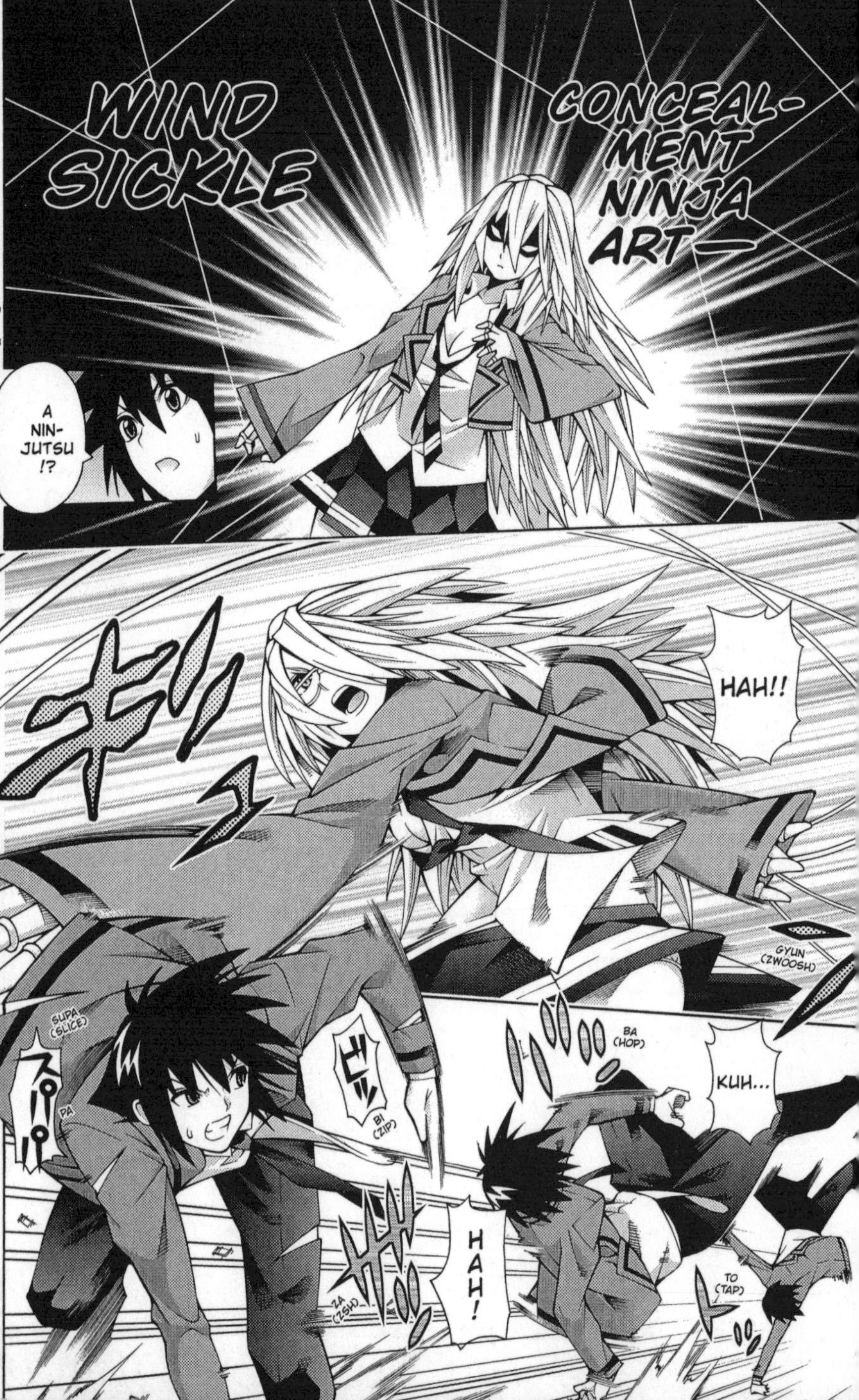
CONCEAL-
MENT
NINJA
ART—
WIND
SICKLE
A NIN-JUTSU !?
HAH!!
GYUN (ZWOOSH)
KUH...
BA (HOP)
TO (TAP)
HAH!
BI (ZIP)
ZA (ZSH)
SUPA (SLICE)
PA

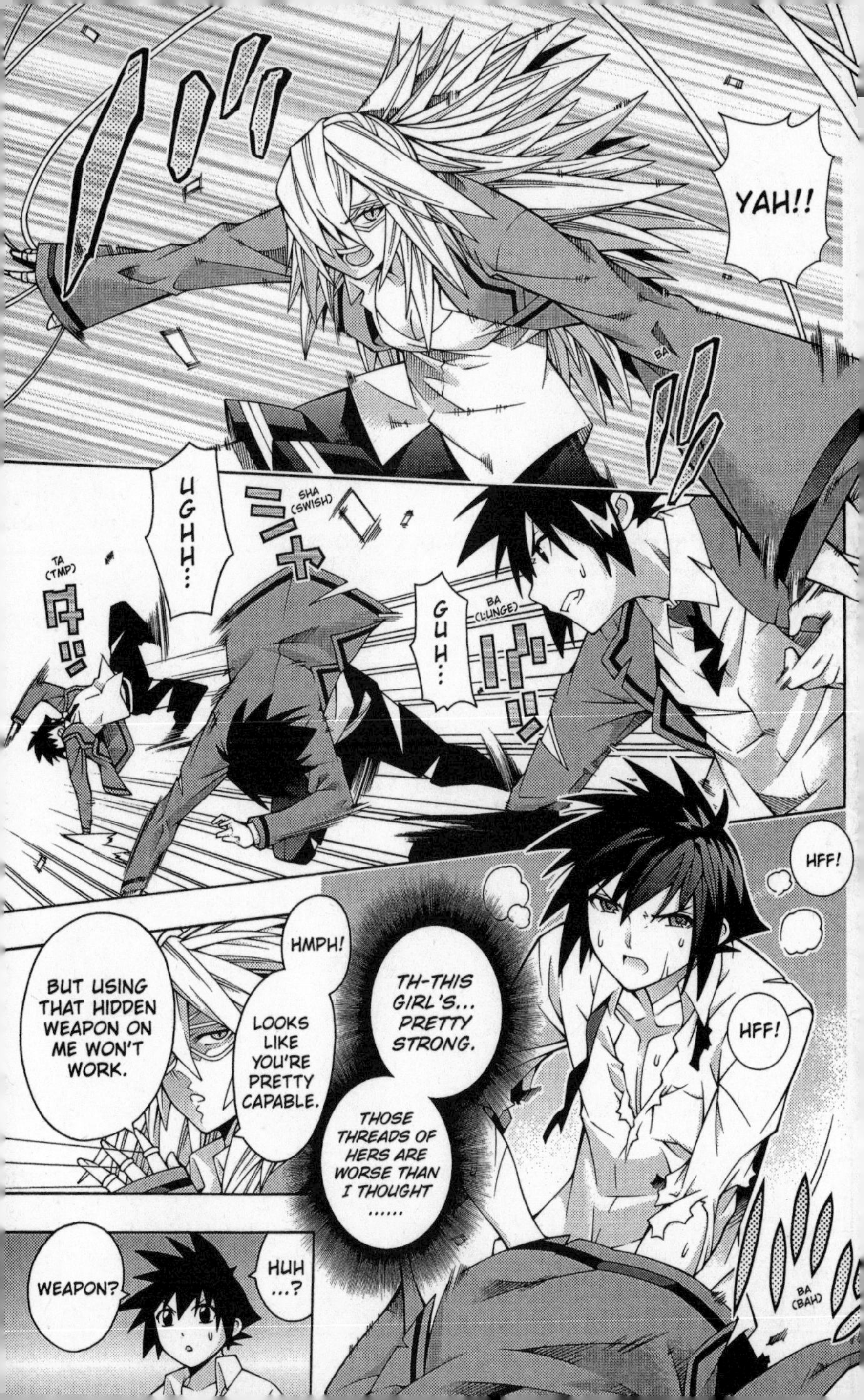
YAH!!
BA
BA (LUNGE)
GUH...
SHA (SWISH)
UGHH...
TA (TMP)
HFF!
HFF!
TH-THIS GIRL'S... PRETTY STRONG.
THOSE THREADS OF HERS ARE WORSE THAN I THOUGHT ......
HMPH!
LOOKS LIKE YOU'RE PRETTY CAPABLE.
BUT USING THAT HIDDEN WEAPON ON ME WON'T WORK.
BA (BAH)
HUH ...?
WEAPON?

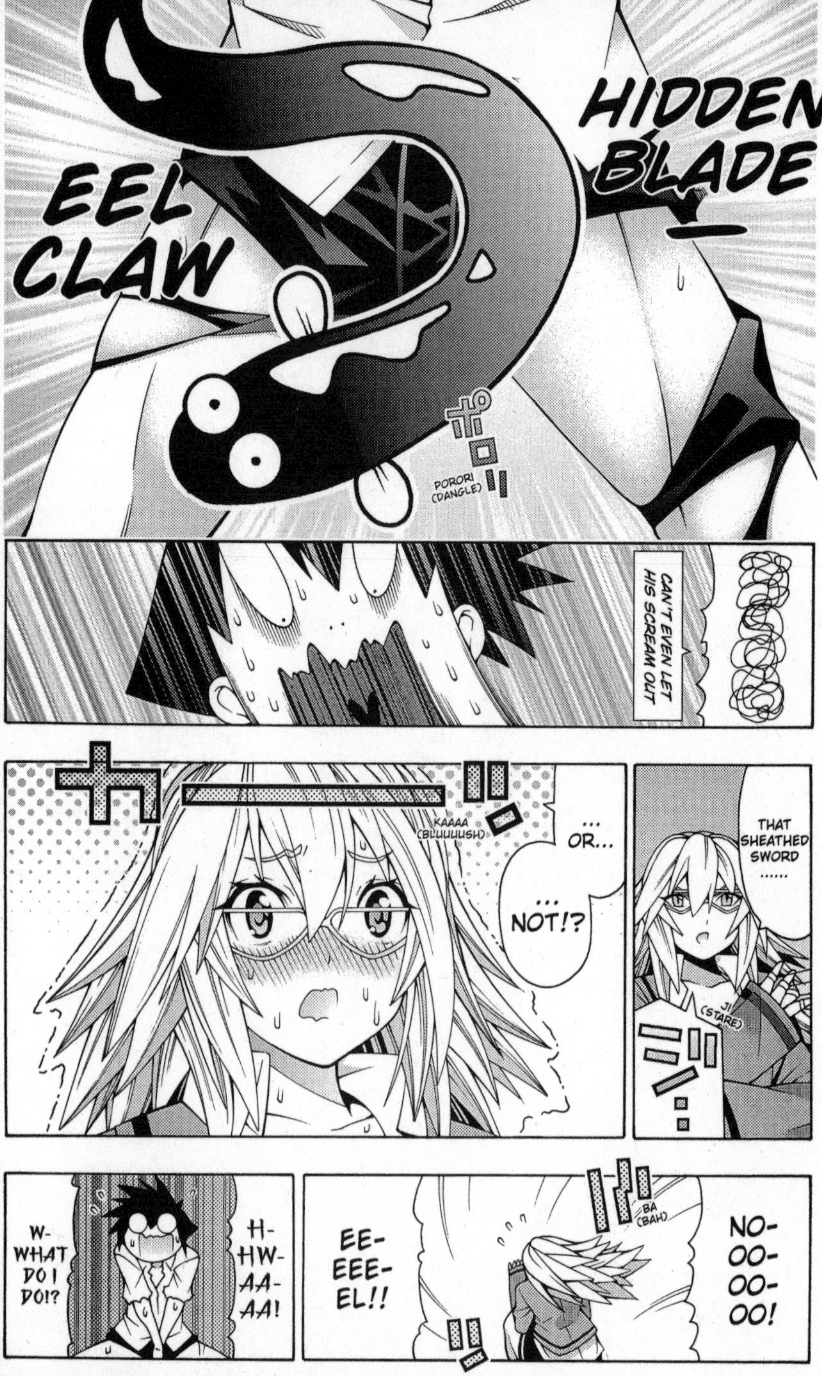
HIDDEN BLADE—
EEL CLAW
PORORI (DANGLE)
CAN'T EVEN LET HIS SCREAM OUT
THAT SHEATHED SWORD ......
JI (STARE)
KAAAA (BLUUUUSH)
... OR...
... NOT!?
NO-OO-OO-OO!
BA (BAH)
EE-EEE-EL!!
H-HW-AA-AA!
W-WHAT DO I DO!?

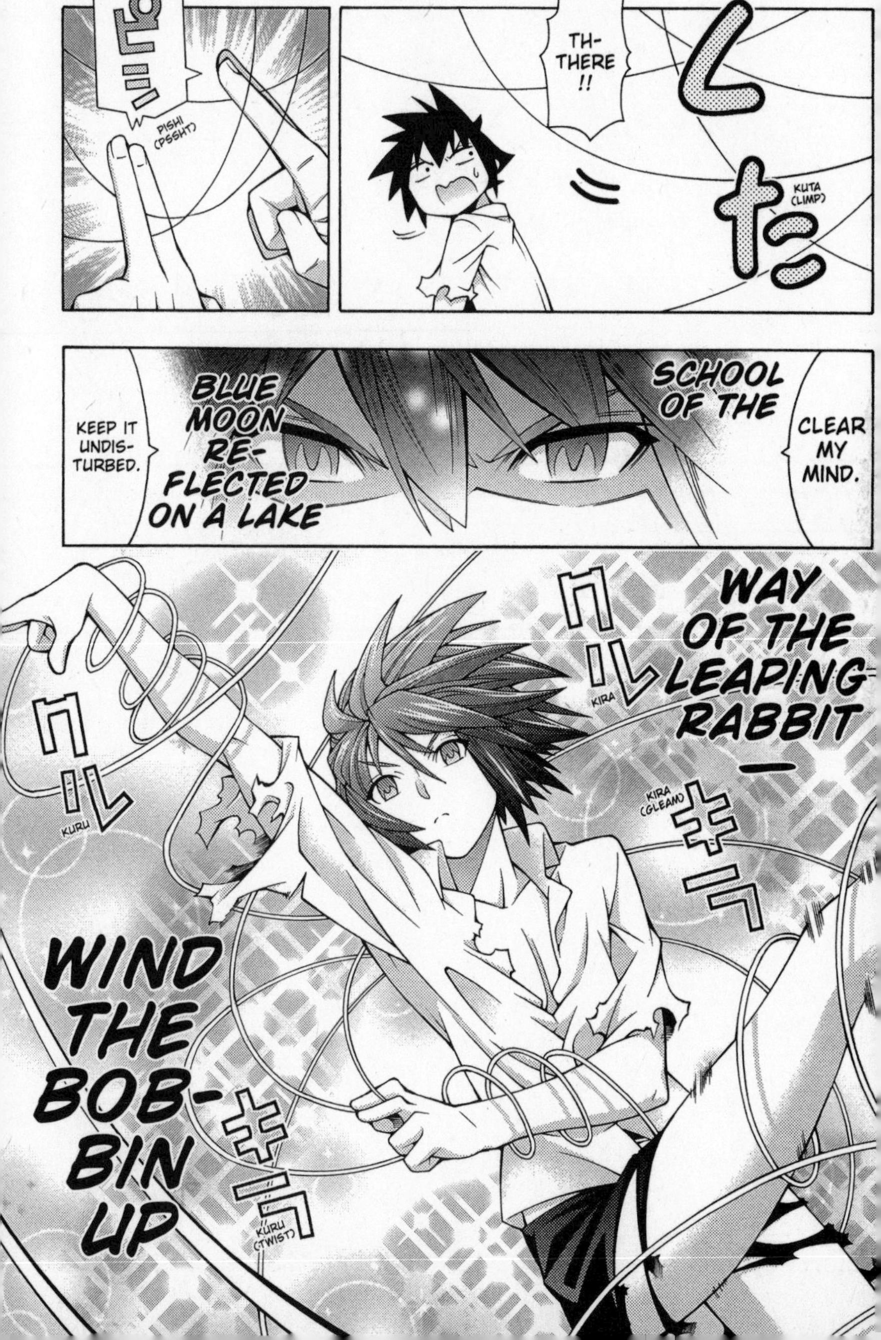
TH-THERE!!
KUTA (LIMP)
PISHI (PSSHT)
CLEAR MY MIND.
SCHOOL OF THE
BLUE MOON RE-FLECTED ON A LAKE
KEEP IT UNDIS-TURBED.
WAY OF THE LEAPING RABBIT—
KIRA
KIRA (GLEAM)
KURU
WIND THE BOB-BIN UP
KURU (TWIST)

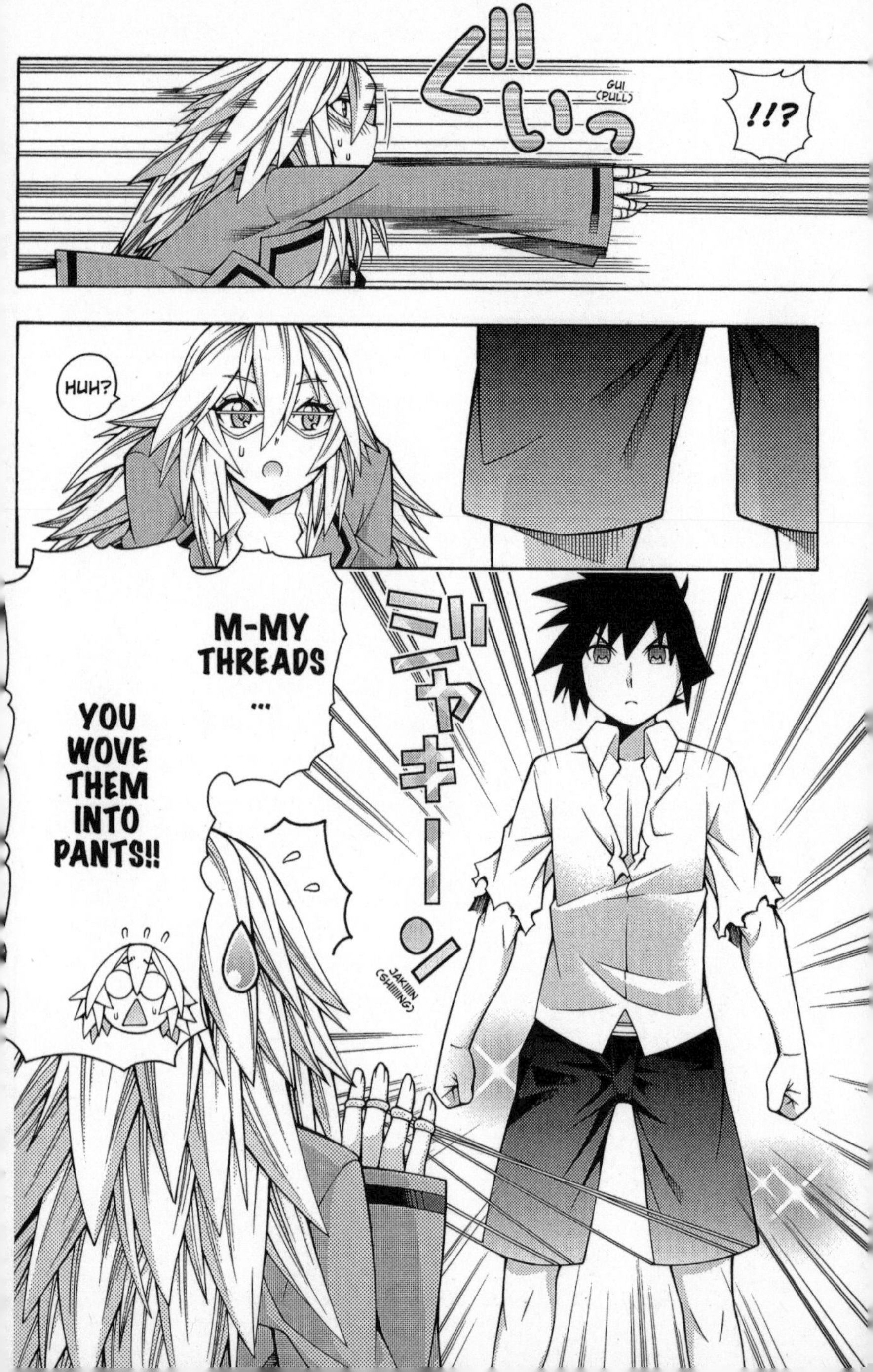
!!?
ぐいっ
GUI (PULL)
HUH?
ジャキーン
JAKIIIN (SHIIIING)
M-MY THREADS ...
YOU WOVE THEM INTO PANTS!!

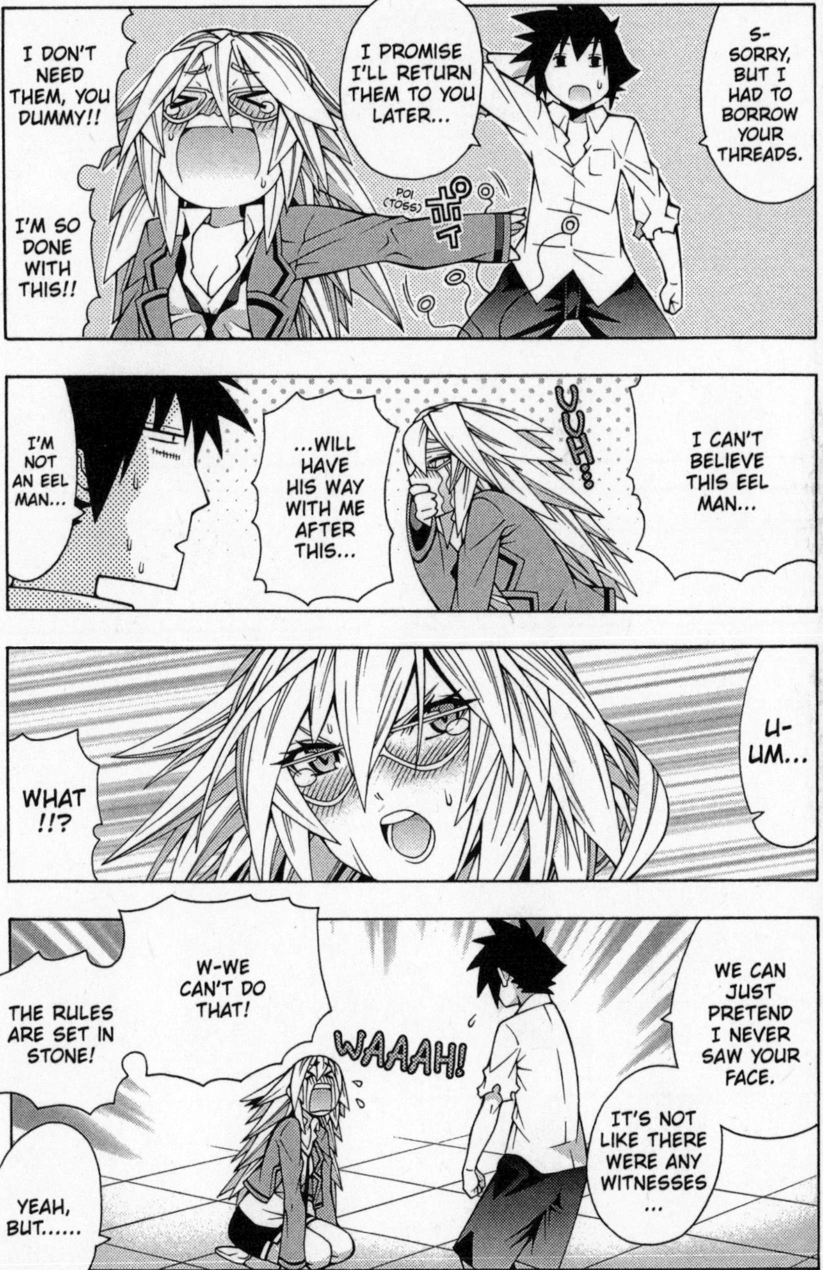
S-SORRY, BUT I HAD TO BORROW YOUR THREADS.
I PROMISE I'LL RETURN THEM TO YOU LATER...
POI (TOSS)
I DON'T NEED THEM, YOU DUMMY!!
I'M SO DONE WITH THIS!!
I CAN'T BELIEVE THIS EEL MAN...
UUH...
...WILL HAVE HIS WAY WITH ME AFTER THIS...
I'M NOT AN EEL MAN...
U-UM...
WHAT!!?
WE CAN JUST PRETEND I NEVER SAW YOUR FACE.
IT'S NOT LIKE THERE WERE ANY WITNESSES...
WAAAH!
W-WE CAN'T DO THAT!
THE RULES ARE SET IN STONE!
YEAH, BUT......

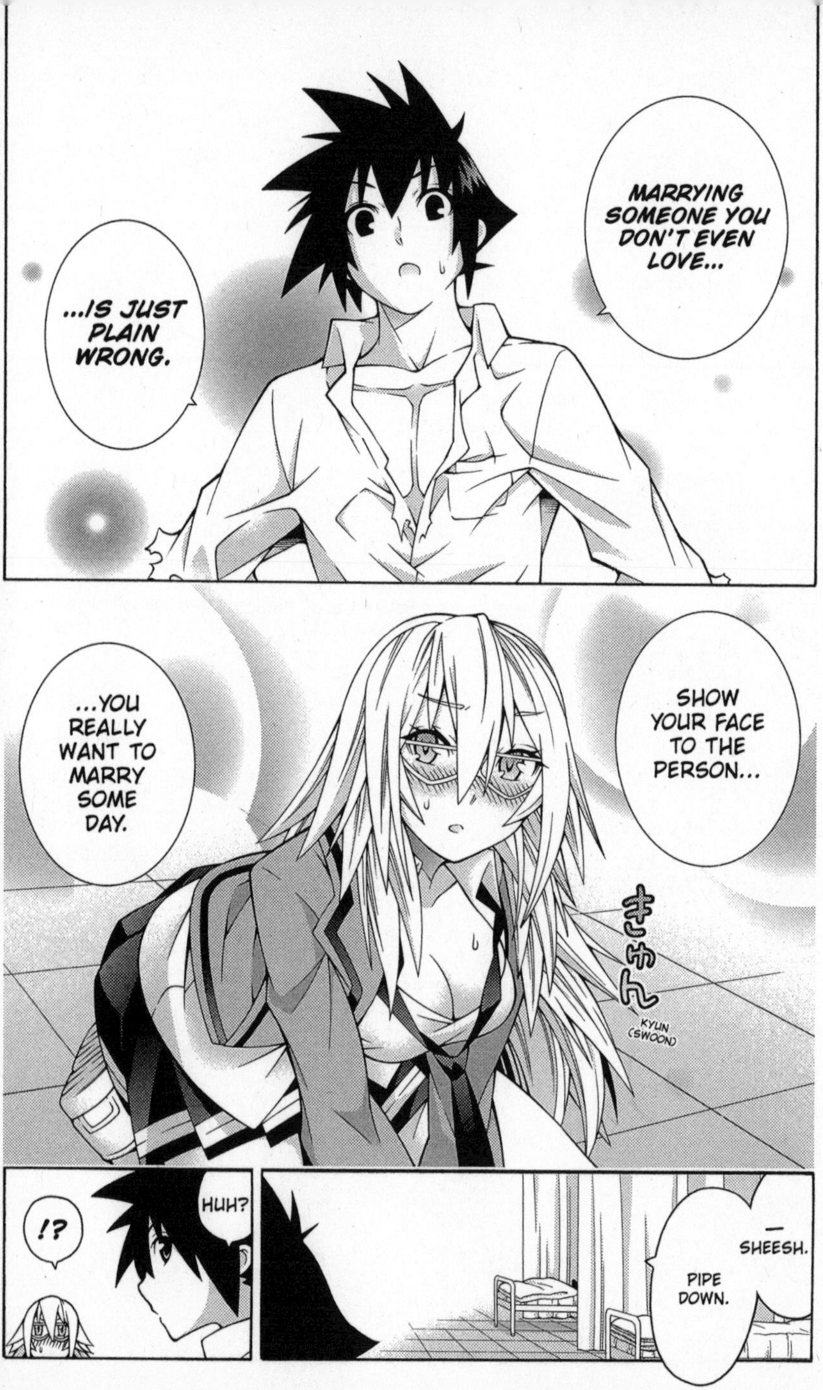
MARRYING SOMEONE YOU DON'T EVEN LOVE...
...IS JUST PLAIN WRONG.
SHOW YOUR FACE TO THE PERSON...
...YOU REALLY WANT TO MARRY SOME DAY.
きゅん
KYUN (SWOON)
—SHEESH.
PIPE DOWN.
HUH?
!?

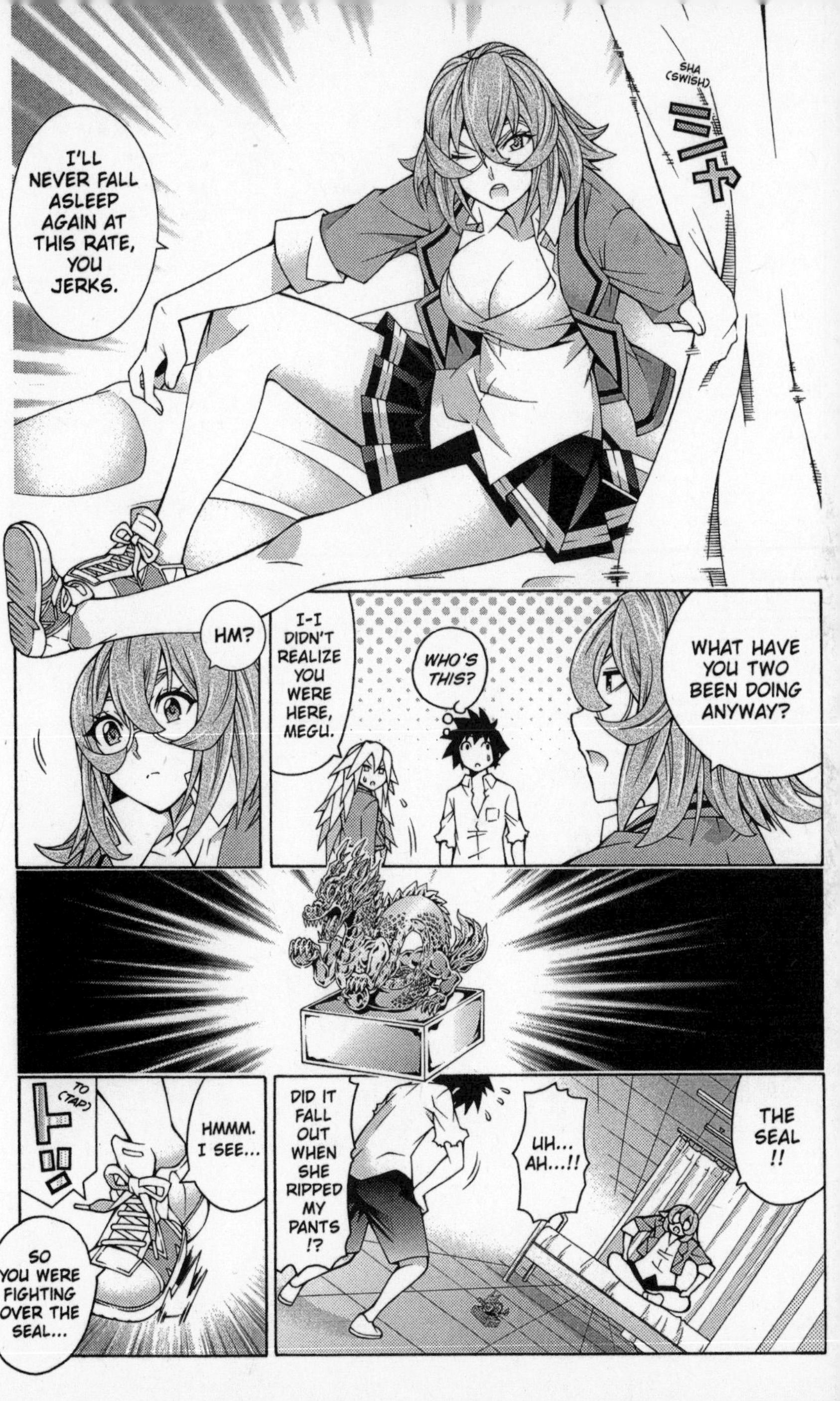
SHA (SWISH)
I'LL NEVER FALL ASLEEP AGAIN AT THIS RATE, YOU JERKS.
WHAT HAVE YOU TWO BEEN DOING ANYWAY?
WHO'S THIS?
I-I DIDN'T REALIZE YOU WERE HERE, MEGU.
HM?
THE SEAL!!
UH... AH...!!
DID IT FALL OUT WHEN SHE RIPPED MY PANTS!?
TO (TAP)
HMMM. I SEE...
SO YOU WERE FIGHTING OVER THE SEAL...

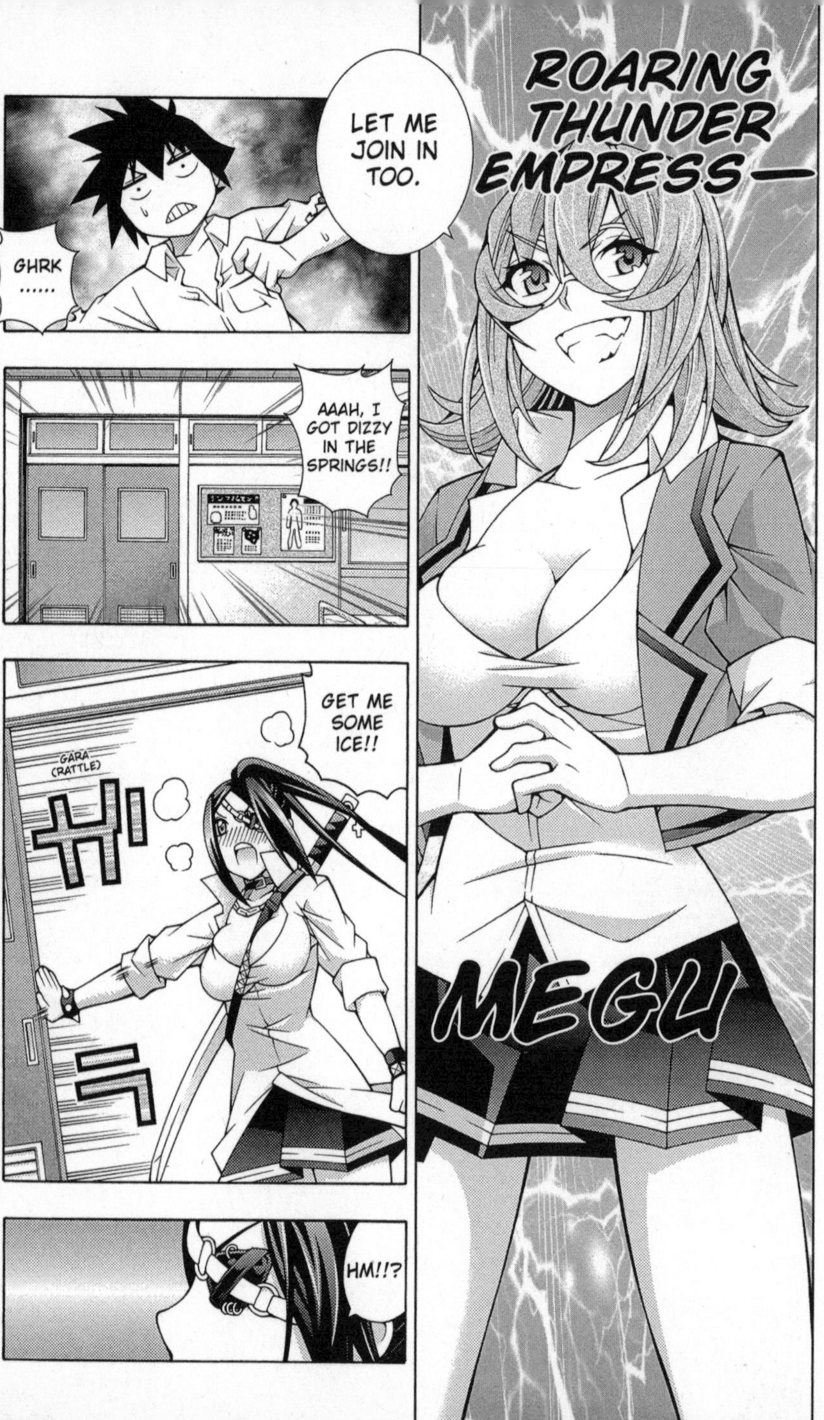
ROARING THUNDER EMPRESS—
MEGU
LET ME JOIN IN TOO.
GHRK ......
AAAH, I GOT DIZZY IN THE SPRINGS!!
GET ME SOME ICE!!
GARA (RATTLE)
HM!!?

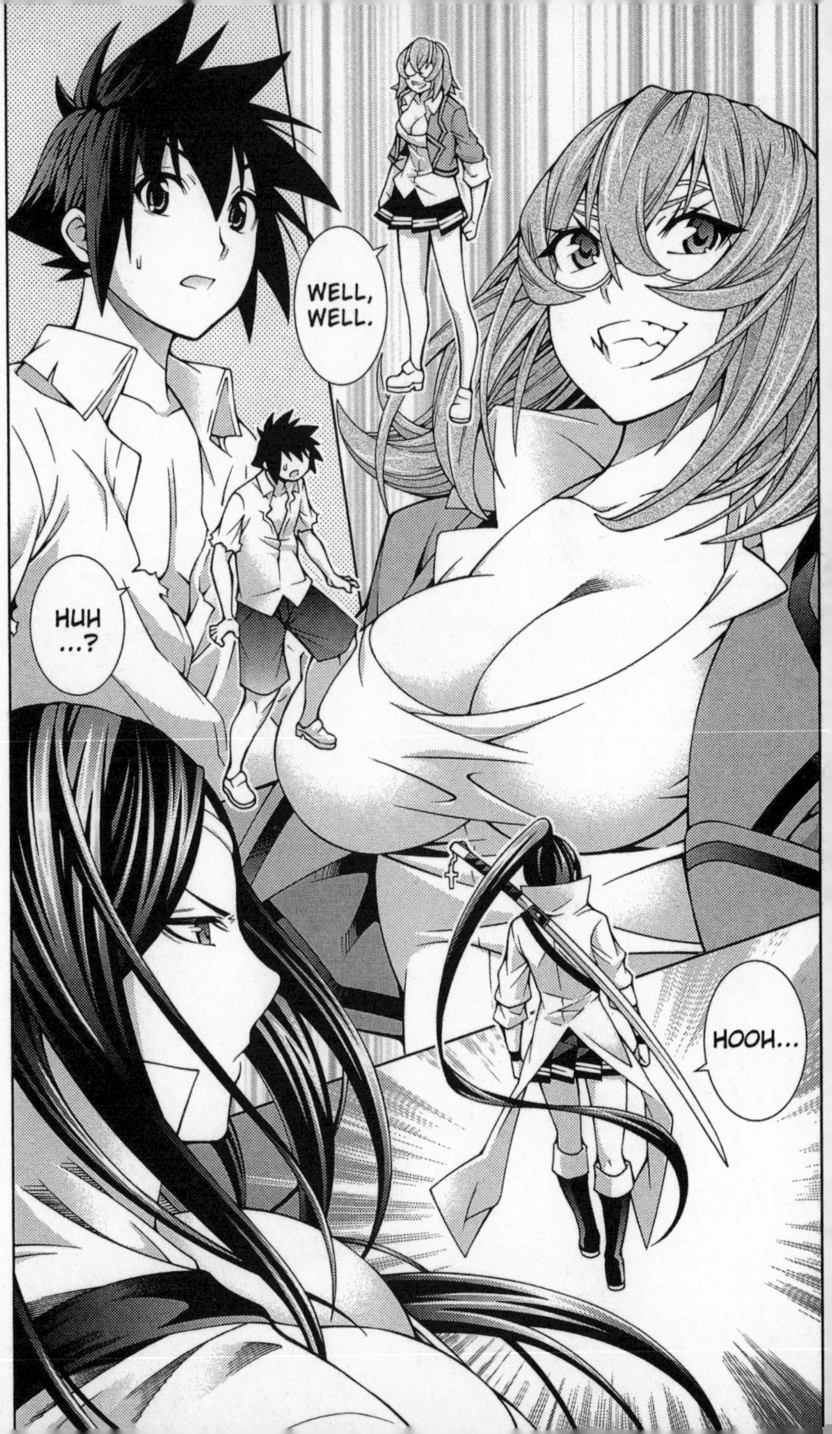
WELL, WELL.
HUH ...?
HOOH...

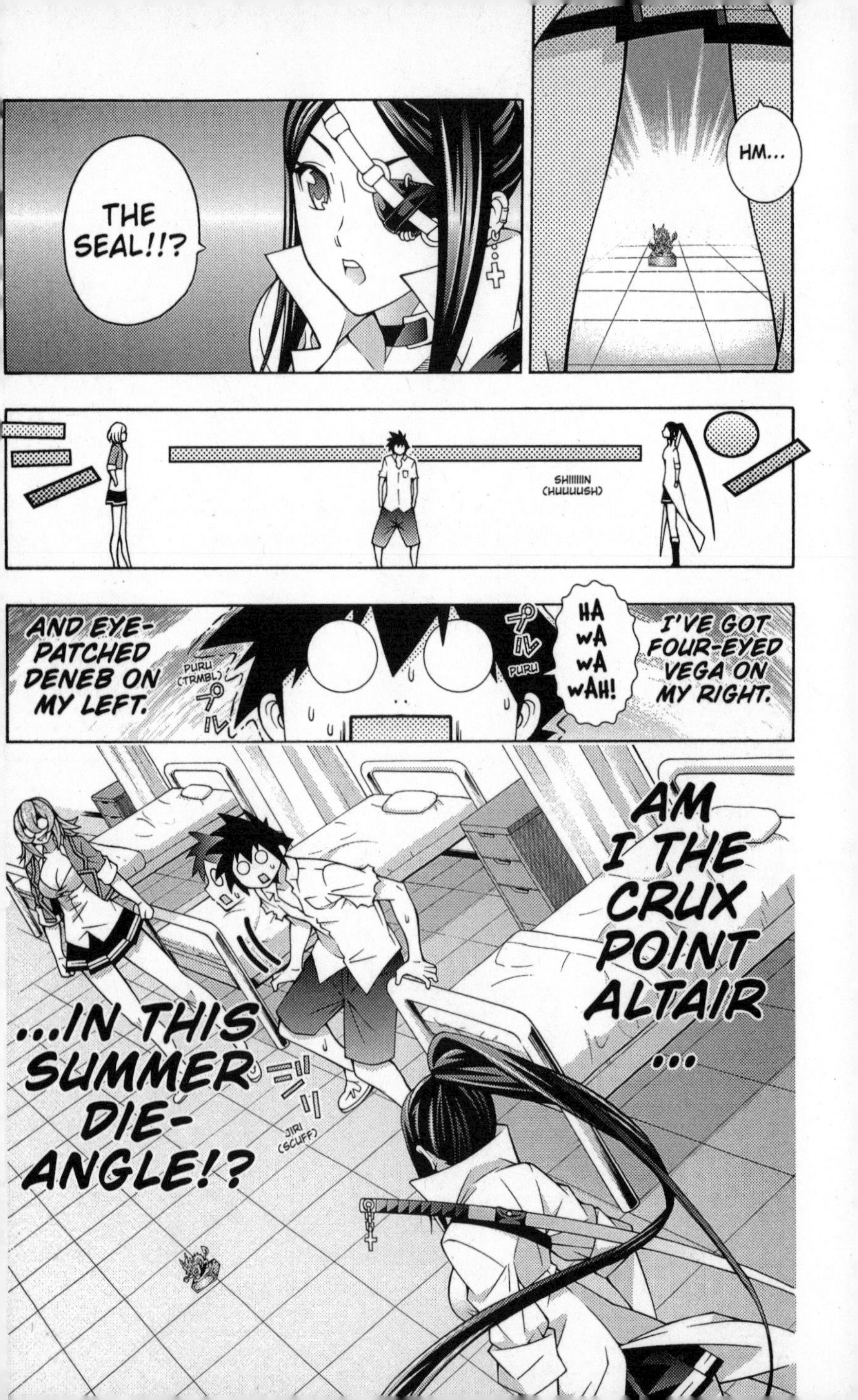
HM...
THE SEAL!!?
SHIIIIIN (HUUUUUSH)
I'VE GOT FOUR-EYED VEGA ON MY RIGHT.
HA wA wA wAH!
PURU
PURU (TRMBL)
AND EYE-PATCHED DENEB ON MY LEFT.
AM I THE CRUX POINT ALTAIR...
...IN THIS SUMMER DIE-ANGLE!?
JIRI (SCUFF)

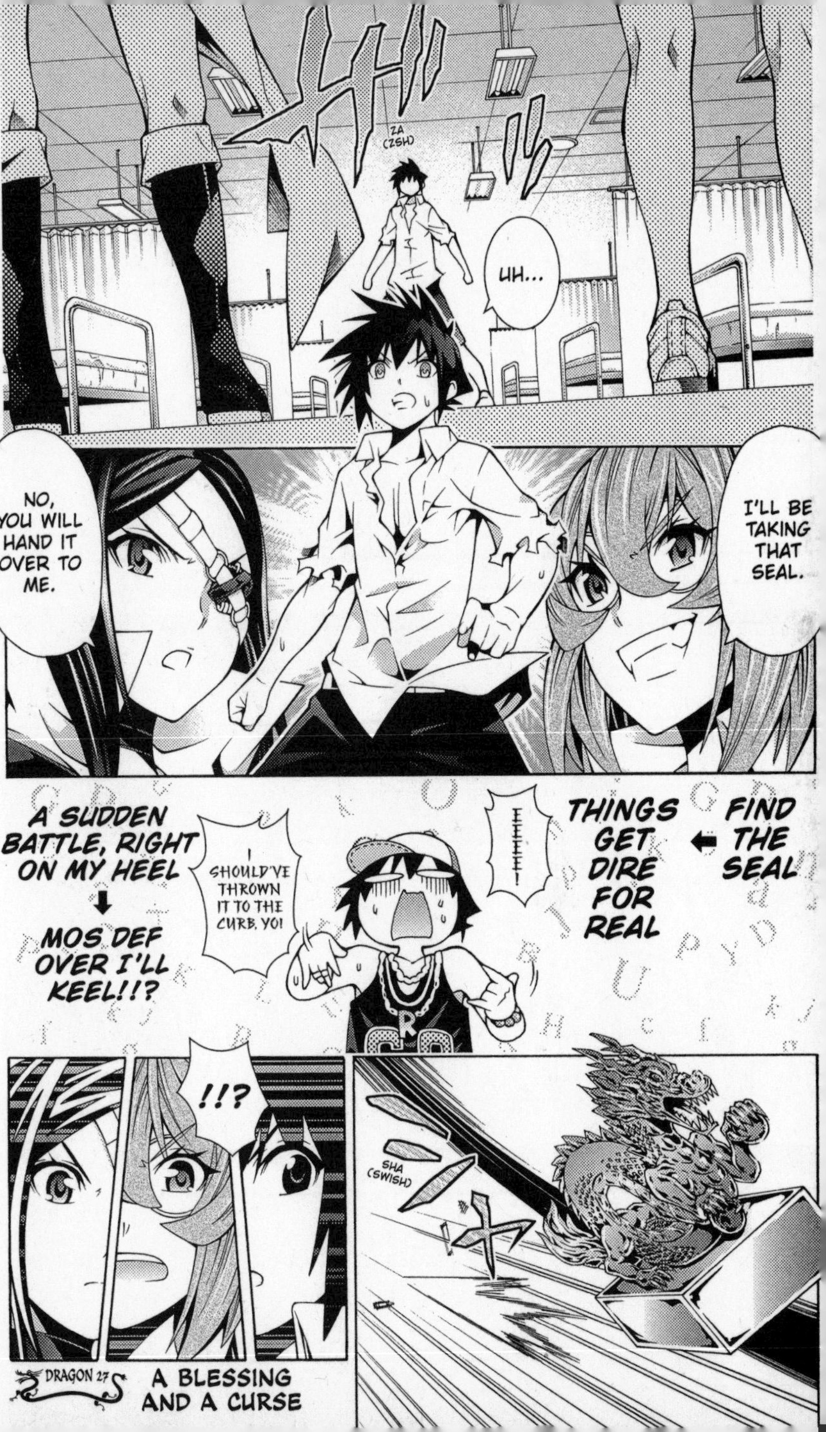
ZA (ZSH)
UH...
I'LL BE TAKING THAT SEAL.
NO, YOU WILL HAND IT OVER TO ME.
FIND THE SEAL ← THINGS GET DIRE FOR REAL
I SHOULD'VE THROWN IT TO THE CURB, YO!
A SUDDEN BATTLE, RIGHT ON MY HEEL ↓ MOS DEF OVER I'LL KEEL!!?
SHA (SWISH)
!!?
DRAGON 27 A BLESSING AND A CURSE

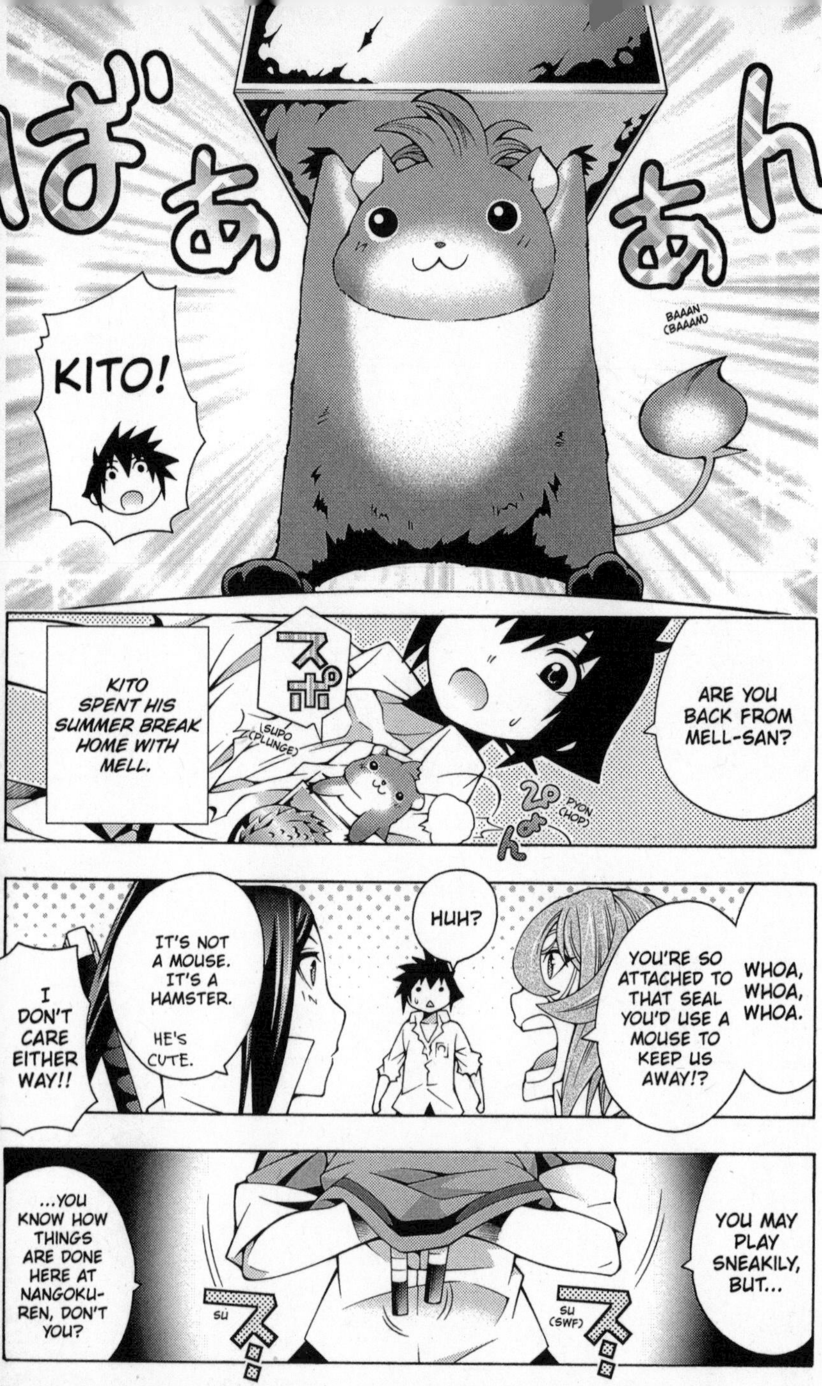
ばぁあん
BAAAN (BAAAM)
KITO!
ARE YOU BACK FROM MELL-SAN?
ぴょん
PYON (HOP)
スポ
SUPO (PLUNGE)
KITO SPENT HIS SUMMER BREAK HOME WITH MELL.
WHOA, WHOA, WHOA.
YOU'RE SO ATTACHED TO THAT SEAL YOU'D USE A MOUSE TO KEEP US AWAY!?
HUH?
IT'S NOT A MOUSE. IT'S A HAMSTER.
HE'S CUTE.
I DON'T CARE EITHER WAY!!
YOU MAY PLAY SNEAKILY, BUT...
すっ
SU (SWF)
すっ
SU
...YOU KNOW HOW THINGS ARE DONE HERE AT NANGOKU-REN, DON'T YOU?

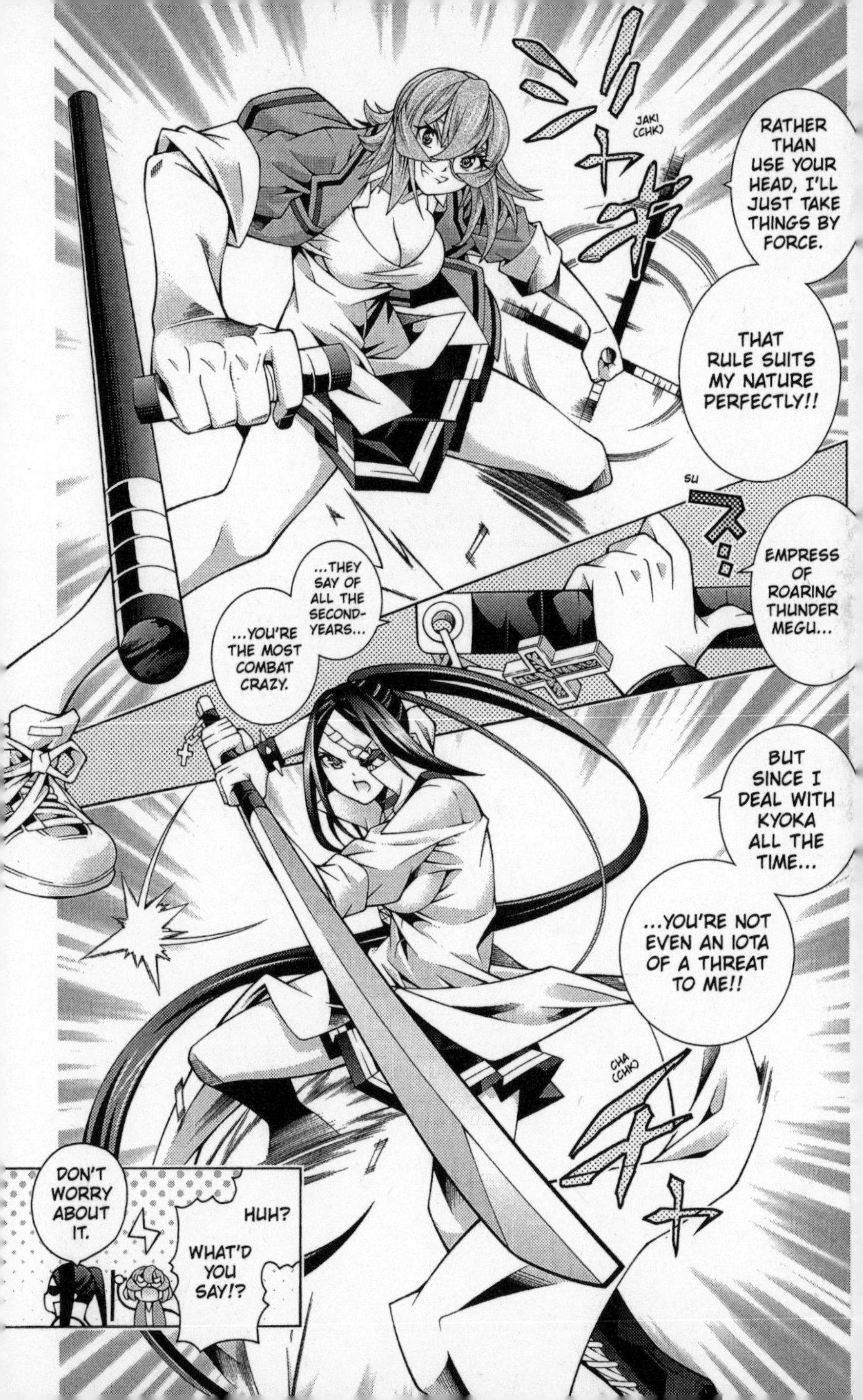
JAKI (CHK)
RATHER THAN USE YOUR HEAD, I'LL JUST TAKE THINGS BY FORCE.
THAT RULE SUITS MY NATURE PERFECTLY!!
SU
EMPRESS OF ROARING THUNDER MEGU...
...THEY SAY OF ALL THE SECOND-YEARS...
...YOU'RE THE MOST COMBAT CRAZY.
BUT SINCE I DEAL WITH KYOKA ALL THE TIME...
...YOU'RE NOT EVEN AN IOTA OF A THREAT TO ME!!
CHA (CHK)
HUH?
WHAT'D YOU SAY!?
DON'T WORRY ABOUT IT.

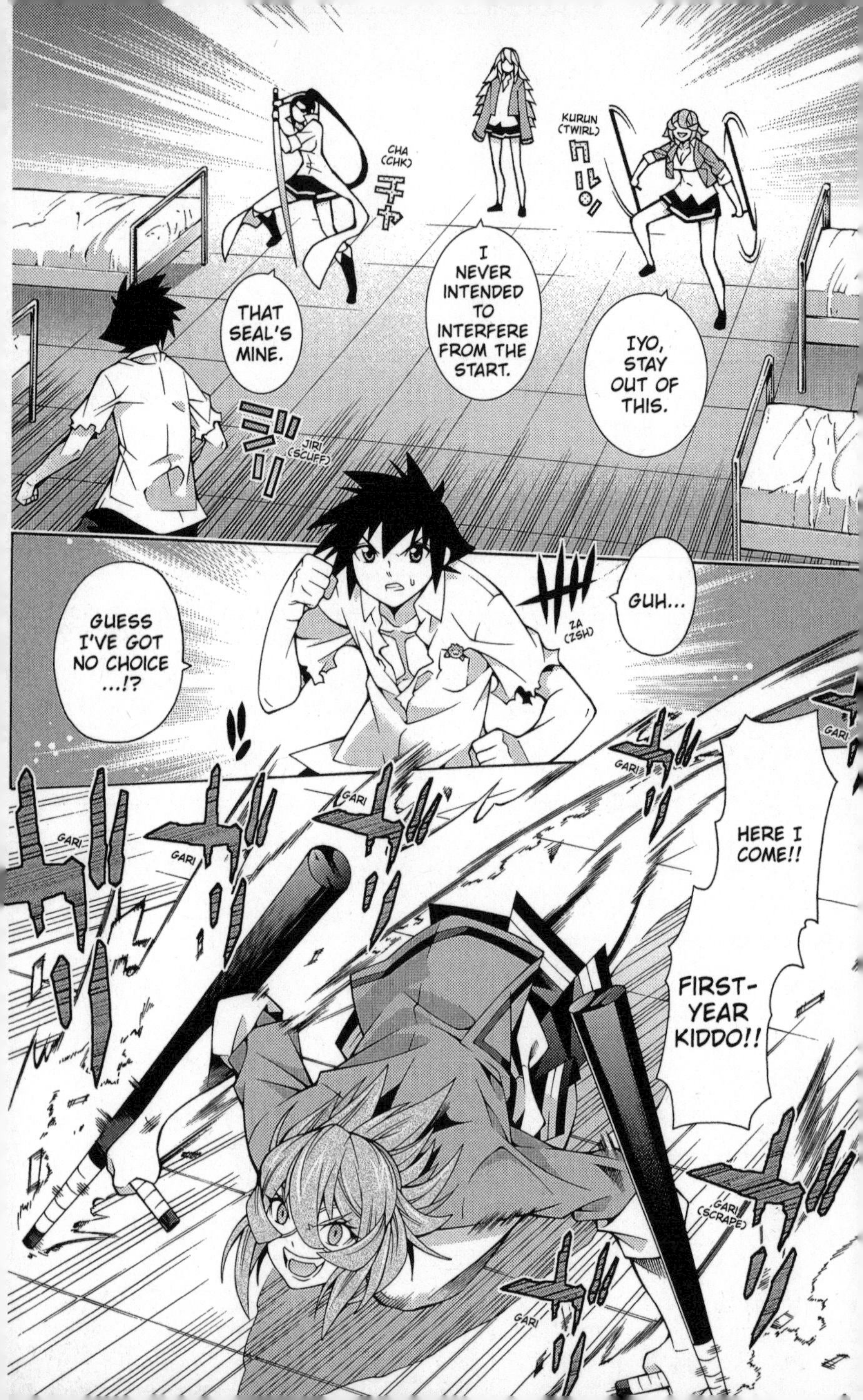
KURUN (TWIRL)
IYO, STAY OUT OF THIS.
I NEVER INTENDED TO INTERFERE FROM THE START.
CHA (CHK)
THAT SEAL'S MINE.
JIRI (SCUFF)
GUH...
ZA (ZSH)
GUESS I'VE GOT NO CHOICE ...!?
HERE I COME!!
FIRST-YEAR KIDDO!!
GARI
GARI
GARI
GARI
GARI
GARI (SCRAPE)
GARI

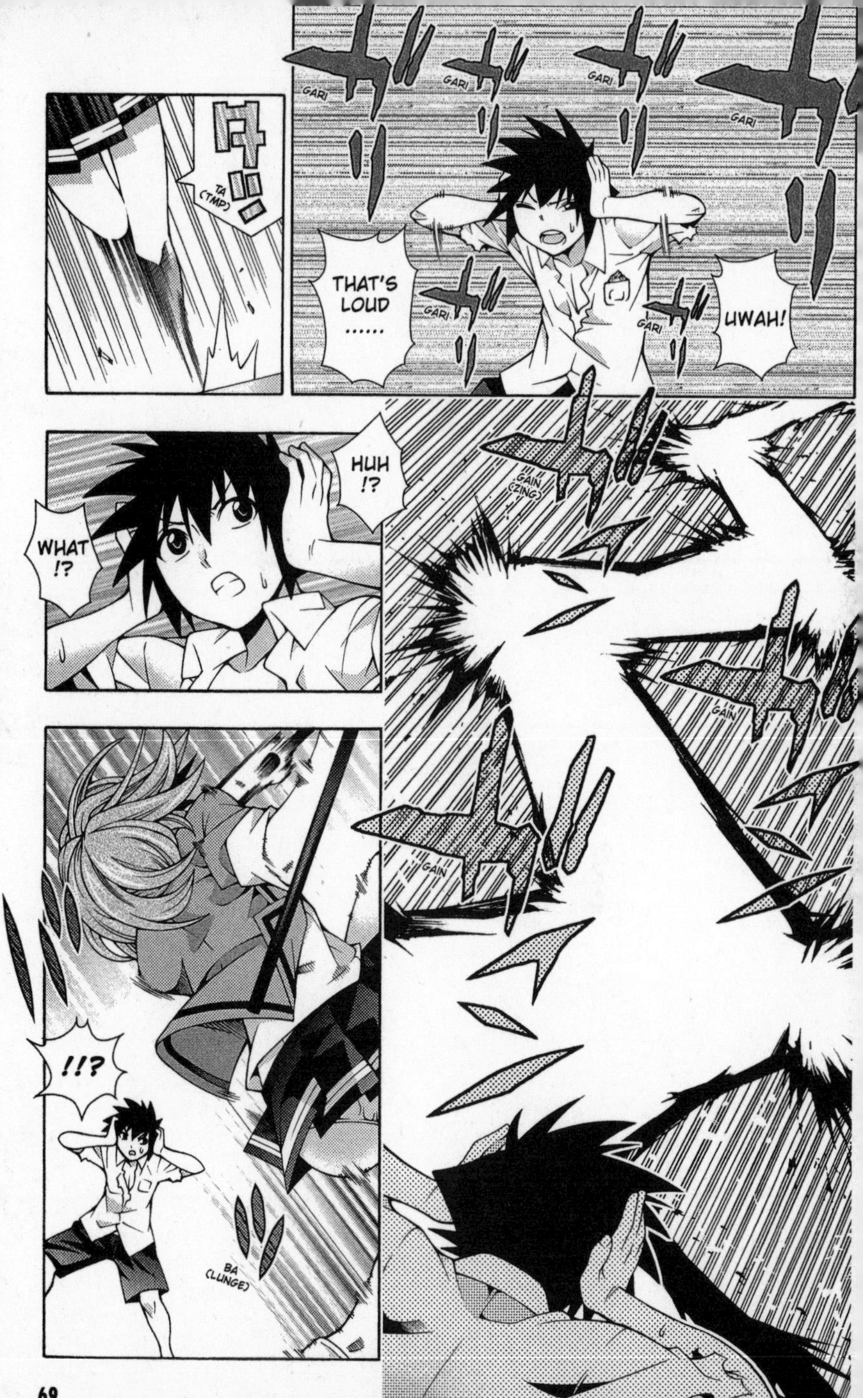
GARI
GARI
GARI
GARI
UWAH!
GARI
GARI
THAT'S LOUD ......
TA (TMP)
GAIN (ZING)
GAIN
GAIN
HUH !?
WHAT !?
!!?
BA (LUNGE)

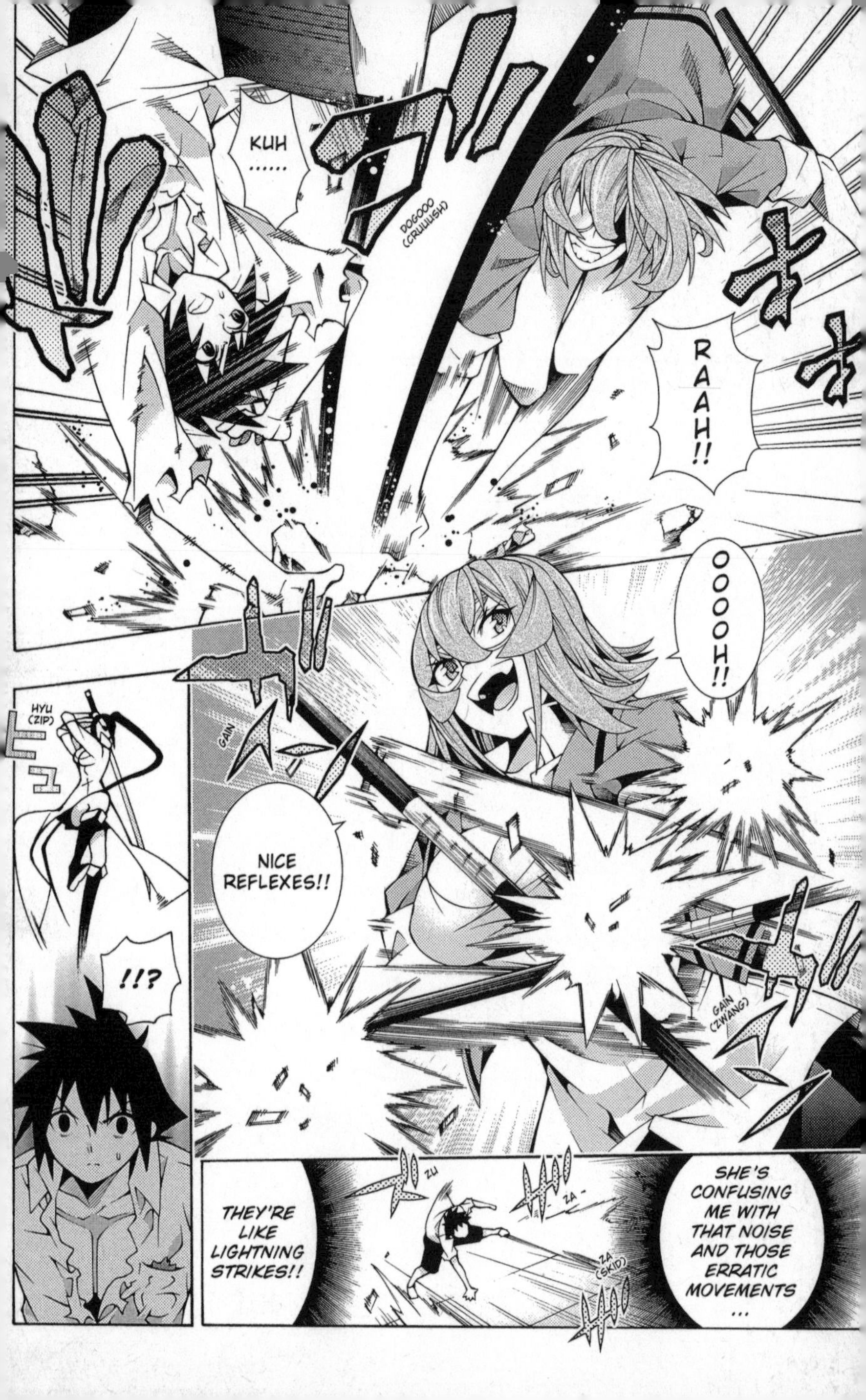
RAAAH!!
DOGOOO (CRUUUSH)
KUH ......
OOOOOH!!
GAIN
NICE REFLEXES!!
GAIN (ZWANG)
SHE'S CONFUSING ME WITH THAT NOISE AND THOSE ERRATIC MOVEMENTS ...
ZA (SKID)
ZA
ZU
THEY'RE LIKE LIGHTNING STRIKES!!
HYU (ZIP)
!!?

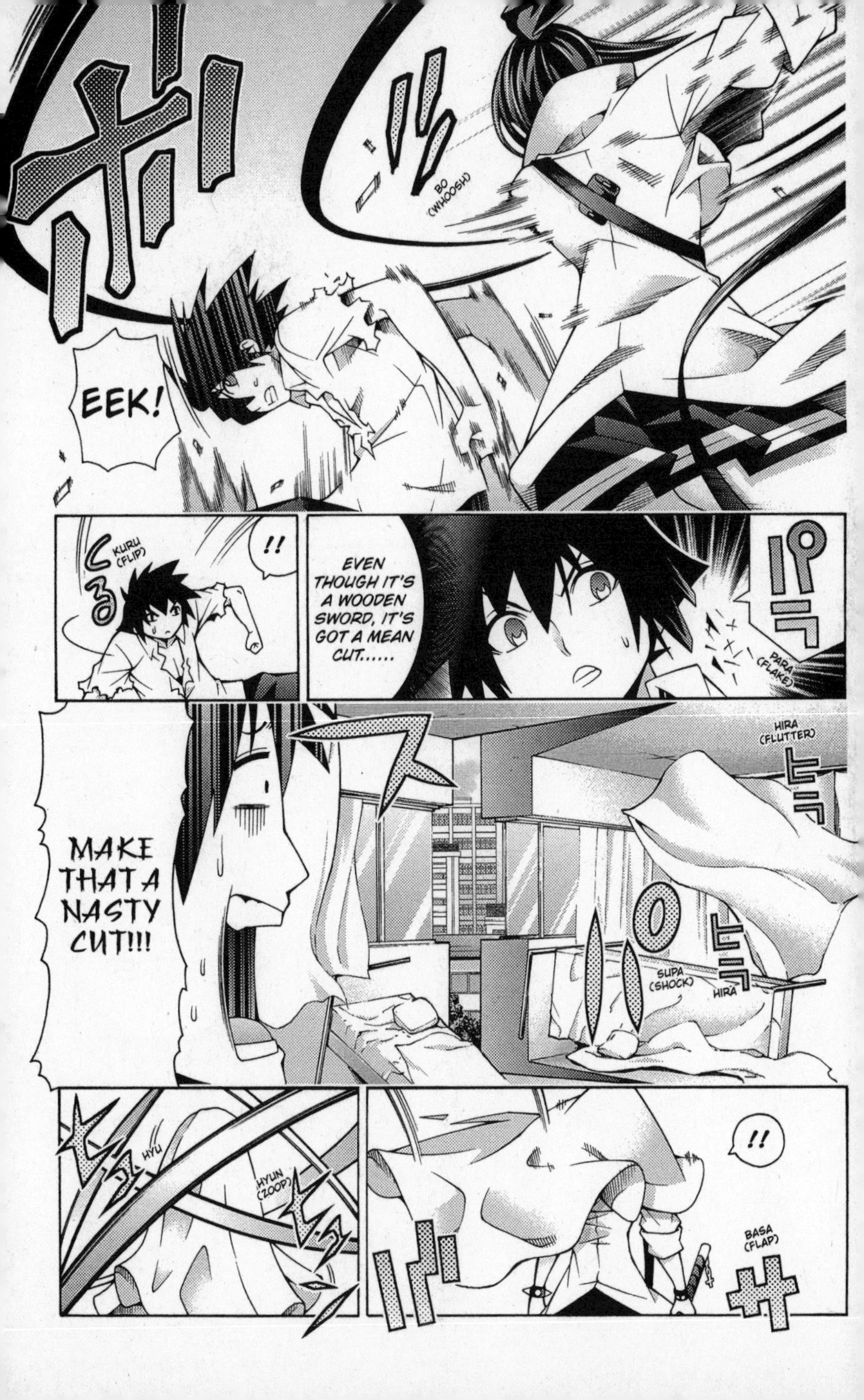
BO
(WHOOSH)
EEK!
PARA
(FLAKE)
EVEN THOUGH IT'S A WOODEN SWORD, IT'S GOT A MEAN CUT......
!!
KURU
(FLIP)
HIRA
(FLUTTER)
SUPA
(SHOCK)
HIRA
MAKE THAT A NASTY CUT!!!
!!
BASA
(FLAP)
HYU
HYUN
(ZOOP)

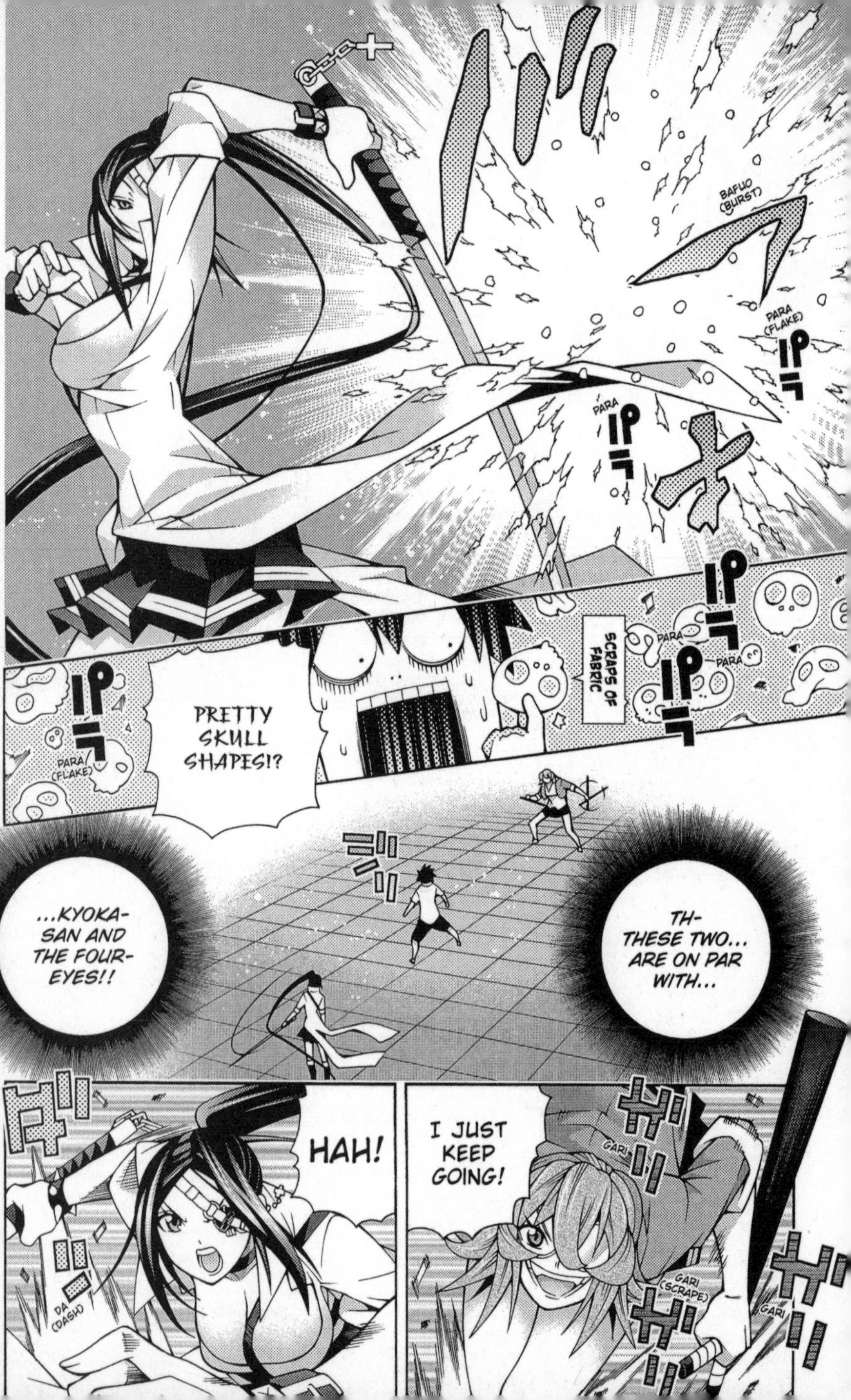
BAFUO (BURST)
PARA (FLAKE)
PARA
SCRAPS OF FABRIC
PARA
PARA
PRETTY SKULL SHAPES!?
PARA (FLAKE)
TH- THESE TWO... ARE ON PAR WITH...
...KYOKA-SAN AND THE FOUR-EYES!!
I JUST KEEP GOING!
GARI
GARI (SCRAPE)
GARI
HAH!
DA (DASH)

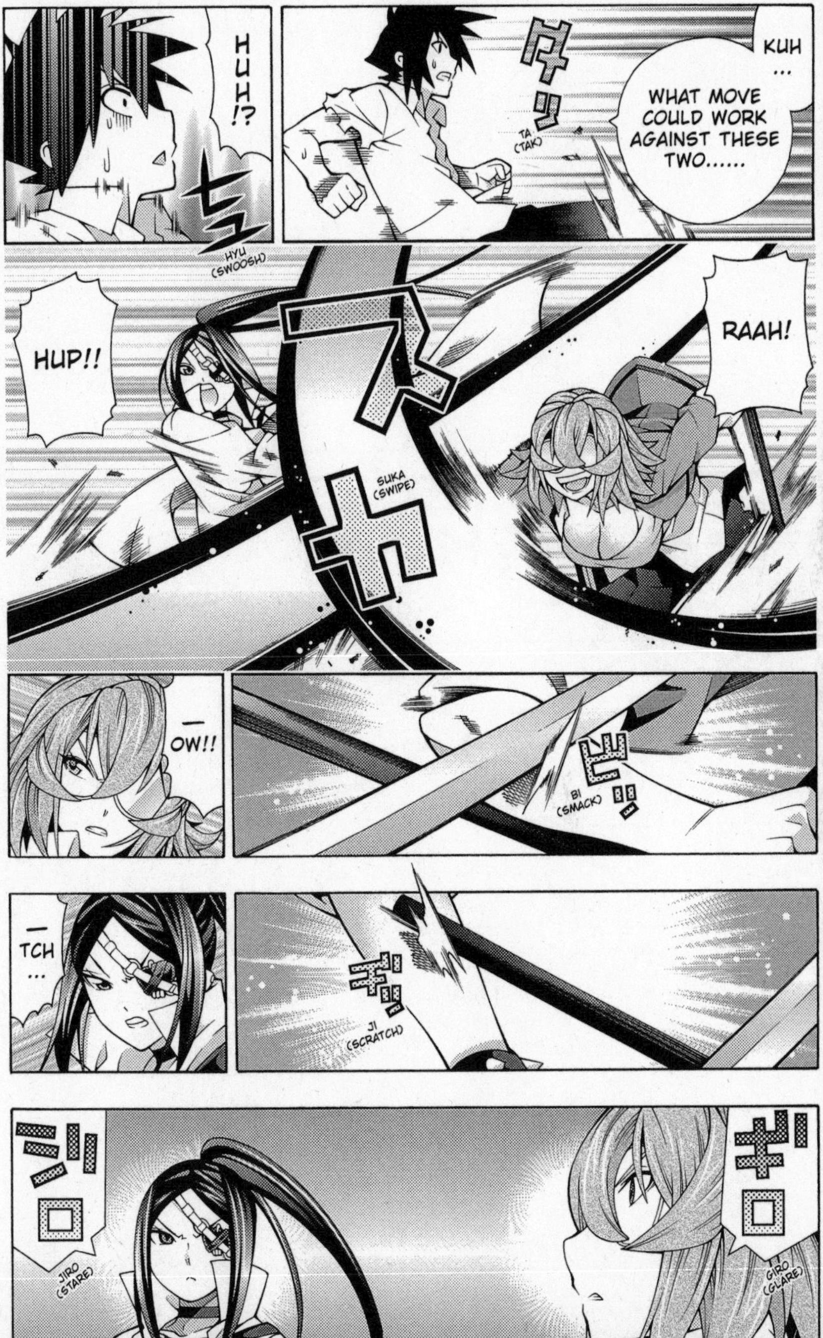
KUH...
WHAT MOVE COULD WORK AGAINST THESE TWO......
TA (TAK)
HUH!?
HYU (SWOOSH)
RAAH!
HUP!!
SUKA (SWIPE)
BI (SMACK)
—OW!!
JI (SCRATCH)
—TCH...
GIRO (GLARE)
JIRO (STARE)

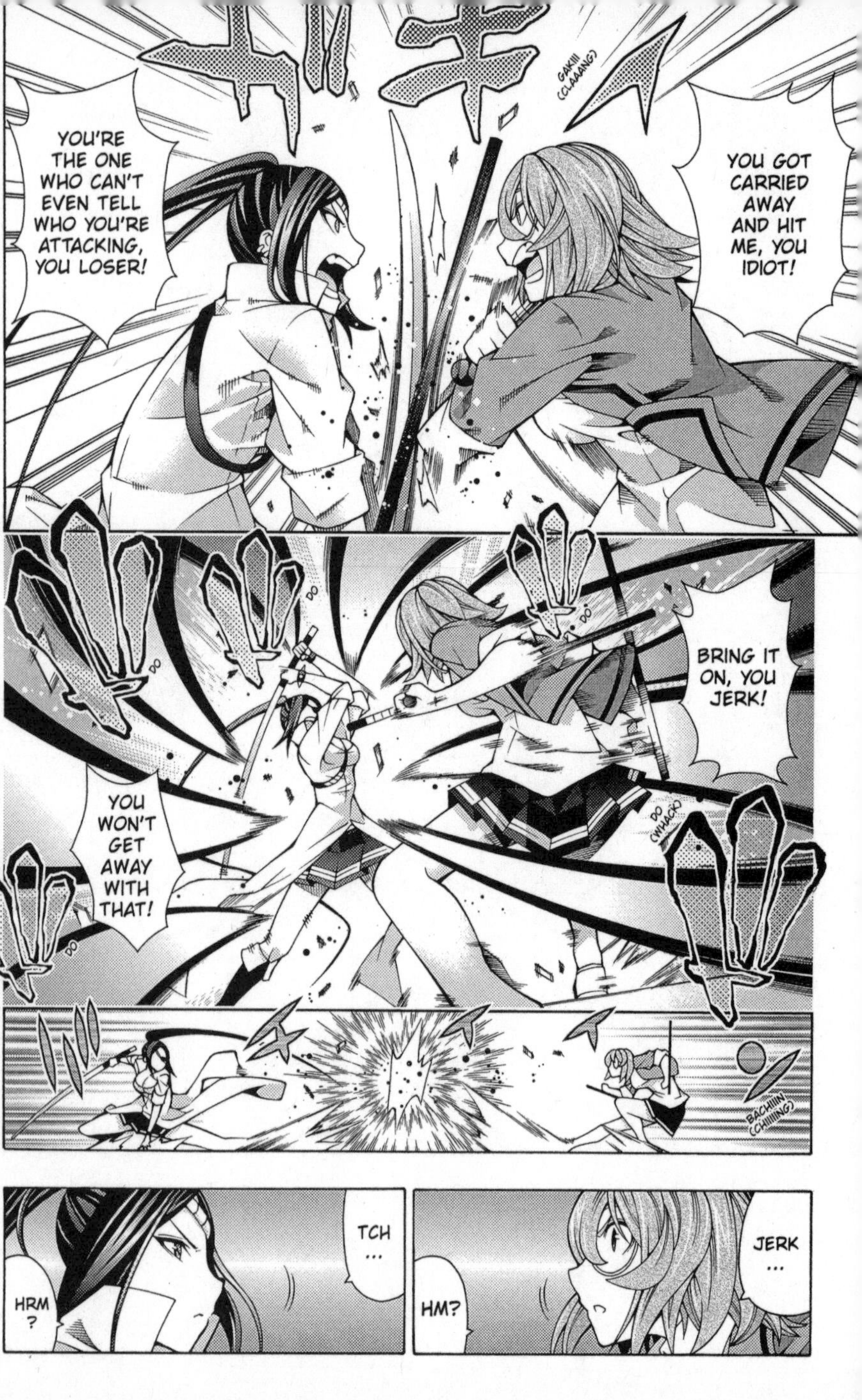
GAKIII (CLAAANG)
YOU GOT CARRIED AWAY AND HIT ME, YOU IDIOT!
YOU'RE THE ONE WHO CAN'T EVEN TELL WHO YOU'RE ATTACKING, YOU LOSER!
BRING IT ON, YOU JERK!
DO
DO (WHACK)
DO
YOU WON'T GET AWAY WITH THAT!
DO
DO
BACHIIIN (CHIIIING)
JERK ...
HM?
TCH ...
HRM ?

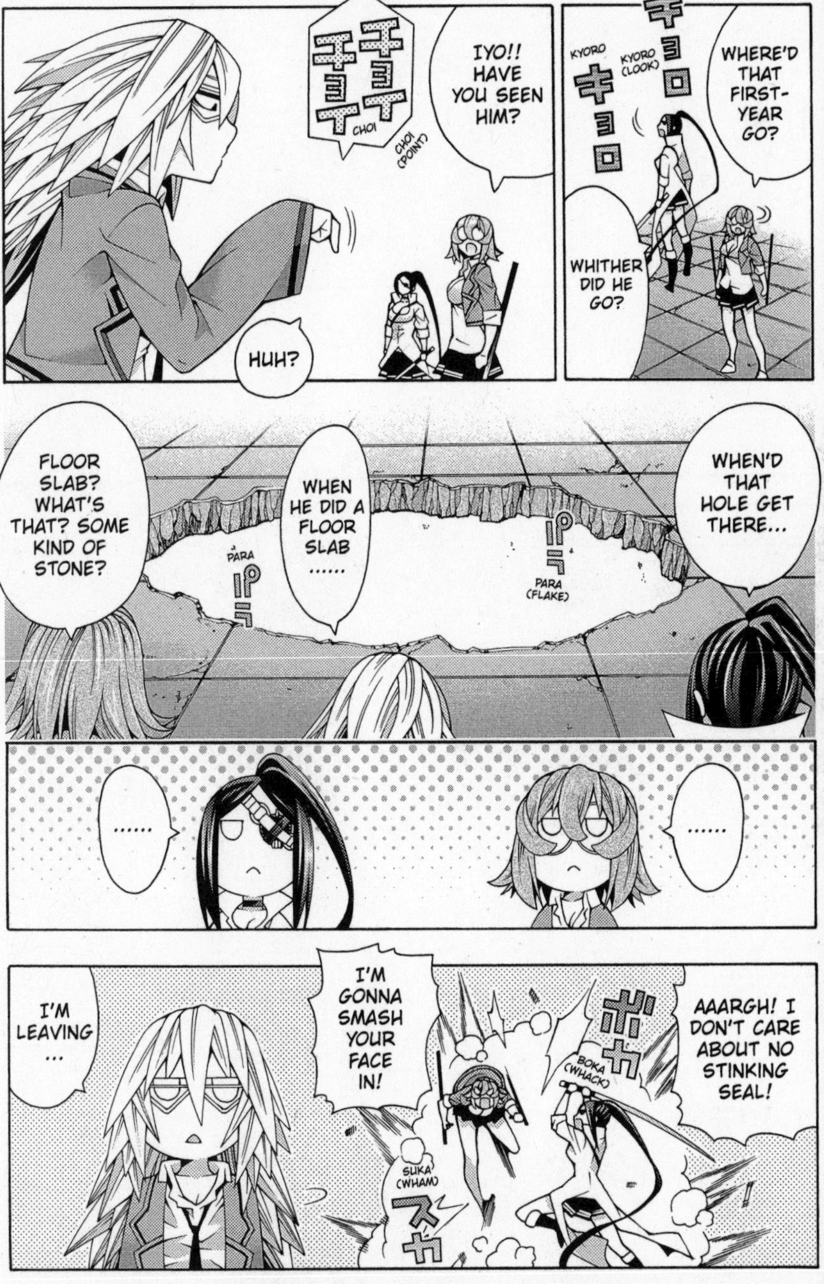

WHERE'D THAT FIRST-YEAR GO?
キョロキョロ
KYORO (LOOK)
KYORO
WHITHER DID HE GO?
IYO!! HAVE YOU SEEN HIM?
チョイチョイ
CHOI (POINT)
CHOI
HUH?
WHEN'D THAT HOLE GET THERE...
パラ
PARA (FLAKE)
WHEN HE DID A FLOOR SLAB ......
パラ
PARA
FLOOR SLAB? WHAT'S THAT? SOME KIND OF STONE?
......
......
AAARGH! I DON'T CARE ABOUT NO STINKING SEAL!
ボカ
BOKA (WHACK)
I'M GONNA SMASH YOUR FACE IN!
スカ
SUKA (WHAM)
I'M LEAVING ...

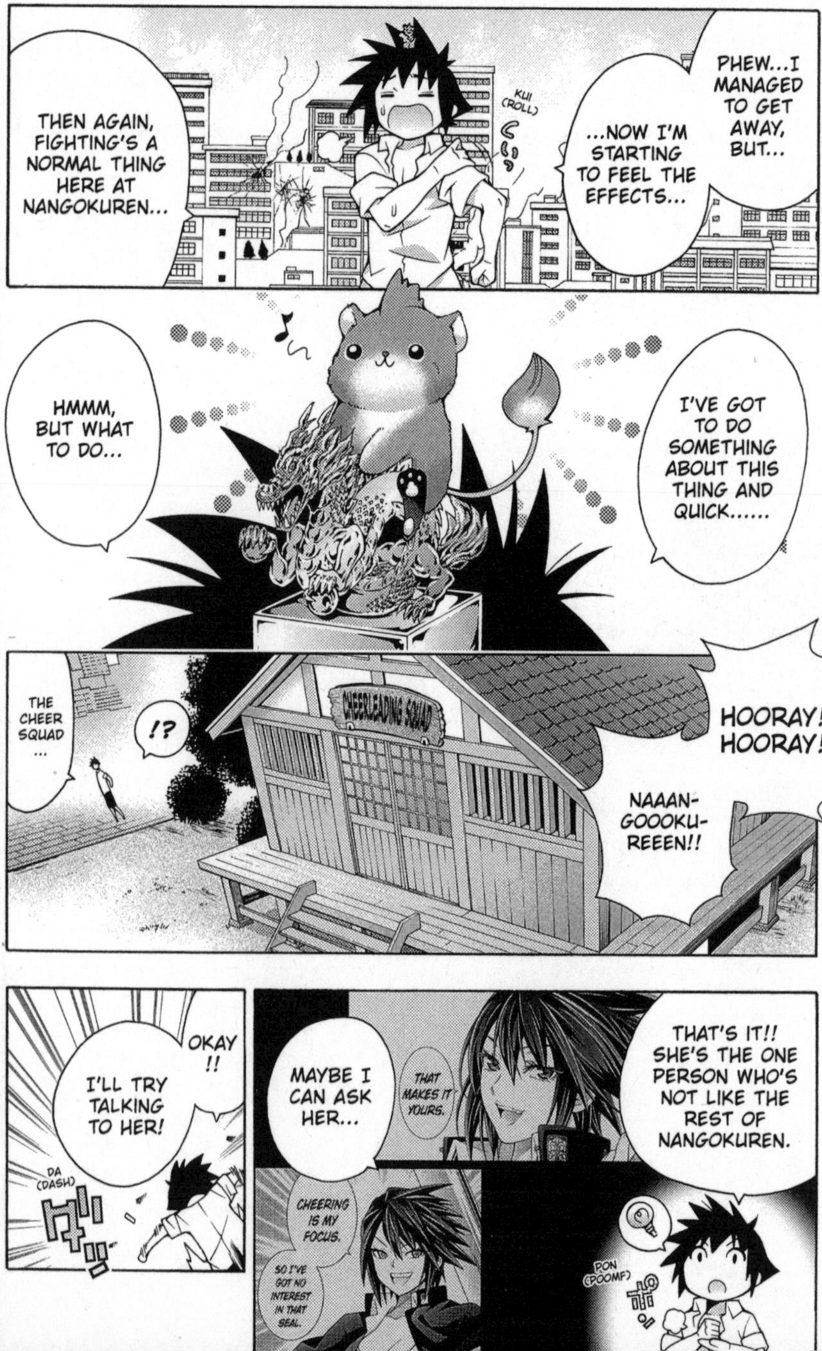
PHEW...I MANAGED TO GET AWAY, BUT...
...NOW I'M STARTING TO FEEL THE EFFECTS...
KUI (ROLL)
THEN AGAIN, FIGHTING'S A NORMAL THING HERE AT NANGOKUREN...
I'VE GOT TO DO SOMETHING ABOUT THIS THING AND QUICK......
HMMM, BUT WHAT TO DO...
HOORAY! HOORAY!
NAAAN-GOOOKU-REEEN!!
CHEERLEADING SQUAD
!?
THE CHEER SQUAD ...
THAT'S IT!! SHE'S THE ONE PERSON WHO'S NOT LIKE THE REST OF NANGOKUREN.
THAT MAKES IT YOURS.
MAYBE I CAN ASK HER...
PON (POOMF)
CHEERING IS MY FOCUS.
SO I'VE GOT NO INTEREST IN THAT SEAL.
OKAY!!
I'LL TRY TALKING TO HER!
DA (DASH)

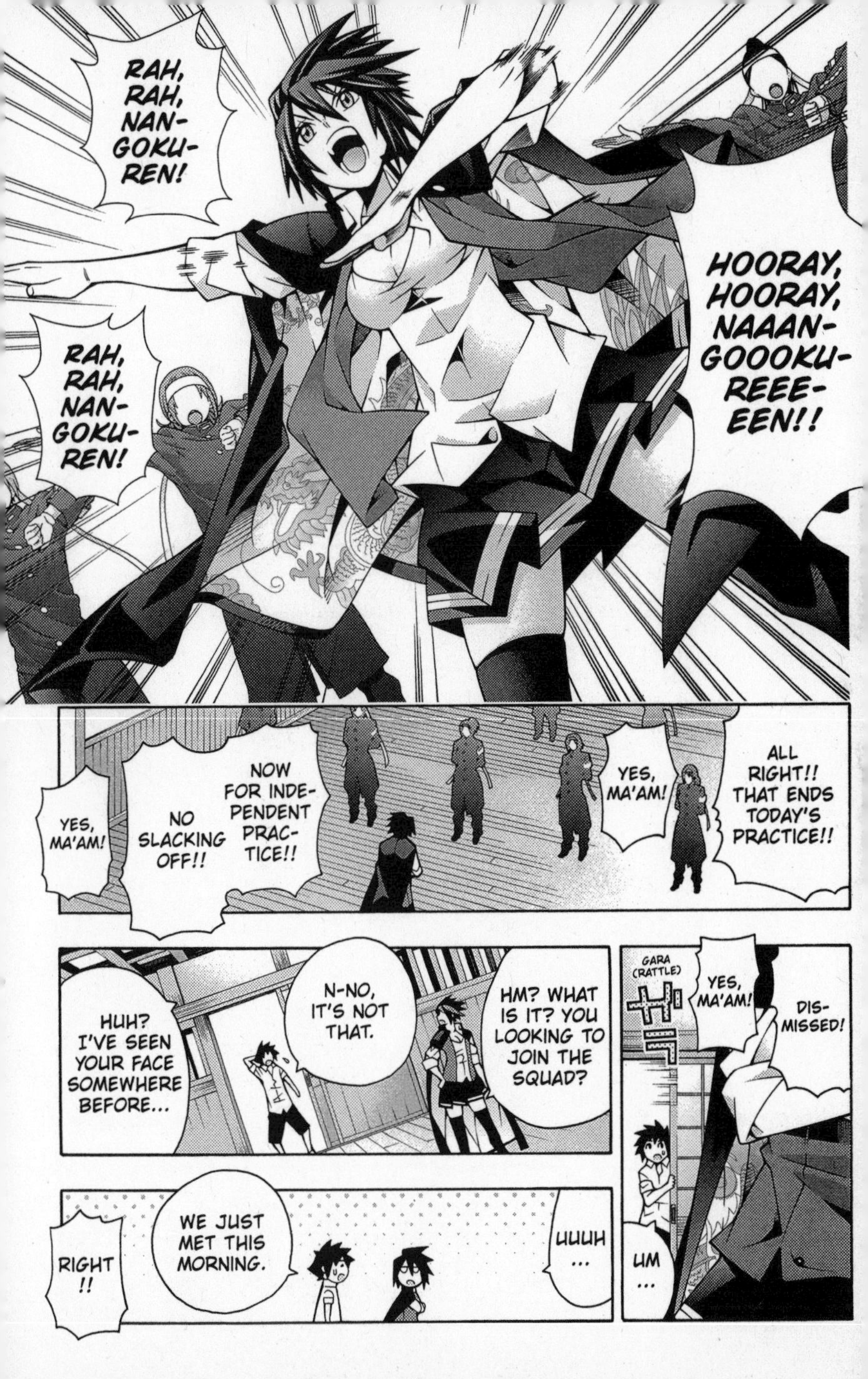
RAH, RAH, NAN-GOKU-REN!
HOORAY, HOORAY, NAAAN-GOOOKU-REEE-EEN!!
RAH, RAH, NAN-GOKU-REN!
ALL RIGHT!! THAT ENDS TODAY'S PRACTICE!!
YES, MA'AM!
NOW FOR INDE-PENDENT PRAC-TICE!!
NO SLACKING OFF!!
YES, MA'AM!
DIS-MISSED!
YES, MA'AM!
GARA (RATTLE)
UM ...
HM? WHAT IS IT? YOU LOOKING TO JOIN THE SQUAD?
N-NO, IT'S NOT THAT.
HUH? I'VE SEEN YOUR FACE SOMEWHERE BEFORE...
UUUH ...
WE JUST MET THIS MORNING.
RIGHT !!

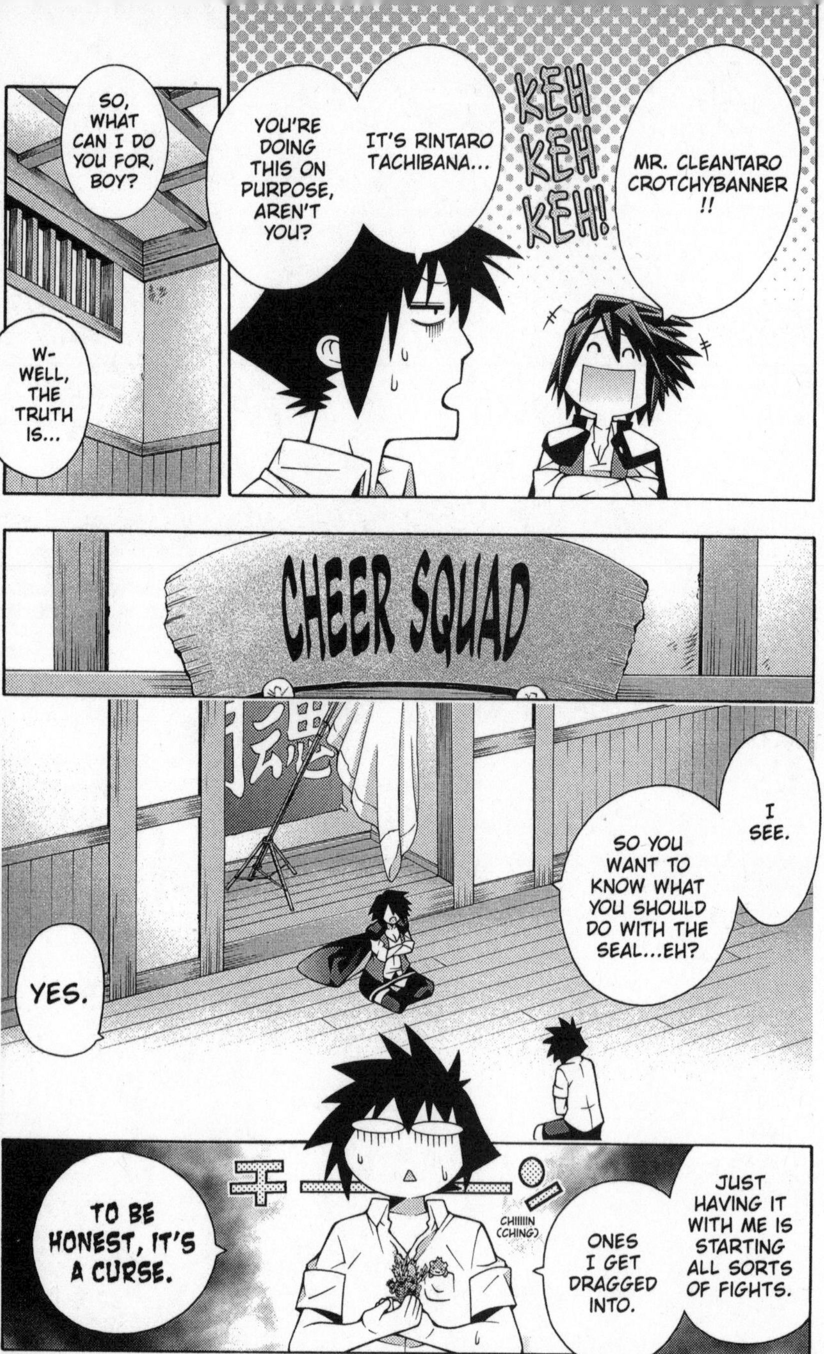
MR. CLEANTARO CROTCHYBANNER !!
KEH KEH KEH!
IT'S RINTARO TACHIBANA...
YOU'RE DOING THIS ON PURPOSE, AREN'T YOU?
SO, WHAT CAN I DO YOU FOR, BOY?
W-WELL, THE TRUTH IS...
CHEER SQUAD
I SEE.
SO YOU WANT TO KNOW WHAT YOU SHOULD DO WITH THE SEAL...EH?
YES.
JUST HAVING IT WITH ME IS STARTING ALL SORTS OF FIGHTS.
ONES I GET DRAGGED INTO.
CHIIIIIN (CHING)
TO BE HONEST, IT'S A CURSE.

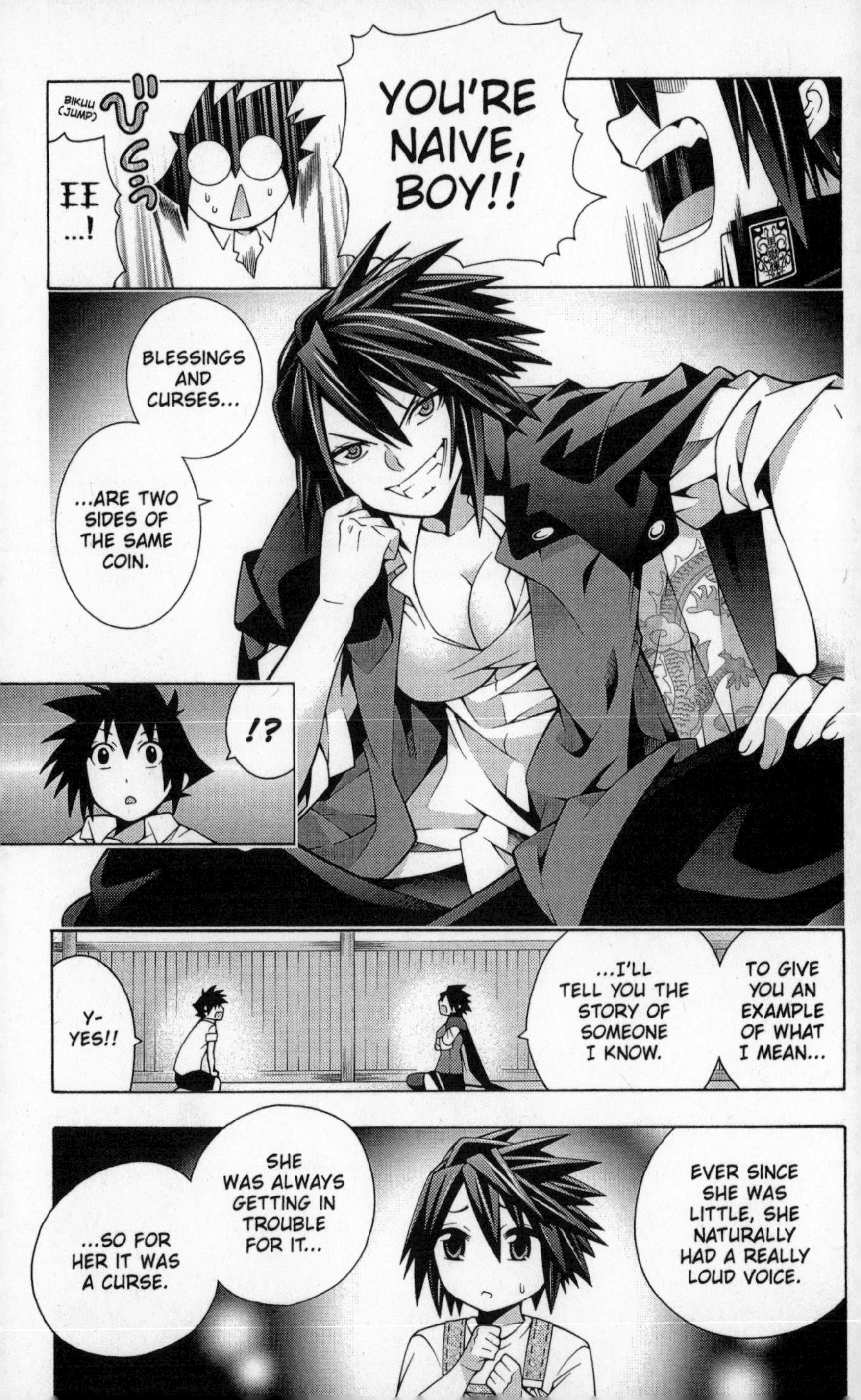
YOU'RE NAIVE, BOY!!
BIKUU (JUMP)
EE ...!
BLESSINGS AND CURSES...
...ARE TWO SIDES OF THE SAME COIN.
!?
TO GIVE YOU AN EXAMPLE OF WHAT I MEAN...
...I'LL TELL YOU THE STORY OF SOMEONE I KNOW.
Y-YES!!
EVER SINCE SHE WAS LITTLE, SHE NATURALLY HAD A REALLY LOUD VOICE.
SHE WAS ALWAYS GETTING IN TROUBLE FOR IT...
...SO FOR HER IT WAS A CURSE.

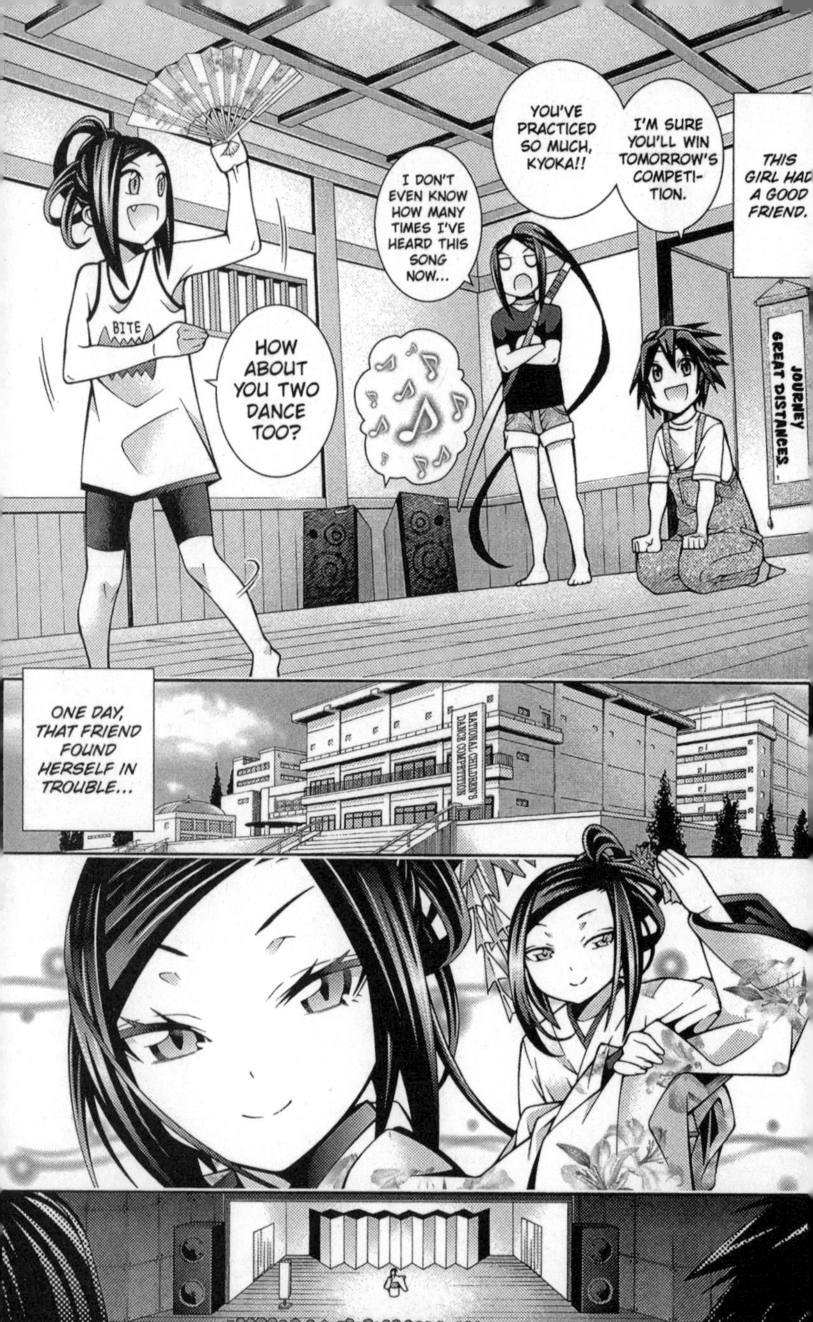
THIS GIRL HAD A GOOD FRIEND.
I'M SURE YOU'LL WIN TOMORROW'S COMPETI- TION.
YOU'VE PRACTICED SO MUCH, KYOKA!!
I DON'T EVEN KNOW HOW MANY TIMES I'VE HEARD THIS SONG NOW...
JOURNEY GREAT DISTANCES.
HOW ABOUT YOU TWO DANCE TOO?
BITE
ONE DAY, THAT FRIEND FOUND HERSELF IN TROUBLE...
NATIONAL CHILDREN'S DANCE COMPETITION

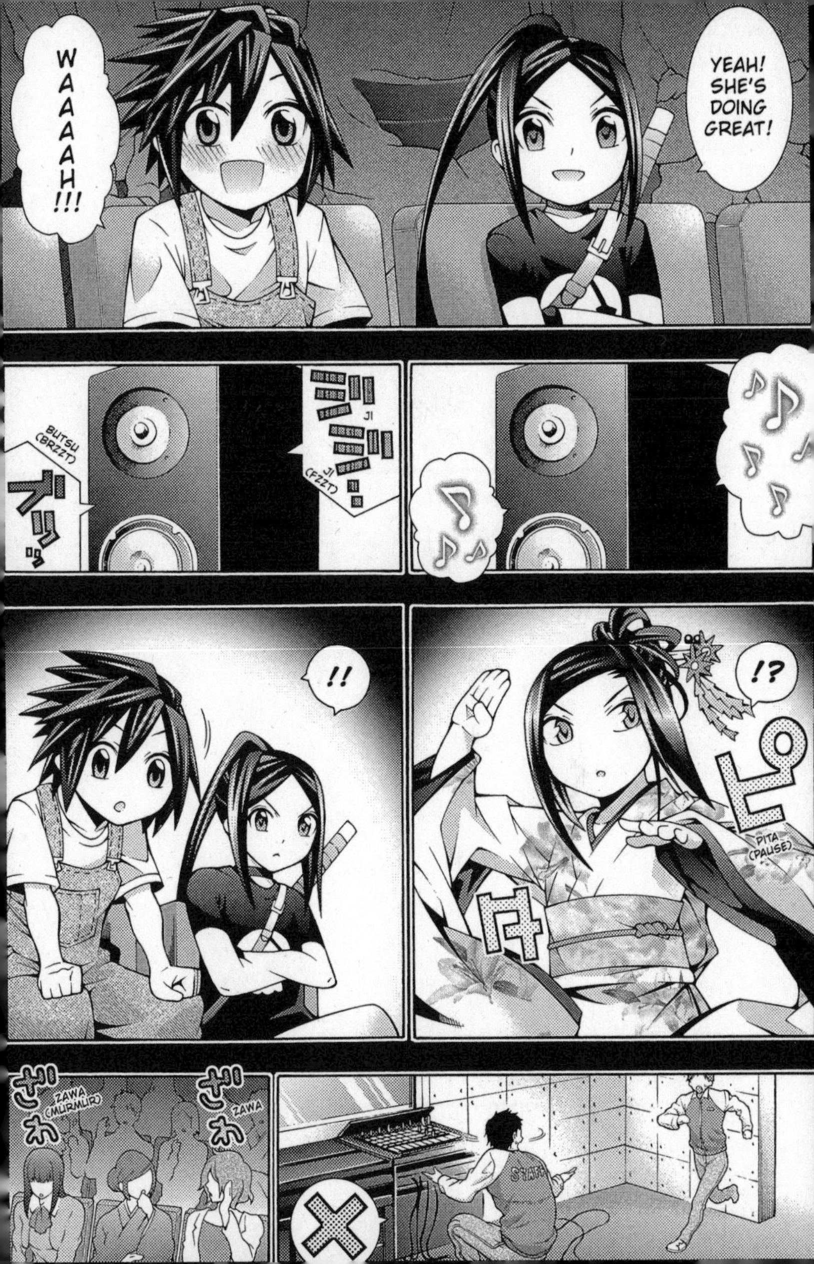
YEAH! SHE'S DOING GREAT!
WAAAAAH!!!
JI JI (FZZT)
BUTSU (BRZZT)
!?
PITA (PAUSE)
!!
ZAWA
ZAWA (MURMUR)

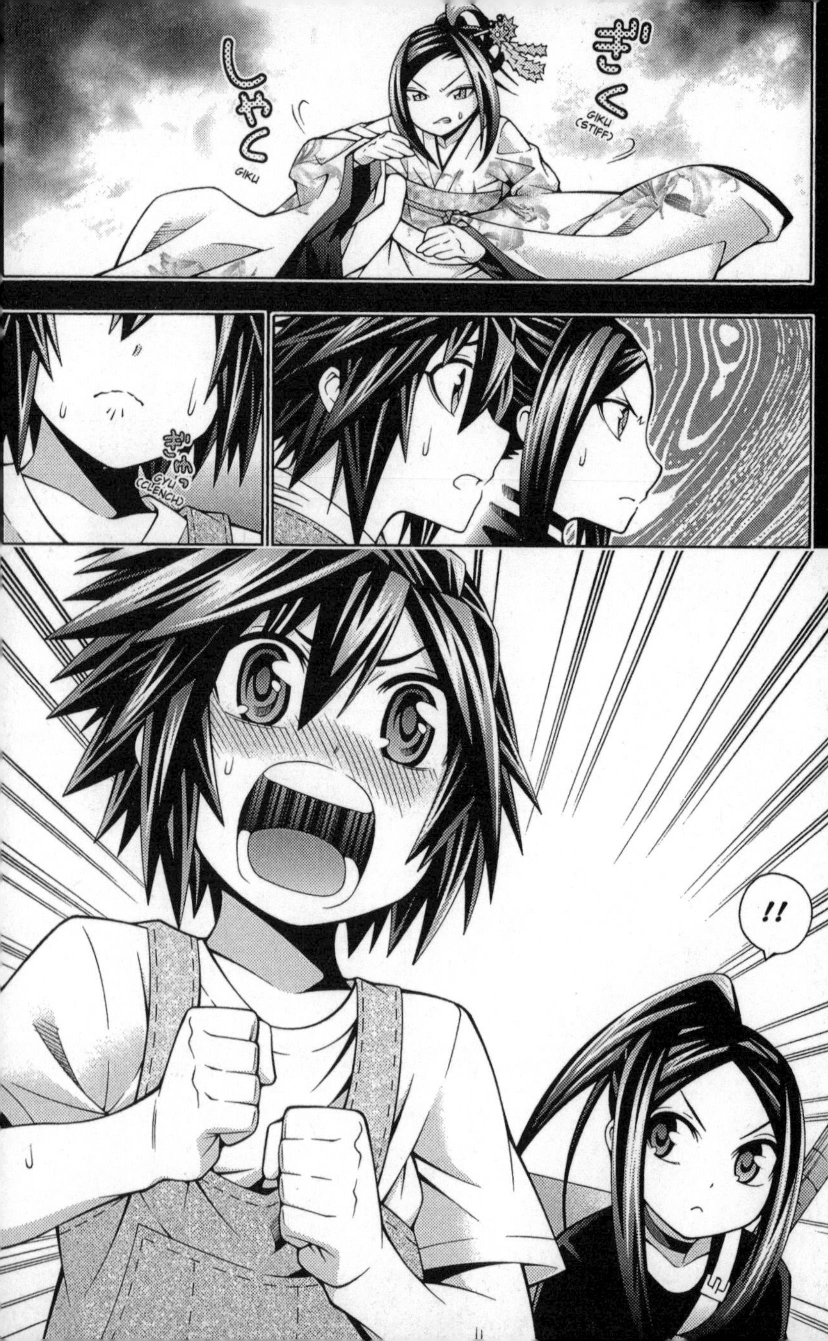
ぎく
GIKU (STIFF)
しゃく
GIKU
ぎゅっ
GYU (CLENCH)
!!

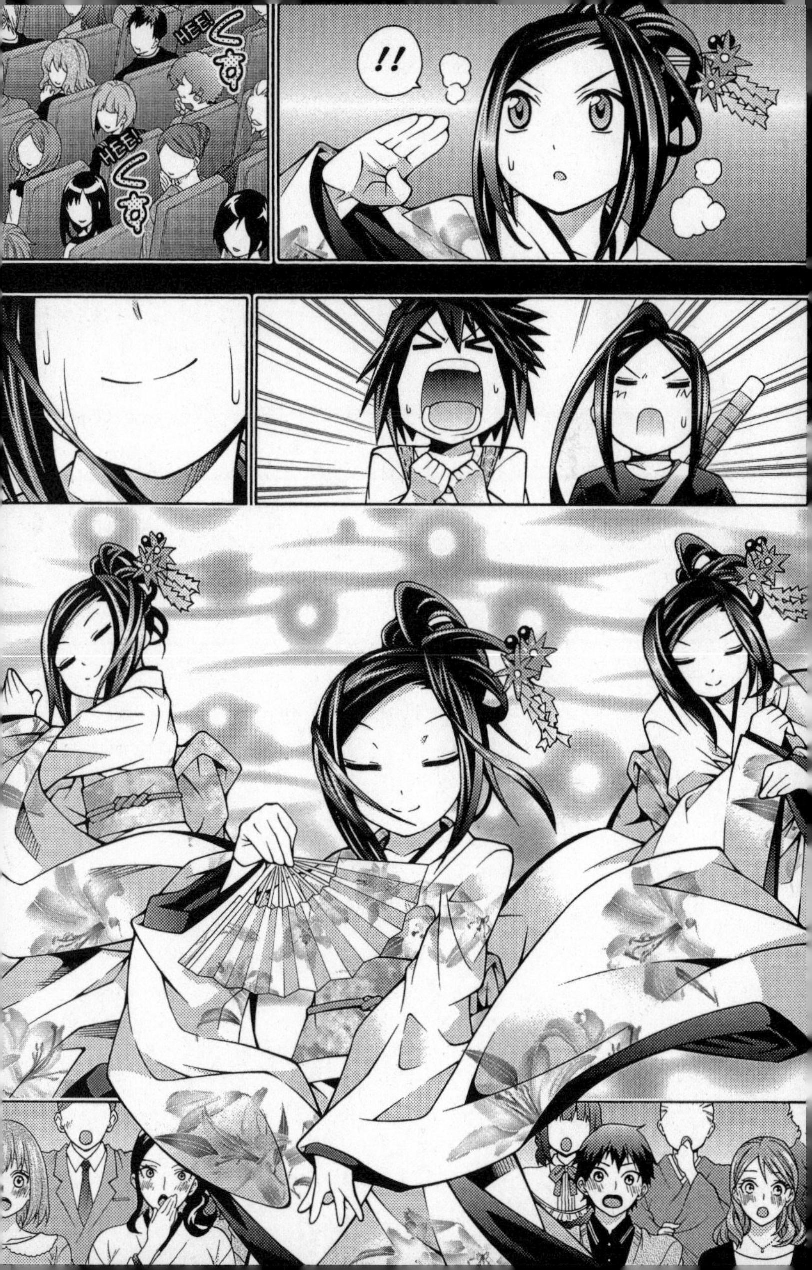
!!
HEE! くす
HEE! くす

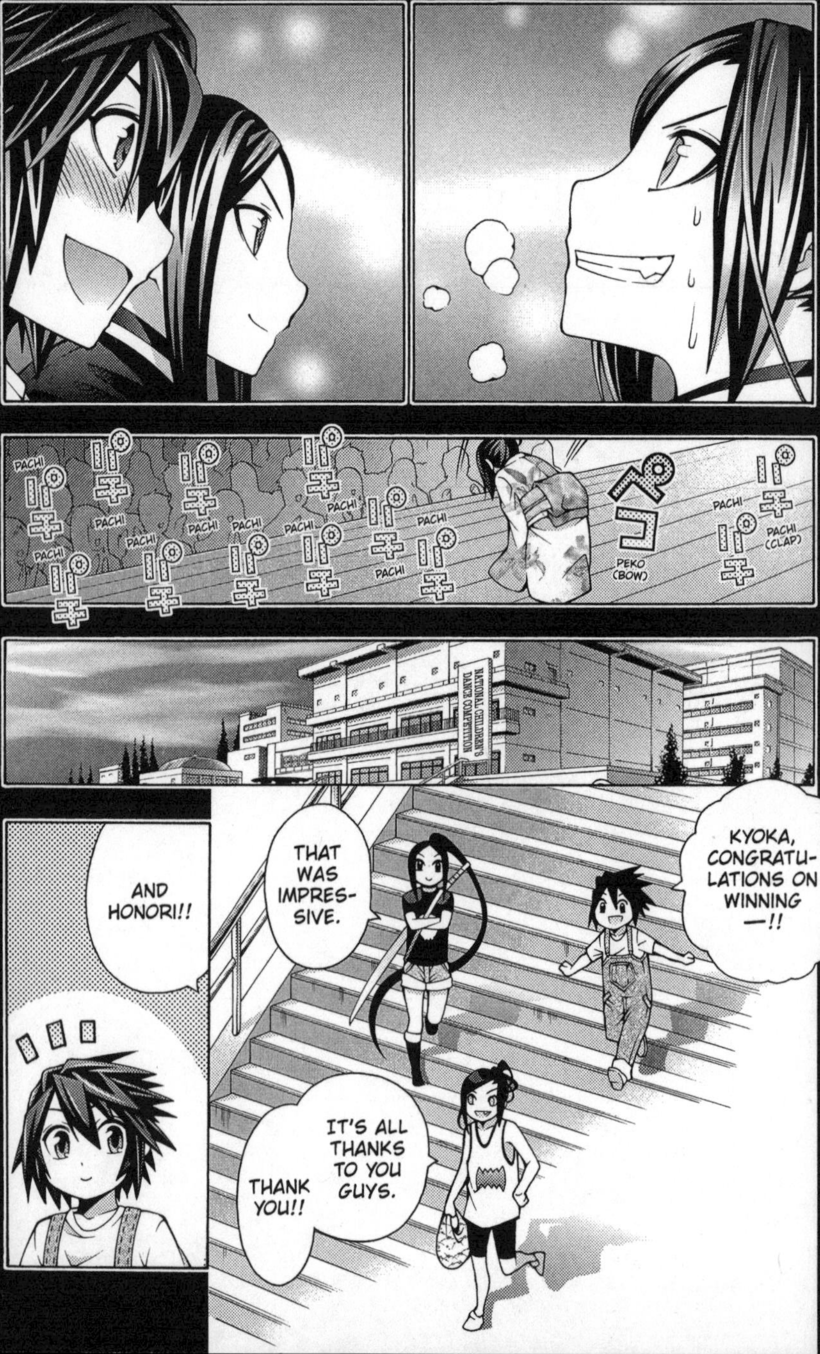
PACHI (CLAP)
PACHI
PEKO (BOW)
PACHI
PACHI
PACHI
PACHI
PACHI
PACHI
PACHI
PACHI
PACHI
NATIONAL CHILDREN'S DANCE COMPETITION
KYOKA, CONGRATULATIONS ON WINNING—!!
THAT WAS IMPRESSIVE.
IT'S ALL THANKS TO YOU GUYS.
THANK YOU!!
AND HONORI!!

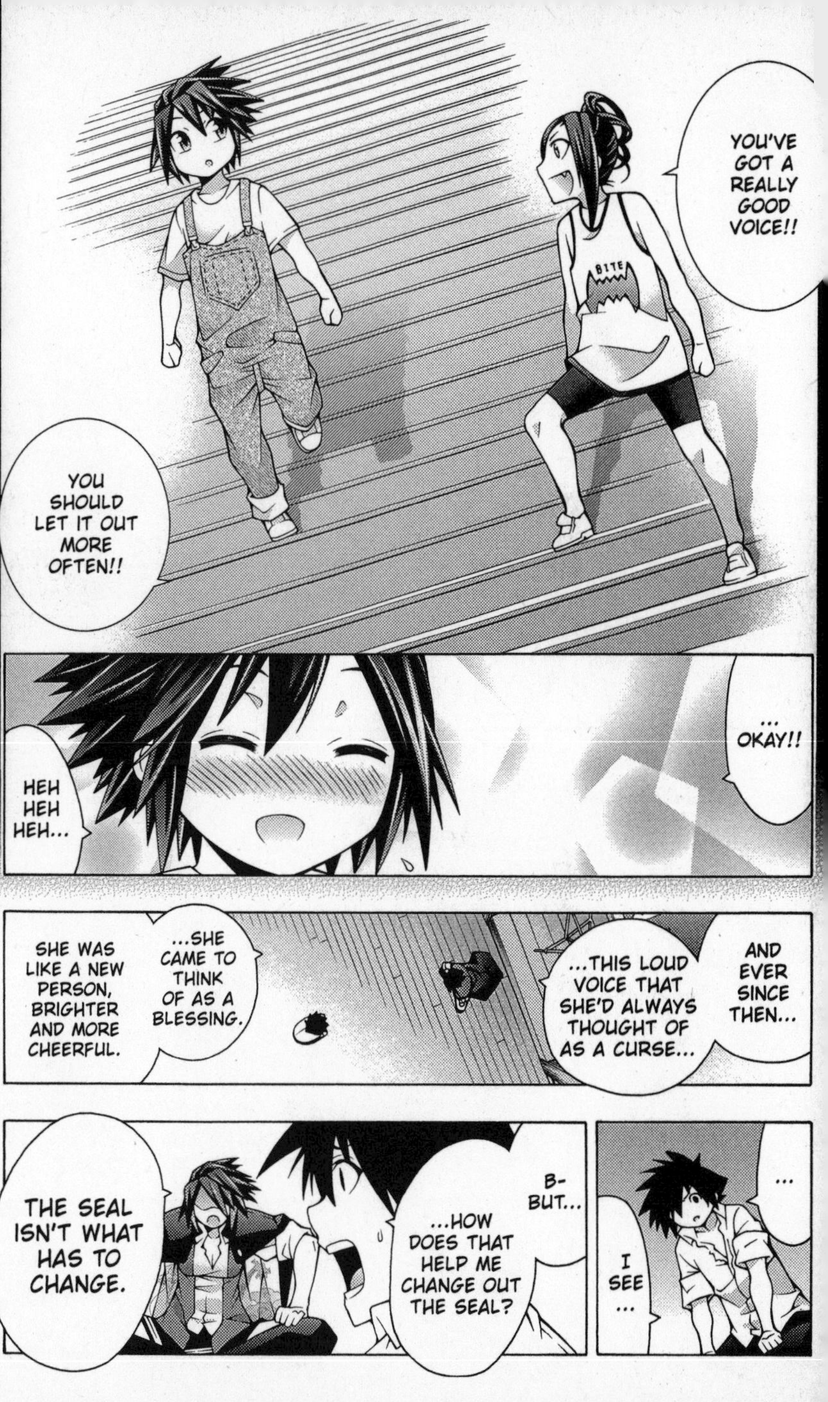
YOU'VE GOT A REALLY GOOD VOICE!!
YOU SHOULD LET IT OUT MORE OFTEN!!
... OKAY!!
HEH HEH HEH...
AND EVER SINCE THEN...
...THIS LOUD VOICE THAT SHE'D ALWAYS THOUGHT OF AS A CURSE...
...SHE CAME TO THINK OF AS A BLESSING.
SHE WAS LIKE A NEW PERSON, BRIGHTER AND MORE CHEERFUL.
...
I SEE ...
B- BUT...
...HOW DOES THAT HELP ME CHANGE OUT THE SEAL?
THE SEAL ISN'T WHAT HAS TO CHANGE.

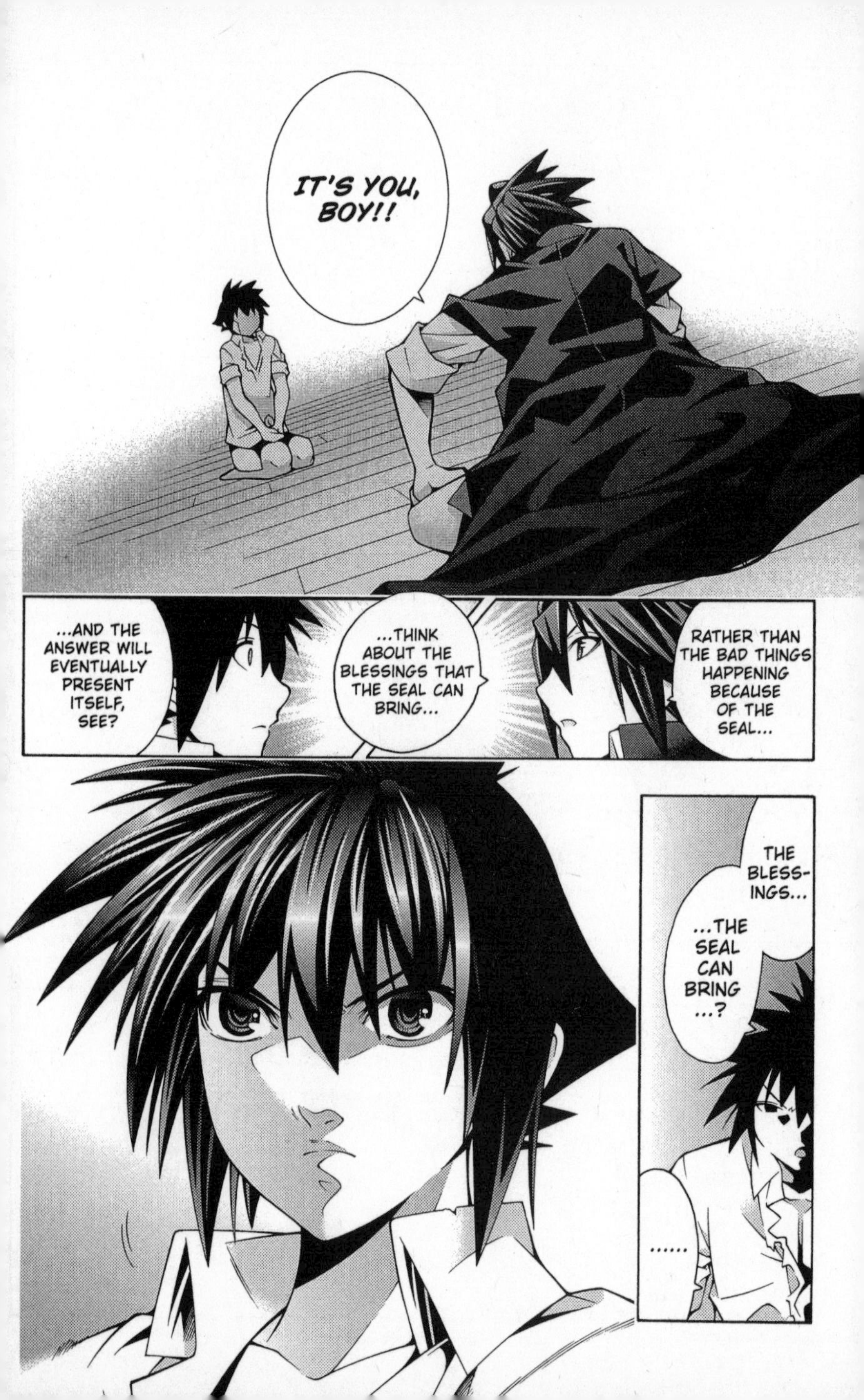
IT'S YOU, BOY!!
RATHER THAN THE BAD THINGS HAPPENING BECAUSE OF THE SEAL...
...THINK ABOUT THE BLESSINGS THAT THE SEAL CAN BRING...
...AND THE ANSWER WILL EVENTUALLY PRESENT ITSELF, SEE?
THE BLESS-INGS...
...THE SEAL CAN BRING ...?
......

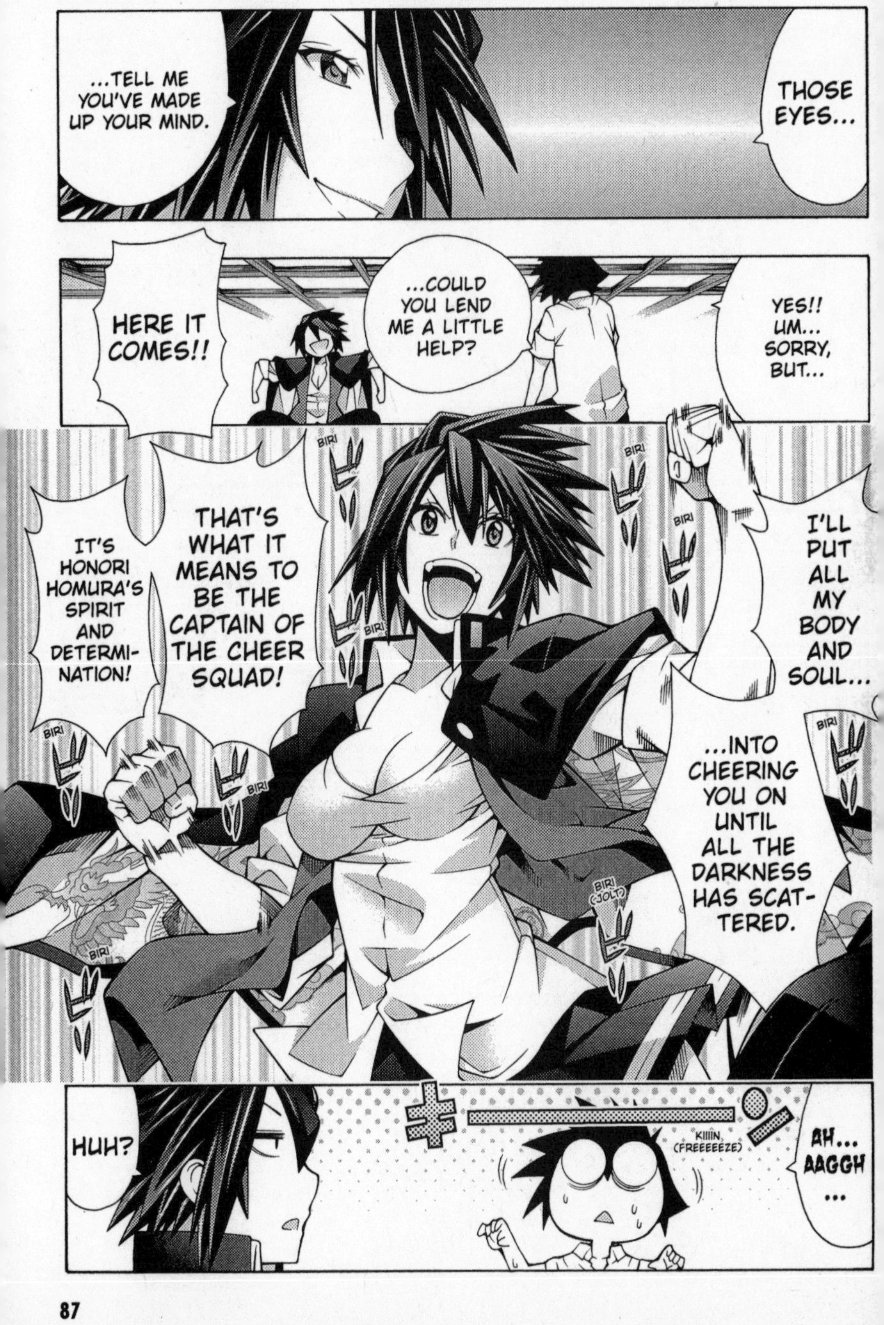
THOSE EYES...
...TELL ME YOU'VE MADE UP YOUR MIND.
YES!! UM... SORRY, BUT...
...COULD YOU LEND ME A LITTLE HELP?
HERE IT COMES!!
I'LL PUT ALL MY BODY AND SOUL...
...INTO CHEERING YOU ON UNTIL ALL THE DARKNESS HAS SCATTERED.
BIRI
BIRI
BIRI
THAT'S WHAT IT MEANS TO BE THE CAPTAIN OF THE CHEER SQUAD!
IT'S HONORI HOMURA'S SPIRIT AND DETERMINATION!
BIRI
BIRI (JOLT)
BIRI
BIRI
BIRI
AH... AAGGH ...
KIIIN (FREEEEEZE)
HUH?

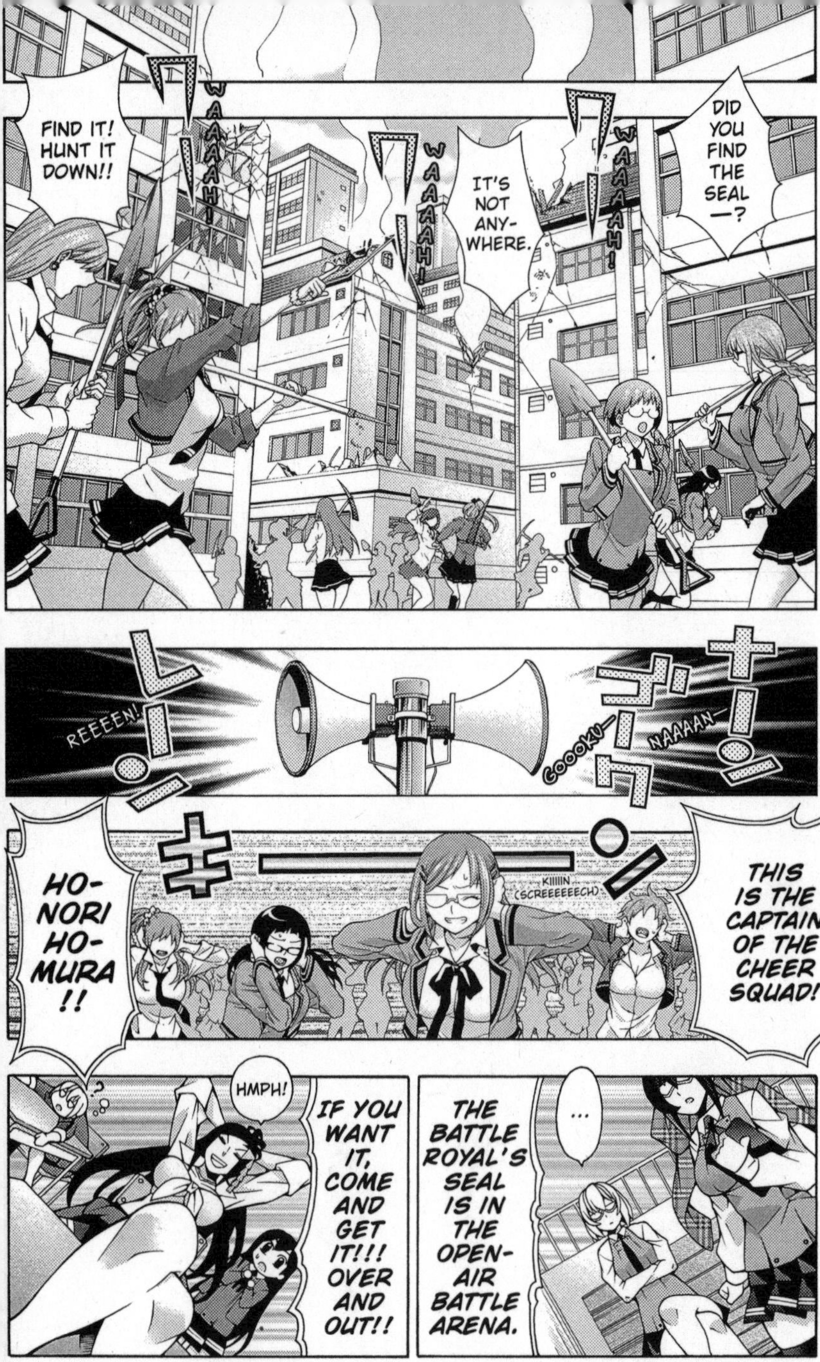
DID YOU FIND THE SEAL—?
WAAAAAH!
IT'S NOT ANYWHERE.
WAAAAAH!
WAAAAH!
FIND IT! HUNT IT DOWN!!
NAAAAN—
GOOOKU—
REEEEN!
THIS IS THE CAPTAIN OF THE CHEER SQUAD!
KIIIIN (SCREEEEEECH)
HO-NORI HO-MURA!!
...
THE BATTLE ROYAL'S SEAL IS IN THE OPEN-AIR BATTLE ARENA.
IF YOU WANT IT, COME AND GET IT!!! OVER AND OUT!!
HMPH!

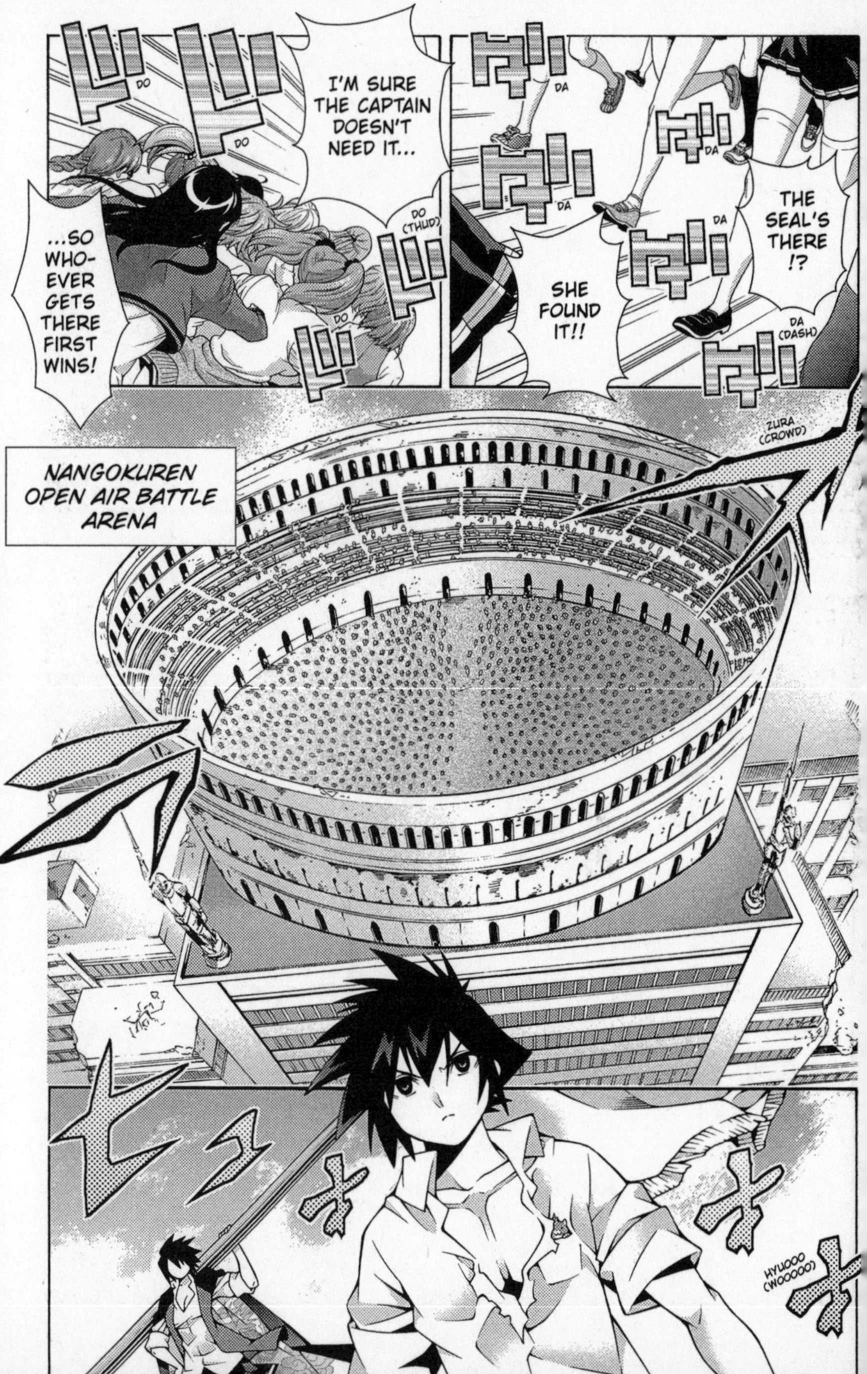
DA
DA
DA
THE SEAL'S THERE !?
DA
SHE FOUND IT!!
DA (DASH)
DO
DO
I'M SURE THE CAPTAIN DOESN'T NEED IT...
DO (THUD)
...SO WHOEVER GETS THERE FIRST WINS!
DO
ZURA (CROWD)
NANGOKUREN OPEN AIR BATTLE ARENA
HYUOOO (WOOOOO)

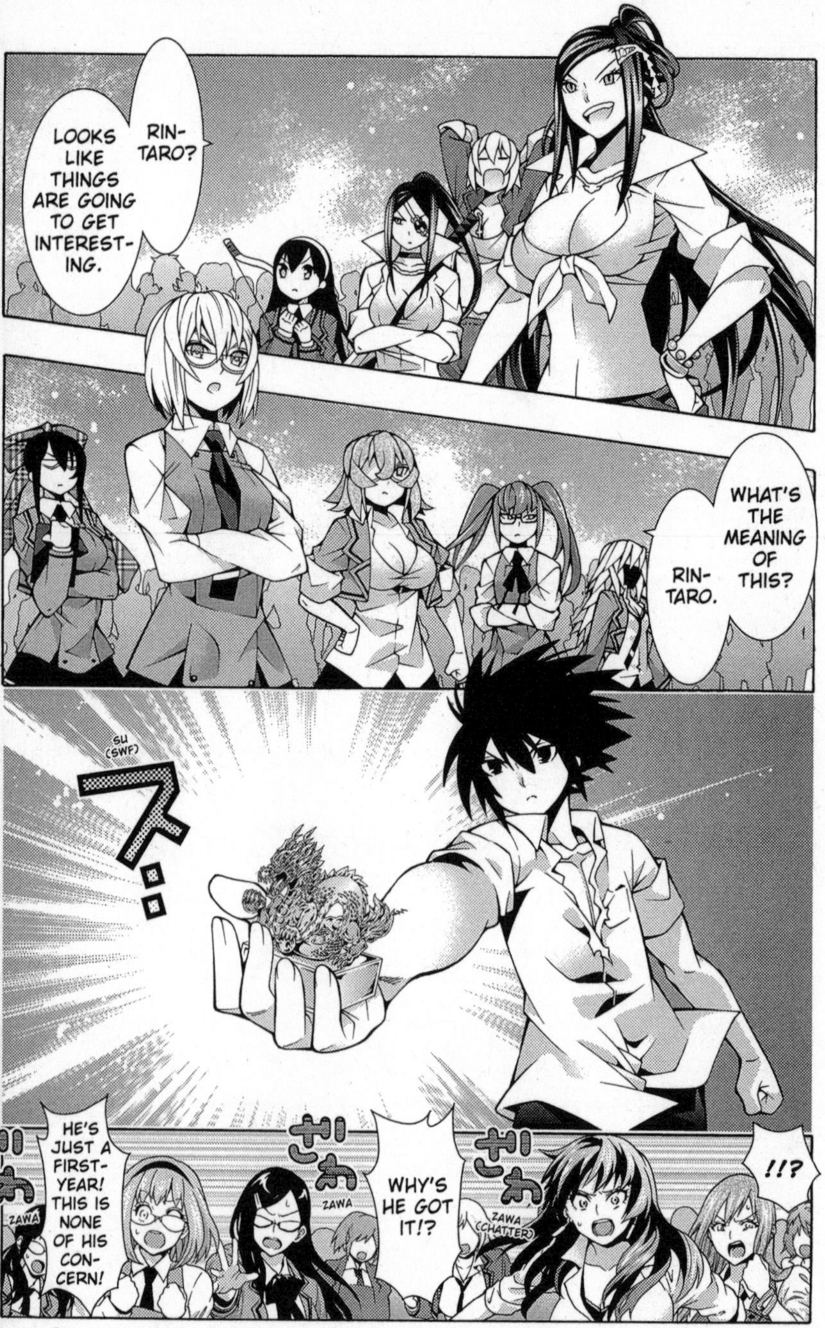

RIN-TARO?
LOOKS LIKE THINGS ARE GOING TO GET INTEREST-ING.
WHAT'S THE MEANING OF THIS?
RIN-TARO.
SU (SWF)
ス
!!?
ざわ
ZAWA (CHATTER)
WHY'S HE GOT IT!?
ざわ
ZAWA
HE'S JUST A FIRST-YEAR! THIS IS NONE OF HIS CON-CERN!
ZAWA

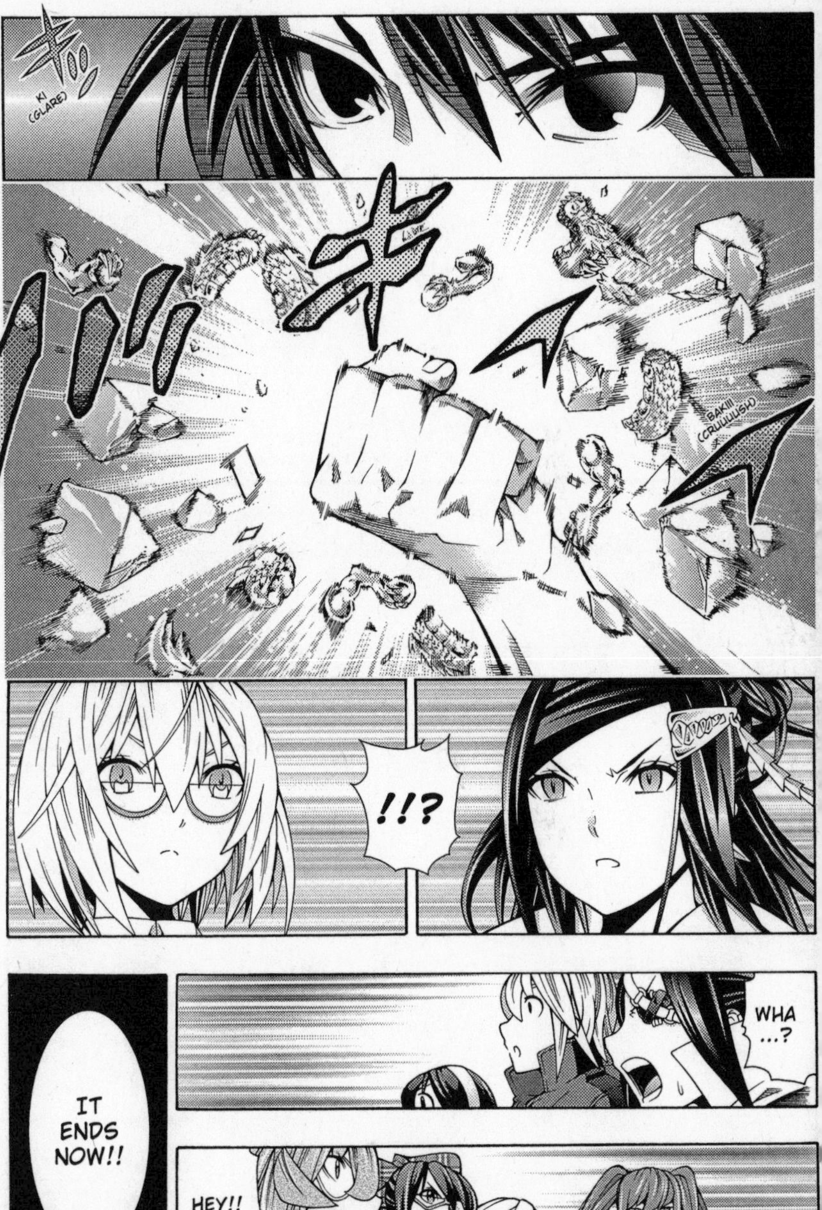
KI (GLARE)
BAKIII (CRUUUUSH)
!!?
WHA ...?
HEY!!
IT ENDS NOW!!

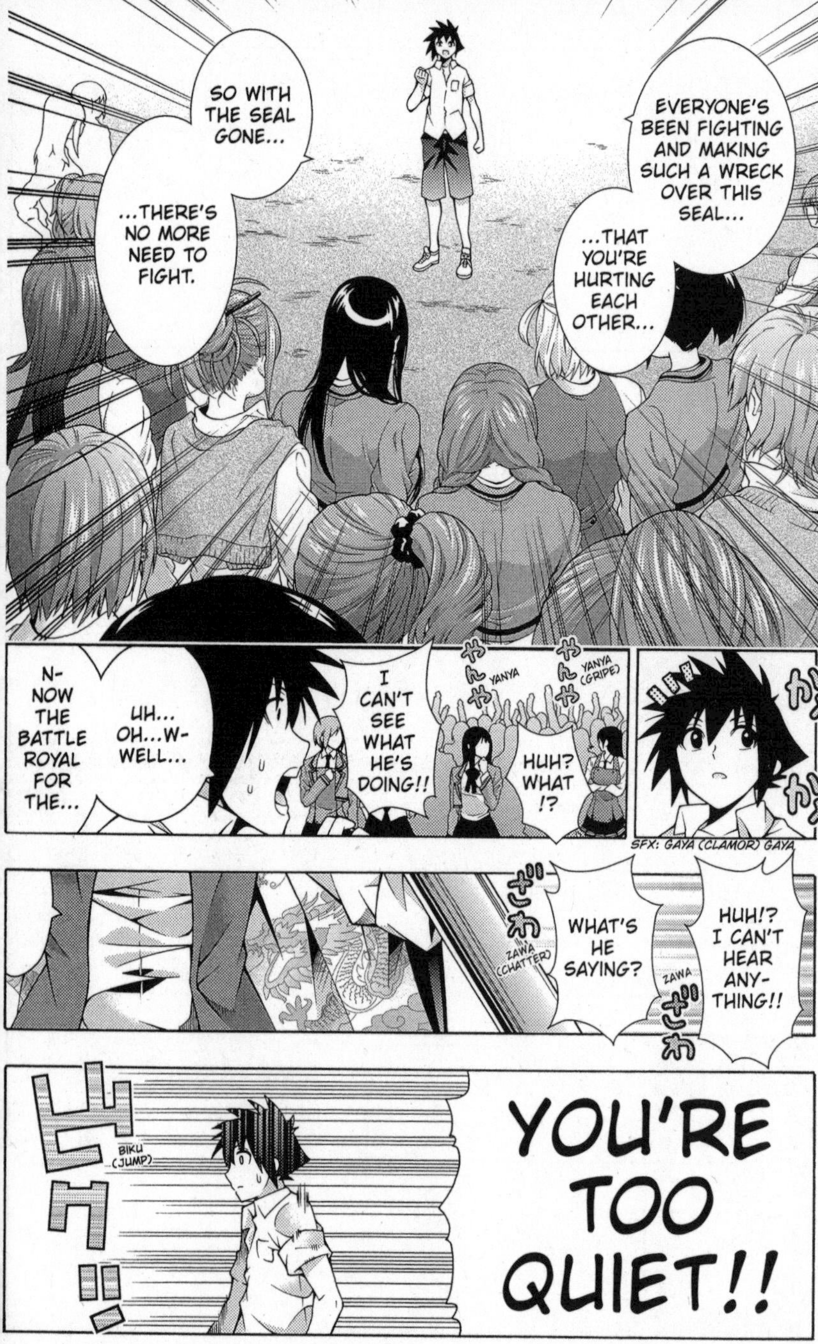
EVERYONE'S BEEN FIGHTING AND MAKING SUCH A WRECK OVER THIS SEAL...
...THAT YOU'RE HURTING EACH OTHER...
SO WITH THE SEAL GONE...
...THERE'S NO MORE NEED TO FIGHT.
SFX: GAYA (CLAMOR) GAYA
YANYA (GRIPE)
YANYA
HUH? WHAT!?
I CAN'T SEE WHAT HE'S DOING!!
UH... OH...W-WELL...
N-NOW THE BATTLE ROYAL FOR THE...
HUH!? I CAN'T HEAR ANY-THING!!
ZAWA
WHAT'S HE SAYING?
ZAWA (CHATTER)
YOU'RE TOO QUIET!!
BIKU (JUMP)

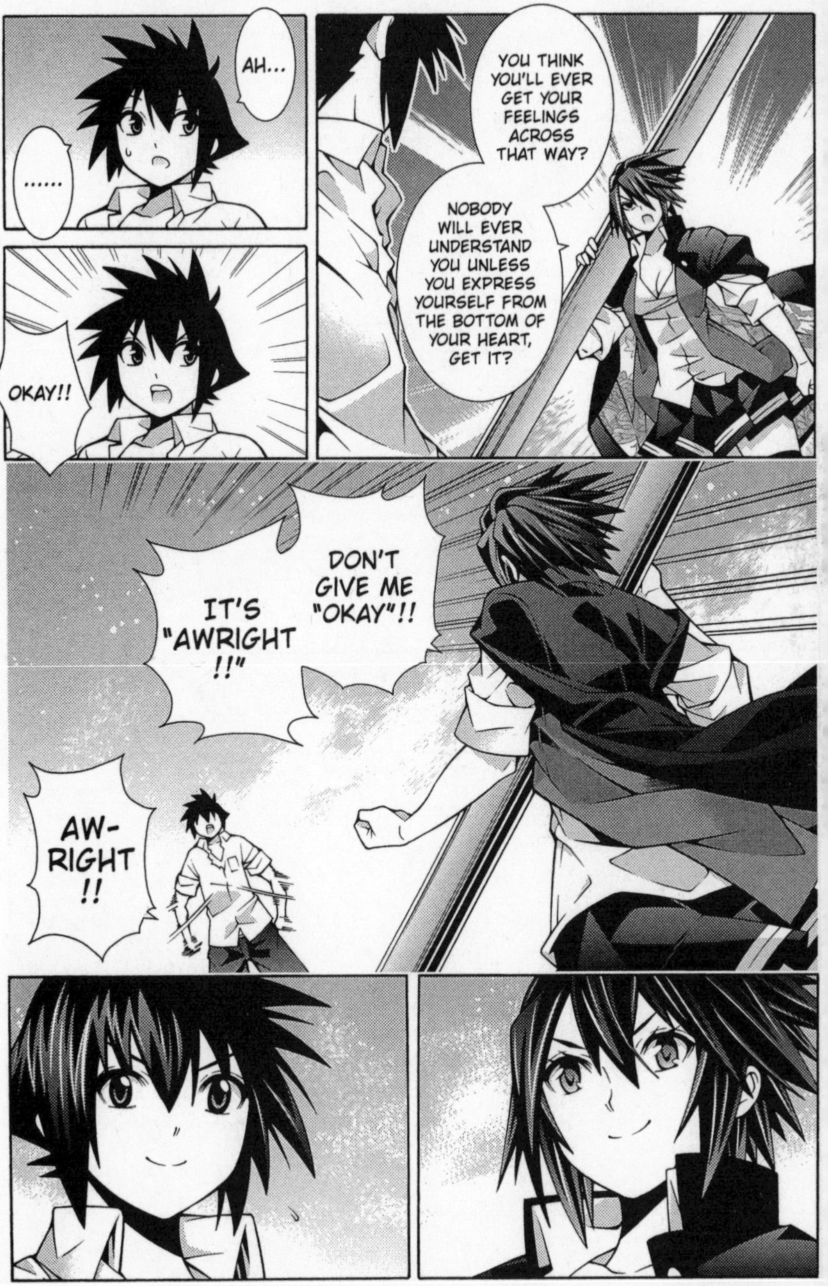
YOU THINK YOU'LL EVER GET YOUR FEELINGS ACROSS THAT WAY?
NOBODY WILL EVER UNDERSTAND YOU UNLESS YOU EXPRESS YOURSELF FROM THE BOTTOM OF YOUR HEART, GET IT?
AH...
......
OKAY!!
DON'T GIVE ME "OKAY"!!
IT'S "AWRIGHT!!"
AW-RIGHT!!

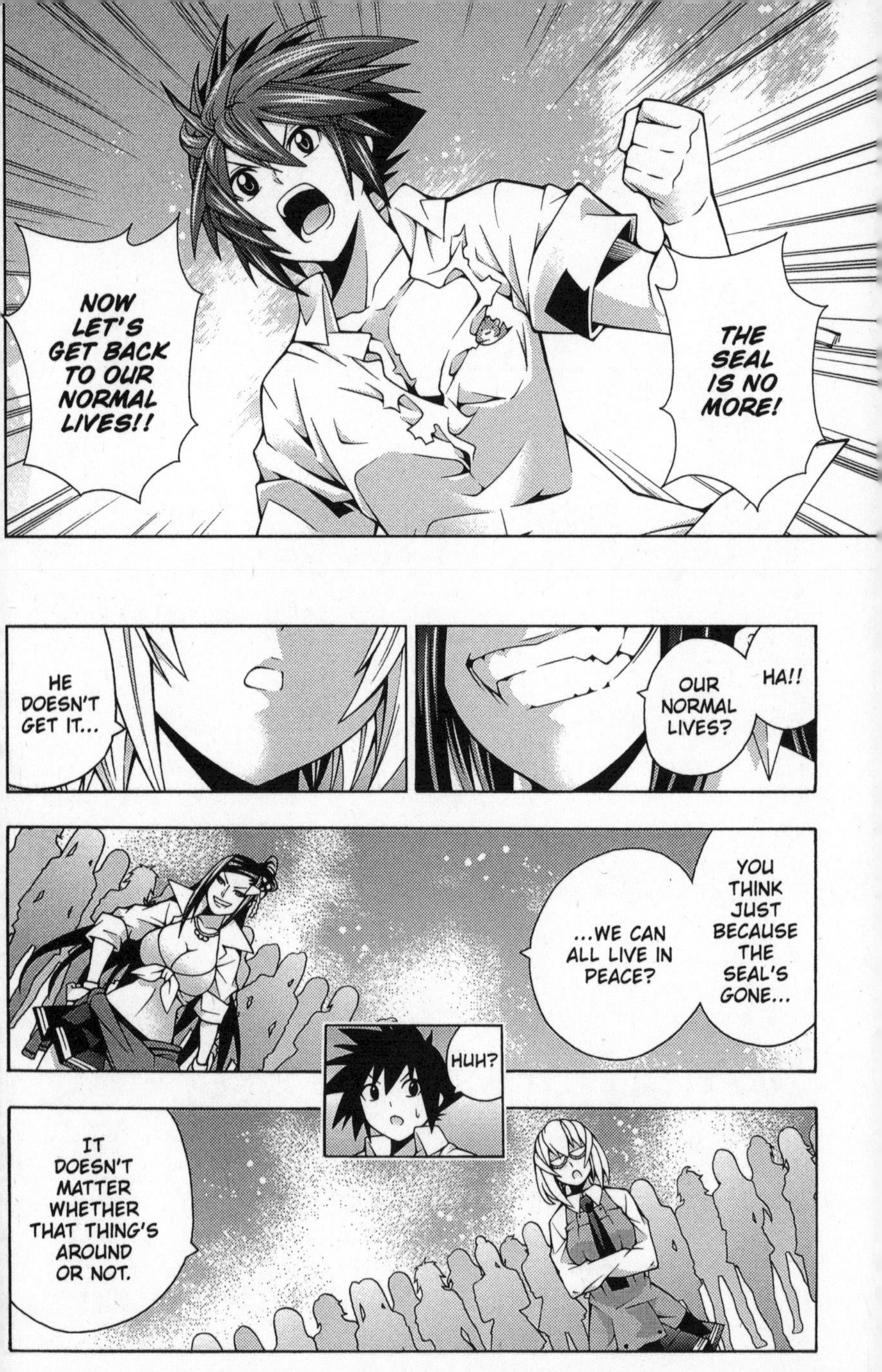
THE SEAL IS NO MORE!
NOW LET'S GET BACK TO OUR NORMAL LIVES!!
HA!!
OUR NORMAL LIVES?
HE DOESN'T GET IT...
YOU THINK JUST BECAUSE THE SEAL'S GONE...
...WE CAN ALL LIVE IN PEACE?
HUH?
IT DOESN'T MATTER WHETHER THAT THING'S AROUND OR NOT.

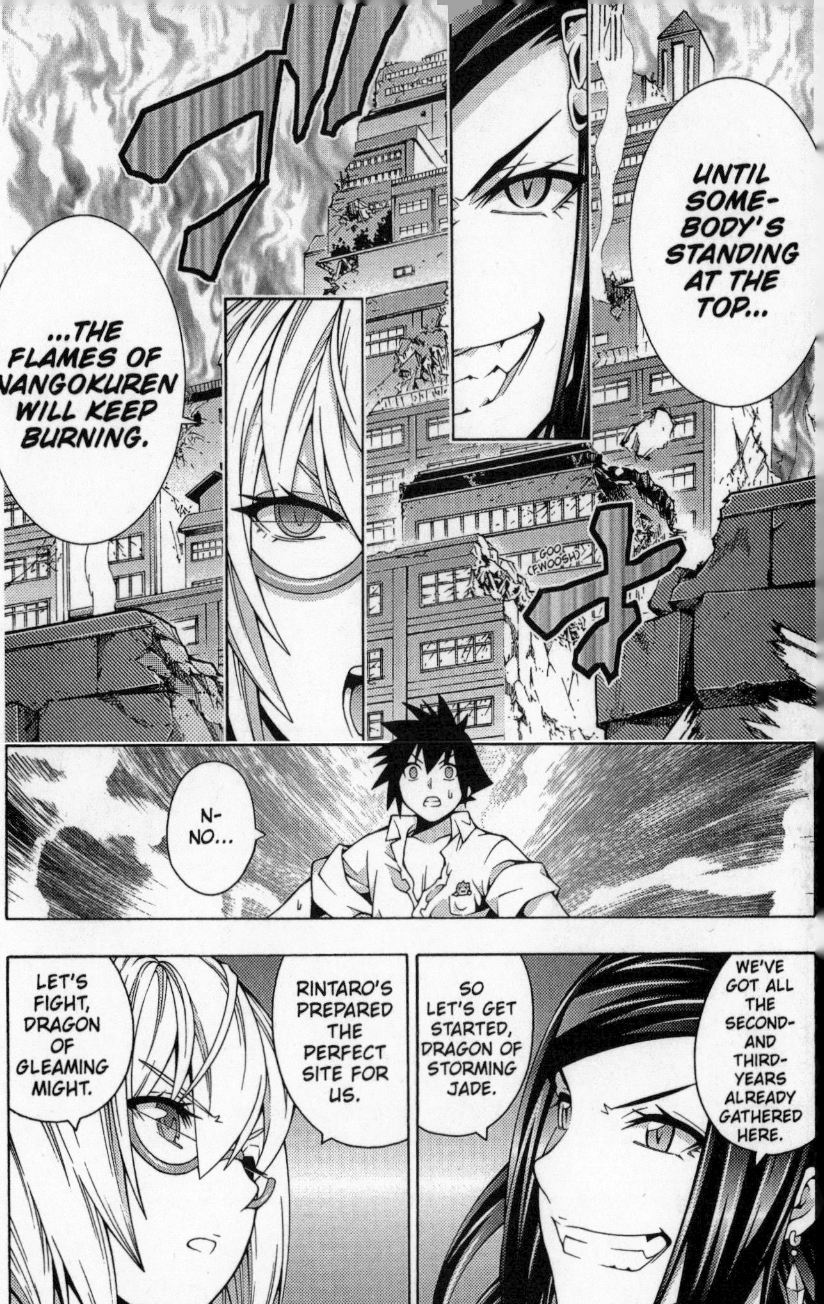
UNTIL SOMEBODY'S STANDING AT THE TOP...
...THE FLAMES OF NANGOKUREN WILL KEEP BURNING.
GOO (FWOOSH)
N- NO...
WE'VE GOT ALL THE SECOND- AND THIRD-YEARS ALREADY GATHERED HERE.
SO LET'S GET STARTED, DRAGON OF STORMING JADE.
RINTARO'S PREPARED THE PERFECT SITE FOR US.
LET'S FIGHT, DRAGON OF GLEAMING MIGHT.

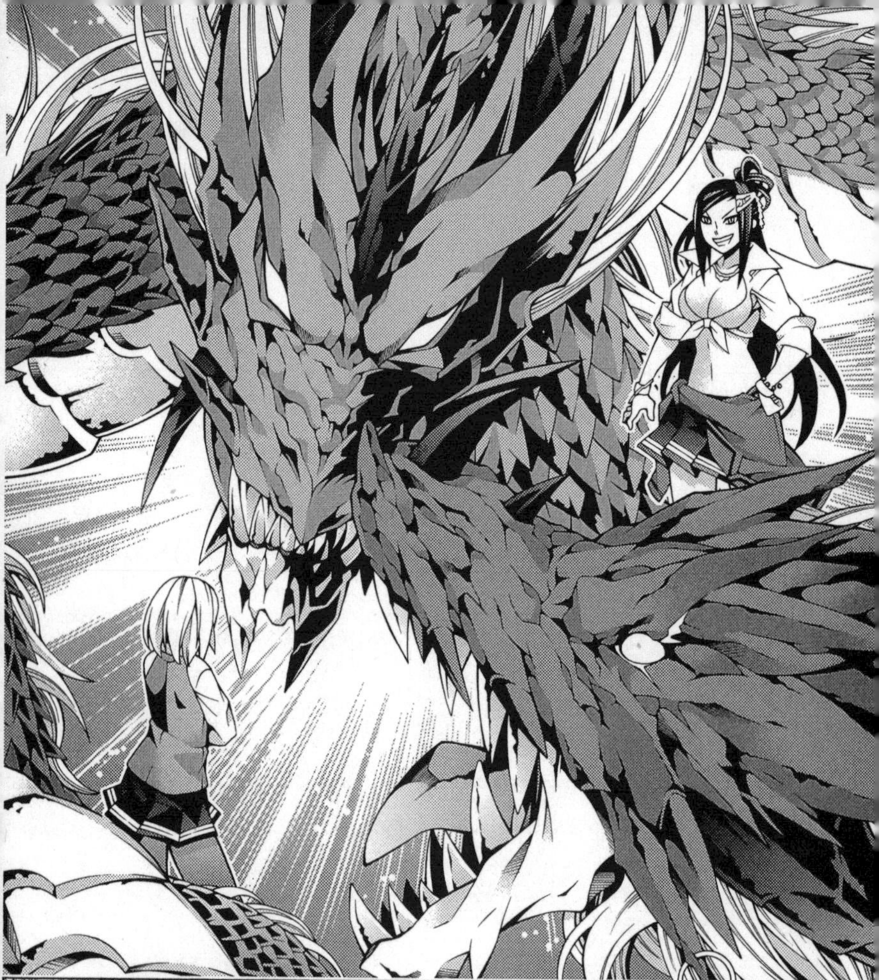

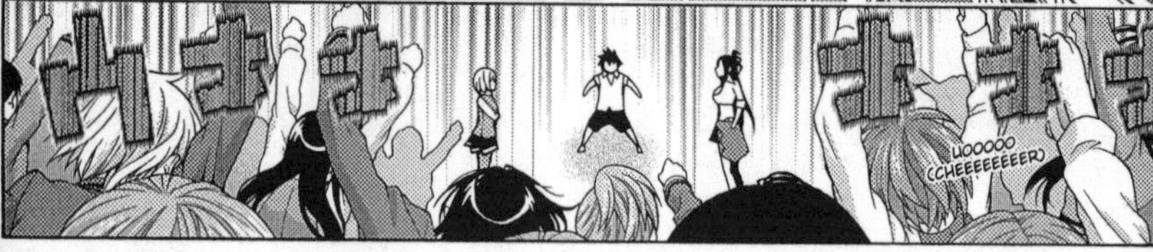
UOOOOO
(CHEEEEEEEER)

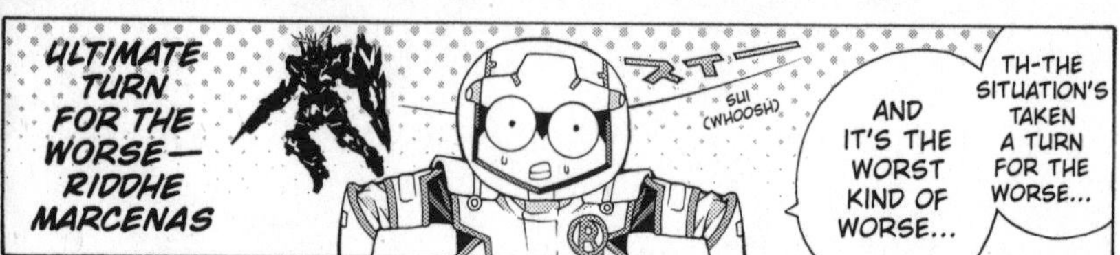
TH-THE SITUATION'S TAKEN A TURN FOR THE WORSE...
AND IT'S THE WORST KIND OF WORSE...
SUI (WHOOSH)
ULTIMATE TURN FOR THE WORSE— RIDDHE MARCENAS

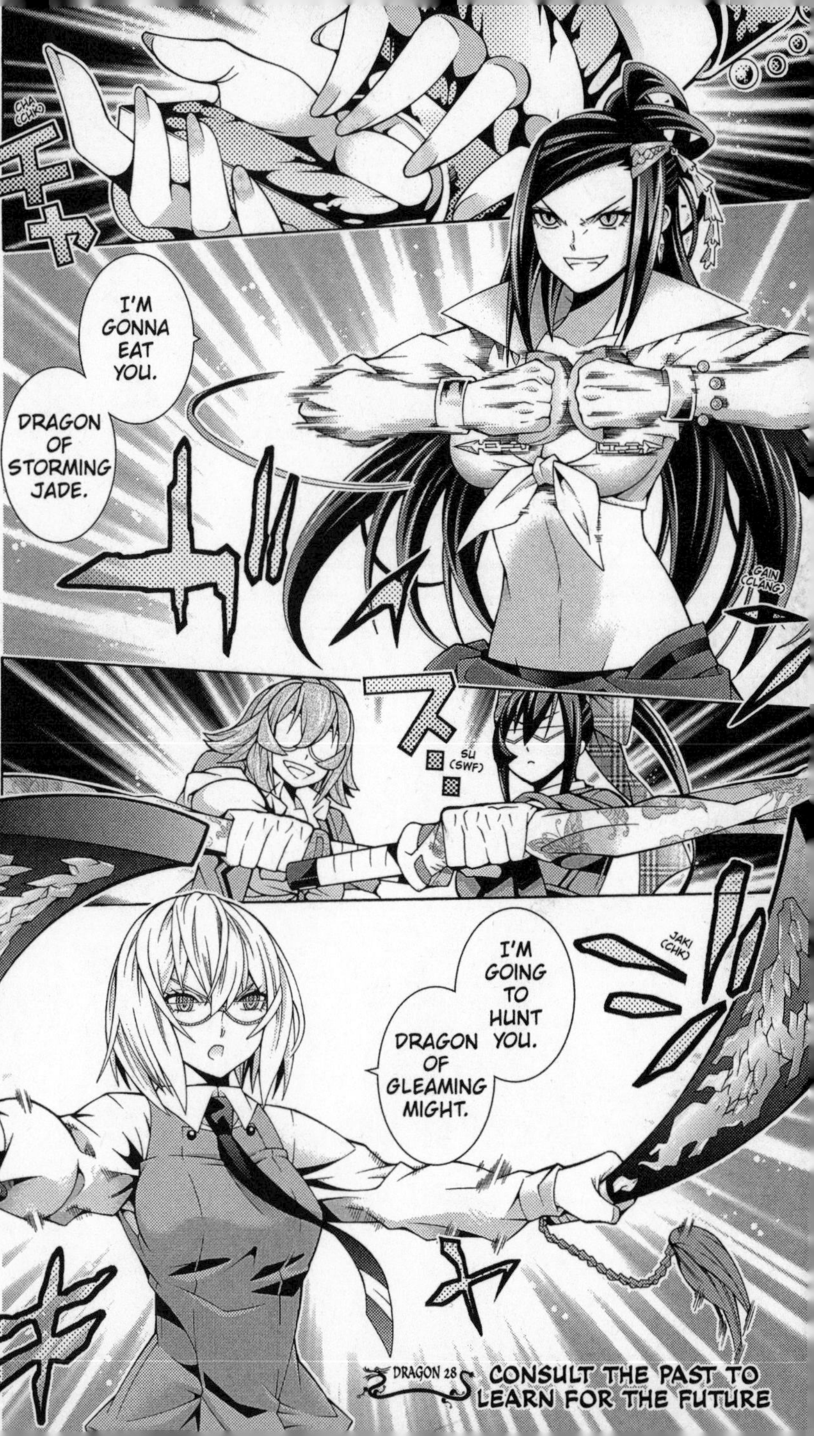
CHA (CHK)
I'M GONNA EAT YOU.
DRAGON OF STORMING JADE.
GAIN (CLANG)
SU (SWF)
I'M GOING TO HUNT YOU.
DRAGON OF GLEAMING MIGHT.
JAKI (CHK)

DRAGON 28 CONSULT THE PAST TO LEARN FOR THE FUTURE

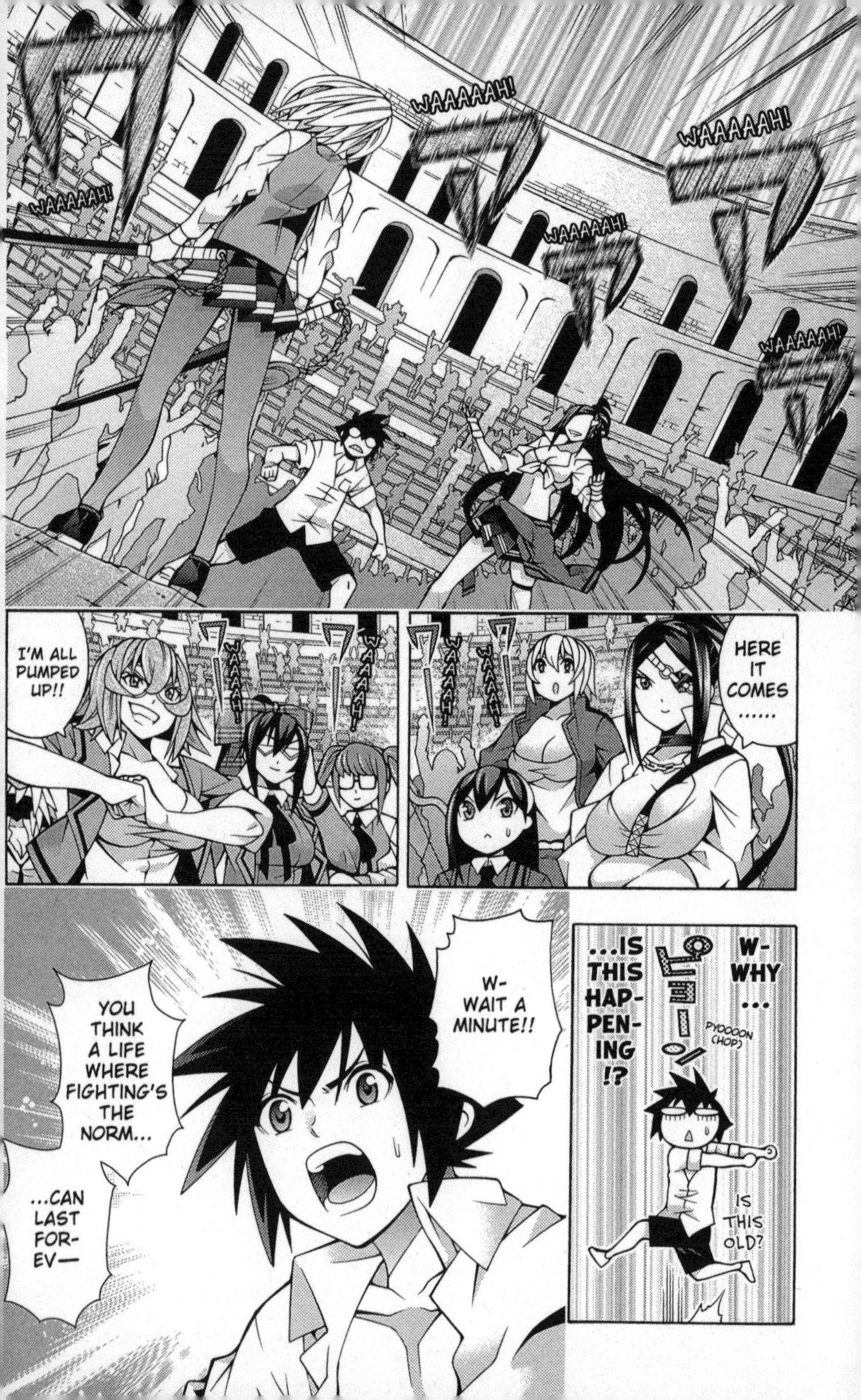
WAAAAAH!
WAAAAAH!
WAAAAAH!
WAAAAAH!
WAAAAAH!
HERE IT COMES......
WAAAAAH!
WAAAAAH!
WAAAAAH!
WAAAAAH!
I'M ALL PUMPED UP!!
W-WHY...
...IS THIS HAP-PEN-ING!?
PYOOOON (HOP)
IS THIS OLD?
W-WAIT A MINUTE!!
YOU THINK A LIFE WHERE FIGHTING'S THE NORM...
...CAN LAST FOR-EV—

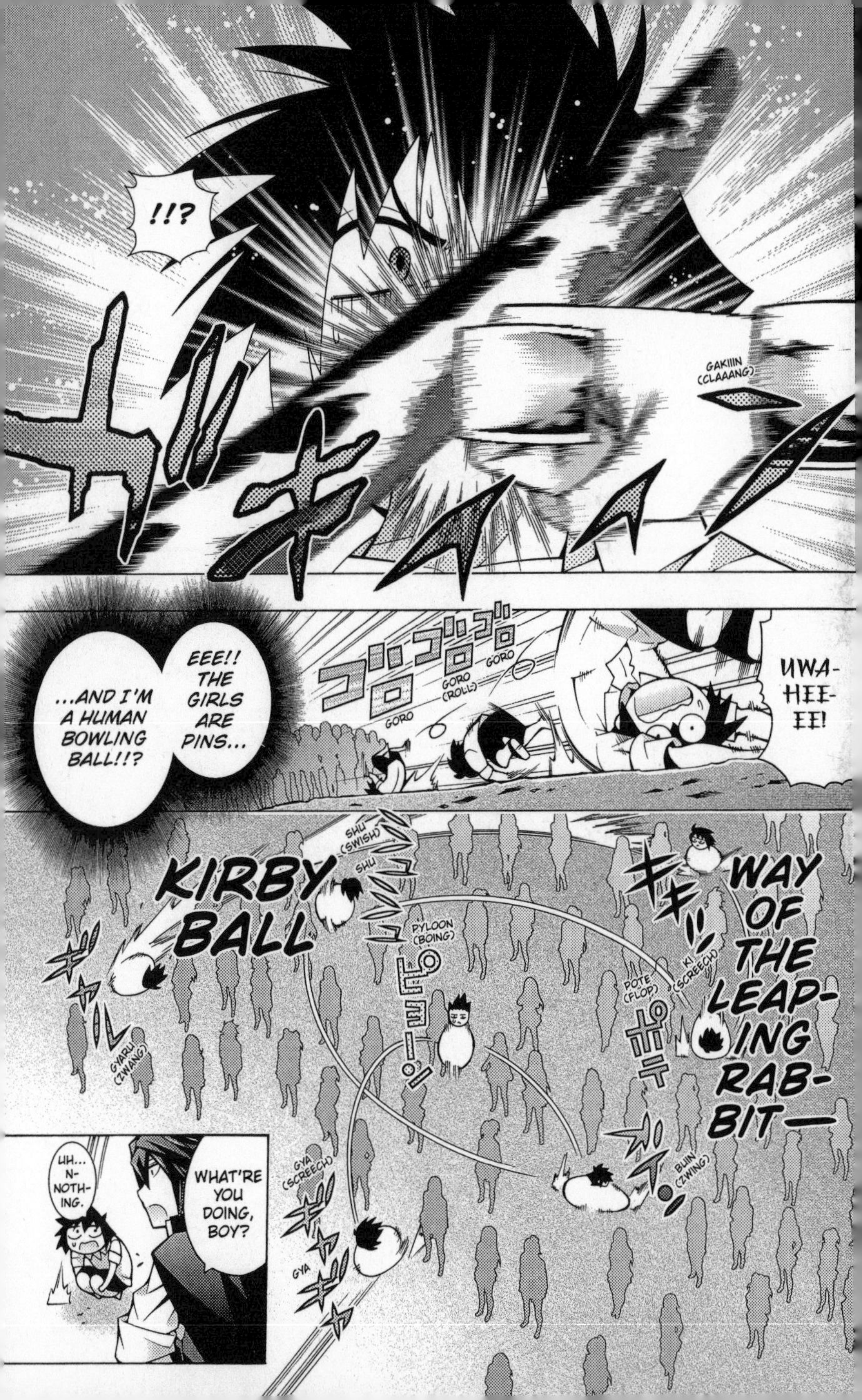
GAKIIIN (CLAAANG)
!!?
UWA-HEE-EE!
GORO GORO (ROLL) GORO
EEE!! THE GIRLS ARE PINS...
...AND I'M A HUMAN BOWLING BALL!!?
WAY OF THE LEAP-ING RAB-BIT—
KI (SCREECH)
POTE (FLOP)
PYLOON (BOING)
SHU (SWISH)
SHU
KIRBY BALL
GYARU (ZWANG)
BUIN (ZWING)
GYA (SCREECH)
GYA
WHAT'RE YOU DOING, BOY?
UH... N-NOTH-ING.

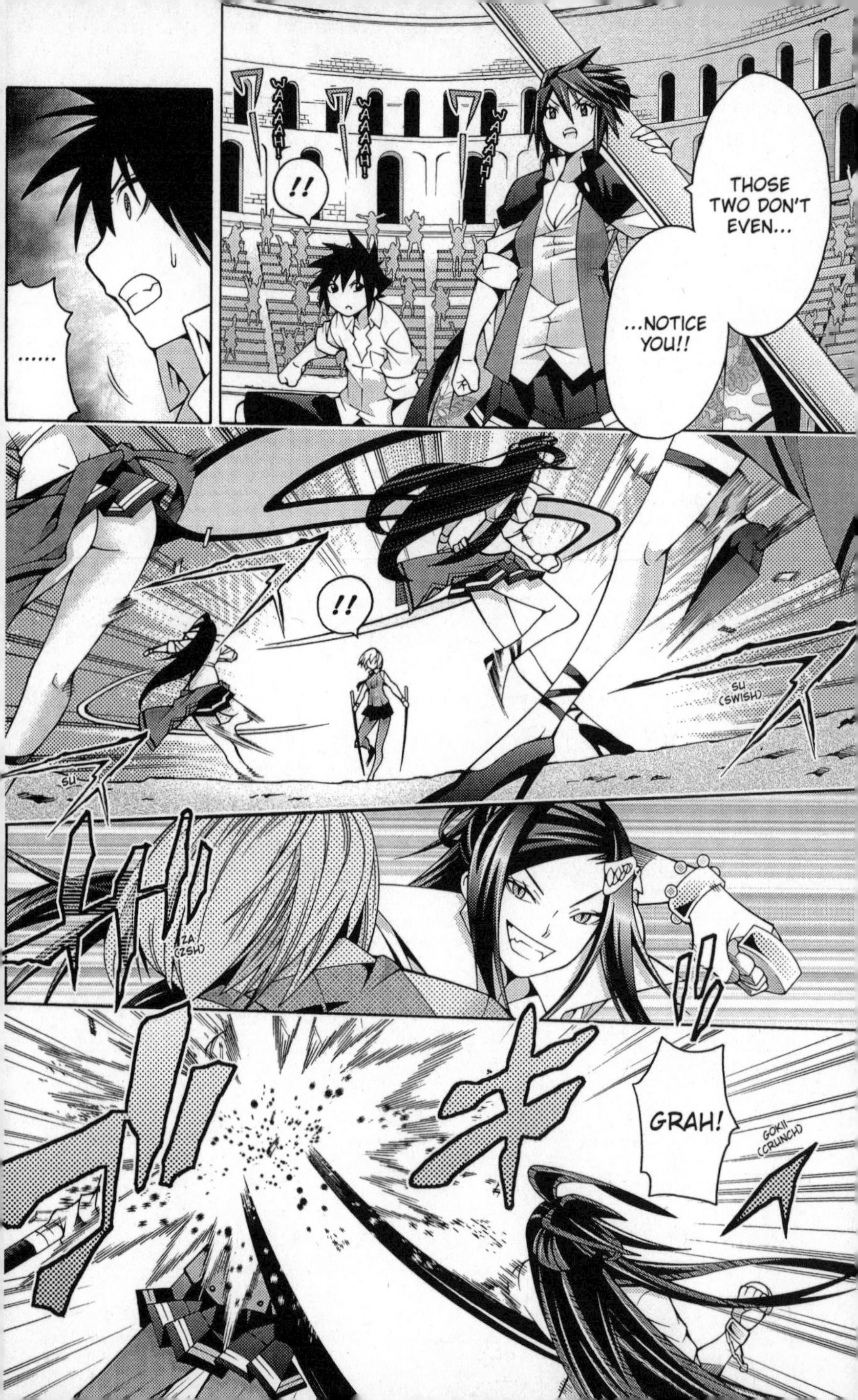
THOSE TWO DON'T EVEN...
...NOTICE YOU!!
WAAAAH!
WAAAAAH!
WAAAAH!
!!
......
SU (SWISH)
!!
SU
ZA (ZSH)
GRAH!
GOKI! (CRUNCH)

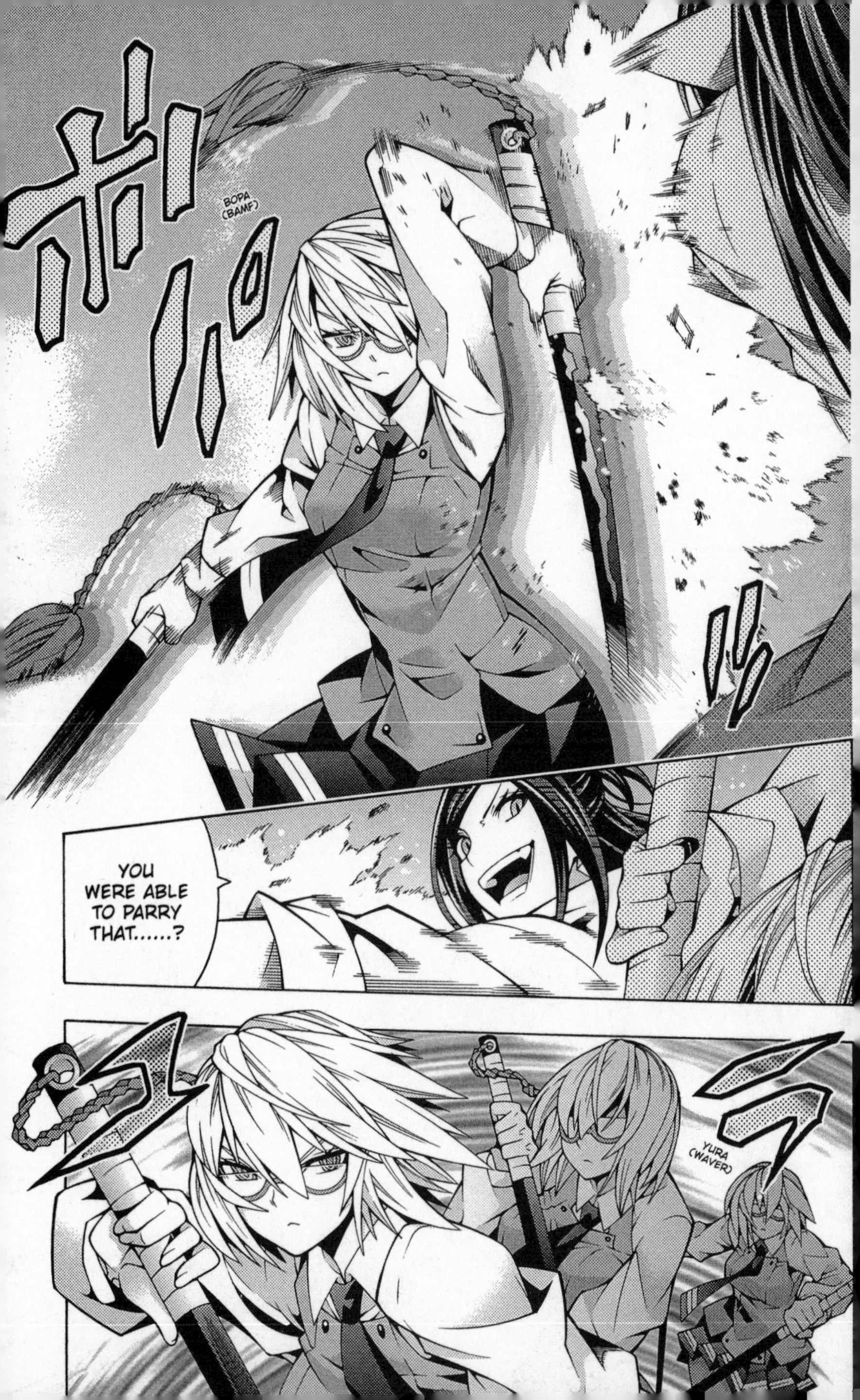
BOPA (BAMF)
YOU WERE ABLE TO PARRY THAT......?
YURA (WAVER)

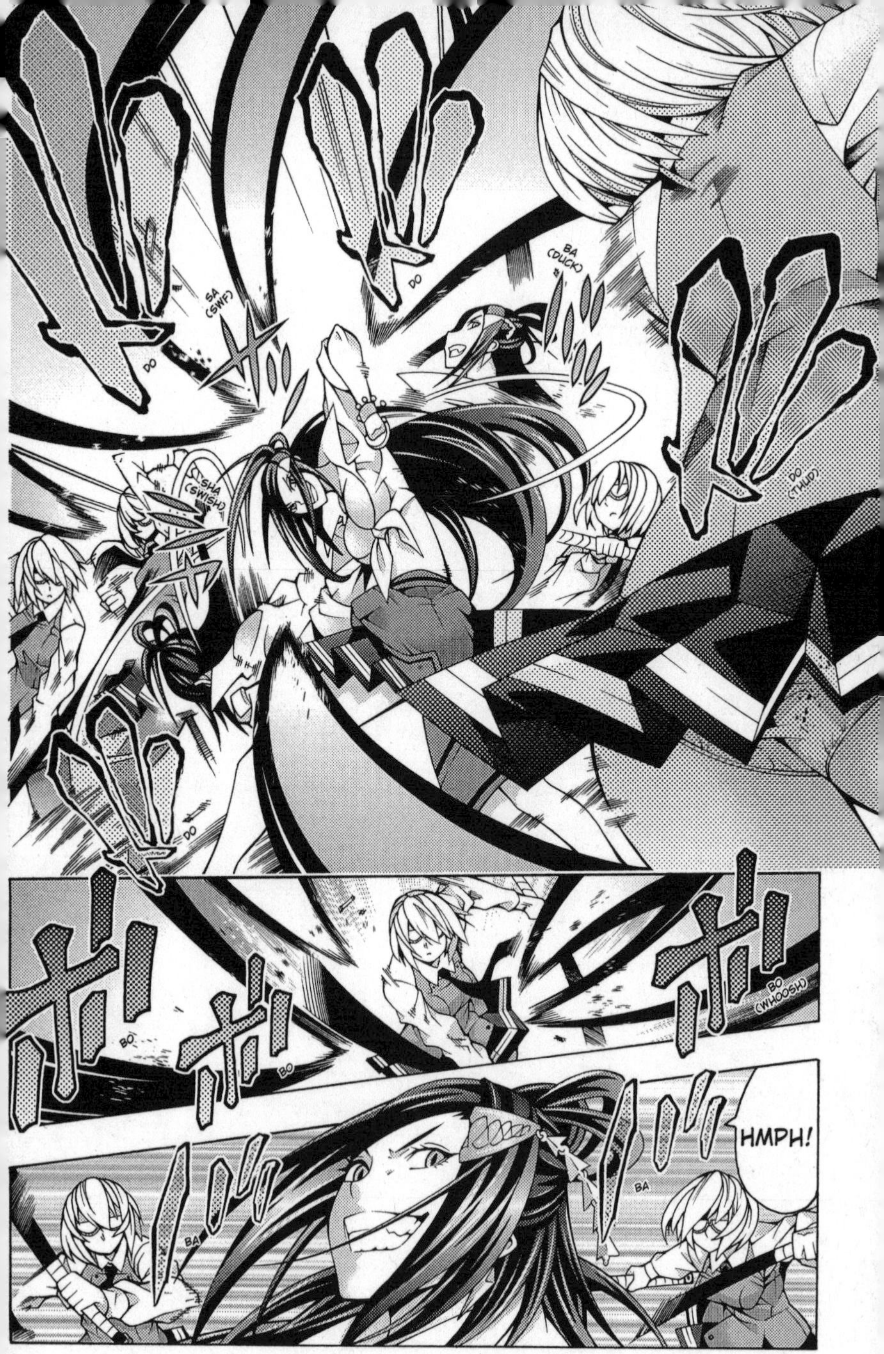
BA (DUCK)
DO
SA (SWF)
DO
DO (THUD)
SHA (SWISH)
DO
BO (WHOOSH)
BO
BO
HMPH!
BA
BA

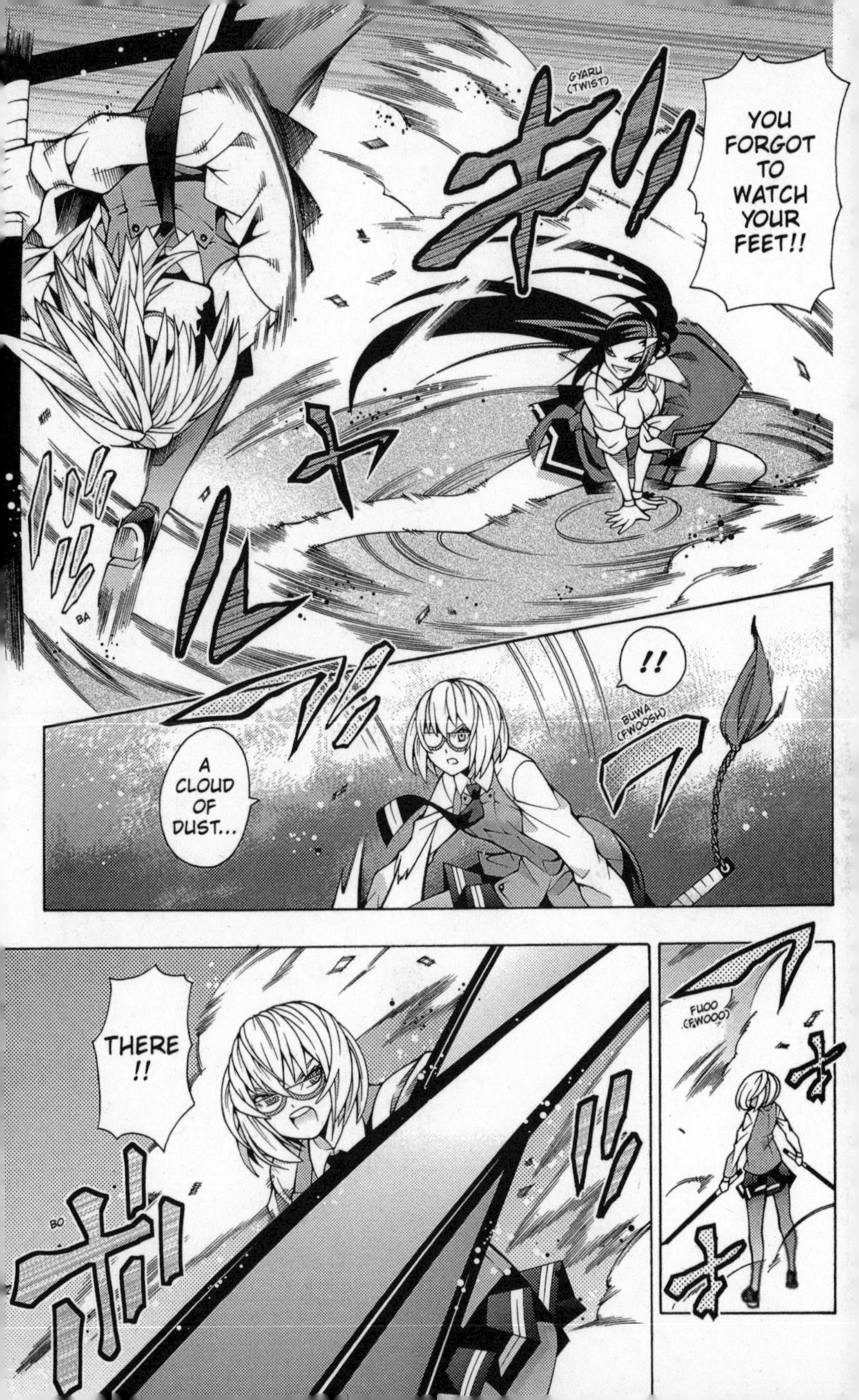
YOU FORGOT TO WATCH YOUR FEET!!
GYARU (TWIST)
BA
!!
BUWA (F.WOOSH)
A CLOUD OF DUST...
FUOO (F.WOOO)
THERE!!
BO

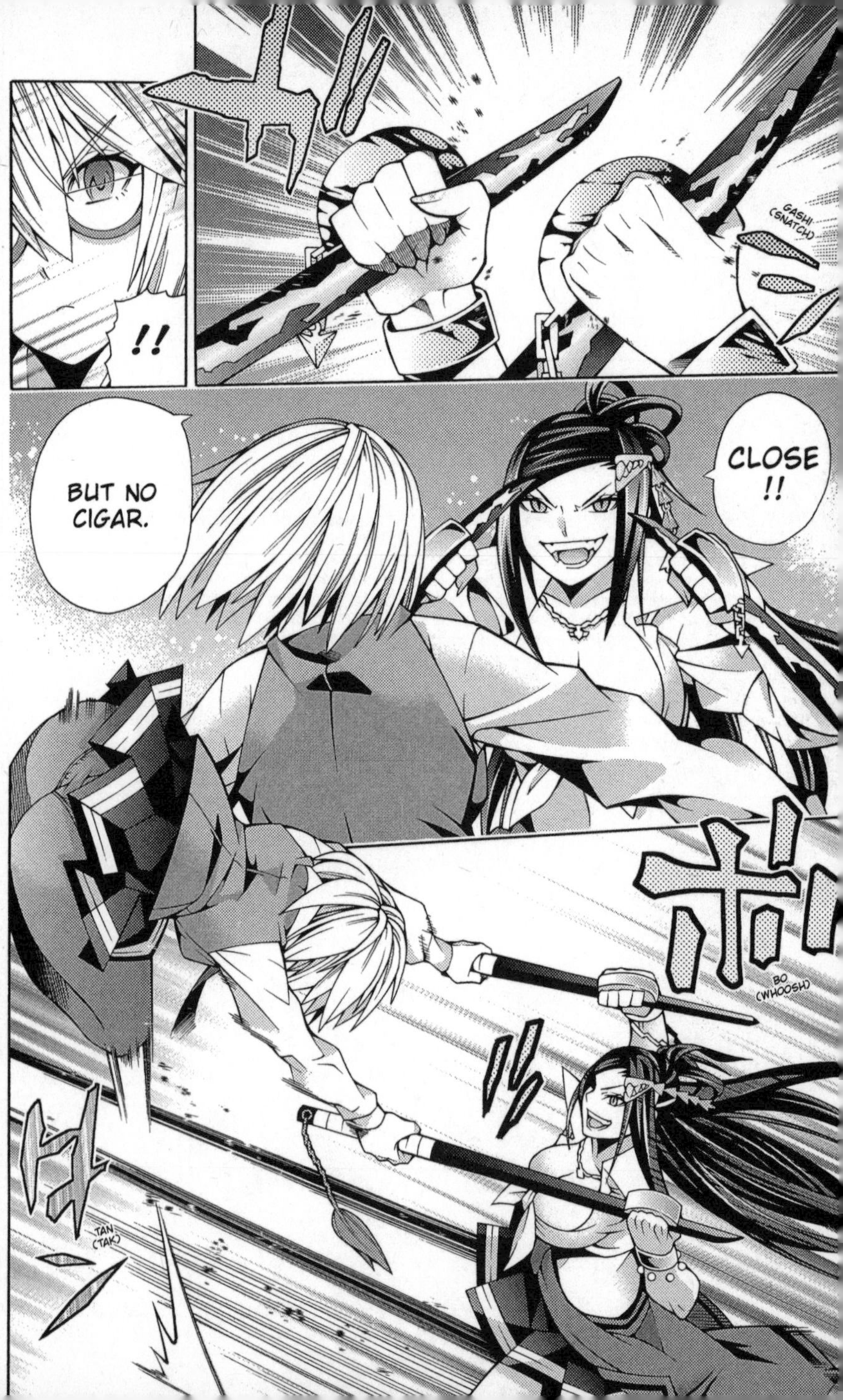
GASHI (SNATCH)
!!
CLOSE !!
BUT NO CIGAR.
BO (WHOOSH)
TAN (TAK)

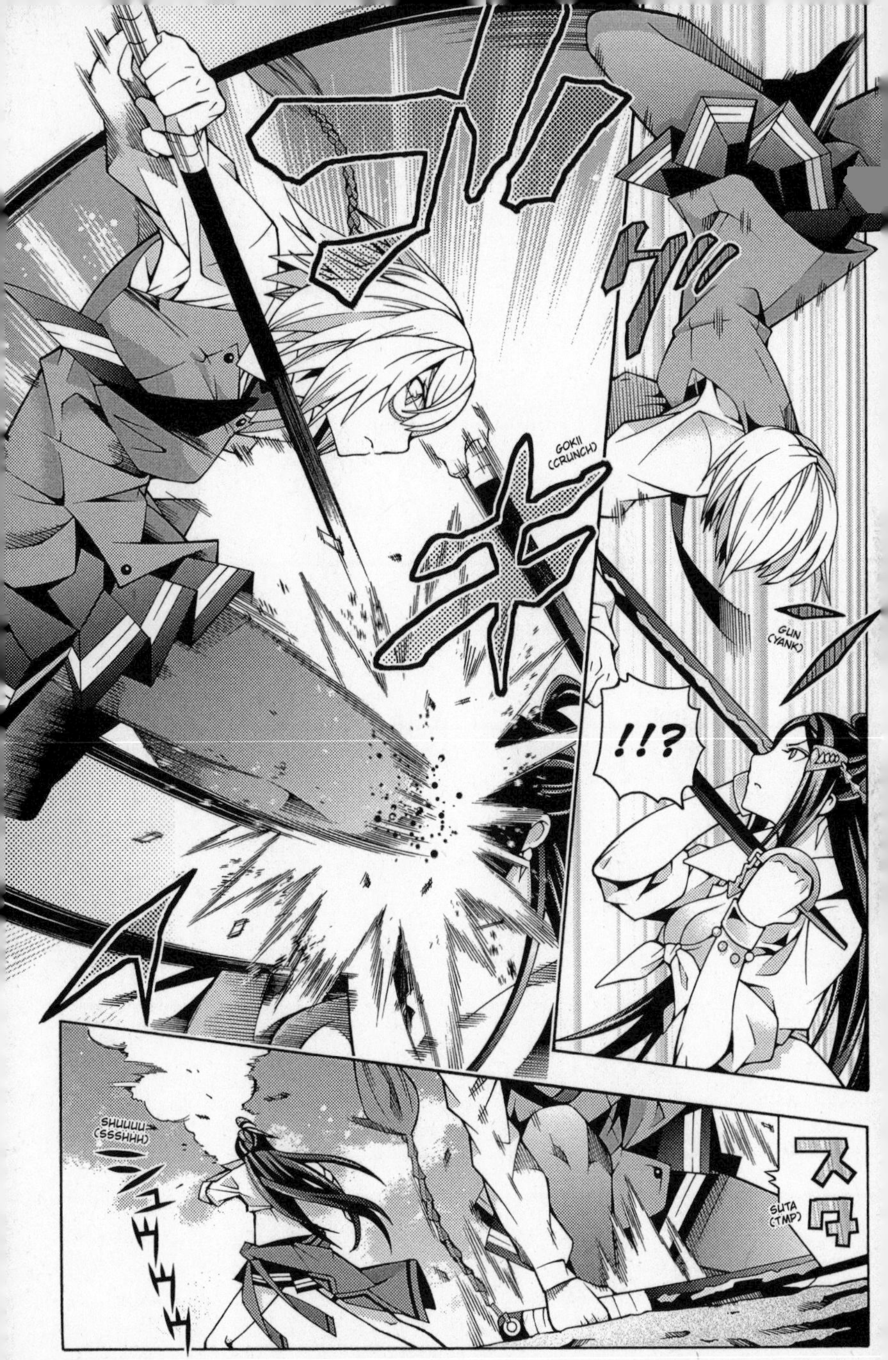
GOKII (CRUNCH)
GUN (YANK)
!!?
SUTA (TMP)
SHUUUU (SSSHHH)

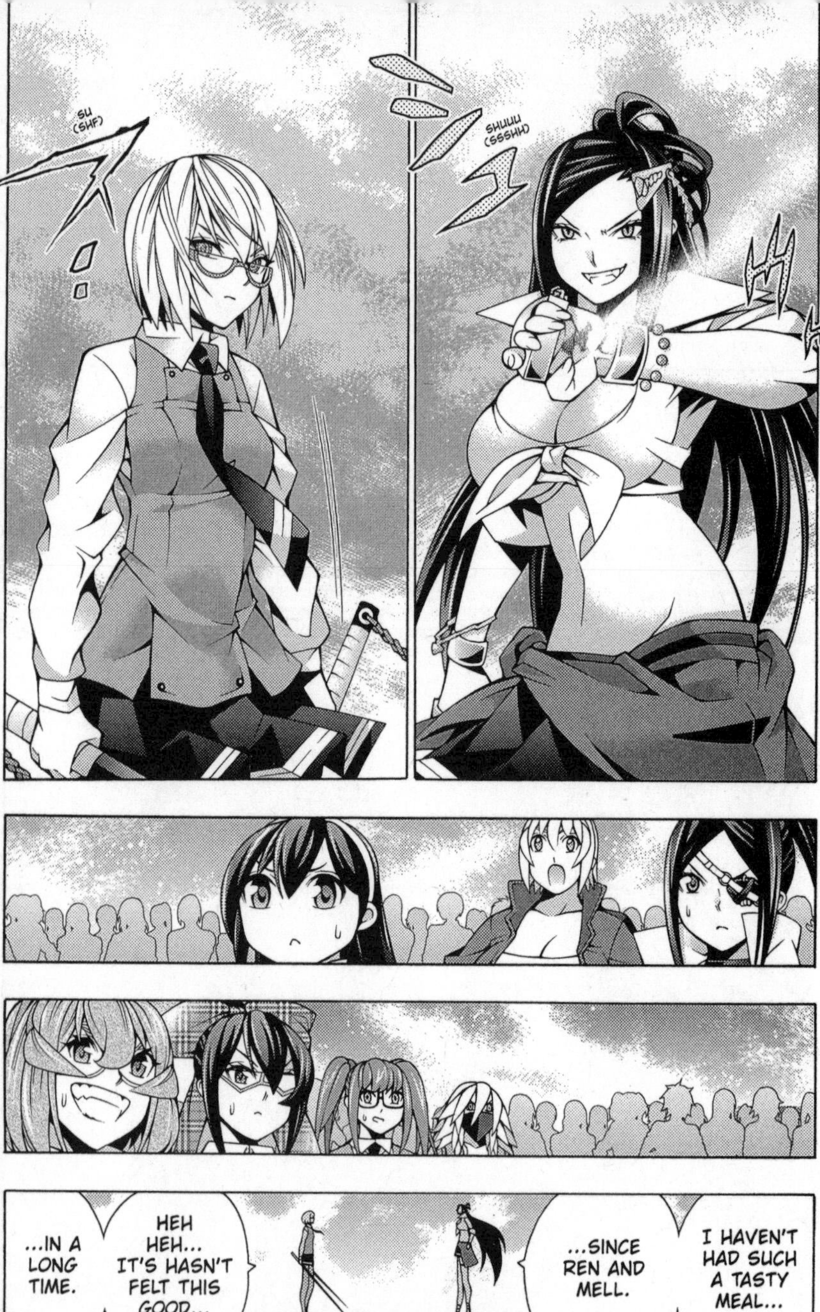
SHUUU (SSSHH)
SU (SHF)
I HAVEN'T HAD SUCH A TASTY MEAL...
...SINCE REN AND MELL.
HEH HEH... IT'S HASN'T FELT THIS GOOD...
...IN A LONG TIME.

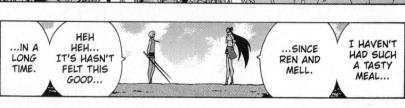

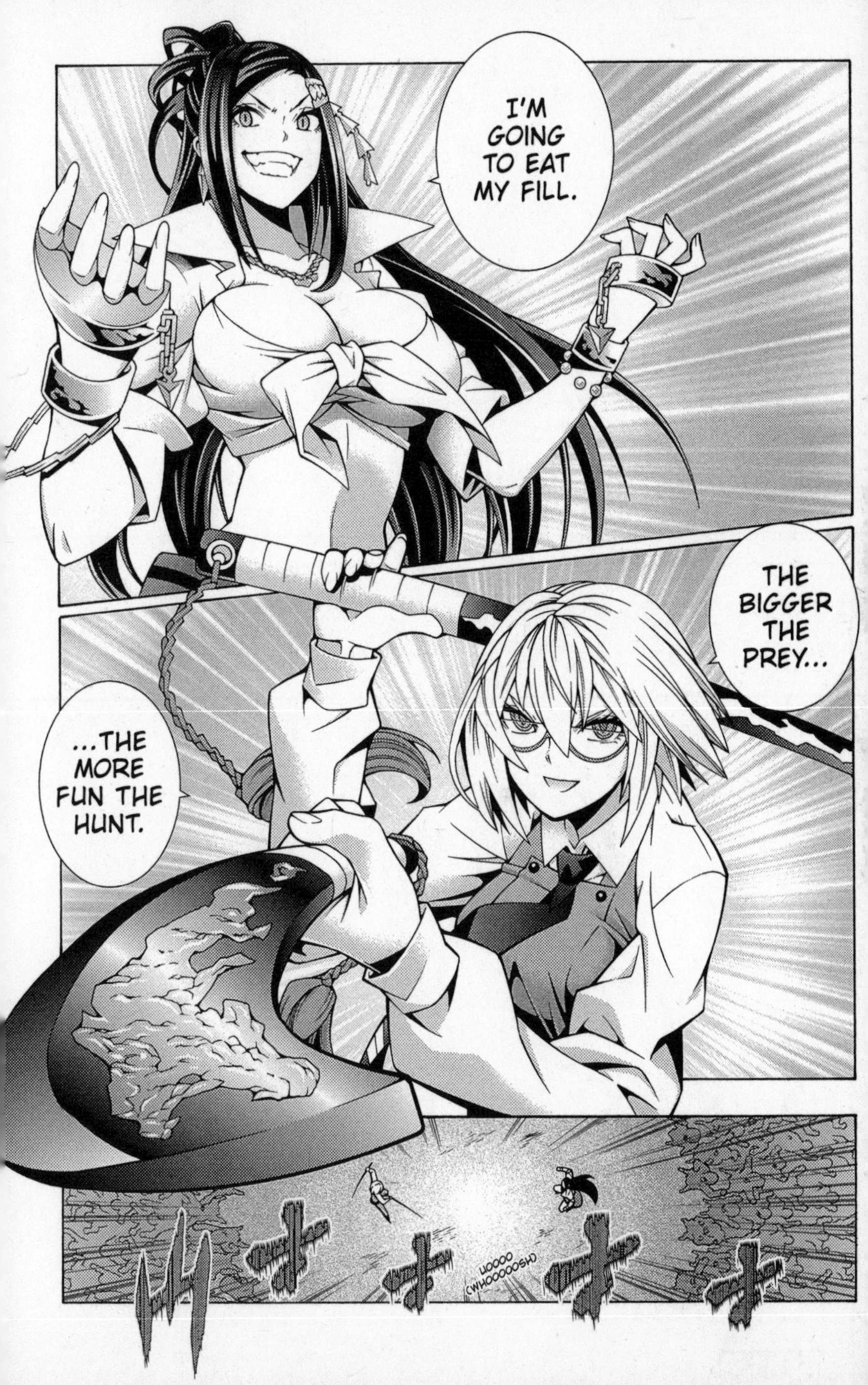
I'M GOING TO EAT MY FILL.
THE BIGGER THE PREY...
...THE MORE FUN THE HUNT.
(WHOOOOOSH)

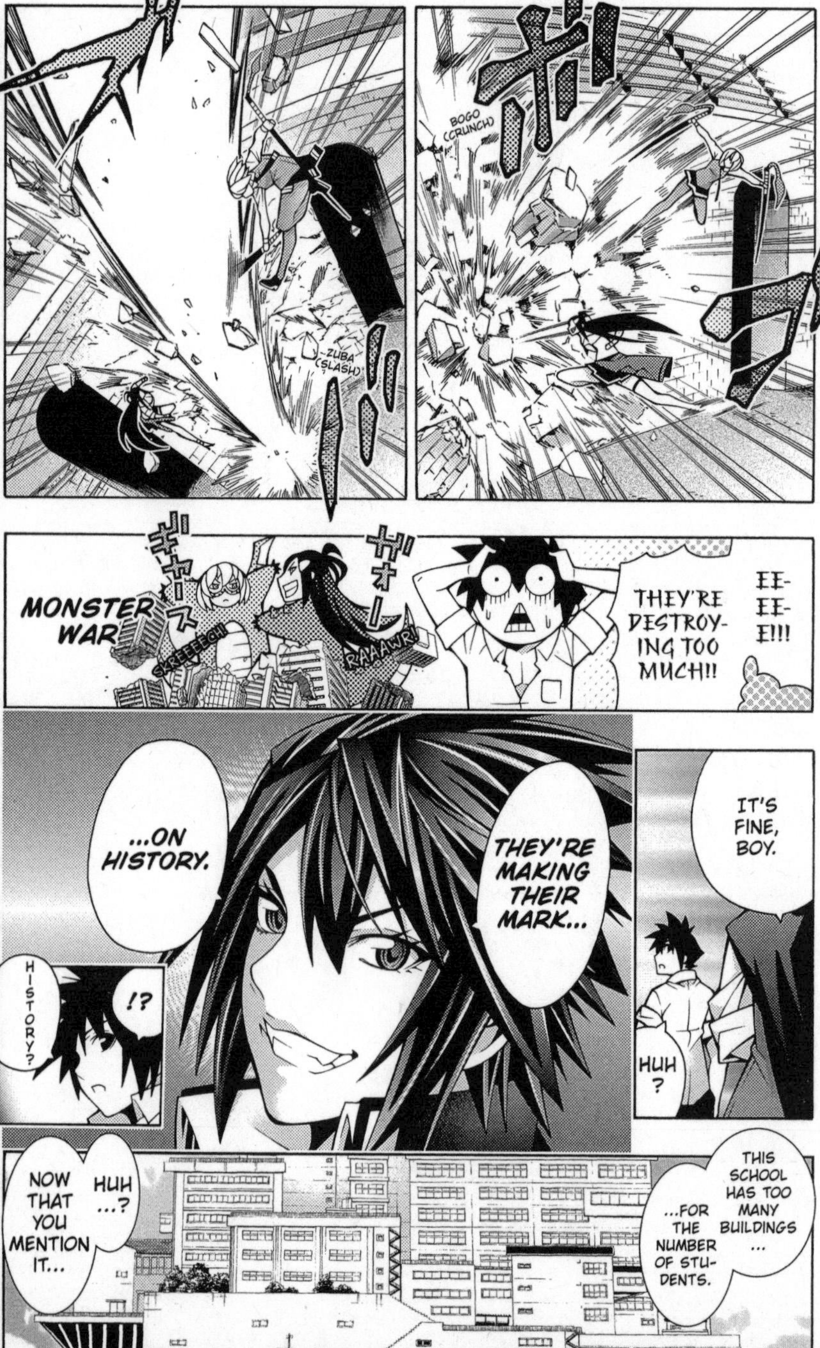
BOGO (CRUNCH)
ZUBA (SLASH)
EE-EE-E!!!
THEY'RE DESTROYING TOO MUCH!!
RAAAWR!
SKREEEEECH!
MONSTER WAR
IT'S FINE, BOY.
HUH?
THEY'RE MAKING THEIR MARK...
...ON HISTORY.
!?
HISTORY?
THIS SCHOOL HAS TOO MANY BUILDINGS...
...FOR THE NUMBER OF STUDENTS.
HUH...?
NOW THAT YOU MENTION IT...

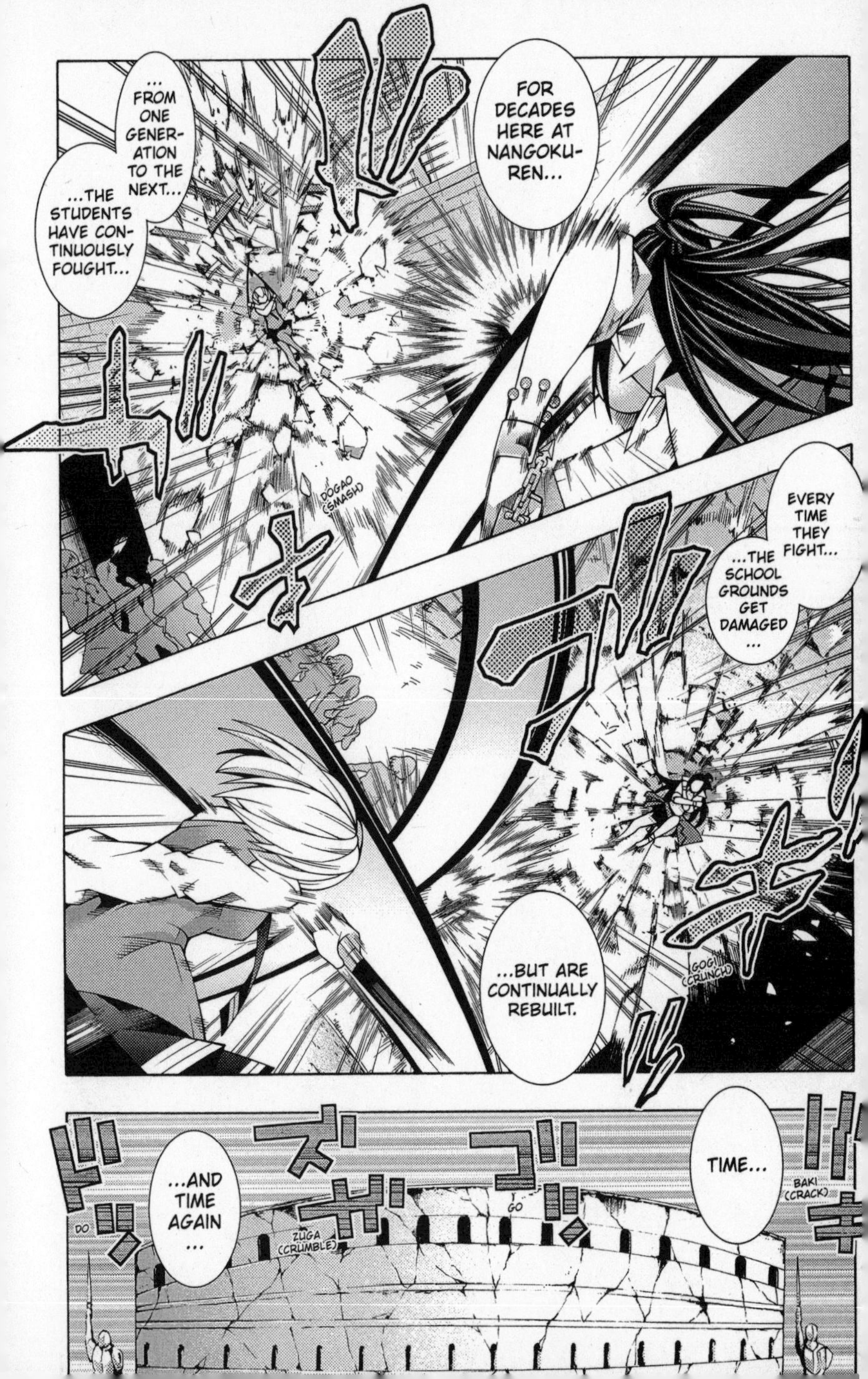
FOR DECADES HERE AT NANGOKU-REN...
...FROM ONE GENERATION TO THE NEXT...
...THE STUDENTS HAVE CONTINUOUSLY FOUGHT...
DOGAO (SMASH)
EVERY TIME THEY FIGHT...
...THE SCHOOL GROUNDS GET DAMAGED ...
...BUT ARE CONTINUALLY REBUILT.
GOGI (CRUNCH)
TIME...
BAKI (CRACK)
GO
ZUGA (CRUMBLE)
...AND TIME AGAIN ...
DO

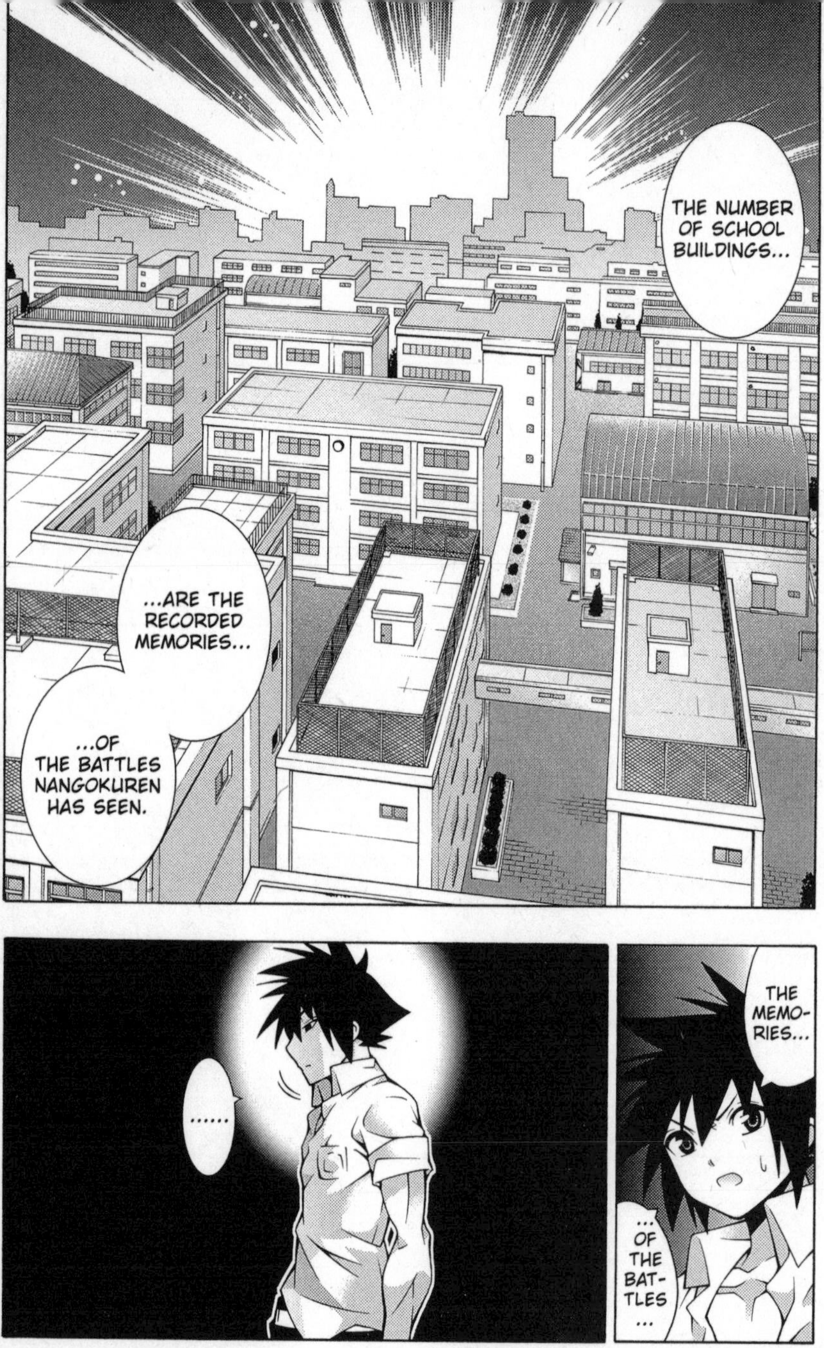
THE NUMBER OF SCHOOL BUILDINGS...
...ARE THE RECORDED MEMORIES...
...OF THE BATTLES NANGOKUREN HAS SEEN.
THE MEMO-RIES...
...OF THE BAT-TLES...
......

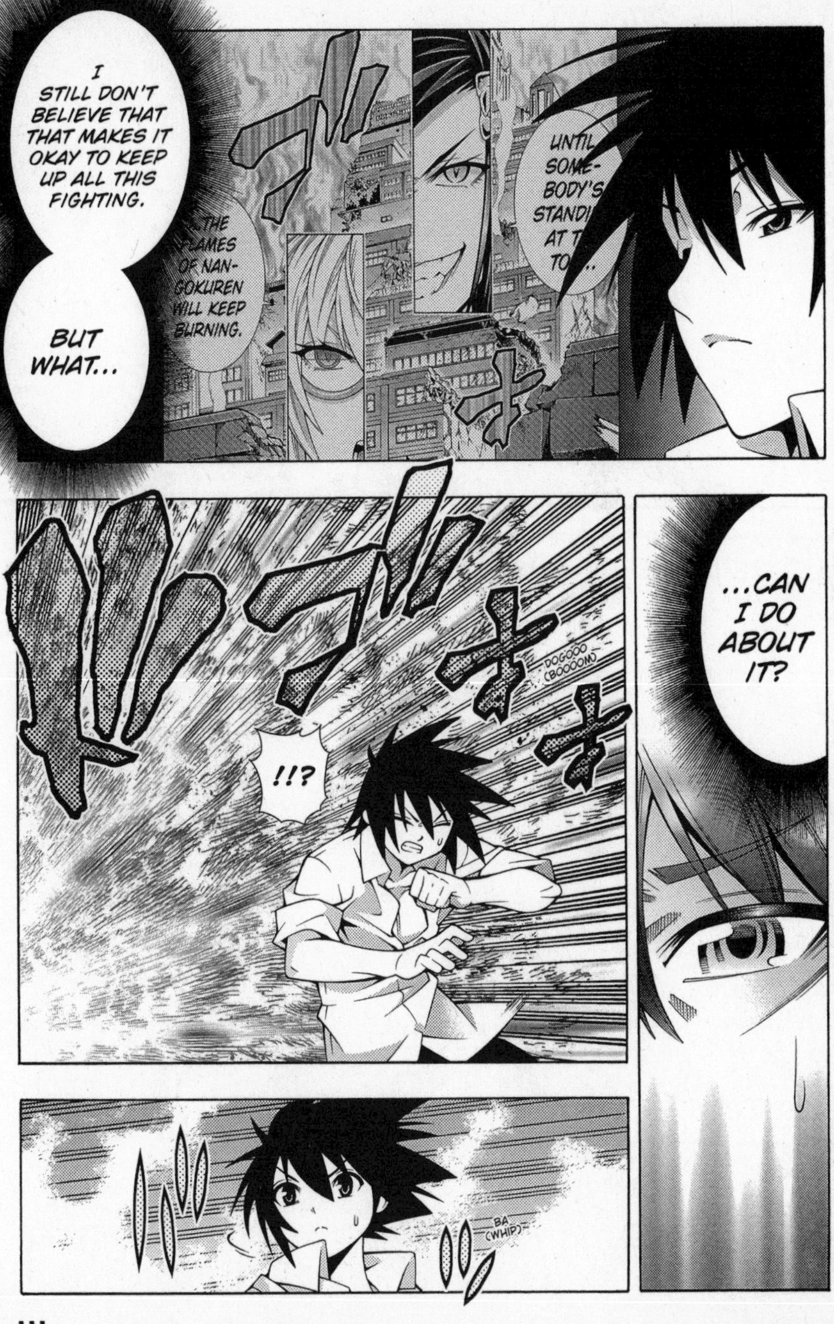
UNTIL SOME-BODY'S STANDI AT T TO...
...THE FLAMES OF NAN-GOKUREN WILL KEEP BURNING.
I STILL DON'T BELIEVE THAT THAT MAKES IT OKAY TO KEEP UP ALL THIS FIGHTING.
BUT WHAT...
...CAN I DO ABOUT IT?
DOGOOO (BOOOOM)
!!?
BA (WHIP)

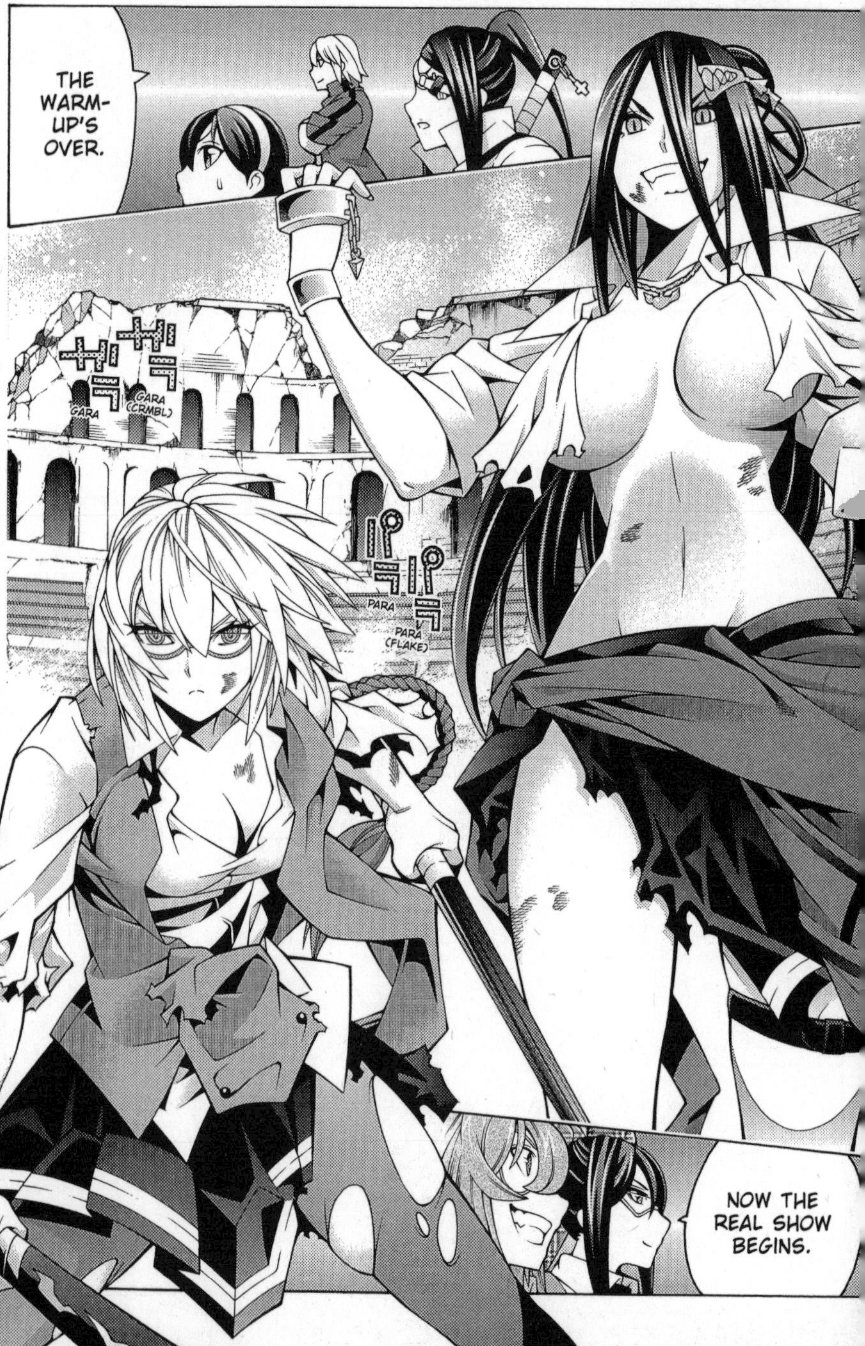
THE WARM-UP'S OVER.
GARA GARA (CRMBL)
PARA PARA (FLAKE)
NOW THE REAL SHOW BEGINS.

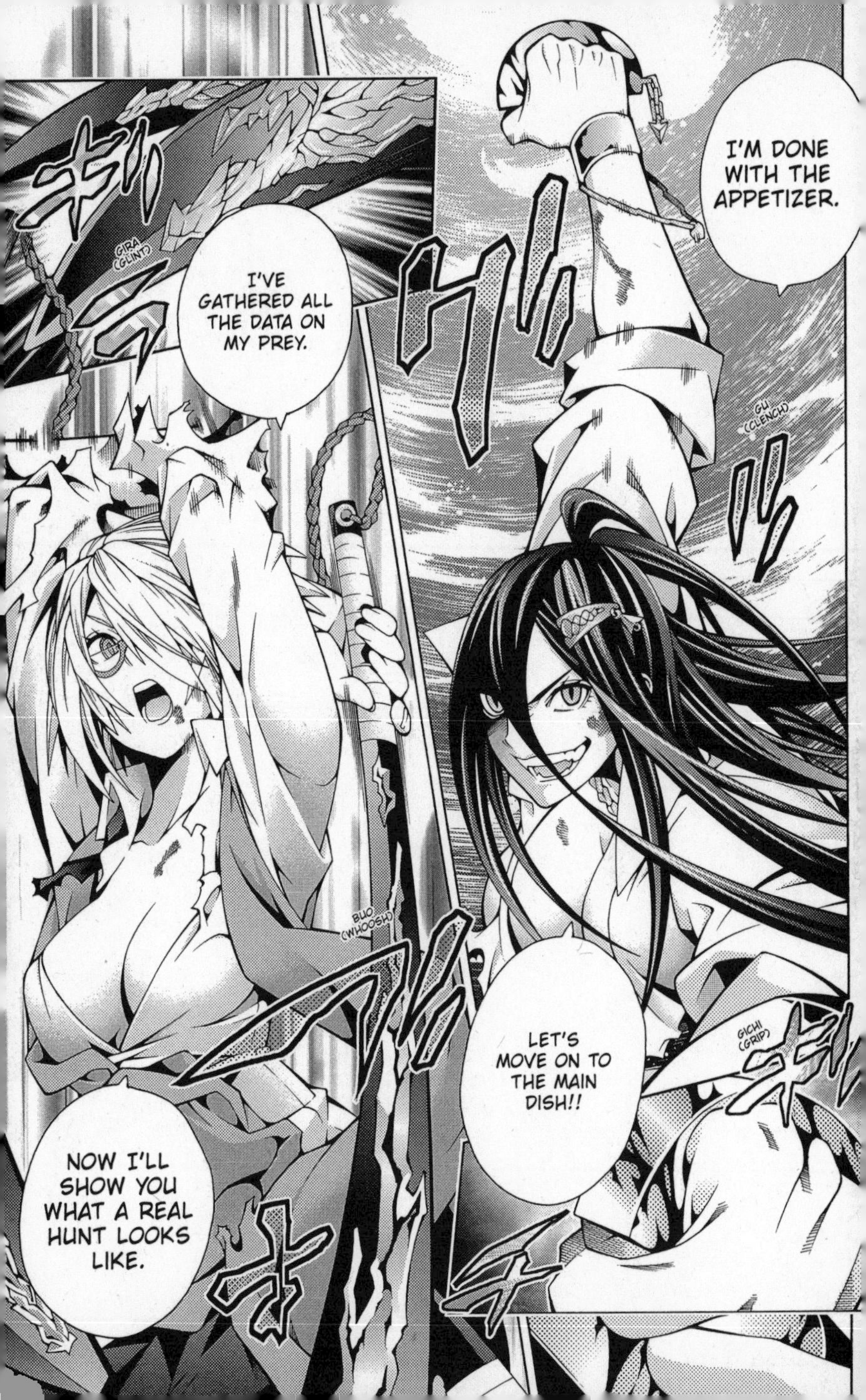
I'M DONE WITH THE APPETIZER.
GU (CLENCH)
LET'S MOVE ON TO THE MAIN DISH!!
GICHI (GRIP)
GIRA (GLINT)
I'VE GATHERED ALL THE DATA ON MY PREY.
BUO (WHOOSH)
NOW I'LL SHOW YOU WHAT A REAL HUNT LOOKS LIKE.

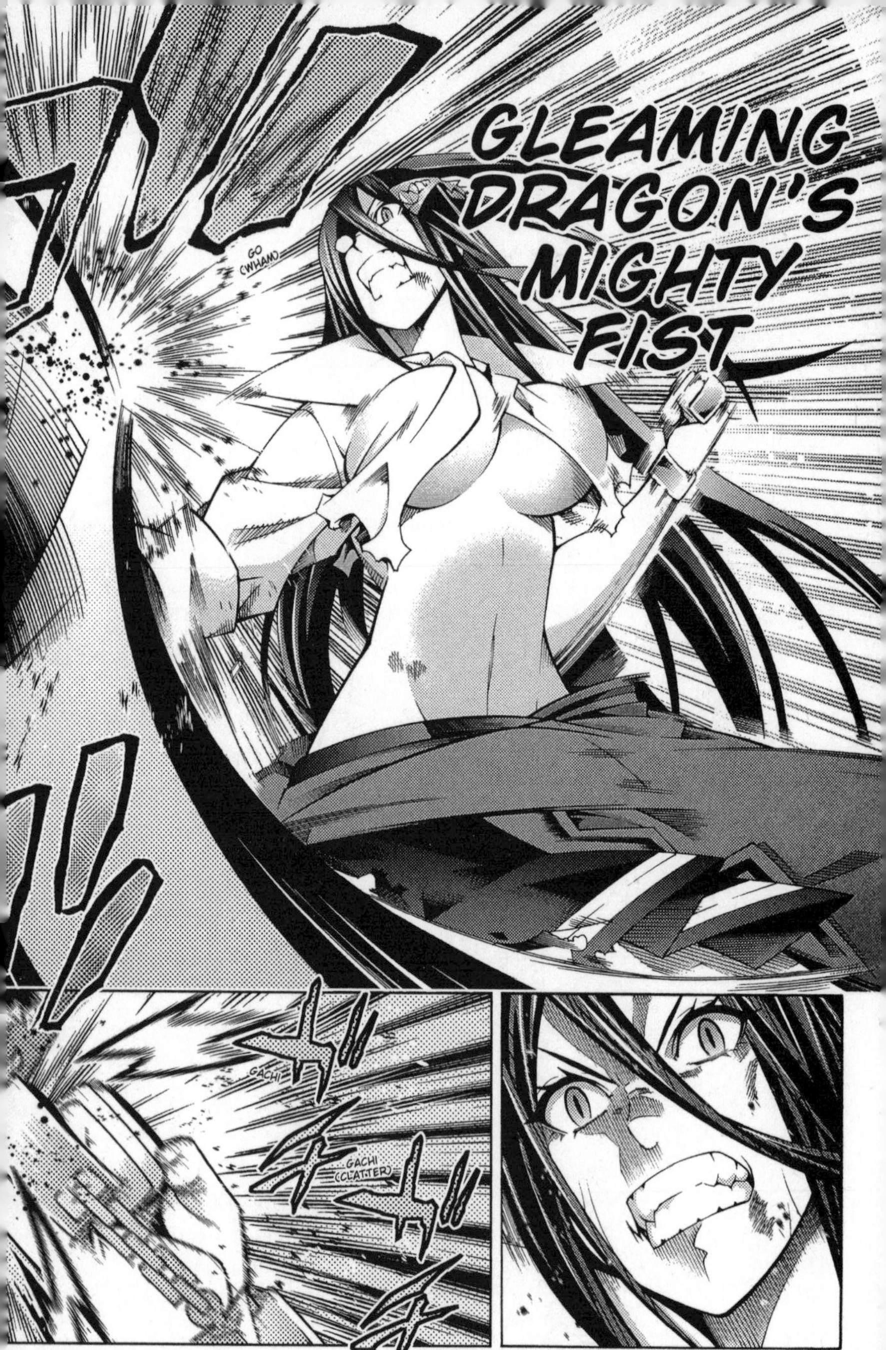
GLEAMING DRAGON'S MIGHTY FIST
GO (WHAM)
GACHI
GACHI (CLATTER)

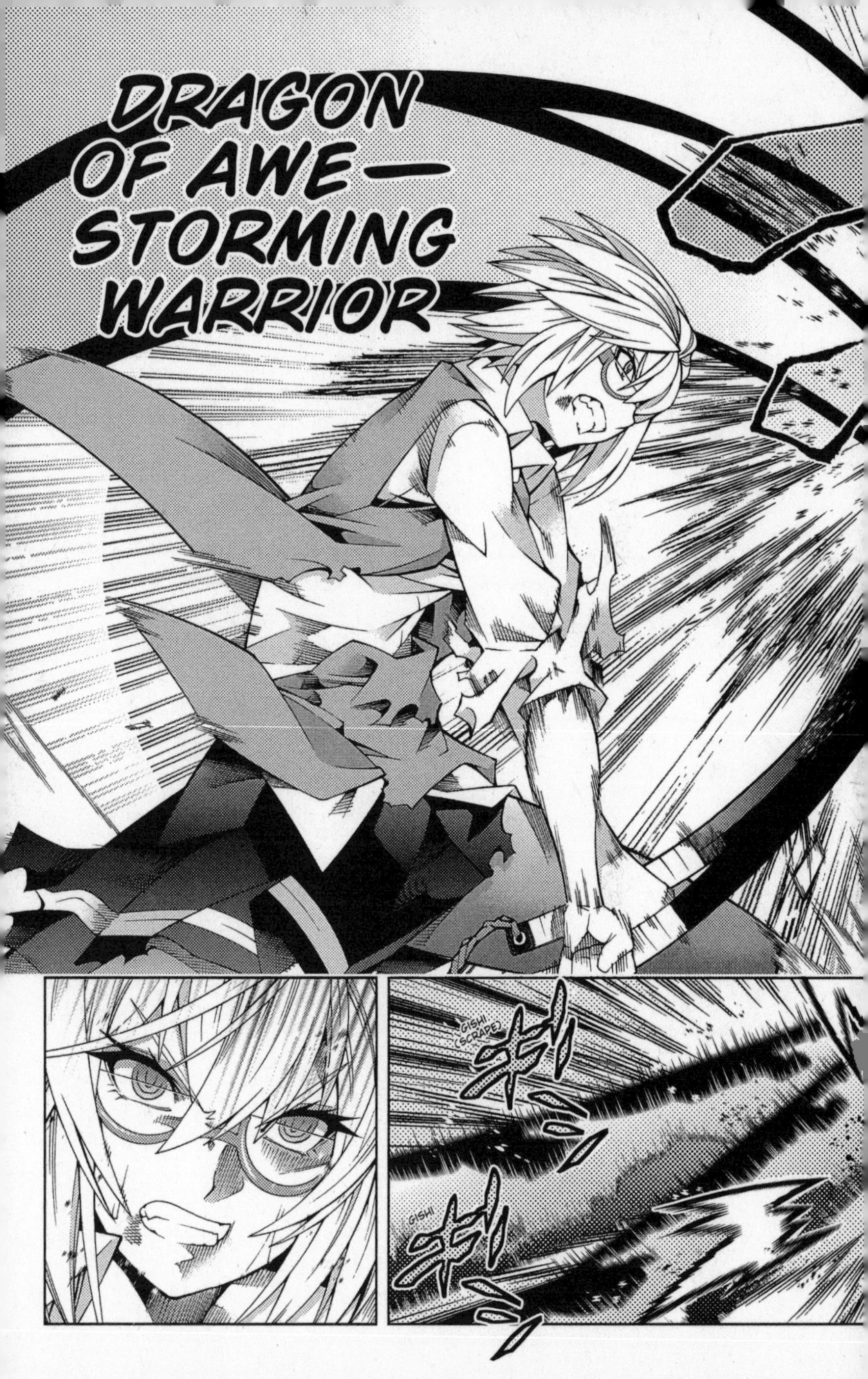
DRAGON OF AWE— STORMING WARRIOR
GISHI (SCRAPE)
GISHI

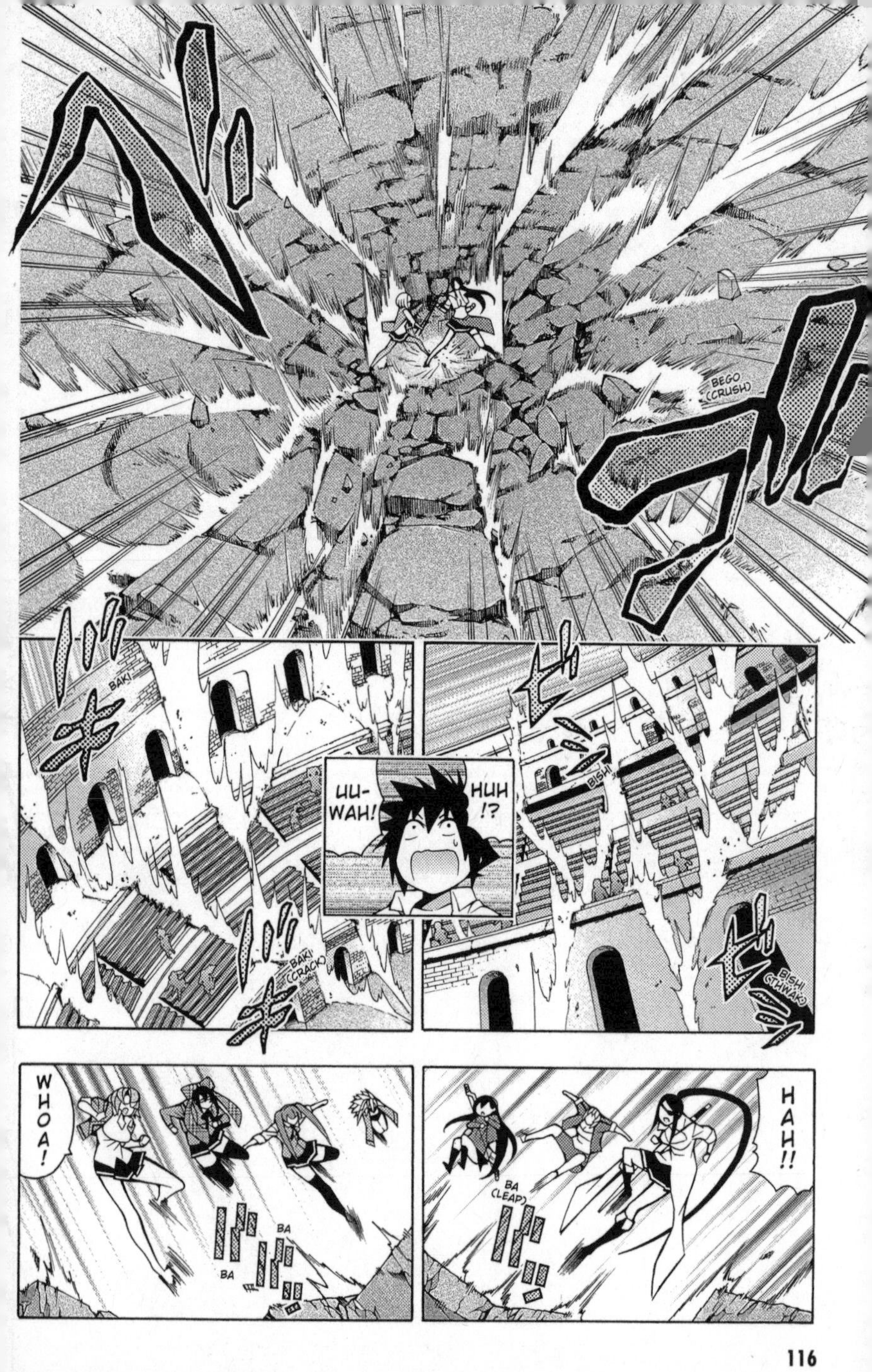
BEGO (CRUSH)
BISHI
BISHI (THWAK)
HUH!?
UU-WAH!
BAKI
BAKI (CRACK)
HAH!!
BA (LEAP)
WHOA!
BA
BA

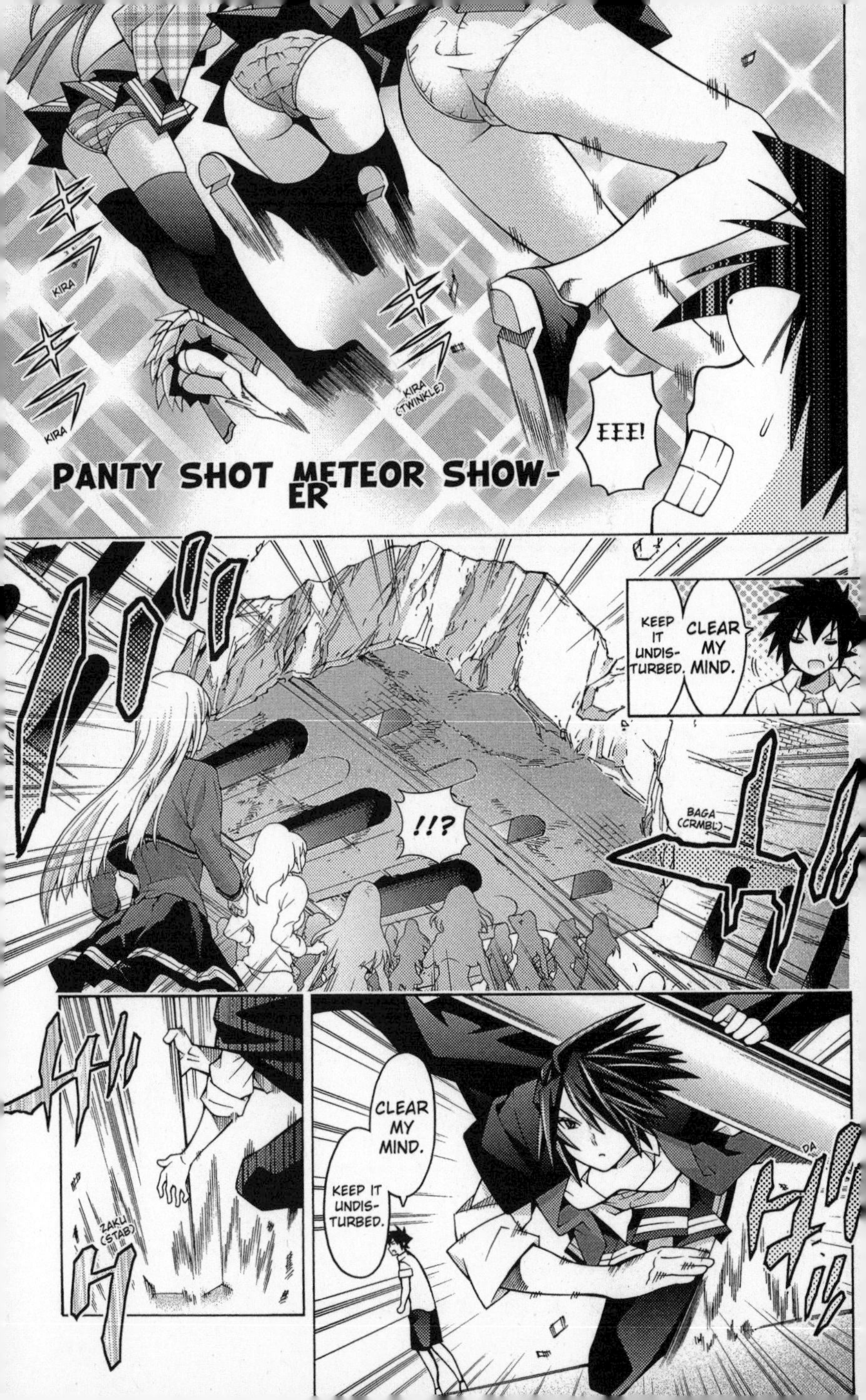
EEE!
KIRA (TWINKLE)
KIRA
KIRA
PANTY SHOT METEOR SHOW-ER
KEEP IT UNDIS-TURBED.
CLEAR MY MIND.
BAGA (CRMBL)
!!?
DA
CLEAR MY MIND.
KEEP IT UNDIS-TURBED.
ZAKU (STAB)

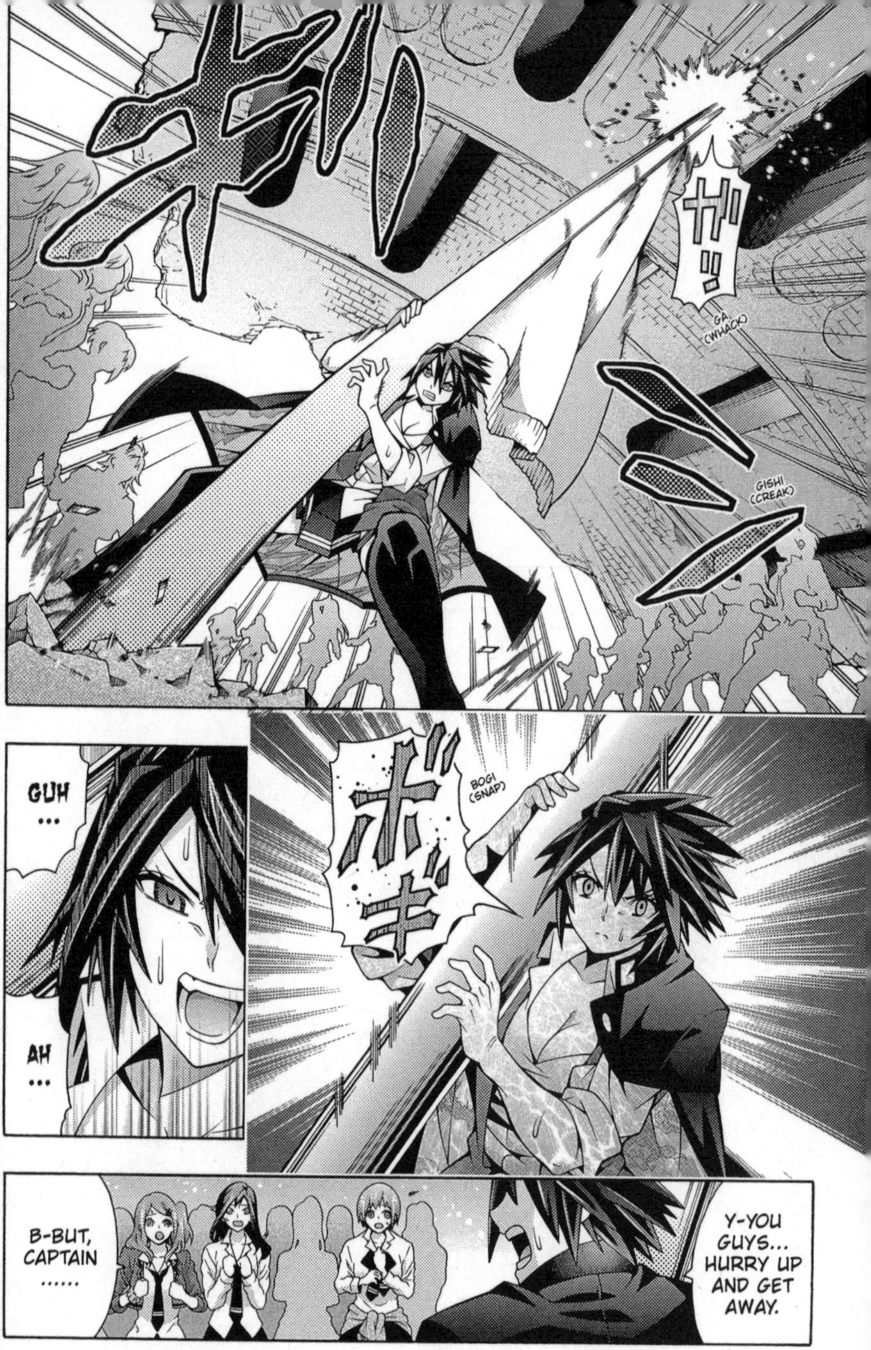
GA (WHACK)
GISHI (CREAK)
BOGI (SNAP)
GUH ...
AH ...
Y-YOU GUYS... HURRY UP AND GET AWAY.
B-BUT, CAPTAIN ......

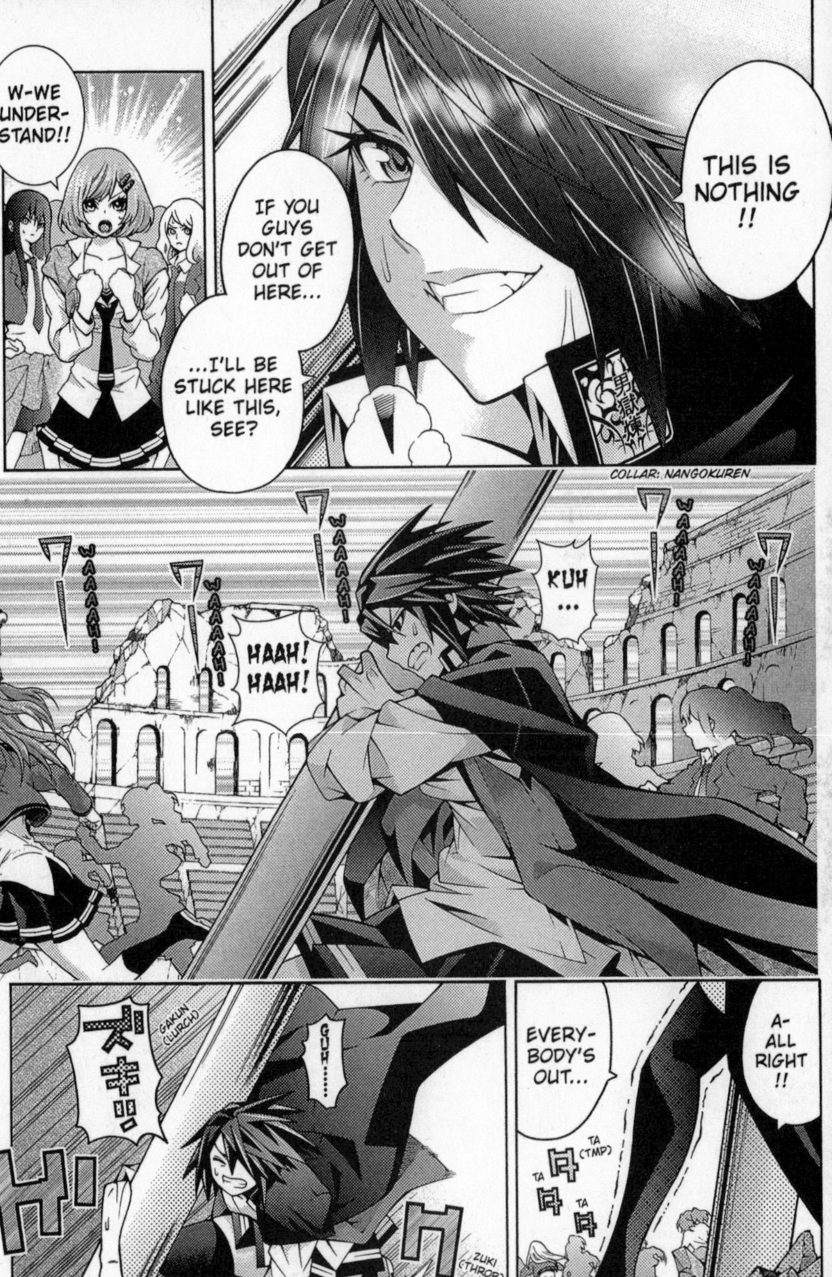
THIS IS NOTHING!!
IF YOU GUYS DON'T GET OUT OF HERE...
...I'LL BE STUCK HERE LIKE THIS, SEE?
COLLAR: NANGOKUREN
W-WE UNDER-STAND!!
WAAAAAH!
WAAAAAH!
KUH...
WAAAAAH!
WAAAAAH!
HAAH! HAAH!
WAAAAAH!
A- ALL RIGHT!!
EVERY-BODY'S OUT...
TA (TMP)
TA
TA
GAKUN (LURCH)
GUH.....
ZUKI (THROB)

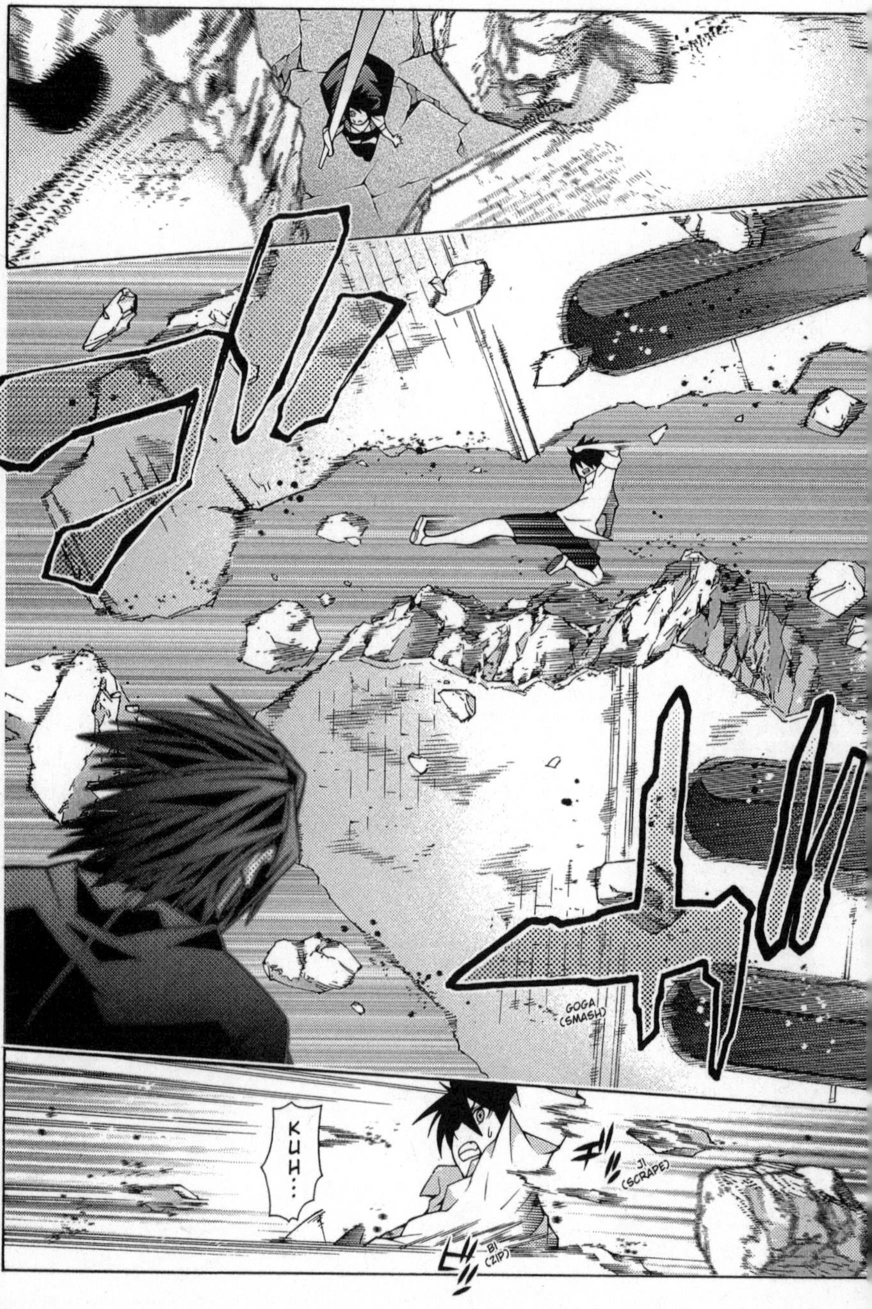
GOGA
(SMASH)
JI
(SCRAPE)
BI
(ZIP)
KUH...

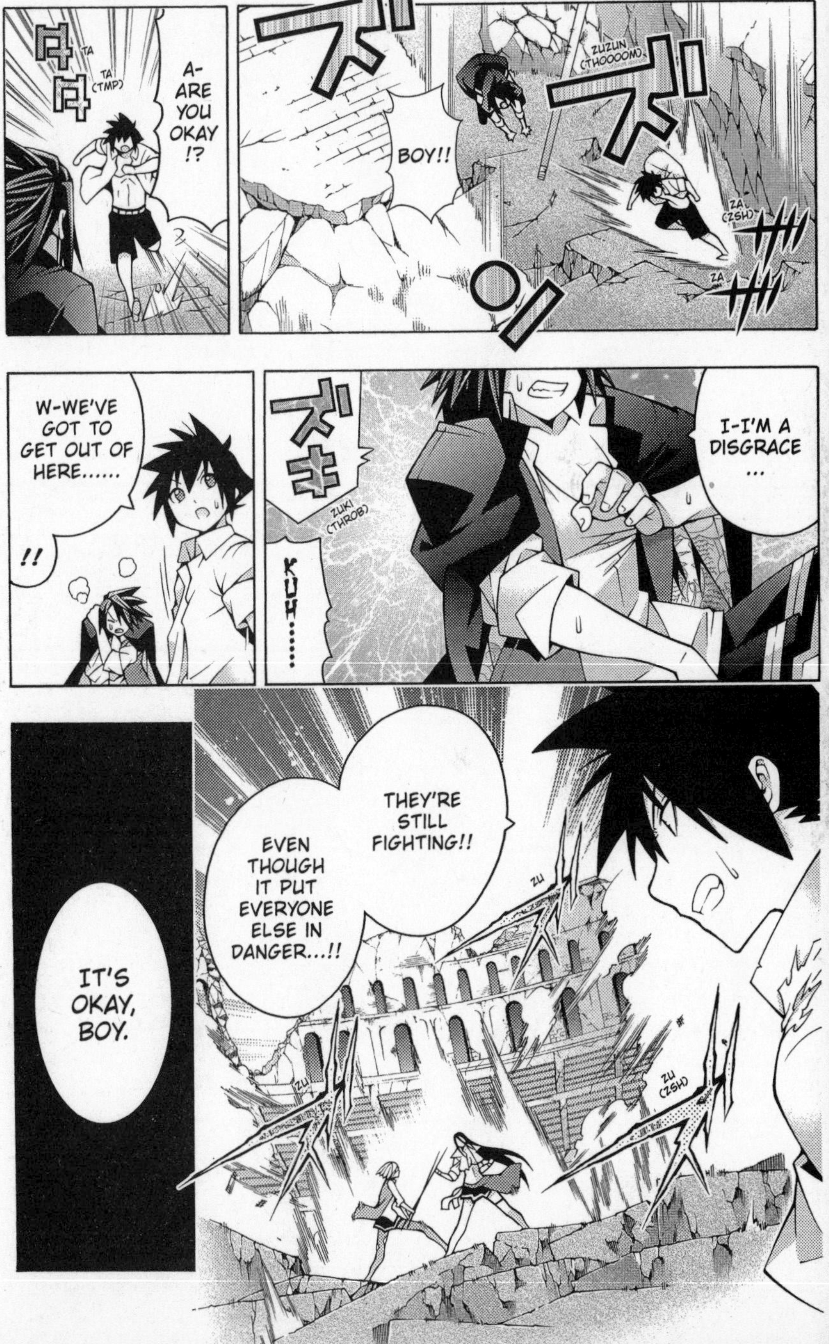
ZUZUN (THOOOOM)
BOY!!
ZA (ZSH)
ZA
TA
TA (TMP)
A- ARE YOU OKAY !?
I-I'M A DISGRACE ...
ZUKI (THROB)
KUH......
W-WE'VE GOT TO GET OUT OF HERE......
!!
THEY'RE STILL FIGHTING!!
EVEN THOUGH IT PUT EVERYONE ELSE IN DANGER...!!
ZU
ZU (ZSH)
ZU
IT'S OKAY, BOY.

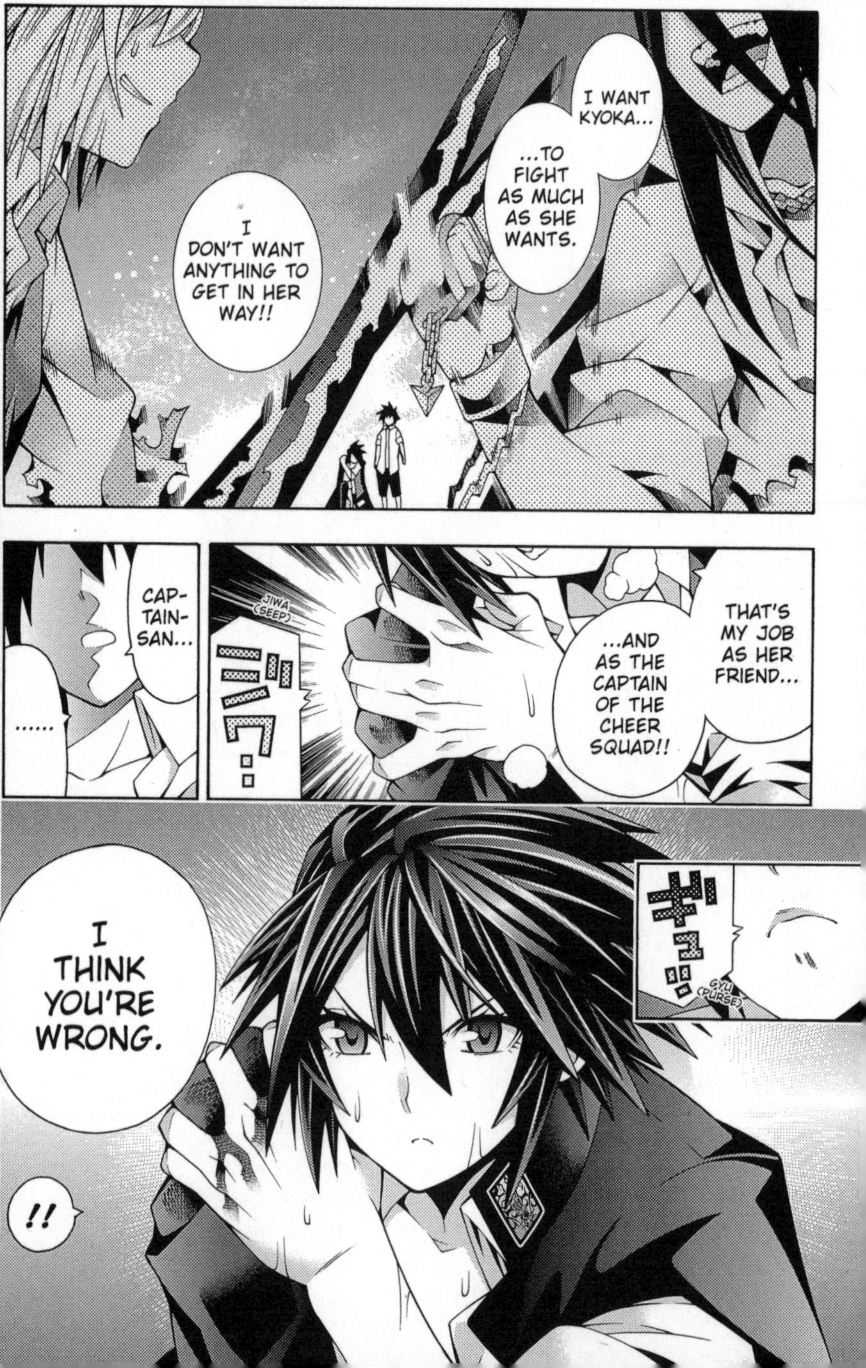
I WANT KYOKA...
...TO FIGHT AS MUCH AS SHE WANTS.
I DON'T WANT ANYTHING TO GET IN HER WAY!!
THAT'S MY JOB AS HER FRIEND...
...AND AS THE CAPTAIN OF THE CHEER SQUAD!!
JIWA (SEEP)
CAP-TAIN-SAN...
......
GYU (PURSE)
I THINK YOU'RE WRONG.
!!

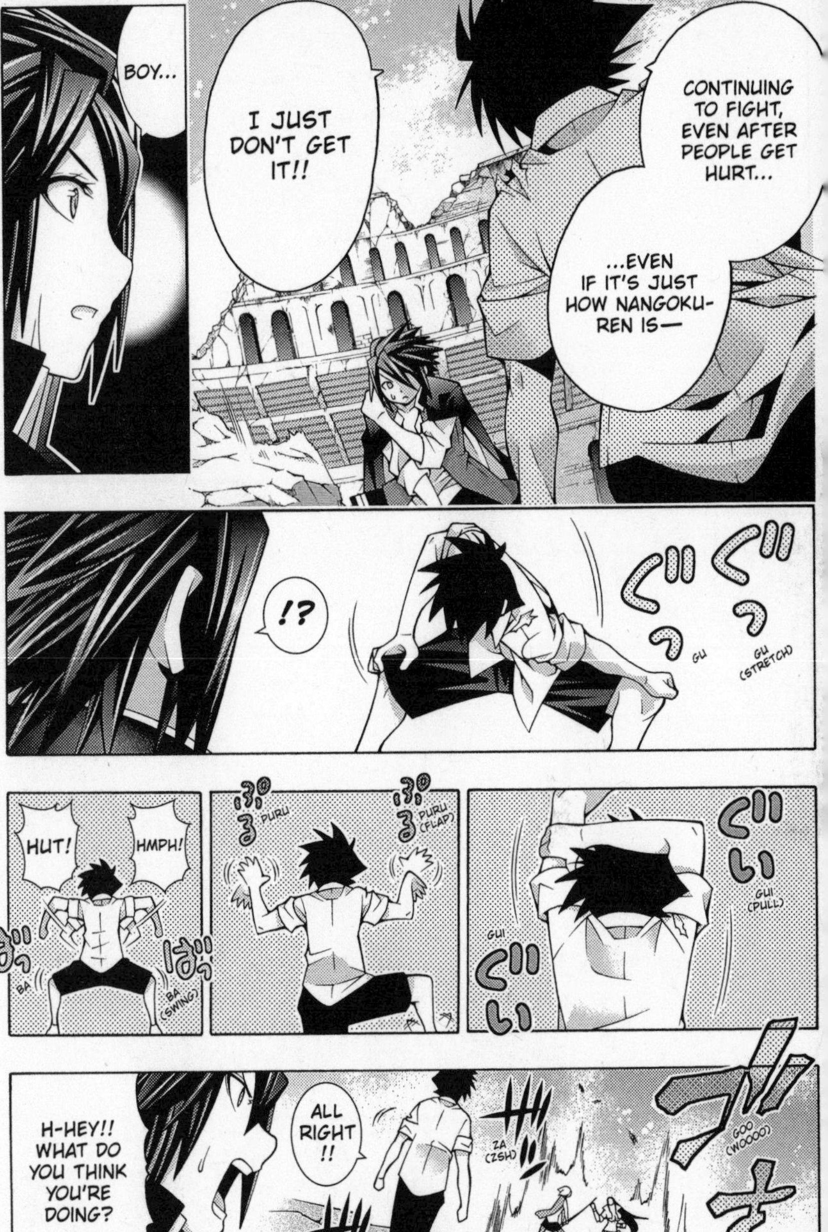
CONTINUING TO FIGHT, EVEN AFTER PEOPLE GET HURT...
...EVEN IF IT'S JUST HOW NANGOKU-REN IS—
I JUST DON'T GET IT!!
BOY...
ぐっ
GU (STRETCH)
ぐっ
GU
!?
ぐい
GUI (PULL)
ぐい
GUI
ぷる
PURU (FLAP)
ぷる
PURU
HMPH!
HUT!
ばっ
BA (SWING)
ばっ
BA
ゴォ
GOO (WOOOO)
ザッ
ZA (ZSH)
ザッ
ZA
ALL RIGHT!!
H-HEY!! WHAT DO YOU THINK YOU'RE DOING?

THE ONE WHO MUST CHANGE...

...IS ME!!

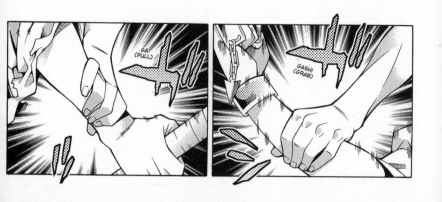

GA
(PULL)

GASHI
(GRAB)

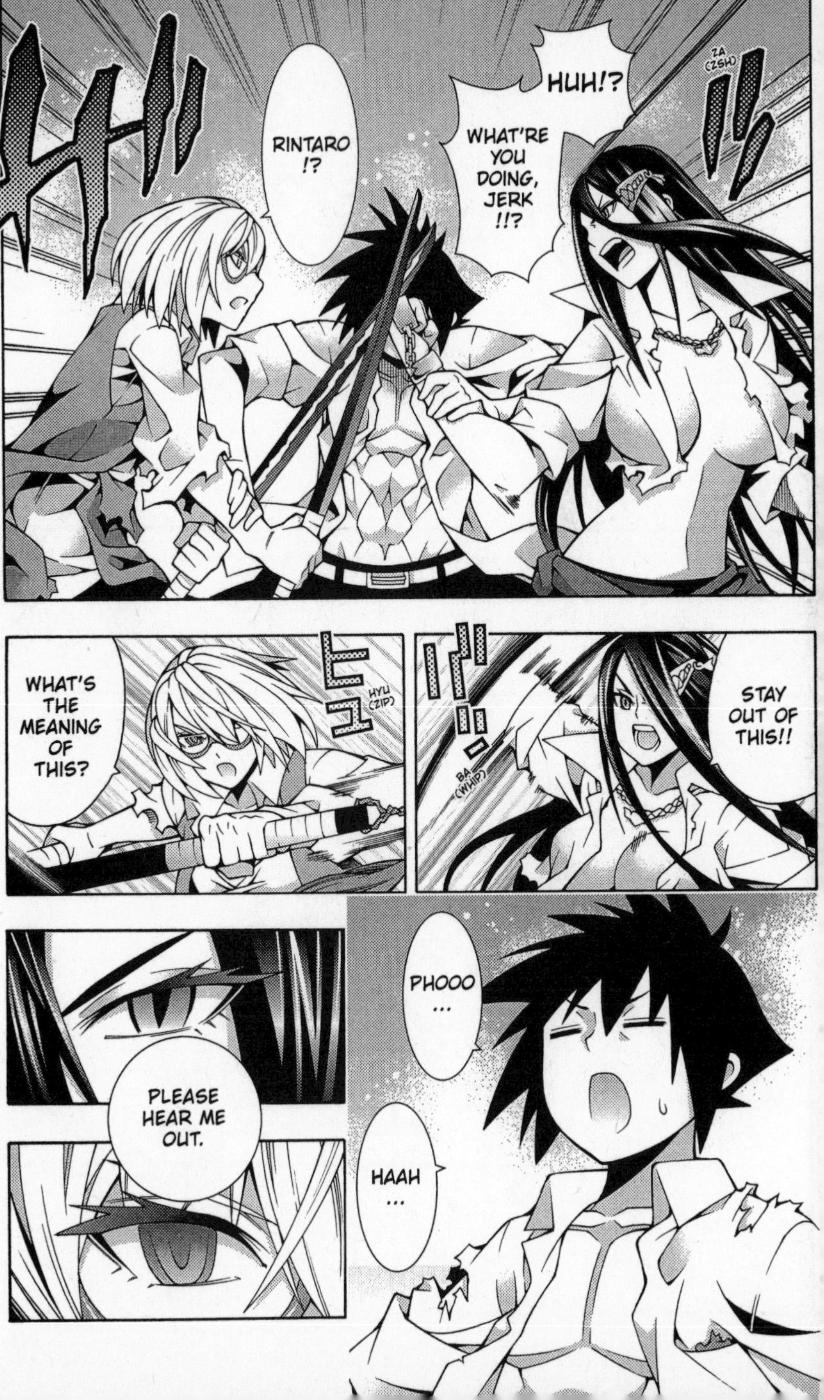
ZA (ZSH)
HUH!?
WHAT'RE YOU DOING, JERK!!?
RINTARO!?
BA (WHIP)
STAY OUT OF THIS!!
HYU (ZIP)
WHAT'S THE MEANING OF THIS?
PHOOO...
HAAH...
PLEASE HEAR ME OUT.

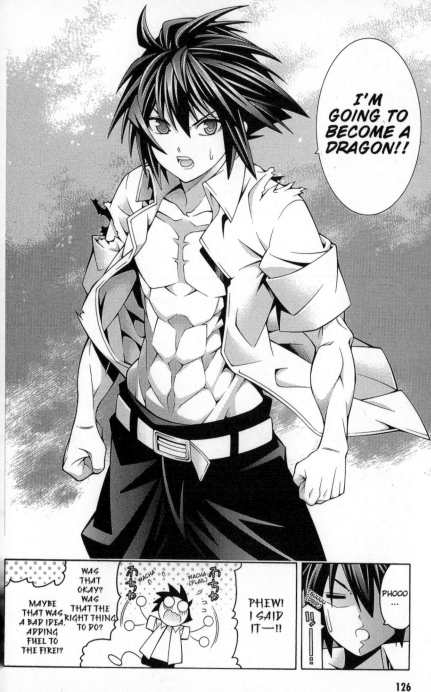

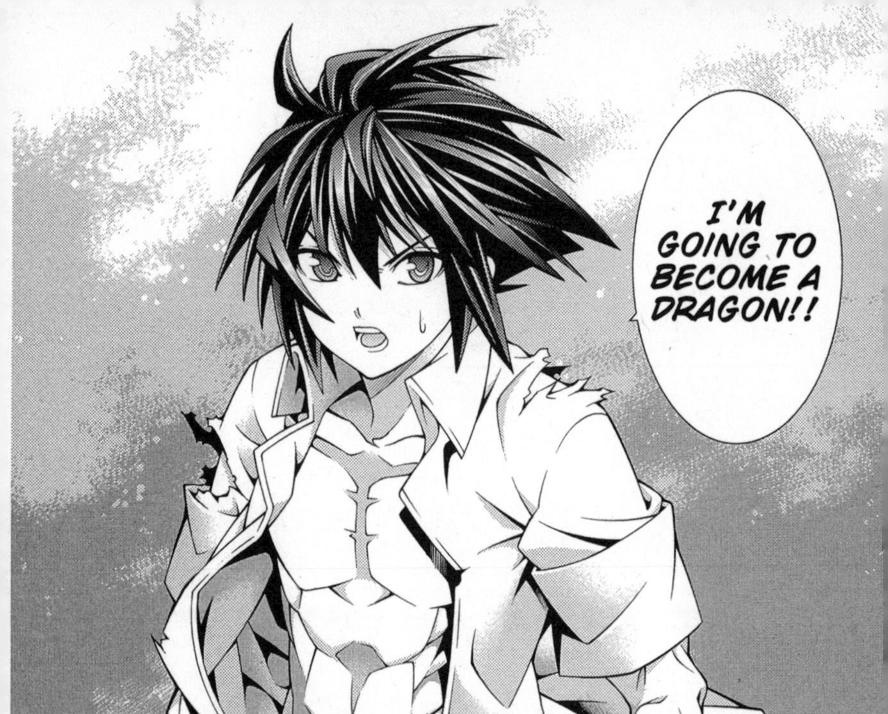
I'M GOING TO BECOME A DRAGON!!

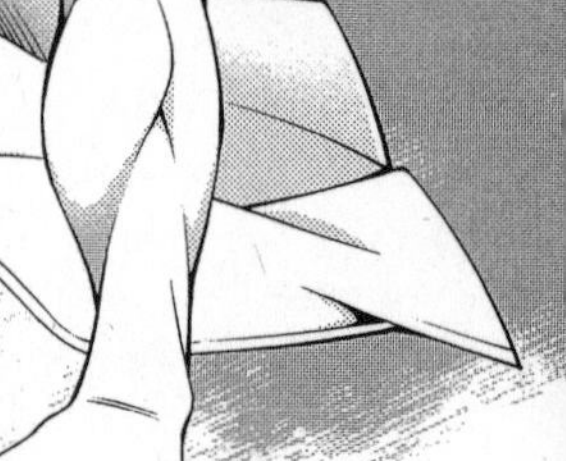
PHOOO ...
TSUUUU (DRIP)

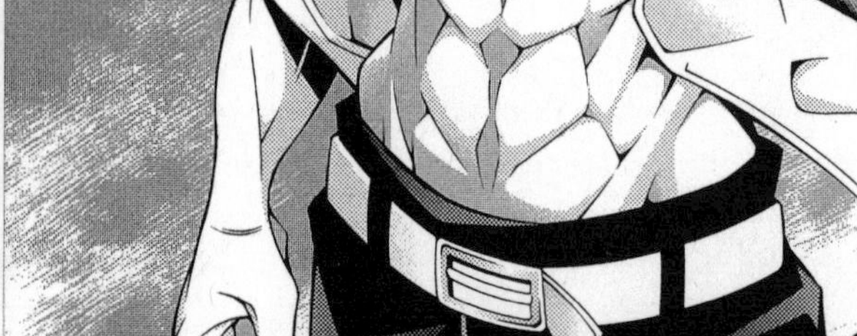
わちゃ
WACHA (FLAIL)
わちゃ
WACHA
PHEW! I SAID IT—!!
WAS THAT OKAY? WAS THAT THE RIGHT THING TO DO?
MAYBE THAT WAS A BAD IDEA, ADDING FUEL TO THE FIRE!?

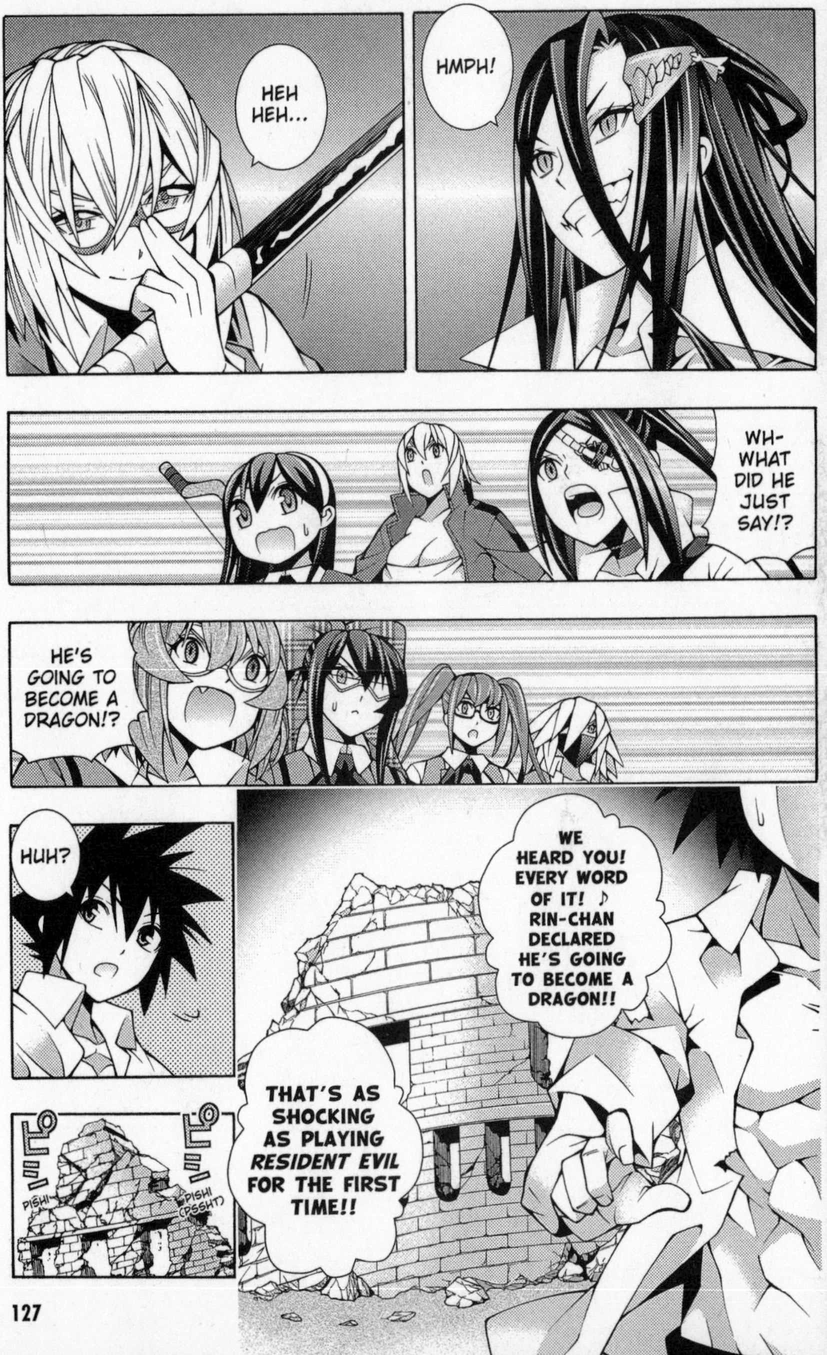
HMPH!
HEH HEH...
WH-WHAT DID HE JUST SAY!?
HE'S GOING TO BECOME A DRAGON!?
WE HEARD YOU! EVERY WORD OF IT! ♪ RIN-CHAN DECLARED HE'S GOING TO BECOME A DRAGON!!
THAT'S AS SHOCKING AS PLAYING *RESIDENT EVIL* FOR THE FIRST TIME!!
HUH?
PISHI
PISHI (PSSHT)

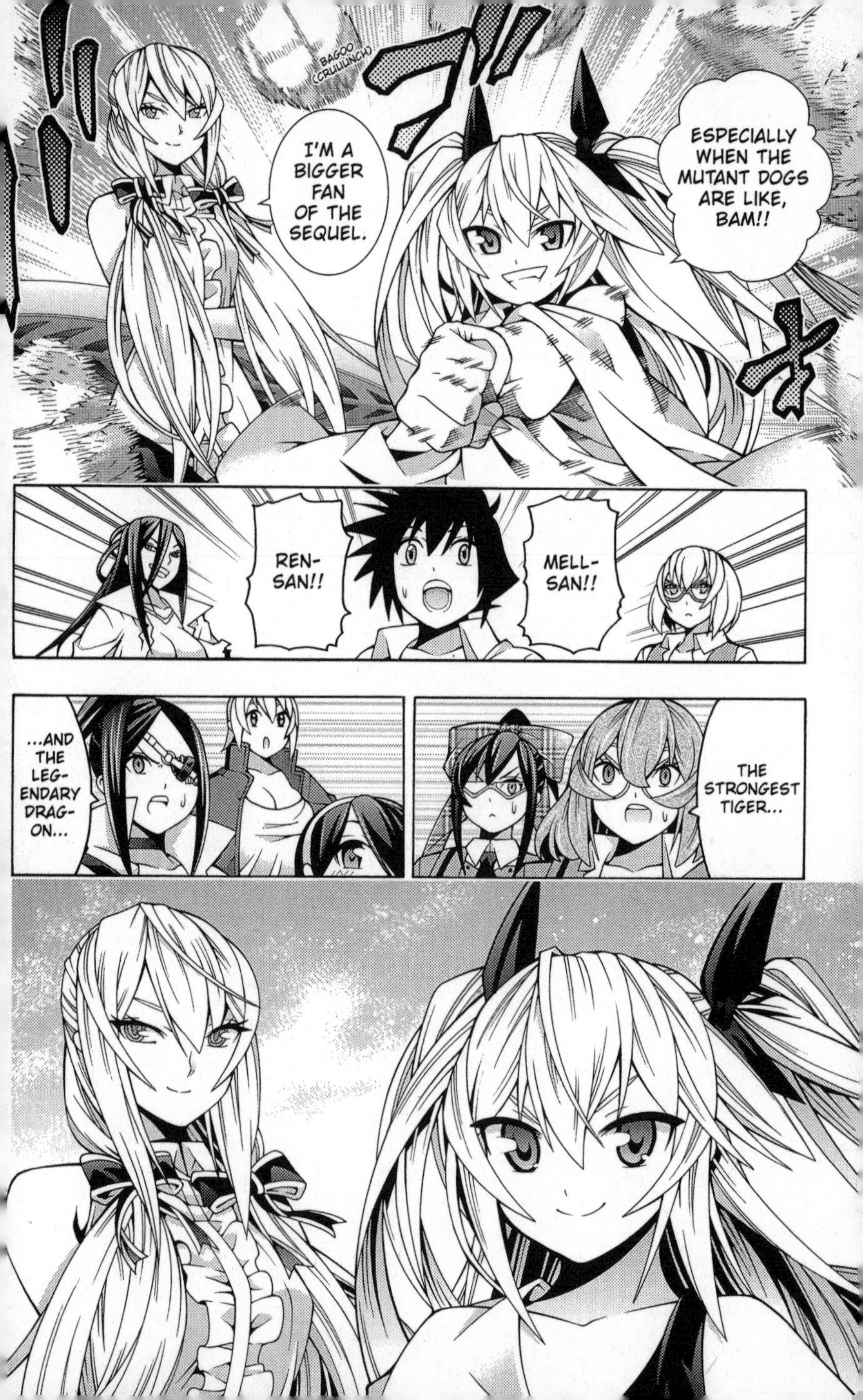
BAGOO (CRUUUNCH)
ESPECIALLY WHEN THE MUTANT DOGS ARE LIKE, BAM!!
I'M A BIGGER FAN OF THE SEQUEL.
MELL-SAN!!
REN-SAN!!
THE STRONGEST TIGER...
...AND THE LEG-ENDARY DRAG-ON...

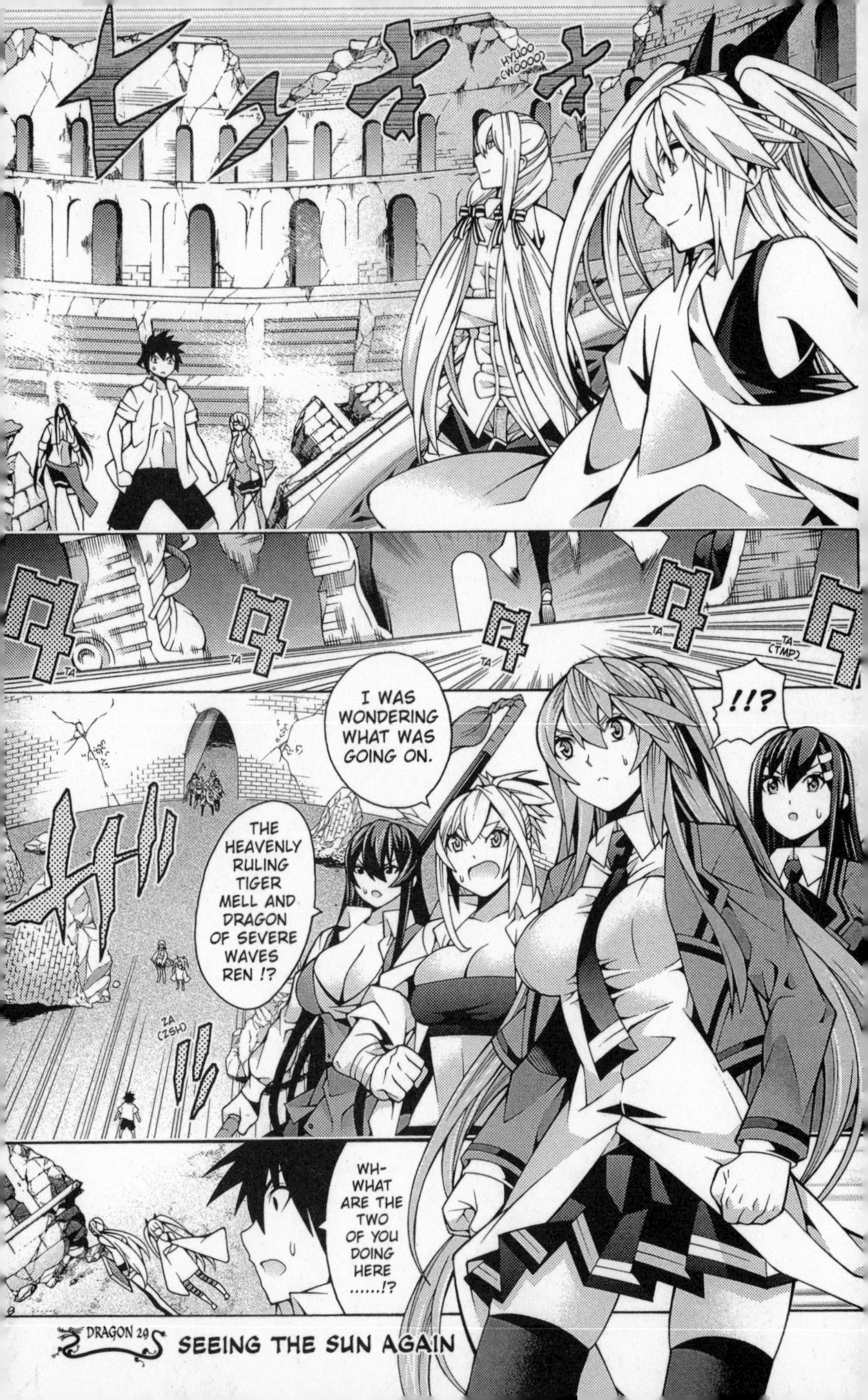
HYUOO (WOOOO)
TA
TA
TA
TA
TA (TMP)
!!?
I WAS WONDERING WHAT WAS GOING ON.
THE HEAVENLY RULING TIGER MELL AND DRAGON OF SEVERE WAVES REN !?
ZA (ZSH)
WH-WHAT ARE THE TWO OF YOU DOING HERE ......!?

DRAGON 29 SEEING THE SUN AGAIN

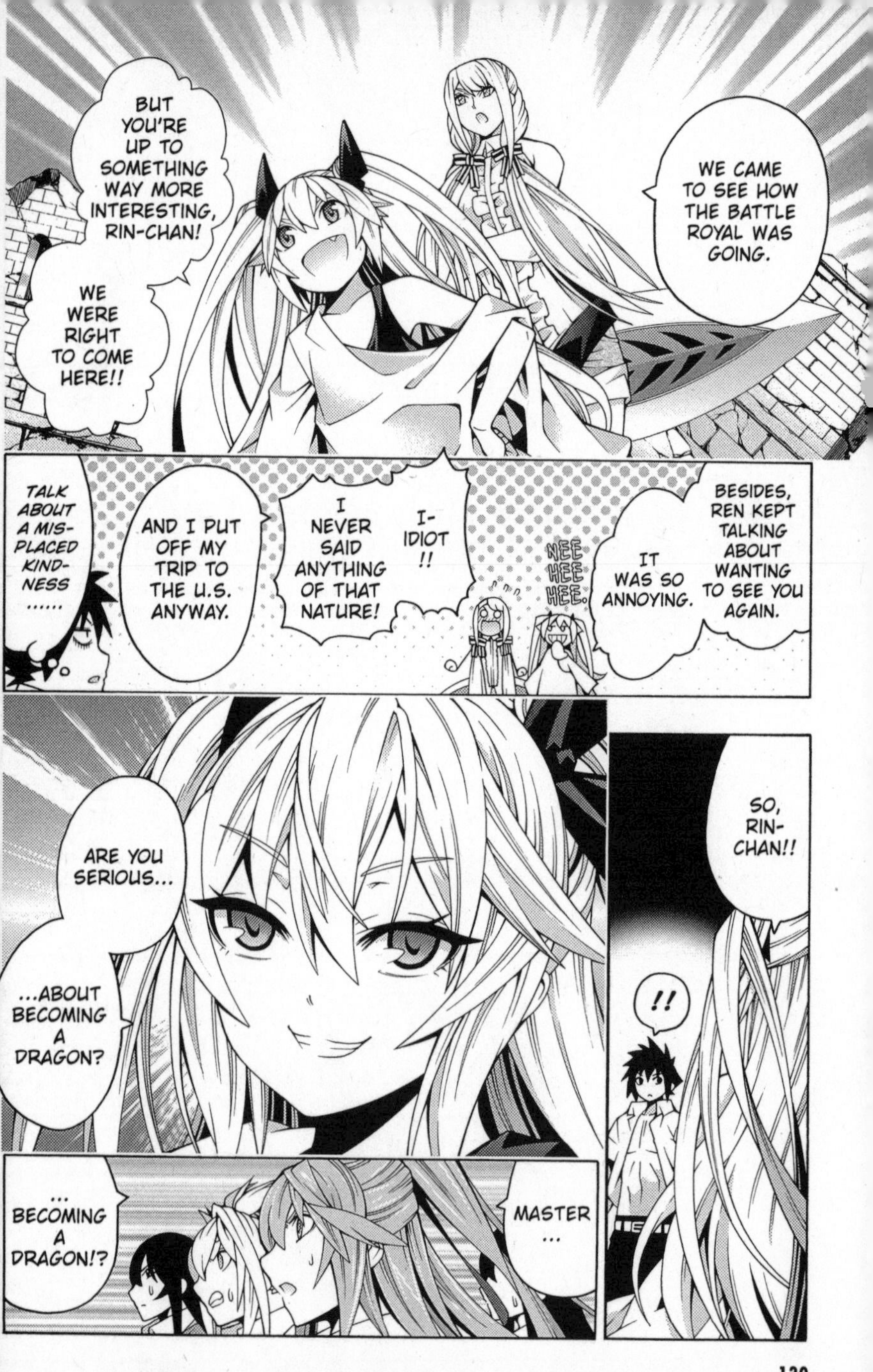
WE CAME TO SEE HOW THE BATTLE ROYAL WAS GOING.
BUT YOU'RE UP TO SOMETHING WAY MORE INTERESTING, RIN-CHAN!
WE WERE RIGHT TO COME HERE!!
BESIDES, REN KEPT TALKING ABOUT WANTING TO SEE YOU AGAIN.
IT WAS SO ANNOYING.
NEE HEE HEE.
I- IDIOT!!
I NEVER SAID ANYTHING OF THAT NATURE!
AND I PUT OFF MY TRIP TO THE U.S. ANYWAY.
TALK ABOUT A MIS-PLACED KIND-NESS ......
SO, RIN-CHAN!!
!!
ARE YOU SERIOUS...
...ABOUT BECOMING A DRAGON?
MASTER ...
... BECOMING A DRAGON!?

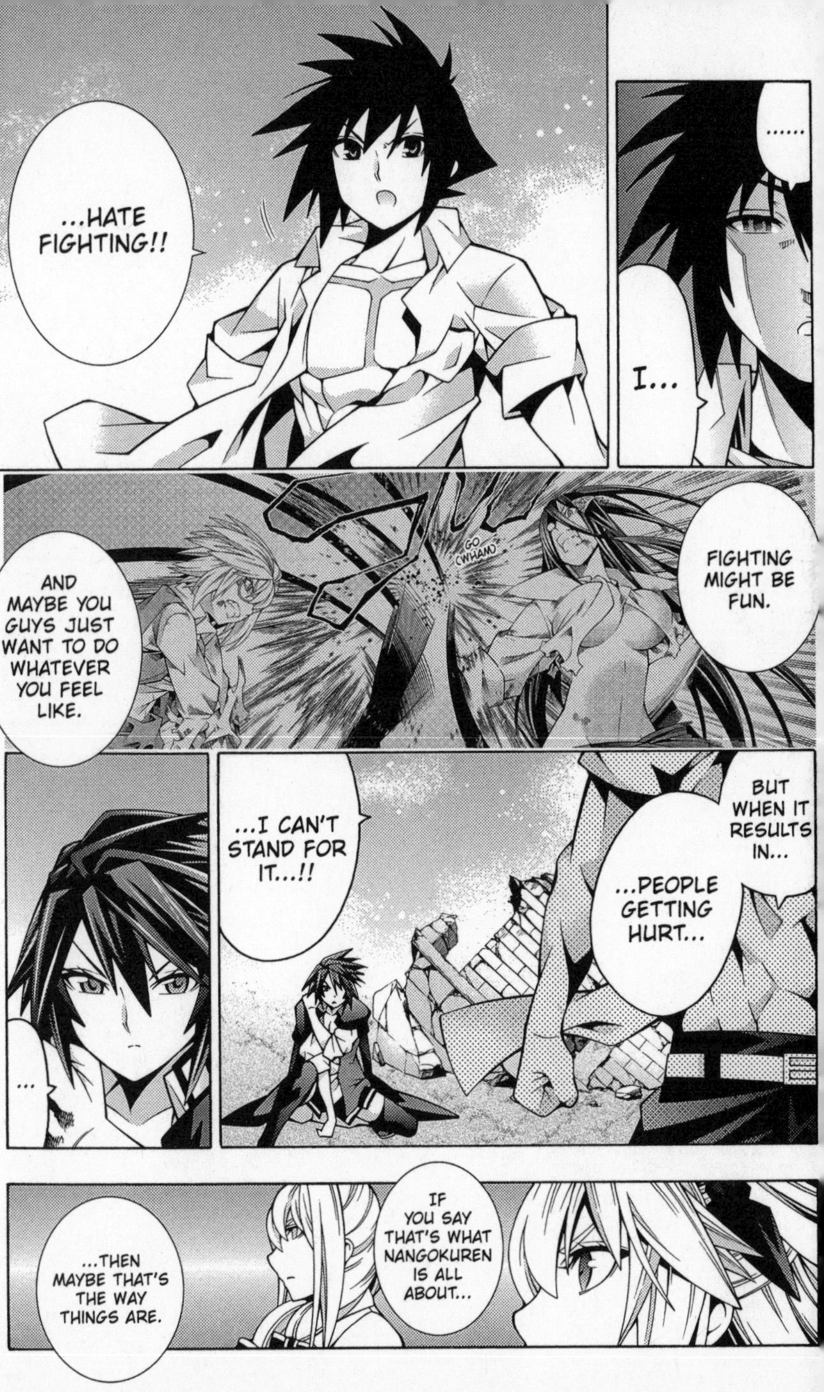
......
I...
...HATE FIGHTING!!
FIGHTING MIGHT BE FUN.
GO (WHAM)
AND MAYBE YOU GUYS JUST WANT TO DO WHATEVER YOU FEEL LIKE.
BUT WHEN IT RESULTS IN...
...PEOPLE GETTING HURT...
...I CAN'T STAND FOR IT...!!
...
IF YOU SAY THAT'S WHAT NANGOKUREN IS ALL ABOUT...
...THEN MAYBE THAT'S THE WAY THINGS ARE.

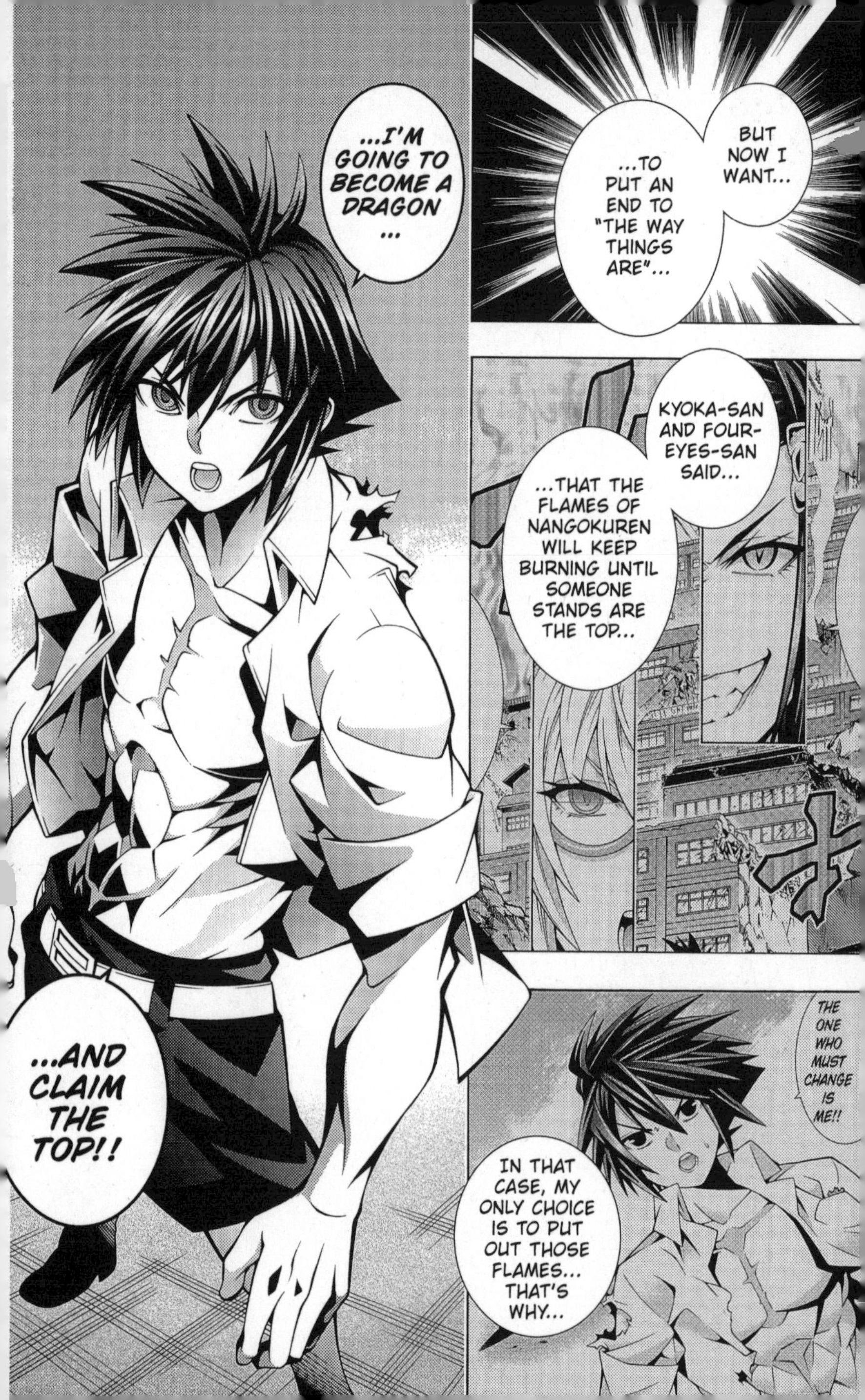
BUT NOW I WANT...
...TO PUT AN END TO "THE WAY THINGS ARE"...
KYOKA-SAN AND FOUR-EYES-SAN SAID...
...THAT THE FLAMES OF NANGOKUREN WILL KEEP BURNING UNTIL SOMEONE STANDS ARE THE TOP...
THE ONE WHO MUST CHANGE IS ME!!
IN THAT CASE, MY ONLY CHOICE IS TO PUT OUT THOSE FLAMES... THAT'S WHY...
...I'M GOING TO BECOME A DRAGON...
...AND CLAIM THE TOP!!

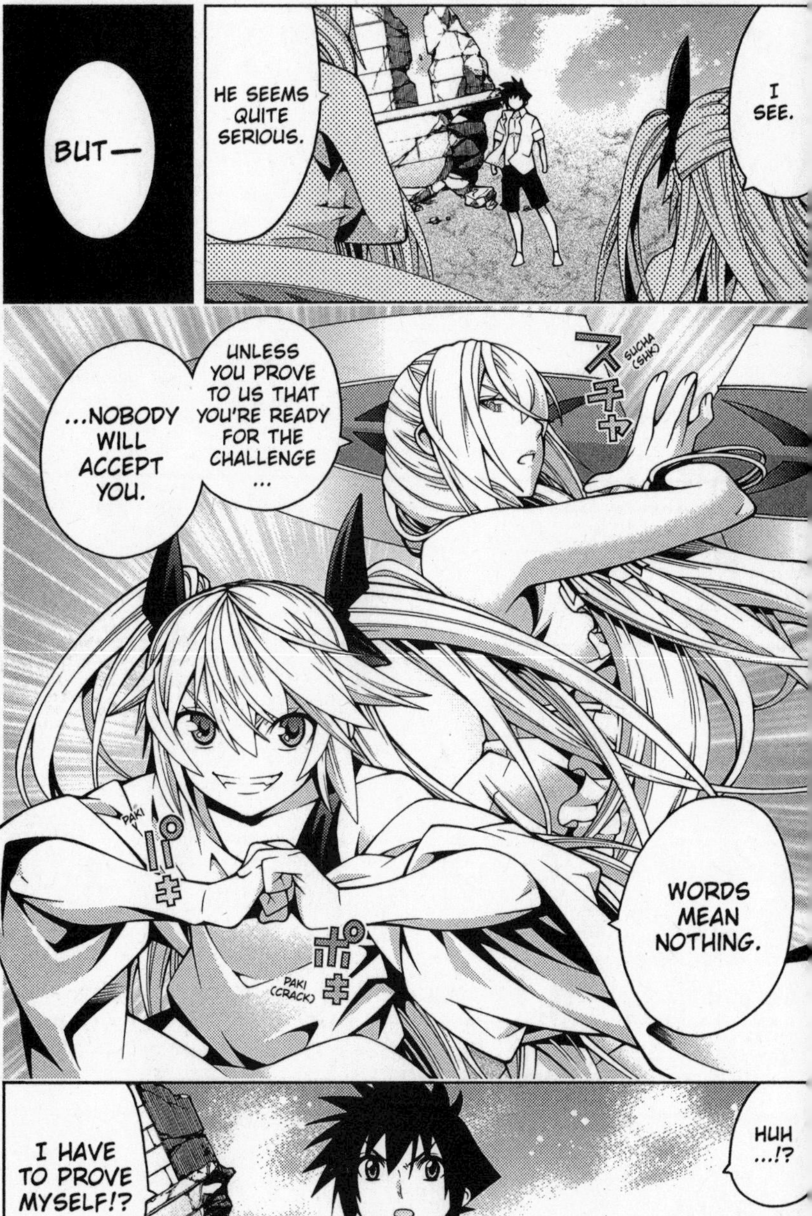
I SEE.
HE SEEMS QUITE SERIOUS.
BUT—
スチャ
SUCHA (SHK)
UNLESS YOU PROVE TO US THAT YOU'RE READY FOR THE CHALLENGE ...
...NOBODY WILL ACCEPT YOU.
WORDS MEAN NOTHING.
パキ
PAKI
ポキ
PAKI (CRACK)
HUH ...!?
I HAVE TO PROVE MYSELF!?

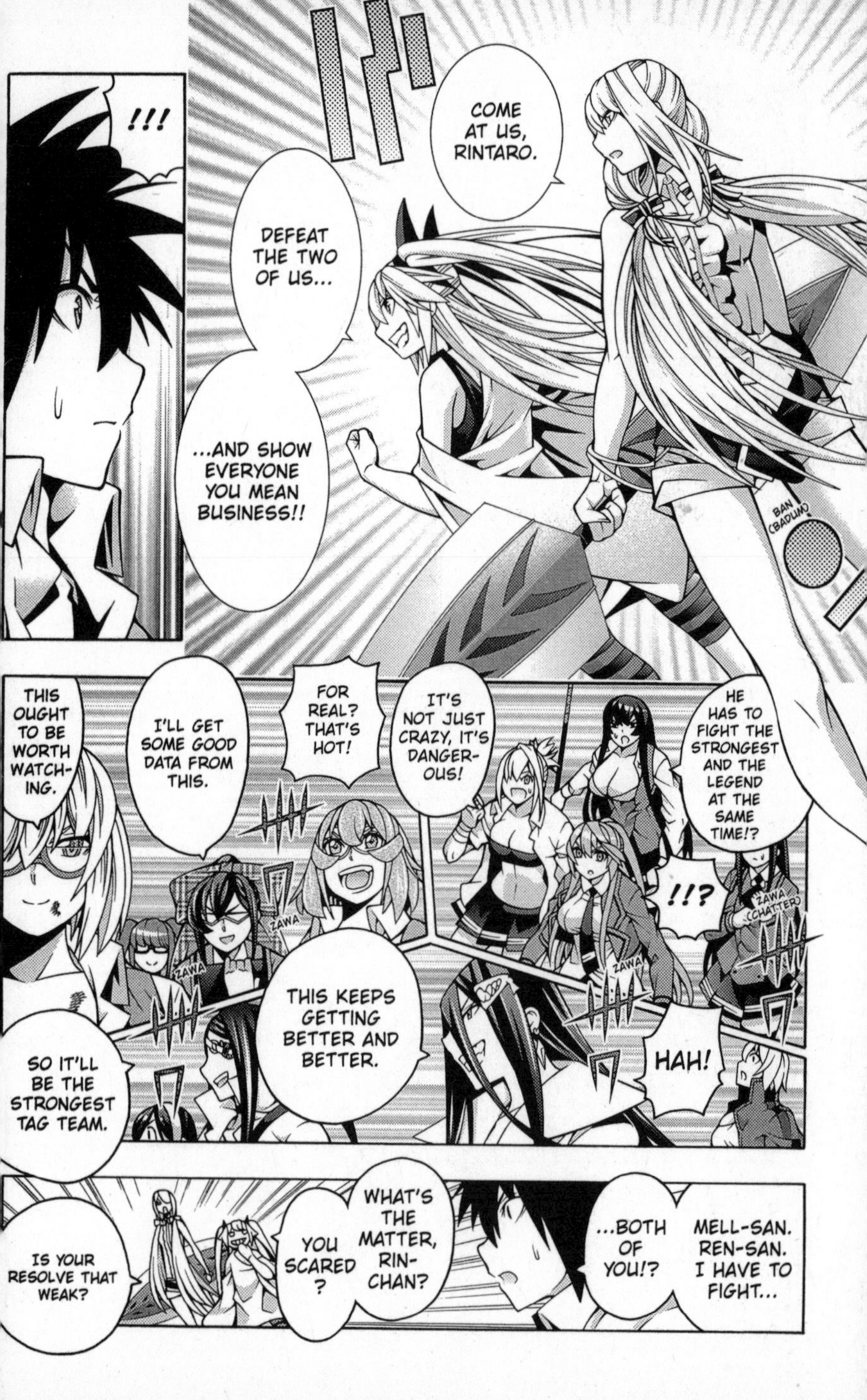
COME AT US, RINTARO.
DEFEAT THE TWO OF US...
...AND SHOW EVERYONE YOU MEAN BUSINESS!!
BAN (BADUM)
!!!
HE HAS TO FIGHT THE STRONGEST AND THE LEGEND AT THE SAME TIME!?
!!?
ZAWA (CHATTER)
IT'S NOT JUST CRAZY, IT'S DANGER-OUS!
FOR REAL? THAT'S HOT!
I'LL GET SOME GOOD DATA FROM THIS.
THIS OUGHT TO BE WORTH WATCH-ING.
ZAWA
ZAWA
HAH!
THIS KEEPS GETTING BETTER AND BETTER.
ZAWA
SO IT'LL BE THE STRONGEST TAG TEAM.
MELL-SAN. REN-SAN. I HAVE TO FIGHT...
...BOTH OF YOU!?
WHAT'S THE MATTER, RIN-CHAN?
YOU SCARED?
IS YOUR RESOLVE THAT WEAK?

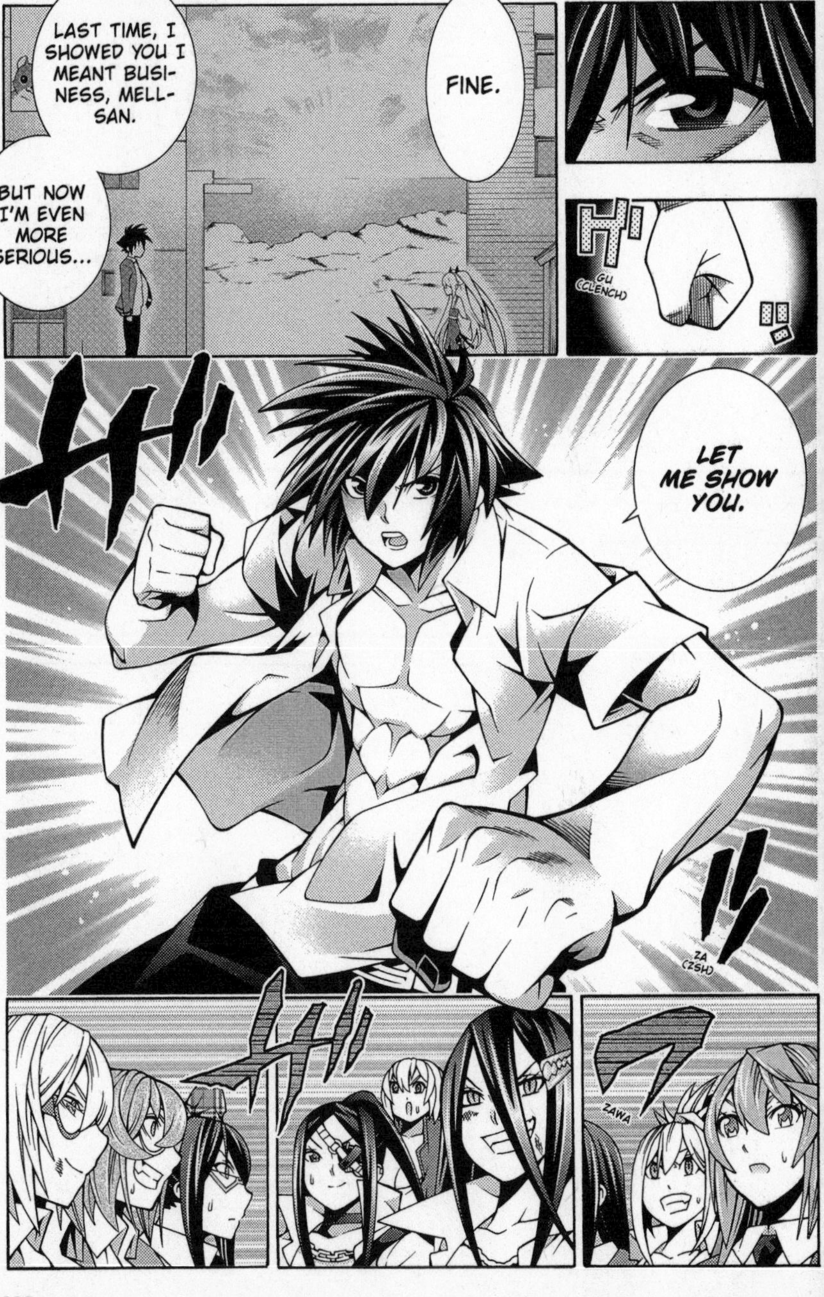
GU (CLENCH)
FINE.
LAST TIME, I SHOWED YOU I MEANT BUSINESS, MELL-SAN.
BUT NOW I'M EVEN MORE SERIOUS...
LET ME SHOW YOU.
ZA (ZSH)
ZAWA

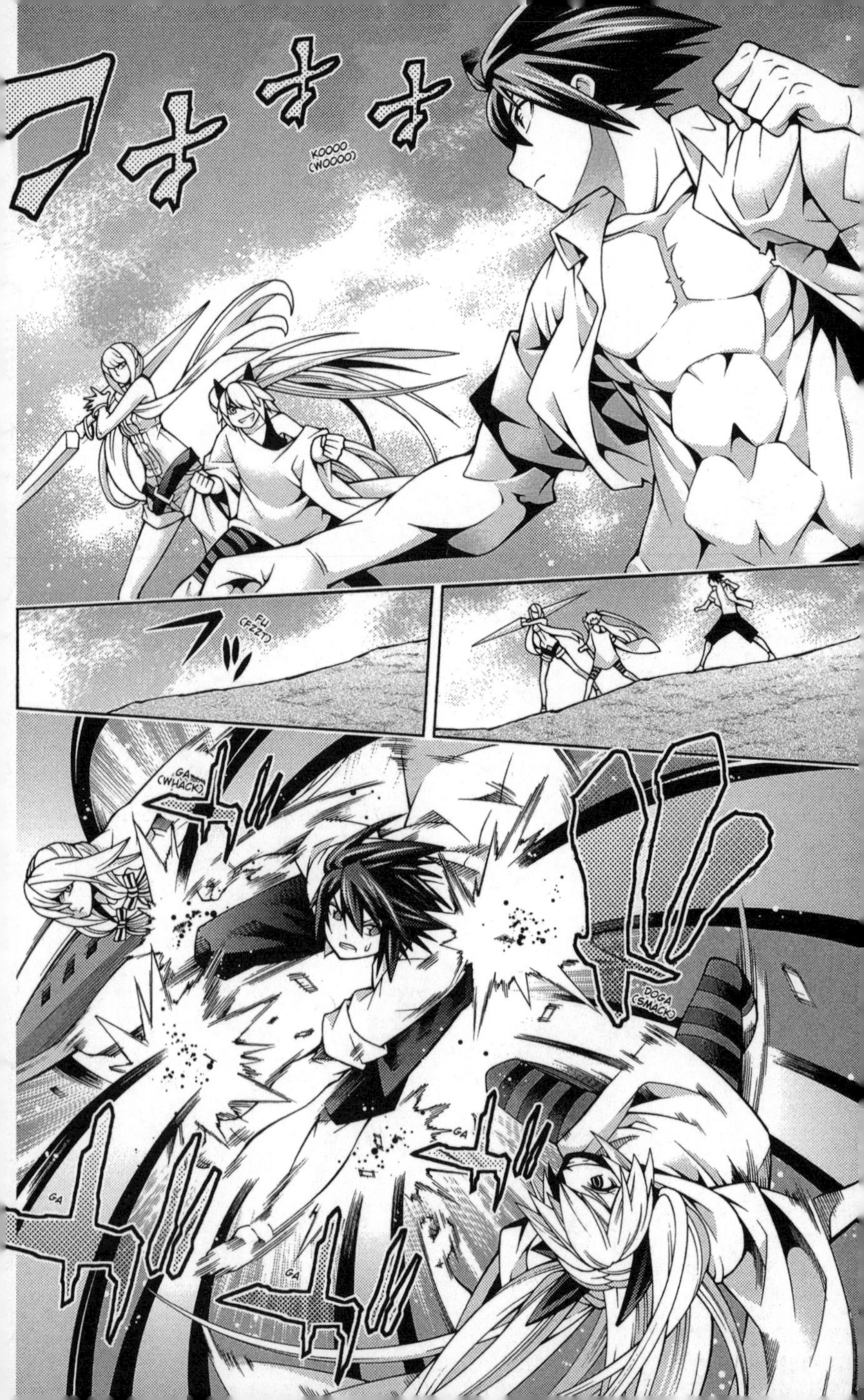
KOOOO
(WOOOO)
FU
(FZZT)
GA
(WHACK)
DOGA
(SMACK)
GA
GA
GA

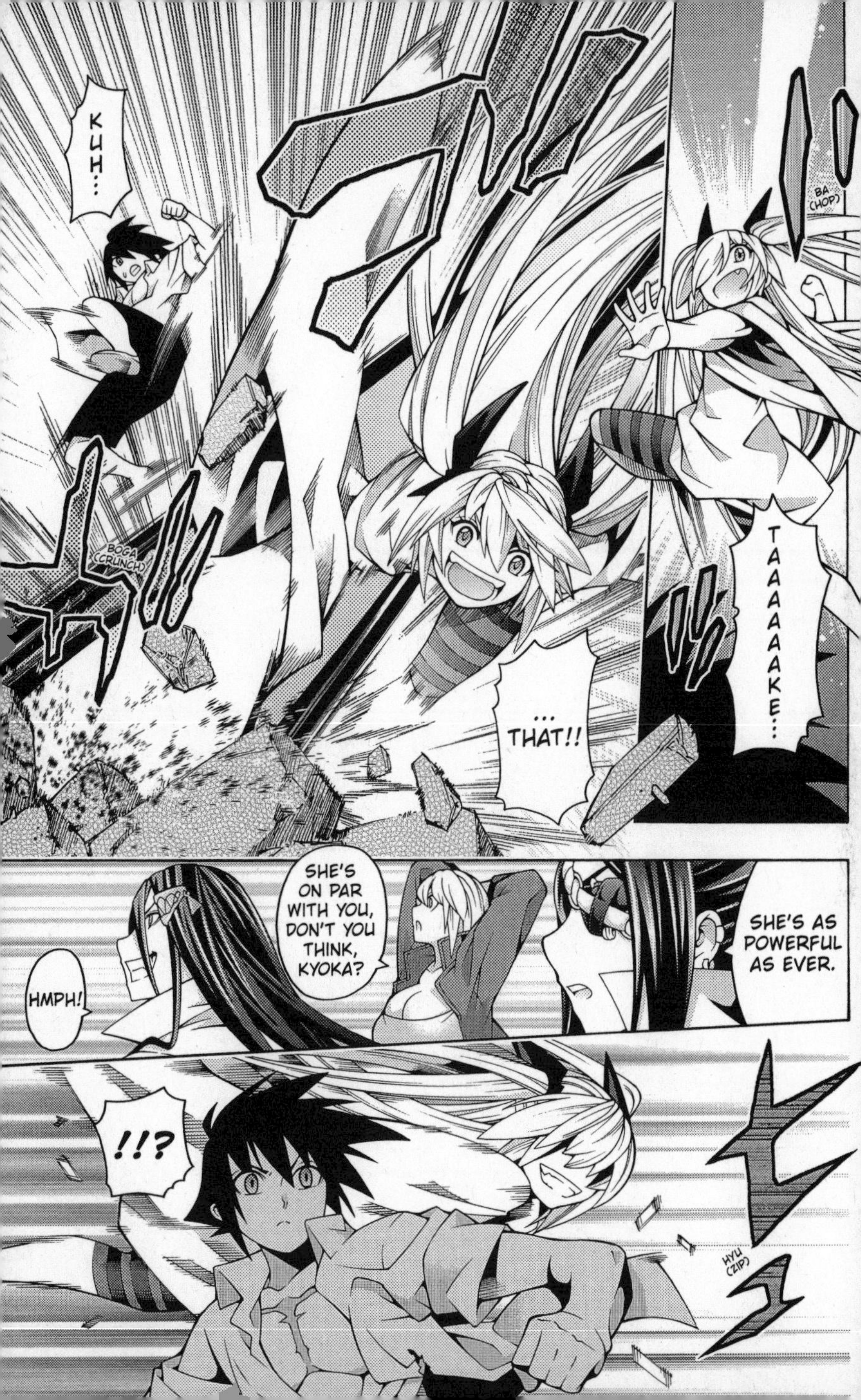
BA (HOP)
TAAAAAAKE...
...THAT!!
KUH...
BOGA (CRUNCH)
SHE'S AS POWERFUL AS EVER.
SHE'S ON PAR WITH YOU, DON'T YOU THINK, KYOKA?
HMPH!
HYU (ZIP)
!!?

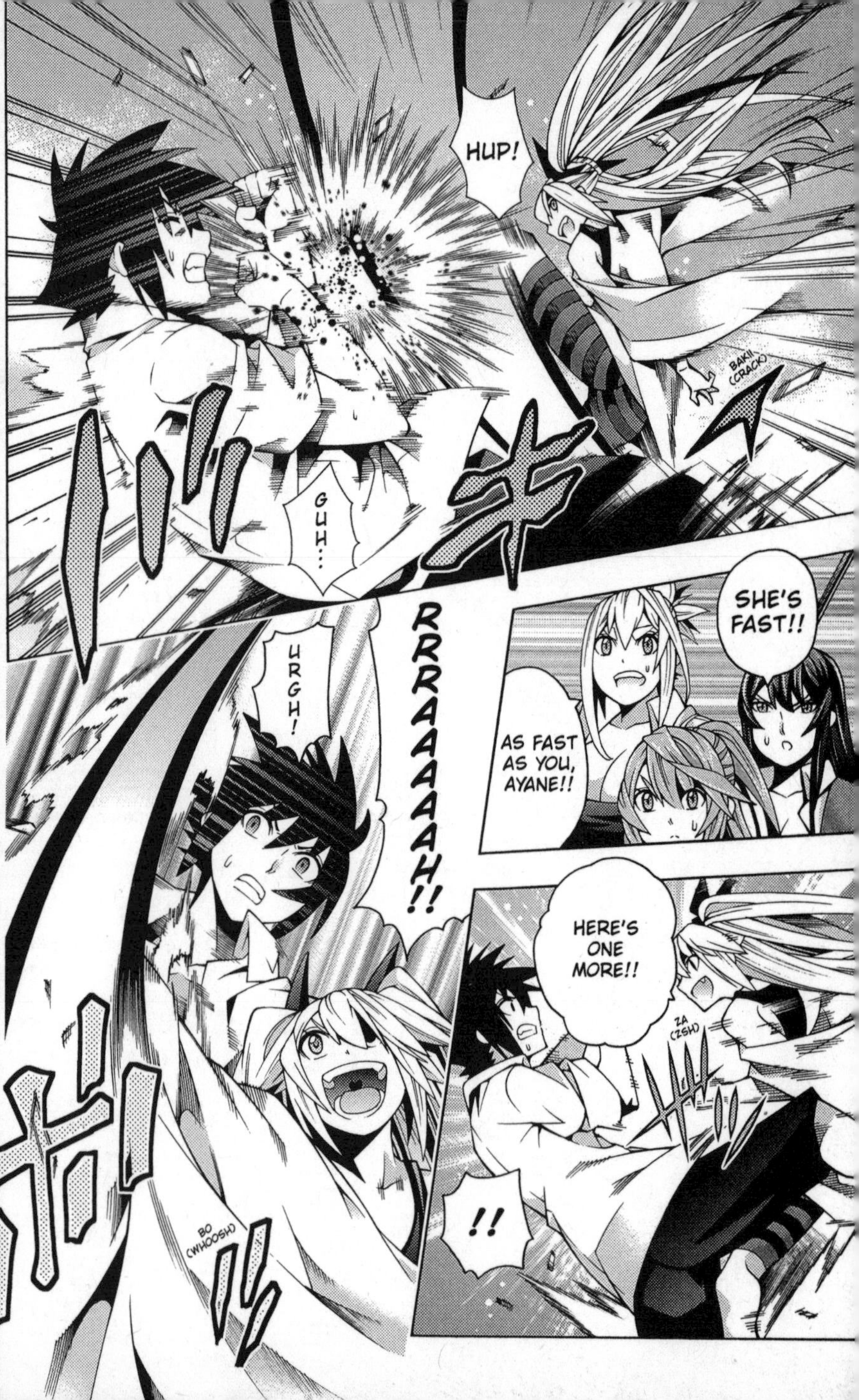
HUP!
BAKI! (CRACK)
GUH...
SHE'S FAST!!
AS FAST AS YOU, AYANE!!
HERE'S ONE MORE!!
ZA (ZSH)
!!
URGH!
RRRAAAAAAAH!!
BO (WHOOSH)

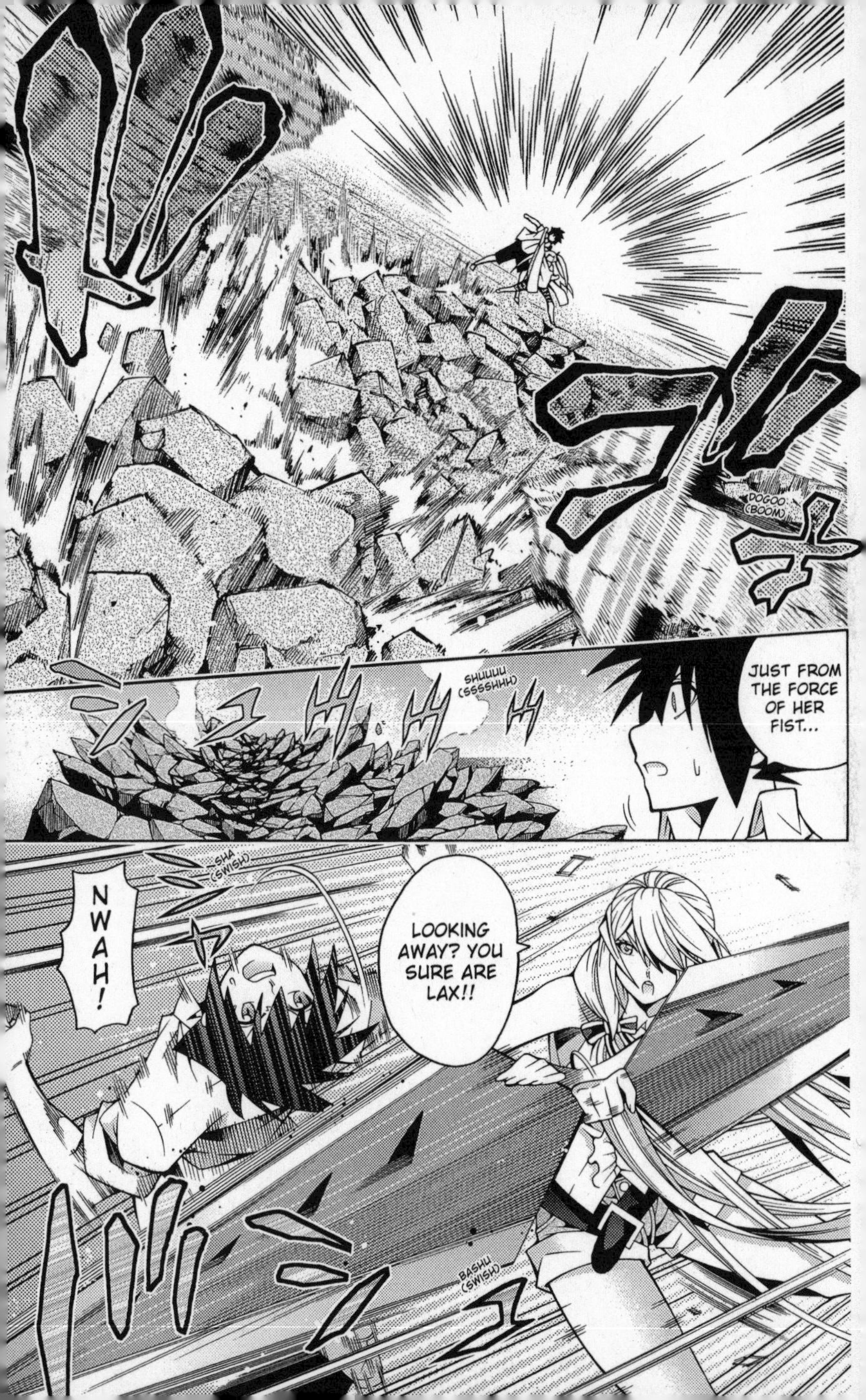
DOGOO (BOOM)
JUST FROM THE FORCE OF HER FIST...
SHUUUU (SSSSHHH)
LOOKING AWAY? YOU SURE ARE LAX!!
SHA (SWISH)
NWAH!
BASHU (SWISH)

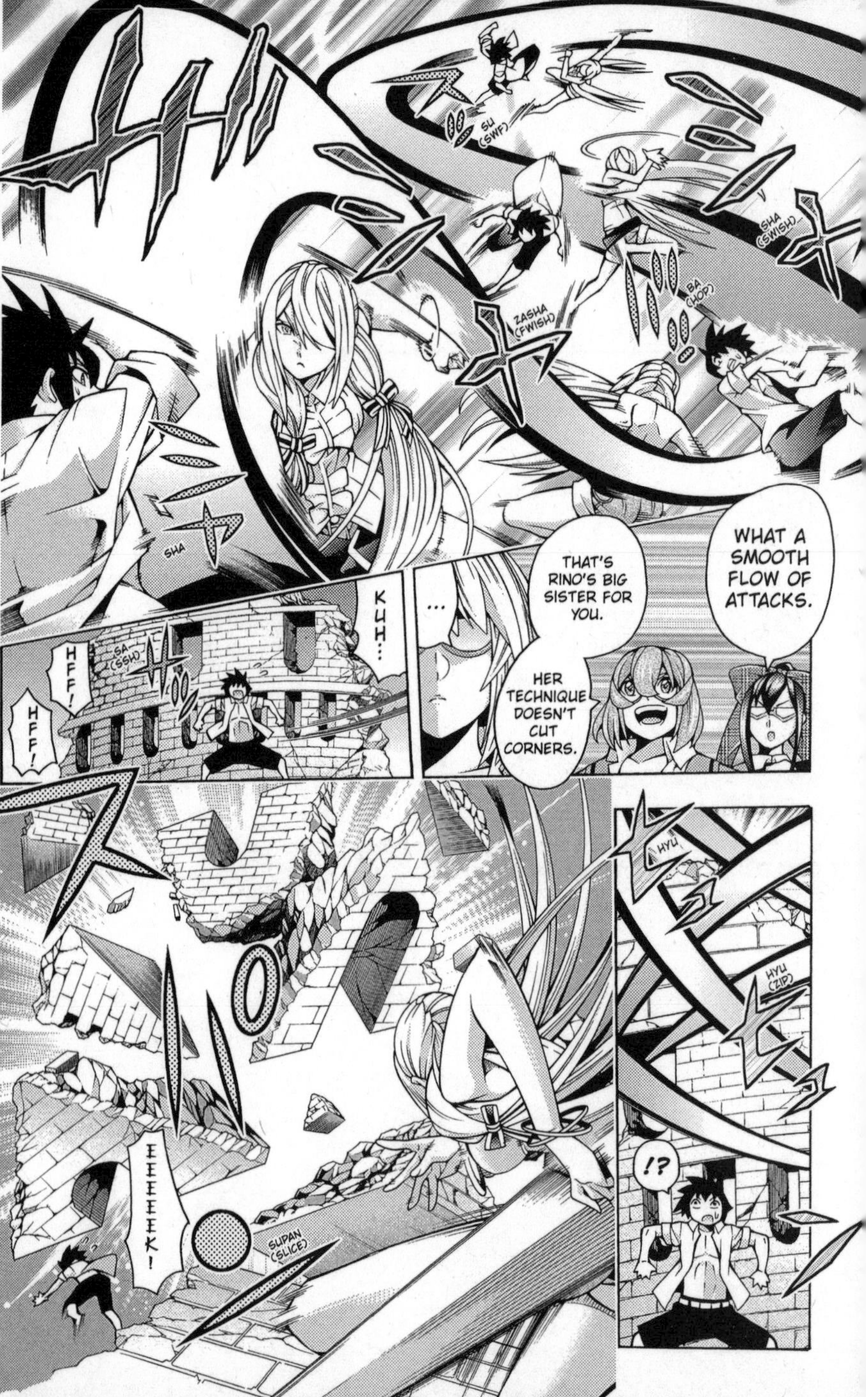
SHA (SWISH)...
BA (HOP)
SU (SWF)
ZASHA (FWISH)
SHA
WHAT A SMOOTH FLOW OF ATTACKS.
THAT'S RINO'S BIG SISTER FOR YOU.
HER TECHNIQUE DOESN'T CUT CORNERS.
...
KUH...
SA (SSH)
HFF!
HFF!
HYU
HYU (ZIP)
!?
SUPAN (SLICE)
EEEEEEK!

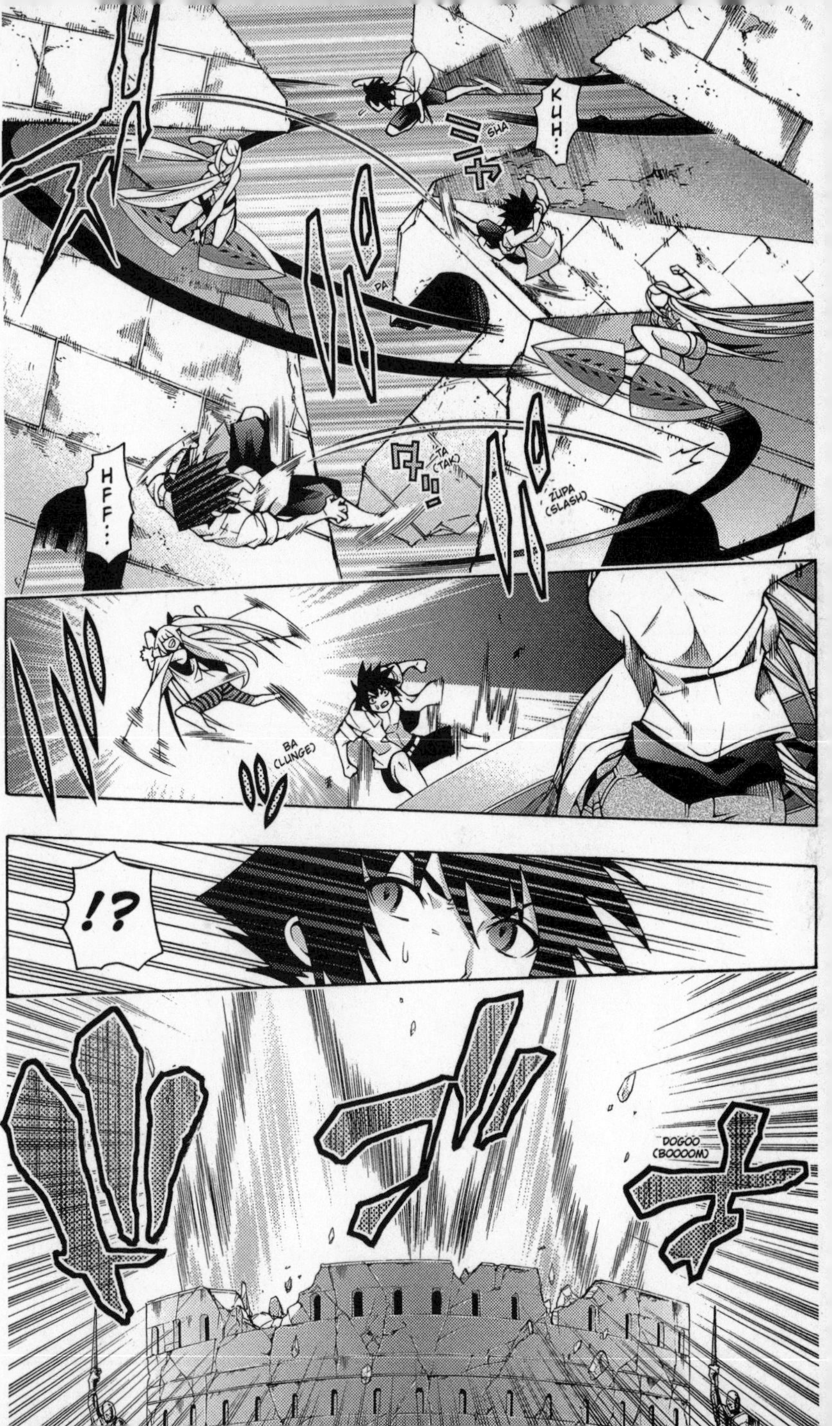
KUH...
SHA
PA
ZUPA (SLASH)
TA (TAK)
HFF...
BA (LUNGE)
!?
DOGOO (BOOOOM)

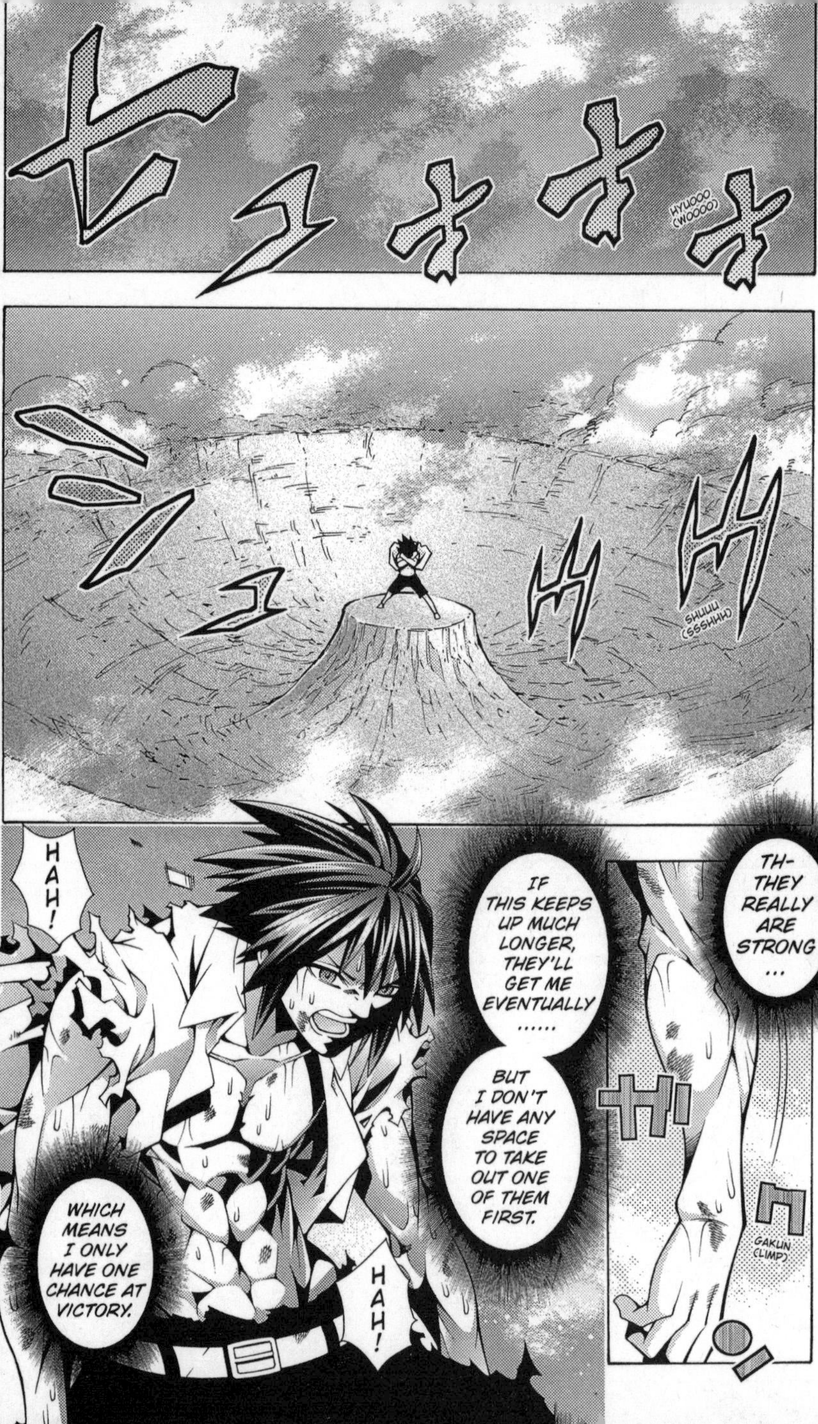
HYUOOO (WOOOO)
SHUUU (SSSHHH)
TH-THEY REALLY ARE STRONG...
GAKUN (LIMP)
HAH!
IF THIS KEEPS UP MUCH LONGER, THEY'LL GET ME EVENTUALLY......
BUT I DON'T HAVE ANY SPACE TO TAKE OUT ONE OF THEM FIRST.
WHICH MEANS I ONLY HAVE ONE CHANCE AT VICTORY.
HAH!

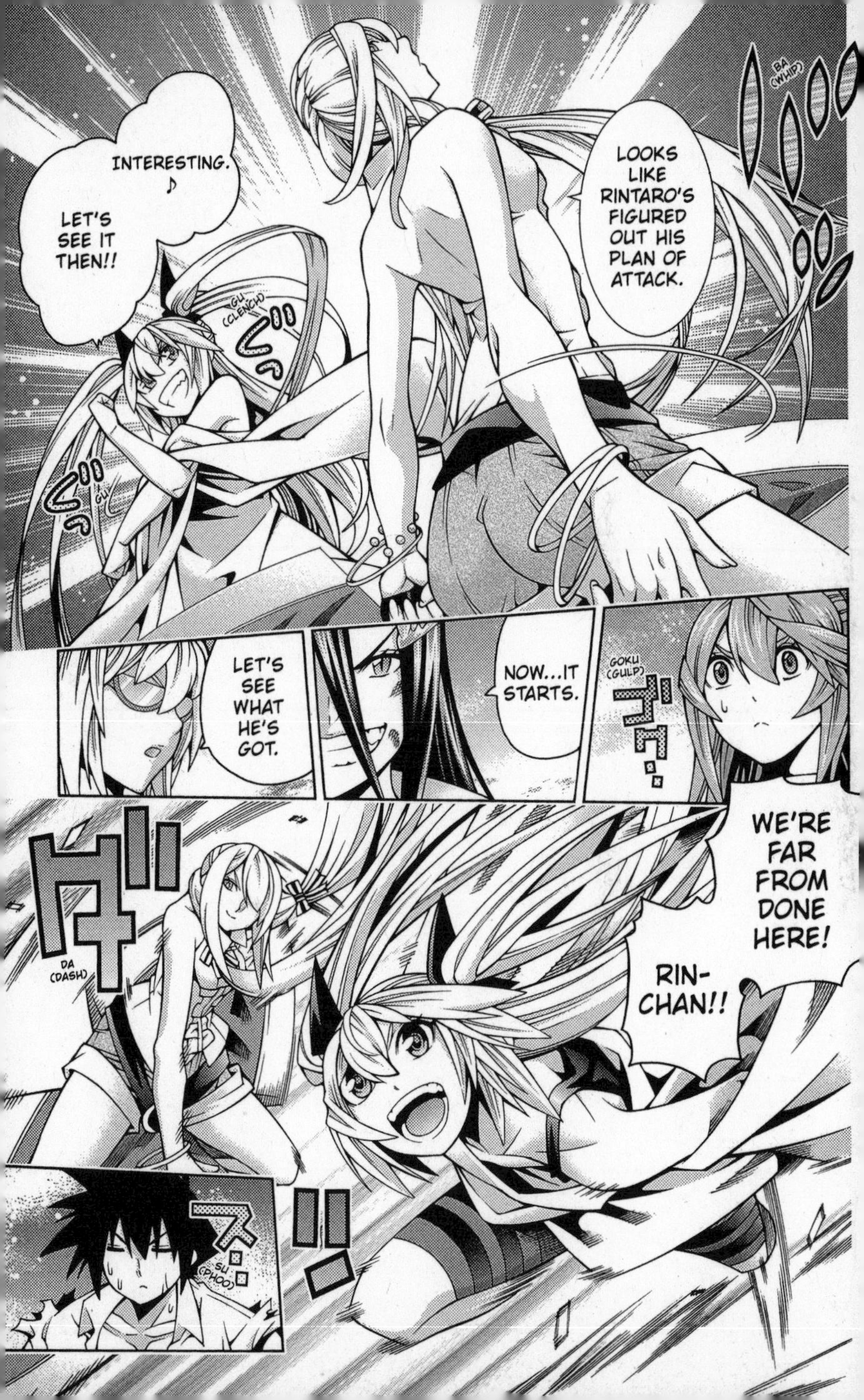
BA (WHIP)
LOOKS LIKE RINTARO'S FIGURED OUT HIS PLAN OF ATTACK.
INTERESTING. ♪
LET'S SEE IT THEN!!
GU (CLENCH)
GU
GOKU (GULP)
NOW...IT STARTS.
LET'S SEE WHAT HE'S GOT.
WE'RE FAR FROM DONE HERE!
RIN-CHAN!!
DA (DASH)
SU (PHOO)

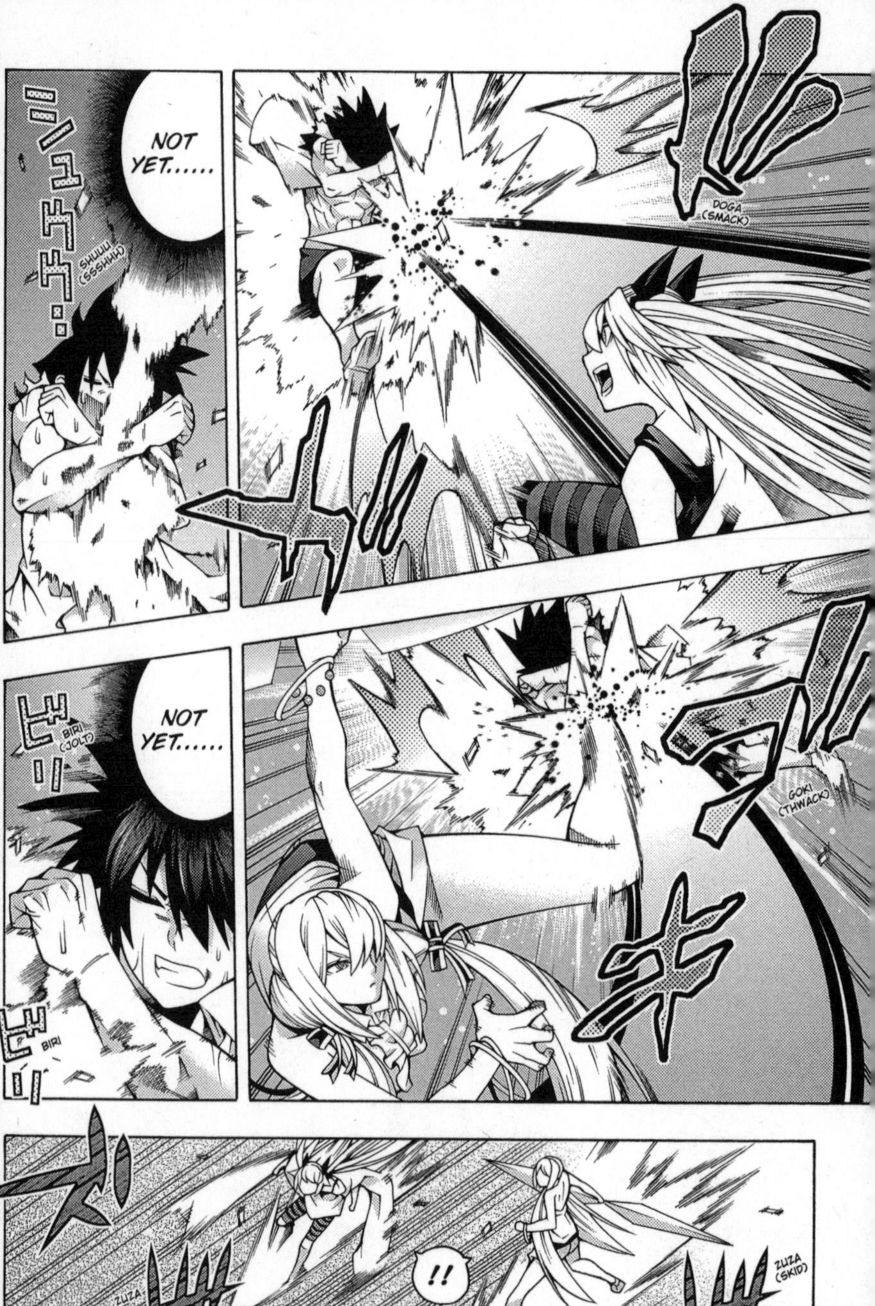
DOGA (SMACK)
NOT YET......
SHUUU (SSSHHH)
GOKI (THWACK)
NOT YET......
BIRI (JOLT)
BIRI
ZUZA (SKID)
!!
ZUZA

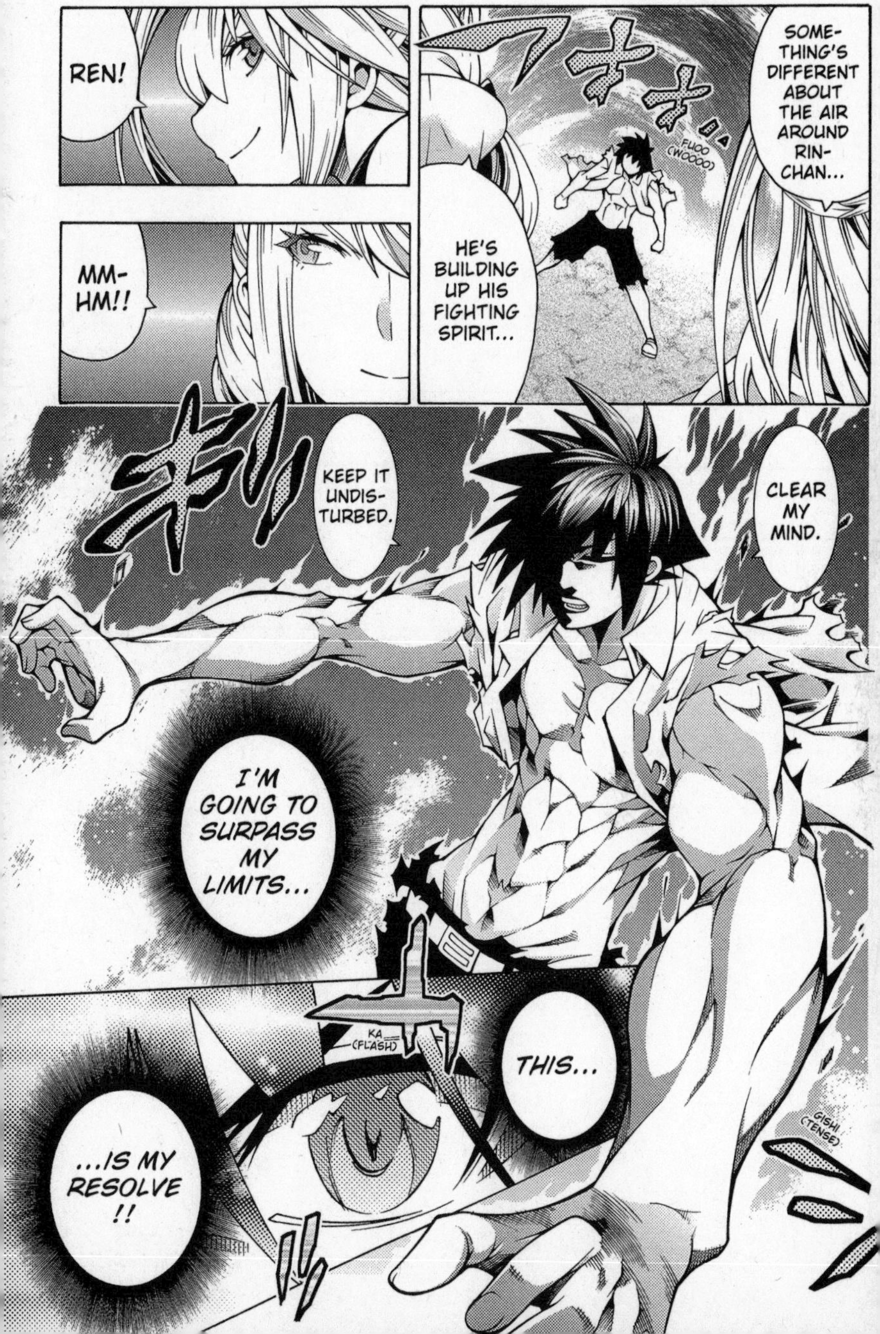
FUOO (WOOOO)
SOME-THING'S DIFFERENT ABOUT THE AIR AROUND RIN-CHAN...
HE'S BUILDING UP HIS FIGHTING SPIRIT...
REN!
MM-HM!!
CLEAR MY MIND.
KEEP IT UNDIS-TURBED.
I'M GOING TO SURPASS MY LIMITS...
GISHI (TENSE)
THIS...
KA (FLASH)
...IS MY RESOLVE!!

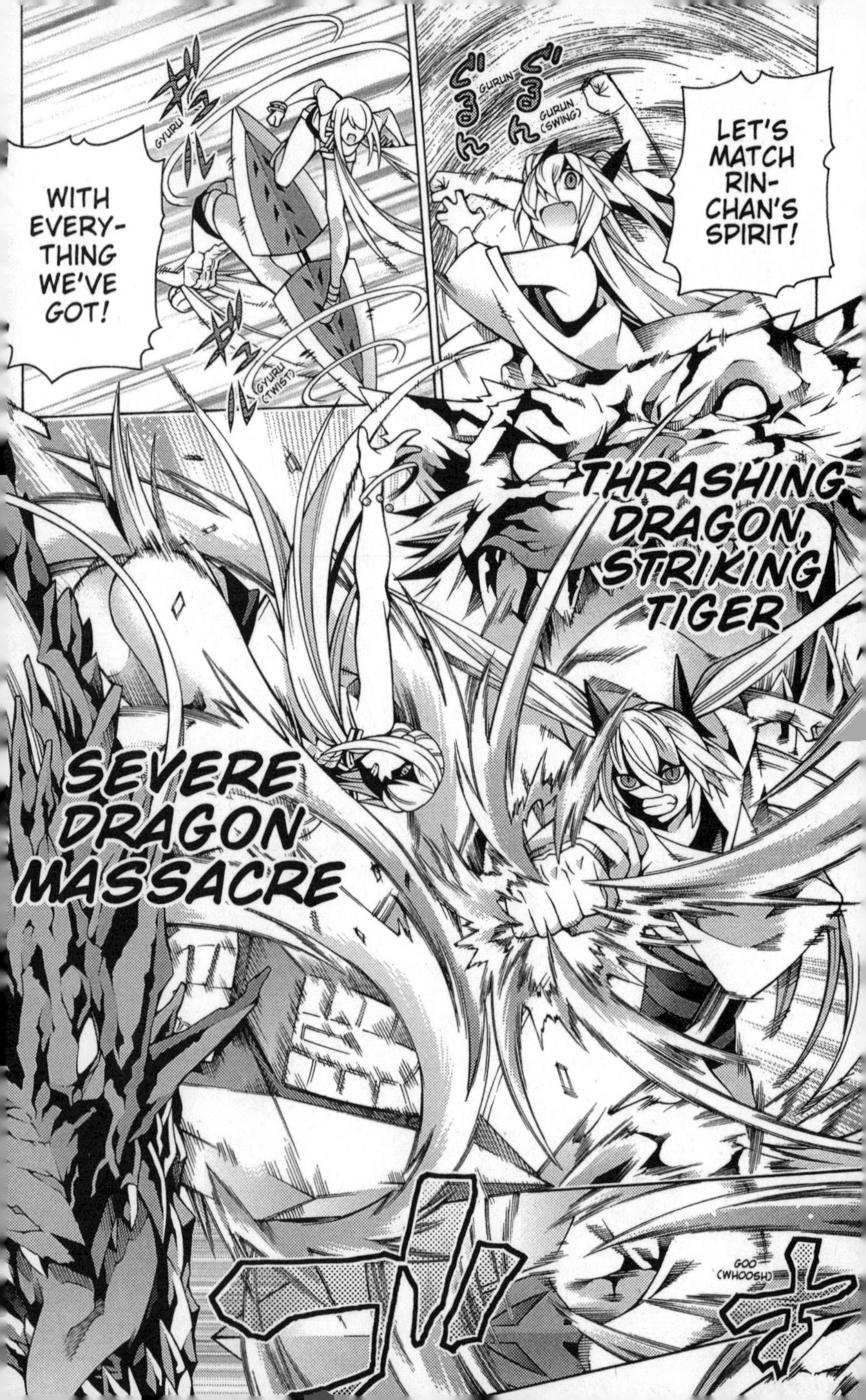
LET'S MATCH RIN-CHAN'S SPIRIT!
ぐるん
GURUN
ぐるん
GURUN (SWING)
WITH EVERY-THING WE'VE GOT!
GYURU
GYURU (TWIST)
THRASHING DRAGON, STRIKING TIGER
SEVERE DRAGON MASSACRE
GOO (WHOOSH)

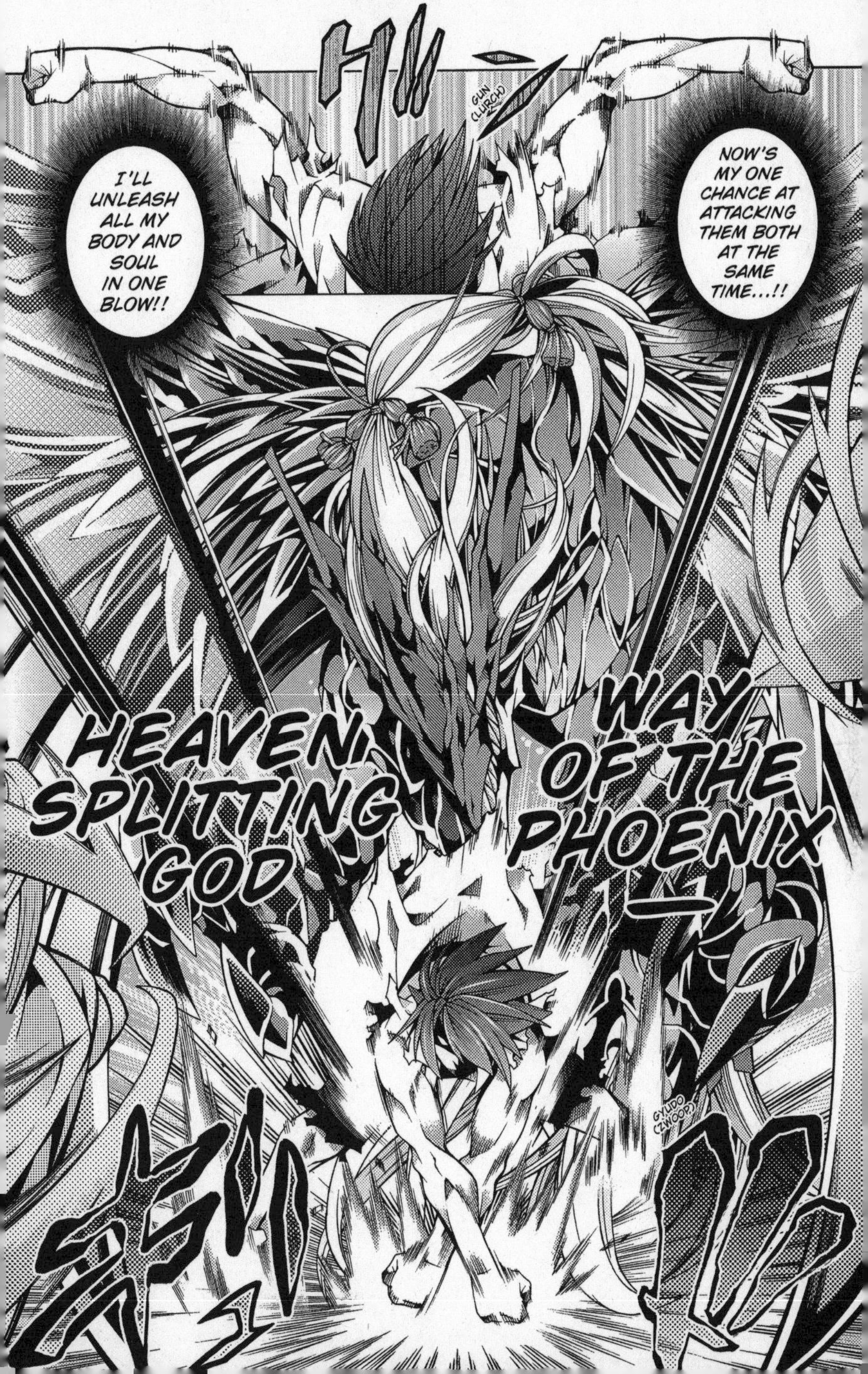
GUN (LURCH)
NOW'S MY ONE CHANCE AT ATTACKING THEM BOTH AT THE SAME TIME...!!
I'LL UNLEASH ALL MY BODY AND SOUL IN ONE BLOW!!
WAY OF THE PHOENIX
HEAVEN SPLITTING GOD
GYUDO (ZWOOP)

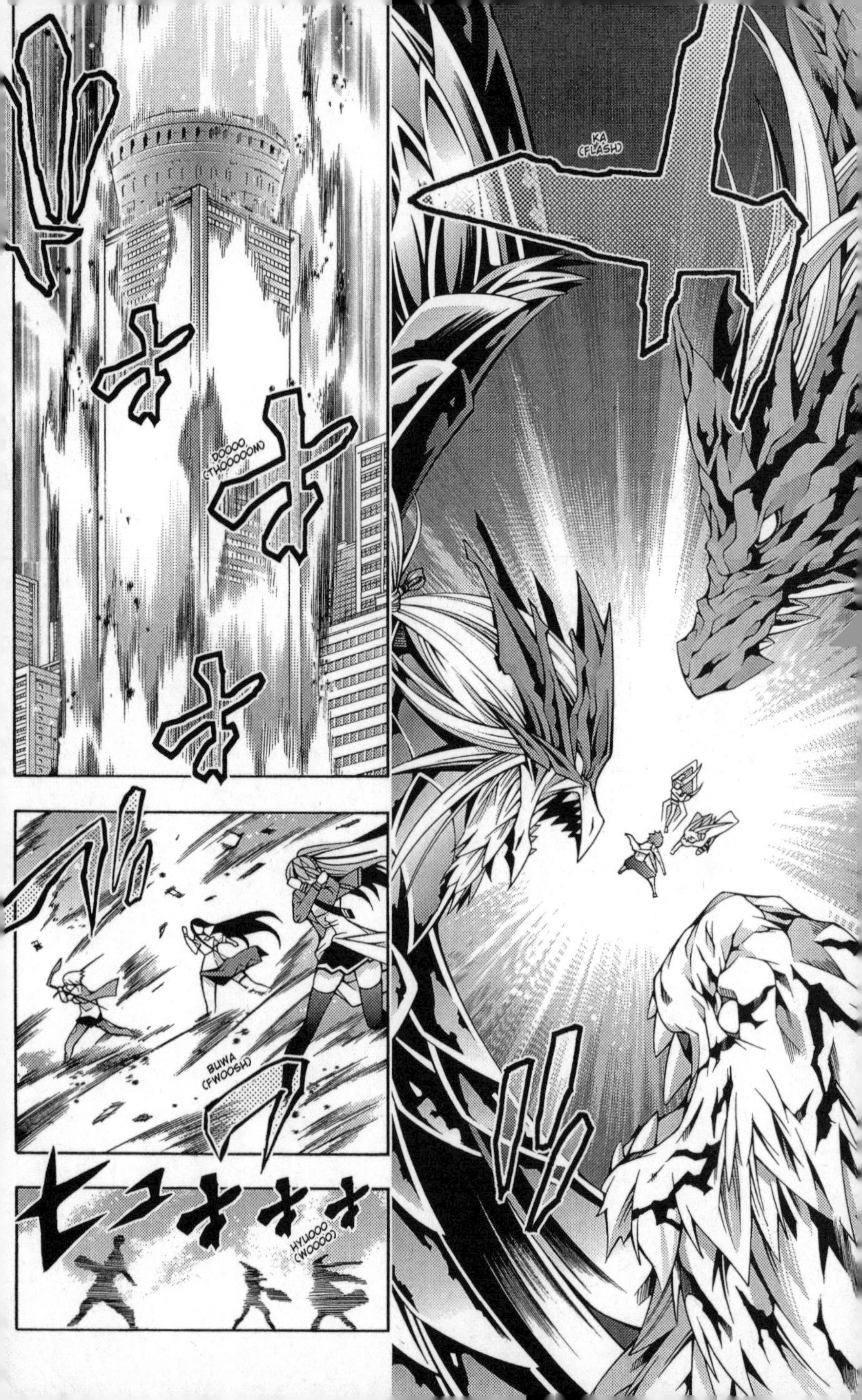
KA (FLASH)
DOOOO (THOOOOOM)
BUWA (FWOOSH)
HYUOOO (WOOOO)

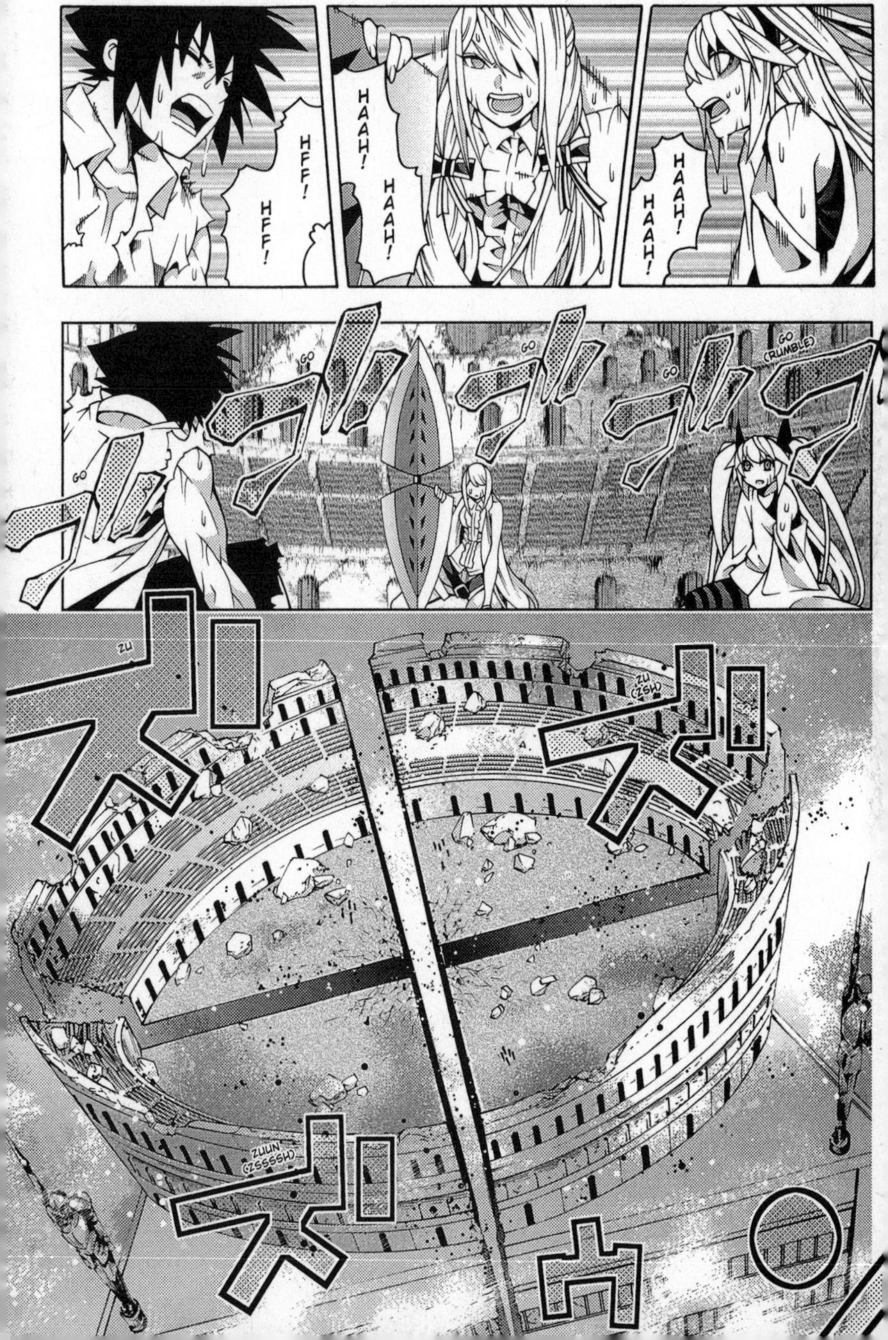
HAAAH!
HAAAH!
HAAAH!
HAAAH!
HFF!
HFF!
GO
GO
GO (RUMBLE)
GO
GO
ZU (ZSH)
ZU
ZUUN (ZSSSSH)

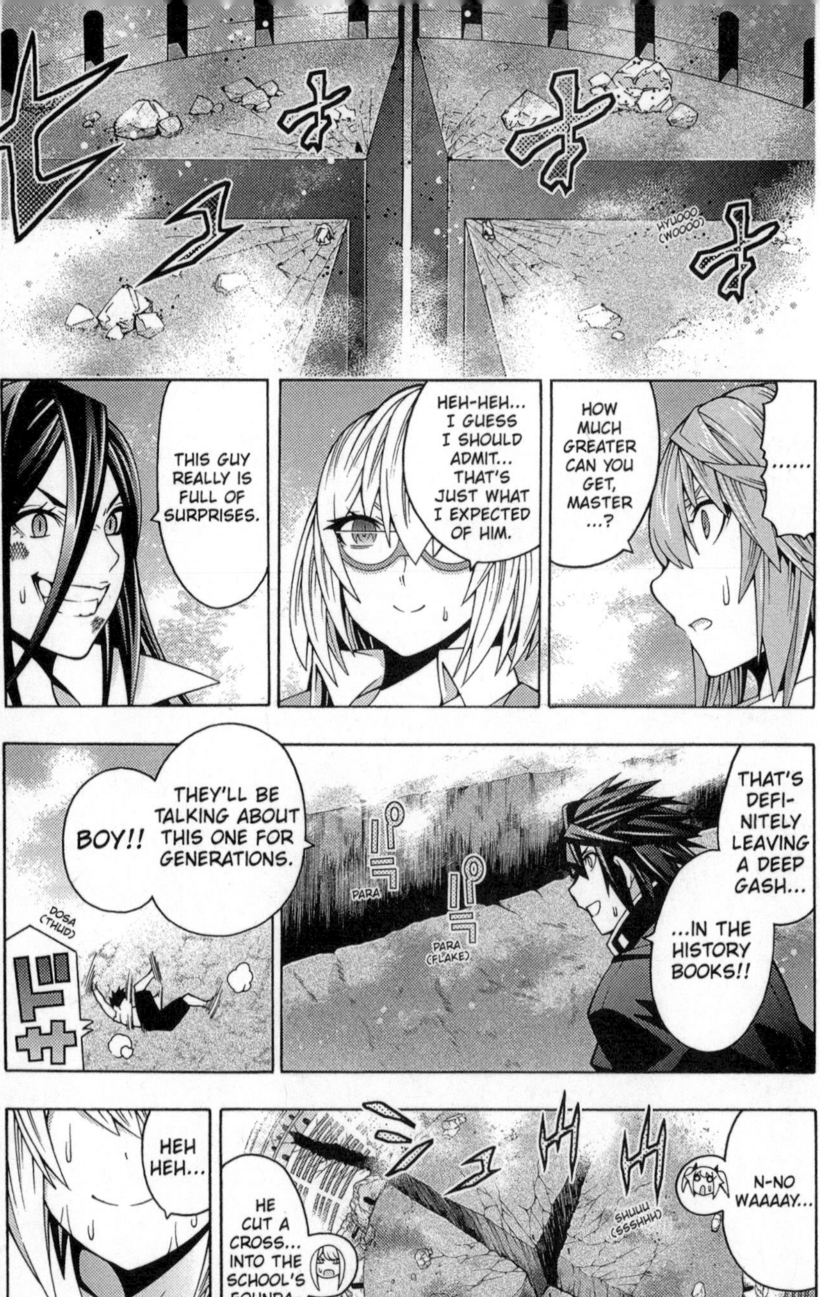
HYUOOO (WOOOO)
......
HOW MUCH GREATER CAN YOU GET, MASTER ...?
HEH-HEH... I GUESS I SHOULD ADMIT... THAT'S JUST WHAT I EXPECTED OF HIM.
THIS GUY REALLY IS FULL OF SURPRISES.
THAT'S DEFINITELY LEAVING A DEEP GASH...
...IN THE HISTORY BOOKS!!
PARA
PARA (FLAKE)
BOY!!
THEY'LL BE TALKING ABOUT THIS ONE FOR GENERATIONS.
DOSA (THUD)
N-NO WAAAAY...
SHUUU (SSSHHH)
HE CUT A CROSS... INTO THE SCHOOL'S FOUNDATION!?
HEH HEH...

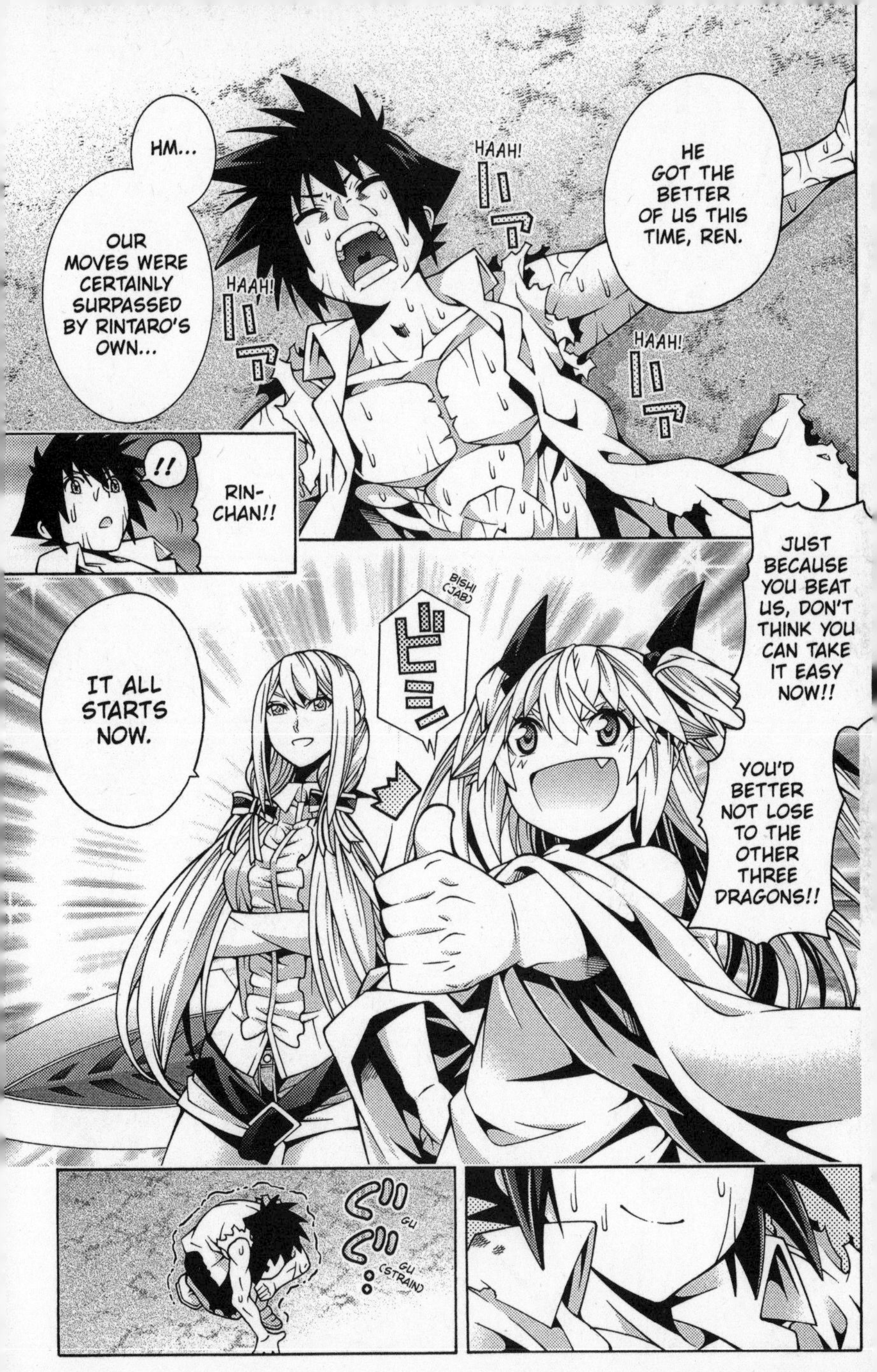
HE GOT THE BETTER OF US THIS TIME, REN.
HAAH!
HAAH!
HAAH!
HM...
OUR MOVES WERE CERTAINLY SURPASSED BY RINTARO'S OWN...
!!
RIN-CHAN!!
JUST BECAUSE YOU BEAT US, DON'T THINK YOU CAN TAKE IT EASY NOW!!
YOU'D BETTER NOT LOSE TO THE OTHER THREE DRAGONS!!
BISHI (JAB)
IT ALL STARTS NOW.
GU
GU (STRAIN)

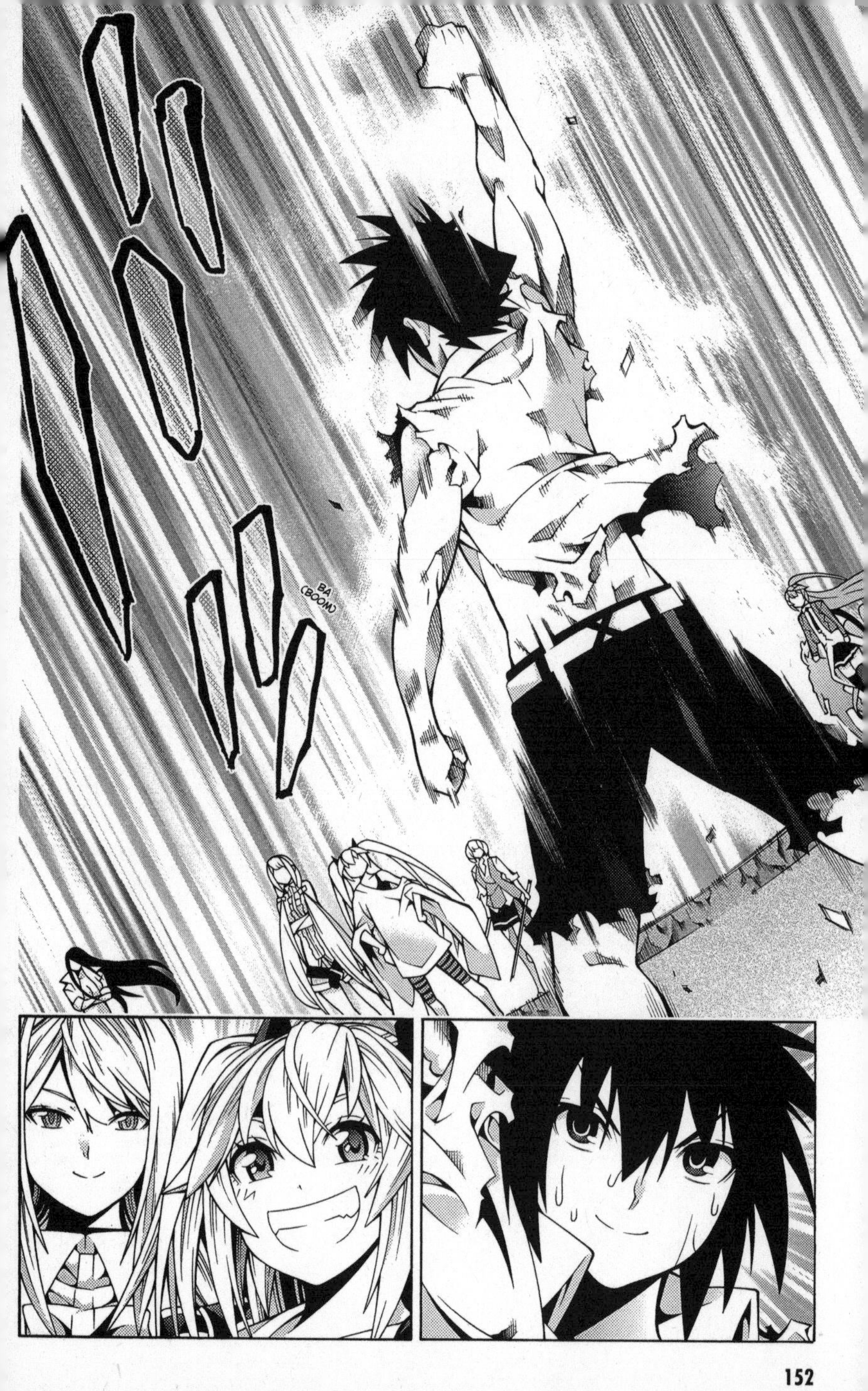
BA
(BOOM)

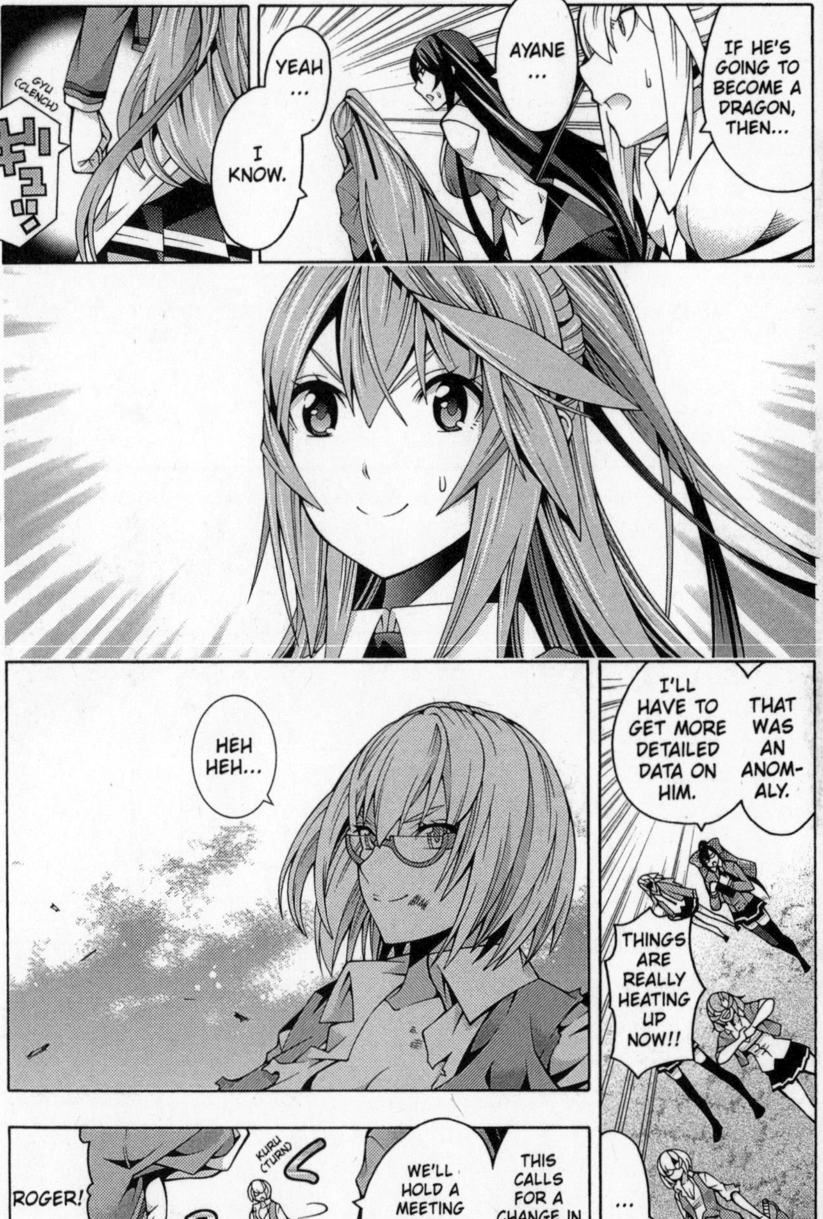
IF HE'S GOING TO BECOME A DRAGON, THEN...
AYANE ...
YEAH ...
I KNOW.
GYU (CLENCH)
THAT WAS AN ANOMALY.
I'LL HAVE TO GET MORE DETAILED DATA ON HIM.
THINGS ARE REALLY HEATING UP NOW!!
...
HEH HEH...
THIS CALLS FOR A CHANGE IN STRATEGY.
WE'LL HOLD A MEETING IN TEN MINUTES.
KURU (TURN)
ROGER!

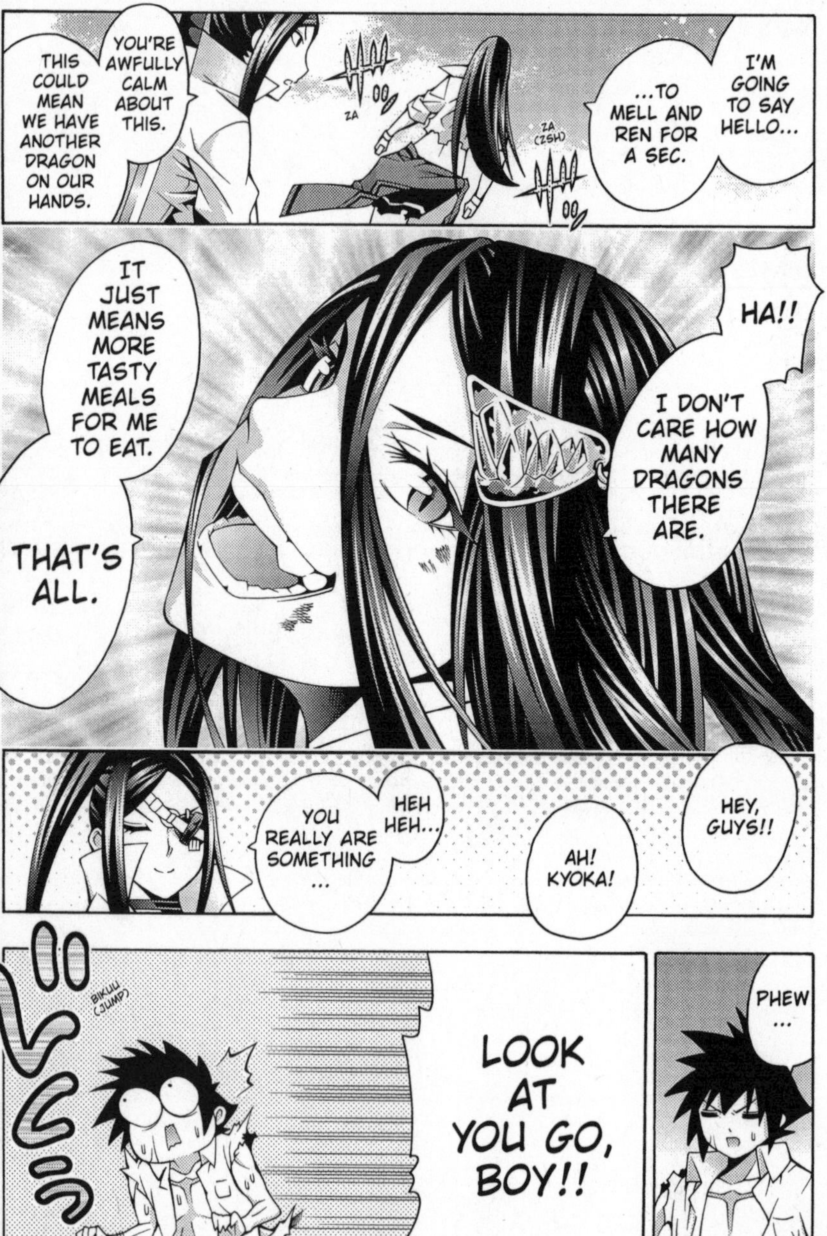
I'M GOING TO SAY HELLO...
...TO MELL AND REN FOR A SEC.
ZA (ZSH)
ZA
YOU'RE AWFULLY CALM ABOUT THIS.
THIS COULD MEAN WE HAVE ANOTHER DRAGON ON OUR HANDS.
HA!!
I DON'T CARE HOW MANY DRAGONS THERE ARE.
IT JUST MEANS MORE TASTY MEALS FOR ME TO EAT.
THAT'S ALL.
HEY, GUYS!!
AH! KYOKA!
HEH HEH...
YOU REALLY ARE SOMETHING...
PHEW...
LOOK AT YOU GO, BOY!!
BIKUU (JUMP)

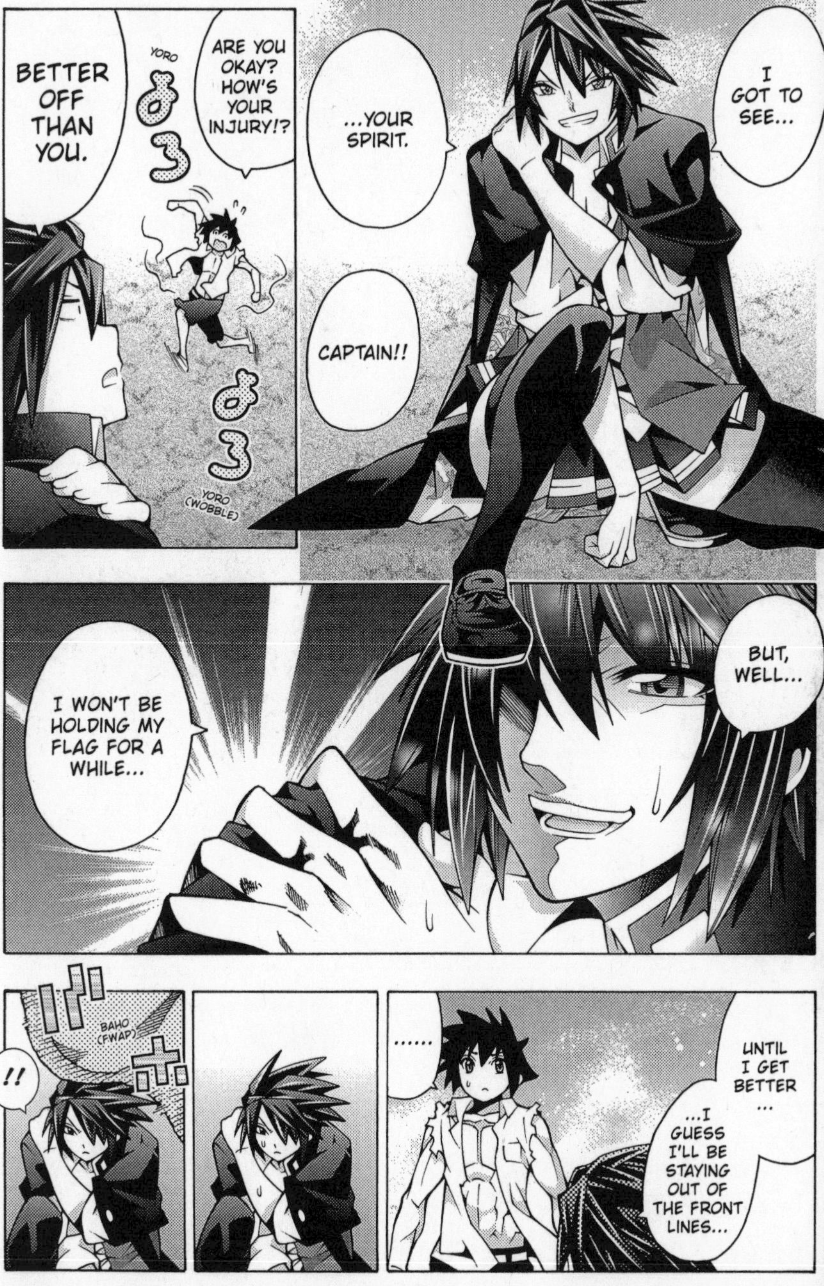
I GOT TO SEE...
...YOUR SPIRIT.
CAPTAIN!!
ARE YOU OKAY? HOW'S YOUR INJURY!?
YORO
YORO (WOBBLE)
BETTER OFF THAN YOU.
BUT, WELL...
I WON'T BE HOLDING MY FLAG FOR A WHILE...
UNTIL I GET BETTER...
...I GUESS I'LL BE STAYING OUT OF THE FRONT LINES...
......
BAHO (FWAP)
!!

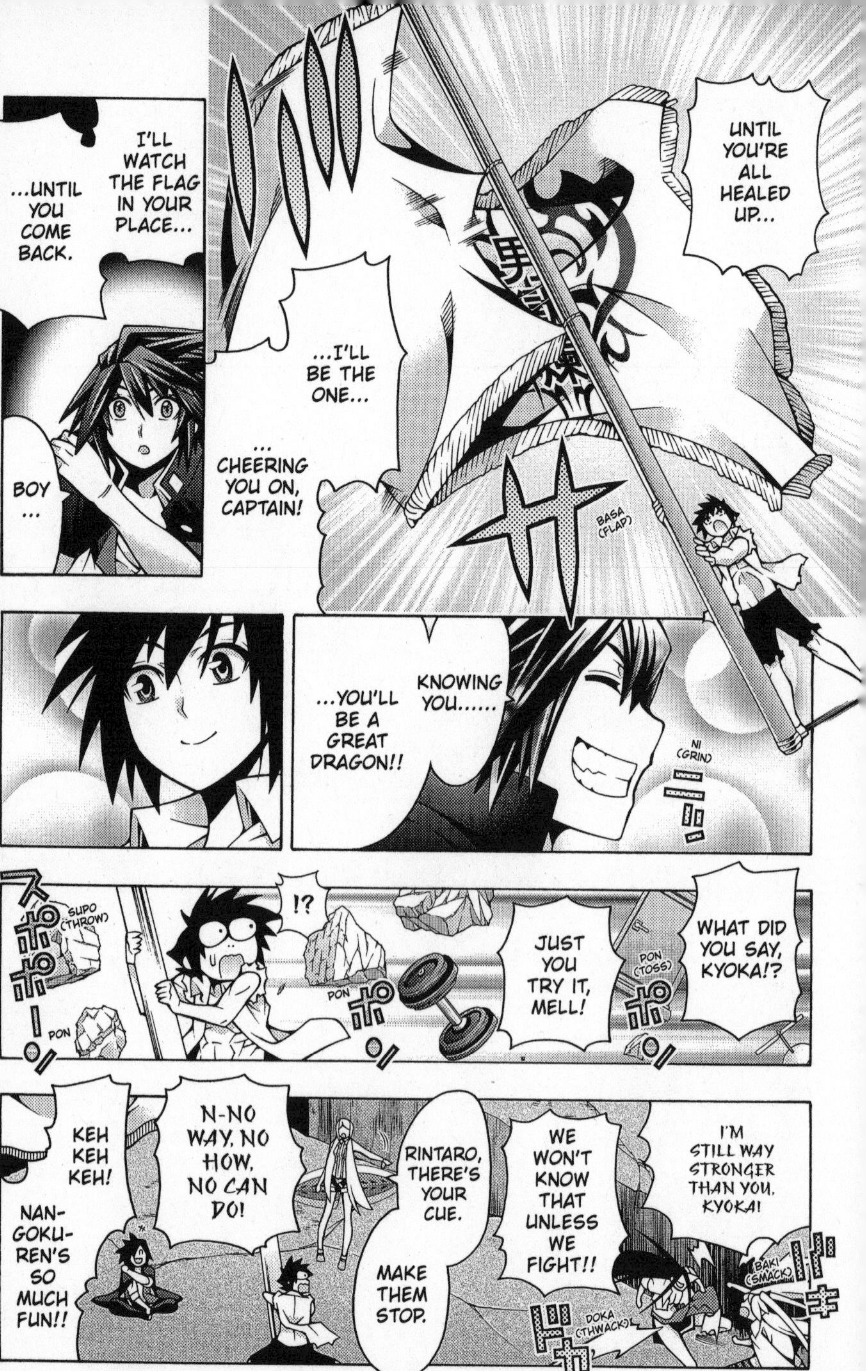
UNTIL YOU'RE ALL HEALED UP...
...I'LL BE THE ONE...
...CHEERING YOU ON, CAPTAIN!
BASA (FLAP)
I'LL WATCH THE FLAG IN YOUR PLACE...
...UNTIL YOU COME BACK.
BOY ...
KNOWING YOU......
...YOU'LL BE A GREAT DRAGON!!
NI (GRIN)
WHAT DID YOU SAY, KYOKA!?
PON (TOSS)
JUST YOU TRY IT, MELL!
PON
!?
SUPO (THROW)
PON
I'M STILL WAY STRONGER THAN YOU, KYOKA!
BAKI (SMACK)
DOKA (THWACK)
WE WON'T KNOW THAT UNLESS WE FIGHT!!
RINTARO, THERE'S YOUR CUE.
MAKE THEM STOP.
N-NO WAY, NO HOW, NO CAN DO!
KEH KEH KEH!
NAN-GOKU-REN'S SO MUCH FUN!!

TO BE CONTINUED

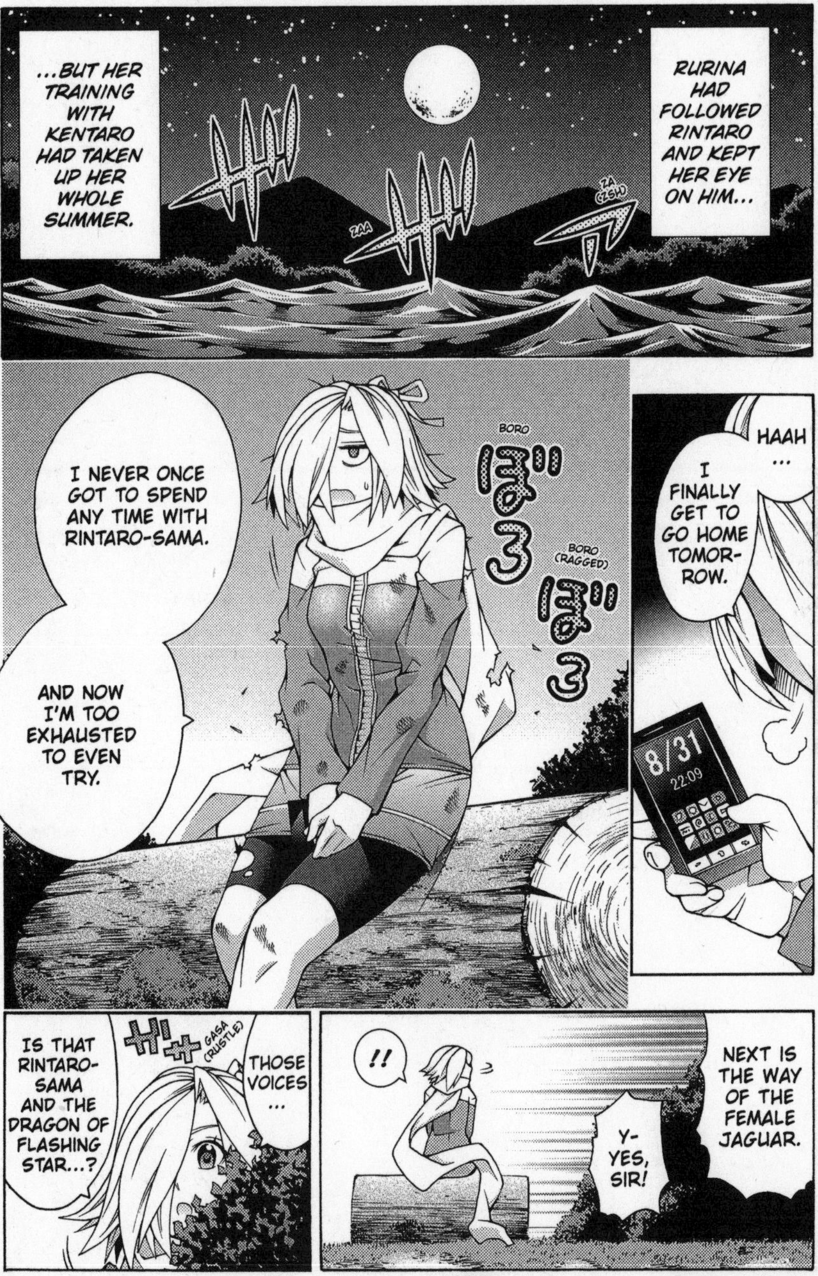
RURINA HAD FOLLOWED RINTARO AND KEPT HER EYE ON HIM...
ZA (ZSH)
ZAA
...BUT HER TRAINING WITH KENTARO HAD TAKEN UP HER WHOLE SUMMER.
HAAH...
I FINALLY GET TO GO HOME TOMORROW.
8/31
22:09
BORO
ぼろ
BORO (RAGGED)
ぼろ
I NEVER ONCE GOT TO SPEND ANY TIME WITH RINTARO-SAMA.
AND NOW I'M TOO EXHAUSTED TO EVEN TRY.
NEXT IS THE WAY OF THE FEMALE JAGUAR.
Y-YES, SIR!
!!
THOSE VOICES...
GASA (RUSTLE)
IS THAT RINTARO-SAMA AND THE DRAGON OF FLASHING STAR...?

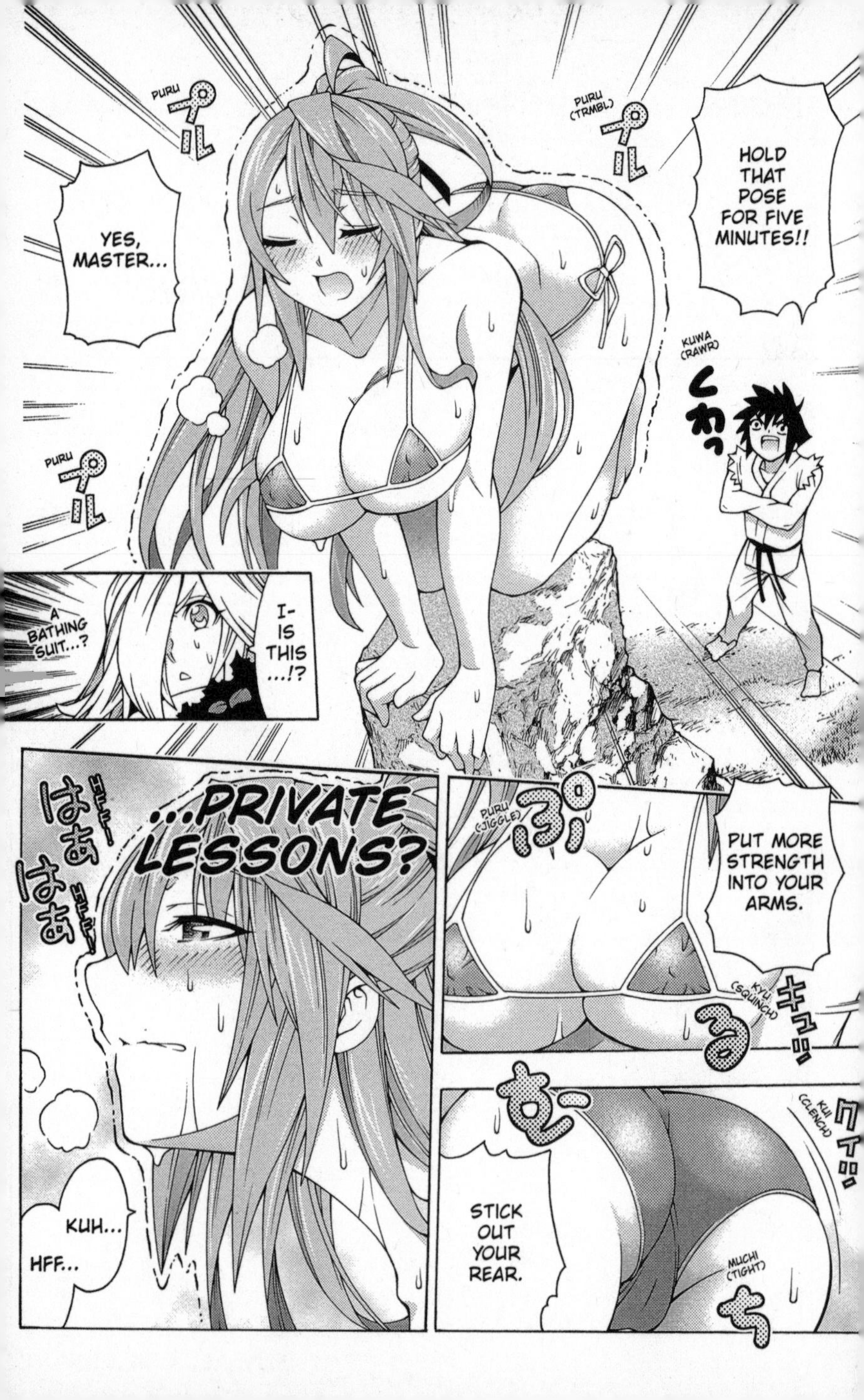
HOLD THAT POSE FOR FIVE MINUTES!!
PURU (TRMBL)
KUWA (RAWR)
PURU
YES, MASTER...
PURU
I- IS THIS ...!?
A BATHING SUIT...?
PUT MORE STRENGTH INTO YOUR ARMS.
PURU (JIGGLE)
KYU (SQUINCH)
KUI (CLENCH)
STICK OUT YOUR REAR.
MUCHI (TIGHT)
...PRIVATE LESSONS?
HFF- HFF-
KUH...
HFF...

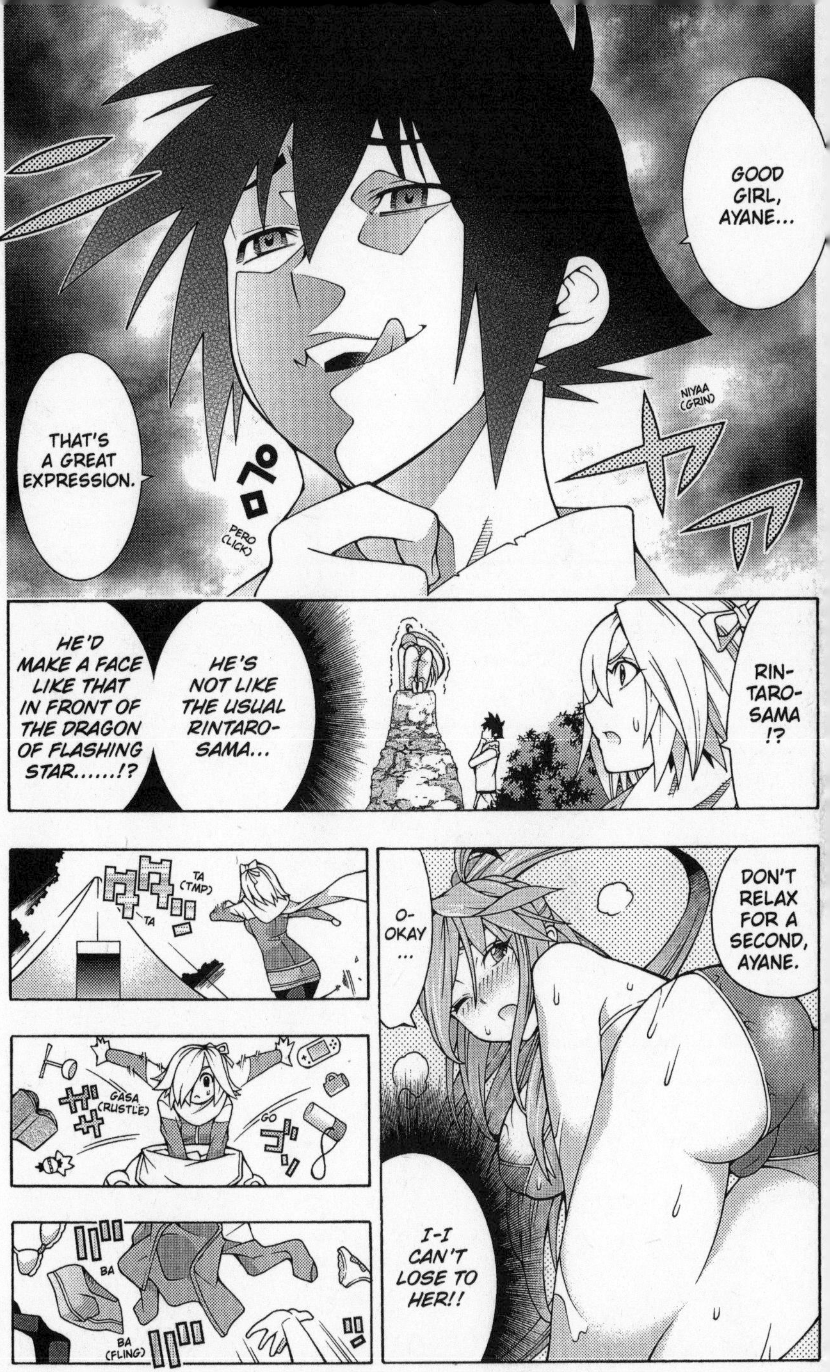
GOOD GIRL, AYANE...
NIYAA (GRIN)
THAT'S A GREAT EXPRESSION.
PERO (LICK)
RIN-TARO-SAMA!?
HE'S NOT LIKE THE USUAL RINTARO-SAMA...
HE'D MAKE A FACE LIKE THAT IN FRONT OF THE DRAGON OF FLASHING STAR......!?
DON'T RELAX FOR A SECOND, AYANE.
O-OKAY...
I-I CAN'T LOSE TO HER!!
TA (TMP)
TA
GASA (RUSTLE)
GO
BA
BA (FLING)

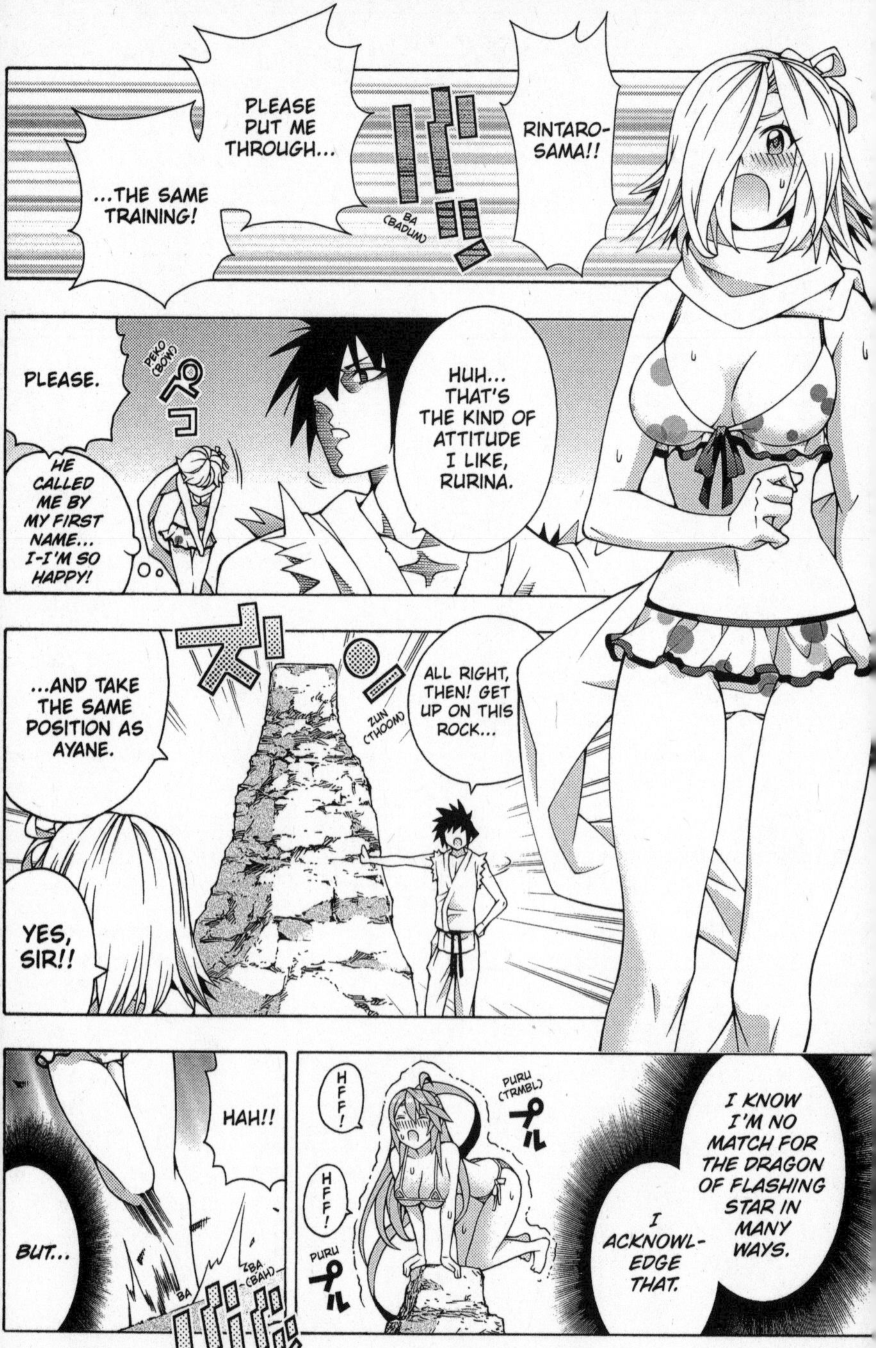
RINTARO-SAMA!!
BA (BADUM)
PLEASE PUT ME THROUGH...
...THE SAME TRAINING!
HUH... THAT'S THE KIND OF ATTITUDE I LIKE, RURINA.
PEKO (BOW)
PLEASE.
HE CALLED ME BY MY FIRST NAME... I-I'M SO HAPPY!
ALL RIGHT, THEN! GET UP ON THIS ROCK...
ZUN (THOOM)
...AND TAKE THE SAME POSITION AS AYANE.
YES, SIR!!
I KNOW I'M NO MATCH FOR THE DRAGON OF FLASHING STAR IN MANY WAYS.
I ACKNOWL-EDGE THAT.
PURU (TRMBL)
HFF!
HFF!
PURU
HAH!!
BA (BAH)
BA
BUT...

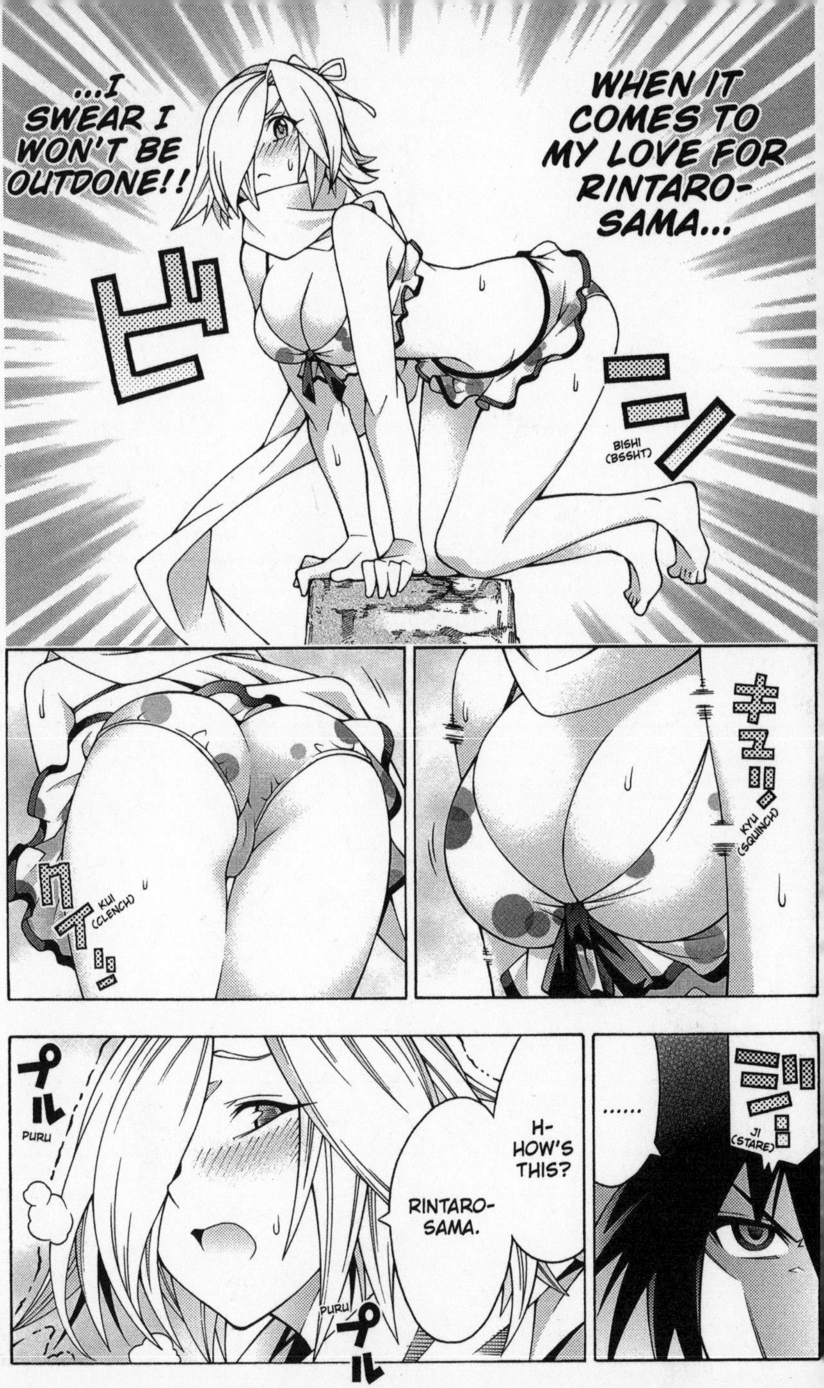
WHEN IT COMES TO MY LOVE FOR RINTARO-SAMA...
...I SWEAR I WON'T BE OUTDONE!!
BISHI (BSSHT)
KYU (SQUINCH)
KUI (CLENCH)
......
JI (STARE)
H-HOW'S THIS?
RINTARO-SAMA.
PURU
PURU

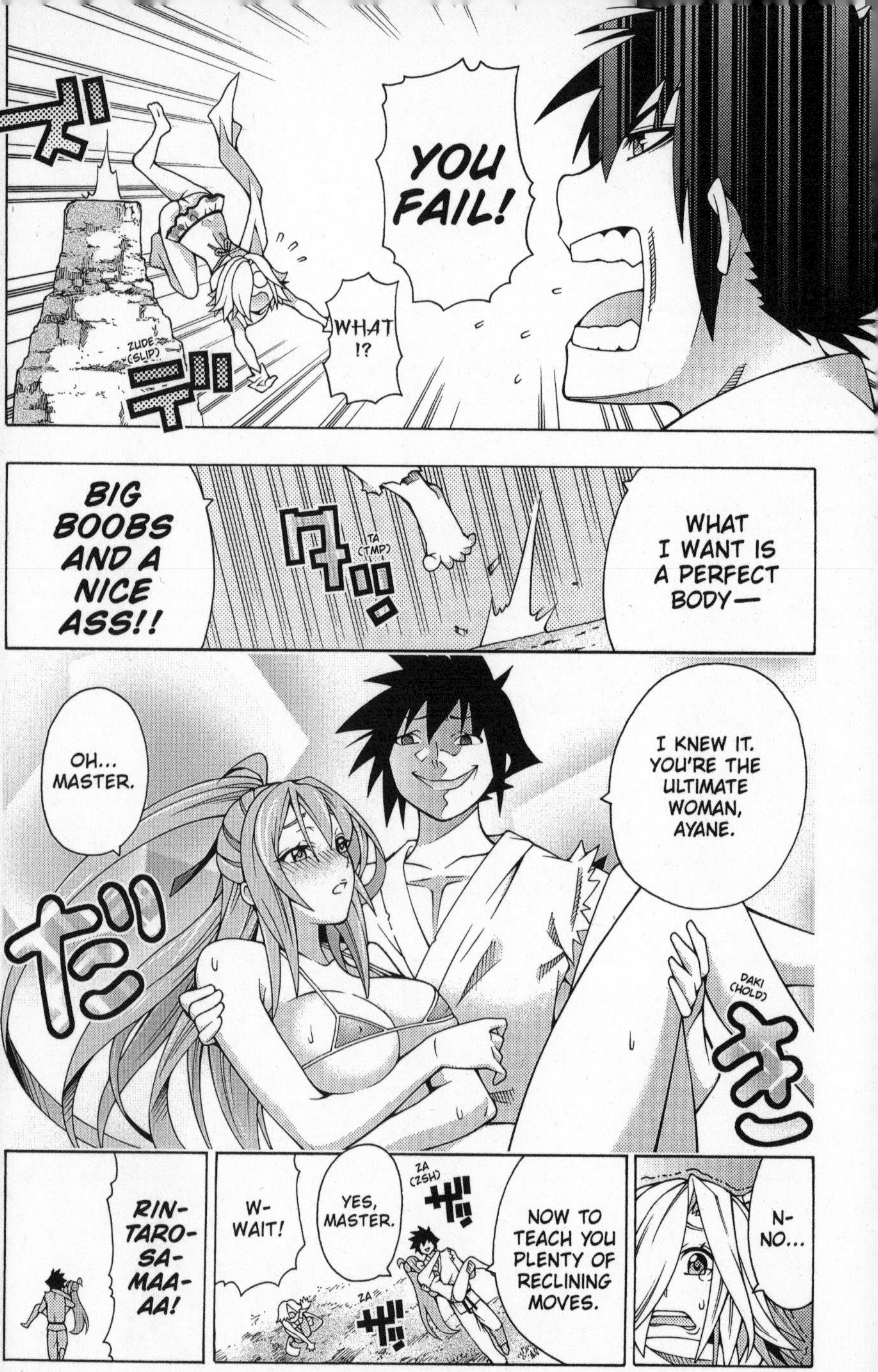
YOU FAIL!
WHAT!?
ZUDE (SLIP)
WHAT I WANT IS A PERFECT BODY—
TA (TMP)
BIG BOOBS AND A NICE ASS!!
I KNEW IT. YOU'RE THE ULTIMATE WOMAN, AYANE.
DAKI (HOLD)
OH... MASTER.
N-NO...
NOW TO TEACH YOU PLENTY OF RECLINING MOVES.
ZA (ZSH)
YES, MASTER.
ZA
W-WAIT!
RIN-TARO-SAMAAAA!

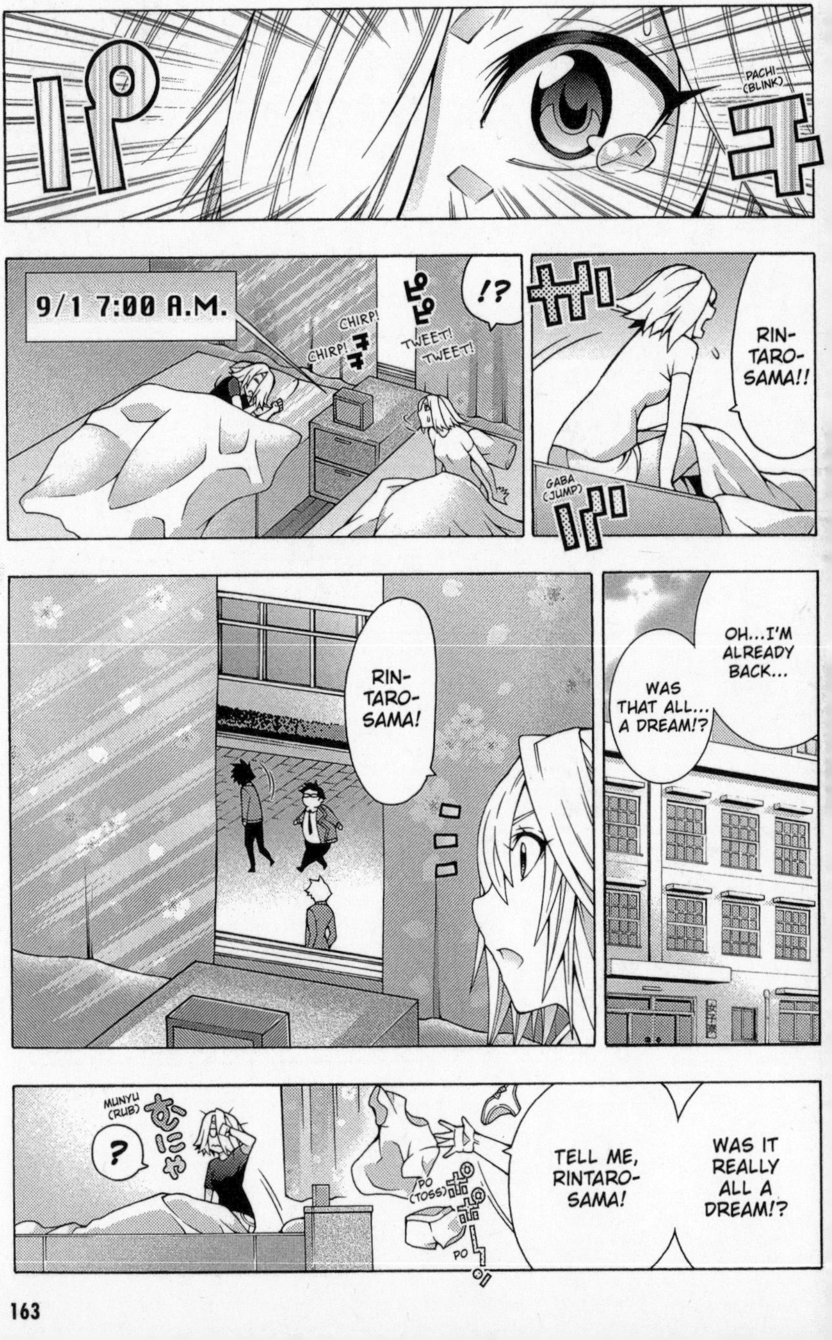
PACHI (BLINK)
RIN-TARO-SAMA!!
GABA (JUMP)
!?
TWEET! TWEET!
CHIRP! CHIRP!
9/1 7:00 A.M.
OH...I'M ALREADY BACK...
WAS THAT ALL... A DREAM!?
RIN-TARO-SAMA!
WAS IT REALLY ALL A DREAM!?
TELL ME, RINTARO-SAMA!
PO (TOSS)
PO
MUNYU (RUB)
?

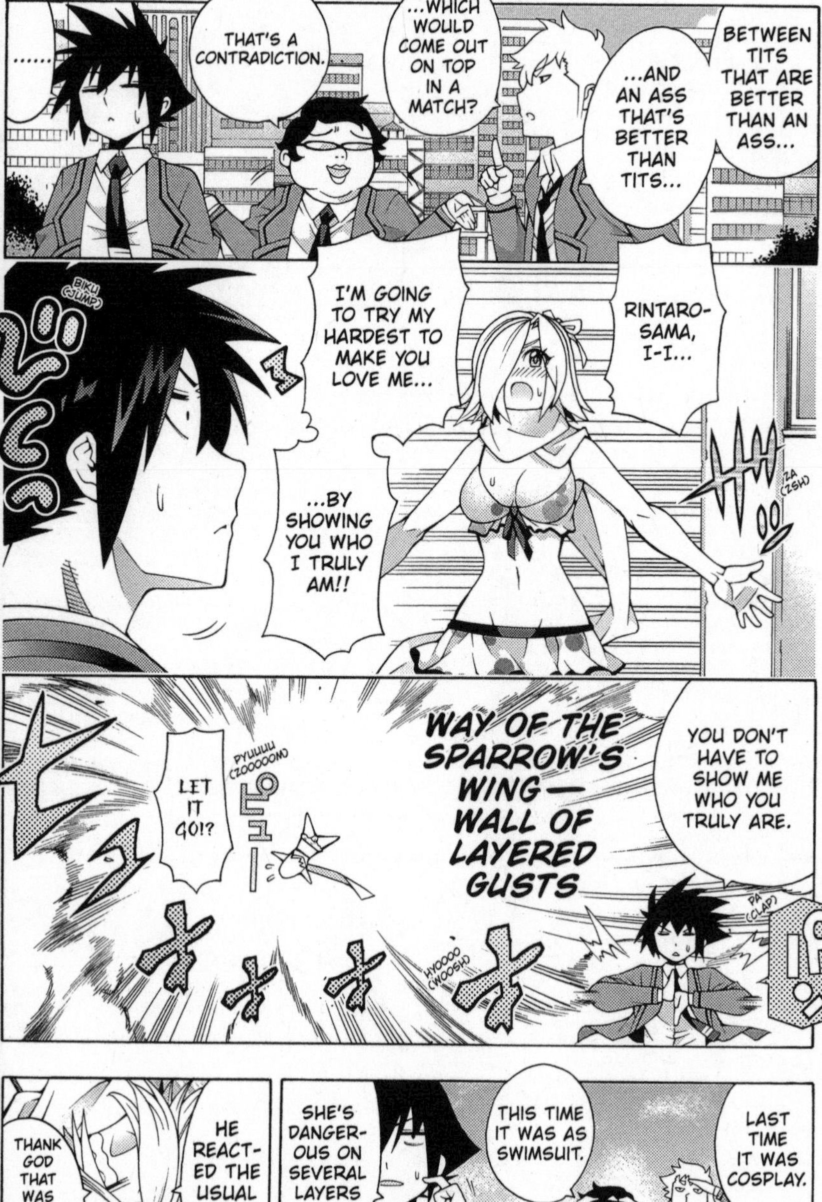
BETWEEN TITS THAT ARE BETTER THAN AN ASS...
...AND AN ASS THAT'S BETTER THAN TITS...
...WHICH WOULD COME OUT ON TOP IN A MATCH?
THAT'S A CONTRADICTION.
......
RINTARO-SAMA, I-I...
ZA (ZSH)
I'M GOING TO TRY MY HARDEST TO MAKE YOU LOVE ME...
...BY SHOWING YOU WHO I TRULY AM!!
BIKU (JUMP)
YOU DON'T HAVE TO SHOW ME WHO YOU TRULY ARE.
PA (CLAP)
!?
WAY OF THE SPARROW'S WING—WALL OF LAYERED GUSTS
HYOOOO (WOOSH)
PYUUUU (ZOOOOOM)
LET IT GO!?
LAST TIME IT WAS COSPLAY.
THIS TIME IT WAS AS SWIMSUIT.
SHE'S DANGER-OUS ON SEVERAL LAYERS...
HE REACT-ED THE USUAL WAY.
THANK GOD THAT WAS ONLY A DREAM...

~ SUPER AFTERWORD TIME ~

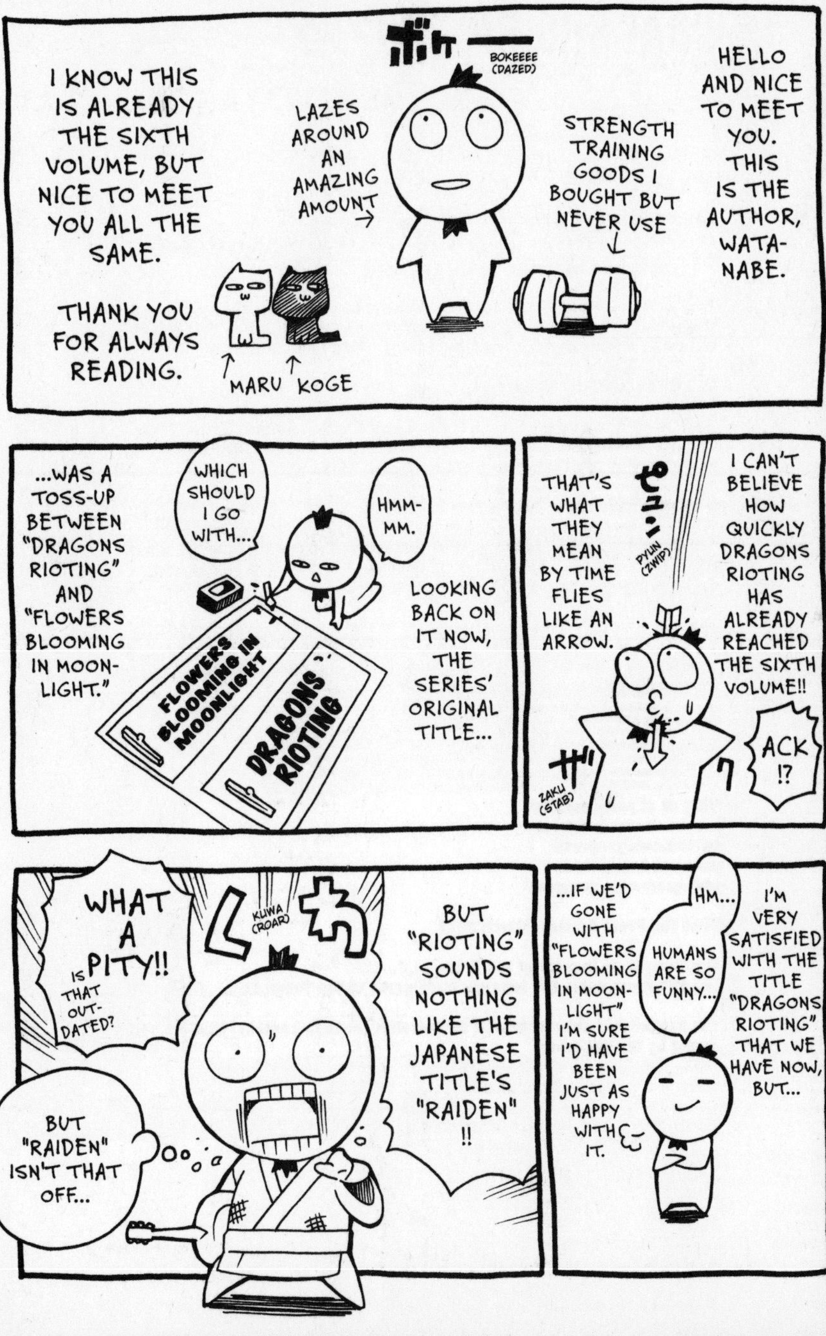
HELLO AND NICE TO MEET YOU. THIS IS THE AUTHOR, WATA-NABE.
ボケー
BOKEEEE (DAZED)
STRENGTH TRAINING GOODS I BOUGHT BUT NEVER USE
LAZES AROUND AN AMAZING AMOUNT
I KNOW THIS IS ALREADY THE SIXTH VOLUME, BUT NICE TO MEET YOU ALL THE SAME.
THANK YOU FOR ALWAYS READING.
MARU
KOGE
I CAN'T BELIEVE HOW QUICKLY DRAGONS RIOTING HAS ALREADY REACHED THE SIXTH VOLUME!!
PYUN (ZWIP)
THAT'S WHAT THEY MEAN BY TIME FLIES LIKE AN ARROW.
ACK !?
ZAKU (STAB)
LOOKING BACK ON IT NOW, THE SERIES' ORIGINAL TITLE...
HMM-MM.
WHICH SHOULD I GO WITH...
...WAS A TOSS-UP BETWEEN "DRAGONS RIOTING" AND "FLOWERS BLOOMING IN MOON-LIGHT."
FLOWERS BLOOMING IN MOONLIGHT
DRAGONS RIOTING
I'M VERY SATISFIED WITH THE TITLE "DRAGONS RIOTING" THAT WE HAVE NOW, BUT...
HM...
...IF WE'D GONE WITH "FLOWERS BLOOMING IN MOON-LIGHT" I'M SURE I'D HAVE BEEN JUST AS HAPPY WITH IT.
HUMANS ARE SO FUNNY...
BUT "RIOTING" SOUNDS NOTHING LIKE THE JAPANESE TITLE'S "RAIDEN" !!
KUWA (ROAR)
WHAT A PITY!!
IS THAT OUT-DATED?
BUT "RAIDEN" ISN'T THAT OFF...

DRAGONS RIOTING ❻

TSUYOSHI WATANABE

Translation: Christine Dashiell

Lettering: Anthony Quintessenza

DRAGONS RIOTING Volume 6
© TSUYOSHI WATANABE 2015
First published in Japan in 2015 by KADOKAWA CORPORATION, Tokyo.
English translation rights arranged with KADOKAWA CORPORATION, Tokyo, through TUTTLE-MORI AGENCY, INC., Tokyo.

English translation © 2017 by Yen Press, LLC

Yen Press
1290 Avenue of the Americas
New York, NY 10104

are not

Library of Congress Control Number: 2015952605

ISBNs: 978-0-316-46924-1 (paperback)
       978-0-316-47092-6 (ebook)

10 9 8 7 6 5 4 3 2 1

BVG

Printed in the United States of America